UNLOCKING THE SECRETS OF SORCERY

Unlocking the Secrets of Sorcery

Clovencrow

CONTENTS

Introduction

This book originally began as my personal Book of Shadows—a collection of information that I have amassed over my many years of study and practice. First and foremost, this is a book about magick. Not Harry Potter magic, not stage magic and not the kind of magick that can be found in most books professing to teach actual magick today. I wrote this book because I was dissatisfied with what magick had become and felt that I needed to reach into other fields in order to create something that was more powerful and authentic. Sure, I will be covering what is typically known as "occult magick"—that is, spells and rituals—but even occult magick must be understood within the context of how the natural world *actually* works in order to be useful.

So, what you see here is the result of over thirty years of research and the study into not only the occult, but also all manner of subjects. Not only is this a guide to those wanting to learn *real* magick, but also I have personally used every single technique in this book and have had success with them. Where there is information that I feel is important but cannot be validated, I have tried to provide the best sources available and give hints about how to proceed so you can uncover these secrets for yourself. In other words, this book is a snapshot of the most important information I have discovered to this date and should not be taken as the final authority.

I have also endeavored to organize this book in the sequence I feel it should be studied. Therefore, it is important that you begin at the beginning and practice every single exercise in sequence in order to get the best results. You should also know that this book contains knowledge that can not only liberate you and heal, but also end lives if abused. I would have it no other way, because I feel that any Sorcerer or Sorceress worth his or her salt should be familiar with both constructive and destructive magick. As such, I take no responsibility for the way you use this knowledge. So if you abuse it, don't be surprised if your neighbors show up at your doorstep with pitchforks and torches wanting to burn you at the stake.

Shall we begin?

The Way of the Sorcerer

Sorcerer: a person who seeks to control and use magic powers; a wizard or magician.

—MERRIAM-WEBSTER DICTIONARY

A long time ago, when most people believed in magick, Witches, Mystics, and Magicians were looked upon with wonder, or even fear, because they were able to shape reality in ways common folk didn't understand. But once we entered the "Age of Enlightenment," people stopped believing in magick, and thus, any who claimed to be a Witch, or Wizard were looked upon as superstitious crackpots, charlatans, or even mentally ill. Unfortunately, this trend has continued to this day. To be honest, it's been *way* too long since the word *magick* has meant anything. This is precisely why I decided to write this book on Sorcery—because, the aim of Sorcery is to *get results*. To the Sorcerer, everything is an act of magick. Therefore, all methods can be used, whether they taken from science, psychology, the occult, or even the art of illusion, as long as those things cause change in conformity with one's *will*.

This not only makes a Sorcerer a caster of spells and performer of esoteric rituals, but it also makes him a scientist and an illusionist—but more importantly, it makes him someone who can back up his words with real power. To the uninitiated masses and even to those who restrict themselves to practicing occult magick only, this may seem like skullduggery or charlatanism. To these people, all I can only say, "So be it," because honestly, anyone making such a statement doesn't really understand what magick is. Magick is what works. Deal with it.

Another important aspect of Sorcery is its lack of religiosity. Sorcerers do not feel compelled to take up a religion, because they know doing so would kill spiritual growth. Instead, they seek to evolve spiritually by collecting truth wherever it can be found. For this very reason, most Sorcerers prefer doing what is right at the time over blindly following some divine edict. This means a Sorcerer is just as willing to use baneful magick as he would be willing to use healing magick—if the situation calls for it. At the core of any Sorcerer is a devotion to discipline and intellectual honesty—because he knows without these two very important attributes, no progress can be made.

TO KNOW, TO DARE, TO WILL, AND TO KEEP SILENT

If there ever was an ideology worth being followed by any serious Sorcerer, it is the Four Powers of the Sphinx, mentioned by the nineteenth-century French occult author and ceremonial Magician Eliphas Levi: to know, to will, to dare, and to keep silent. These rules outline an important way of life that governs the success of any serious practitioner who hopes to achieve great things.

The Sphinx is a type of chimera with the head of a human, torso and front paws of a lion, back side of a bull, and the wings of an eagle. Levi understood the Sphinx to be a representation of profound elemental symbolism that not only relates to the cosmic forces in play in our universe, but states of being, or attitudes that need to be mastered to produce powerful magick. Of the Sphinx, he says this,

> You are called to be king of air, water, earth and fire; but to reign over these four living creatures of symbolism, it is necessary to conquer and enchain them. He who aspires to be a sage and to know the Great Enigma of Nature must be the heir and despoiler of the sphinx: his human head, in

order to possess speech; his eagle's wings, in order to scale the heights; his bull's flanks, in order to furrow the depths; his lion's talons, to make a way on the right and the left, before and behind.

and,

To attain the SANCTUM REGNUM, in other words, the knowledge and power of the Magi, there are four indispensable conditions–an intelligence illuminated by study, an intrepidity which nothing can check, a will which cannot be broken, and a prudence which nothing can corrupt and nothing intoxicate. TO KNOW, TO DARE, TO WILL, TO KEEP SILENCE–such are the four words of the Magus, inscribed upon the four symbolical forms of the sphinx.

—*Transcendental Magic*, ELIPHAS LEVI

So what does all this mean really? What is he talking about? To Know means that it is necessary to study and probe the mysteries—or to be as knowledgeable as one can be about everything possible. To Dare means to be brave, to not be so overcome by fear that you would allow it to govern your life and keep you away from *knowing* and *doing*. To Will is not only to want or give mental attention to the things you want, but is to do so with intention to move forward with action and purpose. And lastly to Keep Silent means to be mentally still of mind so that you can sense the higher forces and listen to your intuition. I am also absolutely sure that To Keep Silent is also a hint that you should *shut up* so that your Will is not polluted and affected by those who may mentally or physically oppose it.

WHAT IS INITIATION?

To be initiated means to symbolically be given membership to a secret order by special rites. Such an order may be a coven or a mystery school, such as the Hermetic Order of the Golden Dawn, the Masons, or any number of esoteric organizations. Although I am not a big fan of this sort of initiation, I understand that everyone on this path, whether a part of an exclusive order or working on their own plan, is in fact on a path of initiation. What I mean is this—life itself is a type of initiation. We struggle to find meaning, to figure out how things work and to find the best way to live life in order to meet these goals. In the process, we must walk a gauntlet fire through a winding path of confusion in order to learn important life lessons that help us become spiritually awakened and evolved—the end result *is* our initiation. And the funny thing is, none of this can be forced or sped up. We all will learn the lessons we need to learn, when the time is right.

In reality, not all but most organizations that offer initiation have little to give except important-sounding titles. Of course, that will give you status, or maybe just the illusion of status, but in the end, all it will do is feed your ego, and this is counterproductive to your mission. The ego is only a small part of who you are, and anything that feeds it will just keep you bound to this lower plane of vibration and hinder enlightenment. So to really become more than what you are and discover what you are fully capable of, you must dispense with titles and overcome egotism.

Think about it this way. What good is a title without real power? The new age and magical community is plagued by people that have titles like "Master," "High Priest/Priestess," and "Frater," who profess to be able to do this and that but are actually unable to deliver. Our goal here is to attain real not imaginary power—and in such case, titles are unnecessary. Let people respect you for what you know and what you can actual do—for that is the mark of a truly initiated Sorcerer.

Personal Development

A lot of people are attracted to magick because of its promise to deliver riches and power—I know I was. Magick is indeed capable of giving you these things. However, wielding such power not only changes your life but also changes the way you look at things. Once you know that your magick is capable of shaping reality in big ways, it becomes apparent how that power affects not only you, but also the environment and people in it. Take changing the weather for example. I once decided that I wanted to cool things down a bit, because the hot summer was making me uncomfortable. My desire to do this was so powerful that I fell asleep dreaming about it. Around three thirty in the morning, I woke up to the boom of thunder as the sky opened up in a torrential downpour—not only did it flood out my bedroom, but also it caused havoc by flooding out parts of the city. Yes, I cooled things down, but how many people did I harm?

Another way magick is transformative is backlash. Thoughtlessly unleashing magick can cause events to cascade in unpredictable ways that will come back to bite you. I once cursed my boss because she was rude and I didn't want to work with her anymore. Being a lazy woman, I decided to enhance her laziness so that she would call in and eventually lose her job. Of course, it worked—but! Everyone else was affected as well. In the next week, half of my coworkers called in. Guess who had to take up the slack—you got it—me! I got what I wanted, but learned a valuable lesson—be careful what you ask for.

So here is my point. Using magick for the wrong reasons can cause harm to yourself and others, so it's a good idea to make sure that your heart is in the right place before you start slinging spells. Knowing when to use your magick to produce the best results for you and those around you is a matter of knowing yourself and understanding your connection to the Source. What you must understand is that everything is connected—so in many cases, what benefits the environment, and all within it, benefits you as well. Knowing this makes it easy to see how making the world a better place for everyone is also helping yourself. But in order to make these determinations clearly, you must be aware of your own faults and be able to reconcile them—and that is called personal development.

MINDFUL EXISTENCE

What does it mean to mindfully exist? A life of mindful existence is a life of generosity, love, and appreciation for nature, and all the life sustained by it. This doesn't mean that you inordinately place the needs of others above your own—after all, you are a part of the loop also. However, as I have stated above, by helping the world and others, you are also helping yourself.

In the world of spirit, like attracts like—you draw in what you put out. Therefore, if you are a generous, loving, and appreciative person, you will be taken care of, loved, and rewarded. I know what you're thinking—it doesn't always work that way! And of course, you are right. However, dishing out love can also be dishing out undesirable truth, a life lesson, or preventing someone from causing harm to themselves or others. The universe as a whole rewards those who do this.

Mindful existence also means living in accord with nature—we must take caution not to pollute and destroy our environment. And by mindfully existing with nature, I don't mean becoming a vegan naturalist or tree-hugging hippie (no insult intend). It just means we must all do our parts. You don't have to throw away your technology and go live out in the woods—that doesn't make sense. But there is no reason to take more than you need and waste. As you do this, you should also make it a point to share your lifestyle with others and teach others who are open to the experience how to do the same—in this way, we can make the world a better place for everyone.

MORALITY

> For what shall it profit a man, if he shall gain the whole world,
> and lose his own soul.
>
> —MARK 8:36

No, I am not Christian, but this quote from the book of Mark rings true. The most important thing about the physical world are the lessons it teaches. Everything is transient, especially our existence here on this plane. It doesn't matter how many bobbles we collect or how shiny they are—we can't take them with us. So then, what is our purpose, and how should we go about comporting ourselves through life?

Although we really can't say for certain what the meaning of life is, one thing is undeniable—the only thing we take with us are our experiences. This means who you are is more valuable than what you own. Even in this life, we can always recover what we lose if we put our mind to it. One might argue that there is a point of no return—that there is no recovering from calamity if you are physically incapable of doing so. But I disagree. People have lost limbs and have even suffered from complete paralysis and have still gone on to live a meaningful and fulfilling lives. Why? Because they were determined and had positive spirits—the mind is a powerful thing indeed! So knowing this, what is the right way to live? Well, magical traditions recognize three paths: the right-hand path, the left-hand path, and the middle path.

The right-hand path is a very ascetic one, meaning wholly focused on becoming one with the Source by conditioning oneself through moderation or even extreme abstinence. Those who follow this path, tend to see the physical world and the basic human desires that motivate us as sinful and impure. Such an individual might decide to be celibate (not marry or have sex), not eat a certain types of food, fast, or even isolate him or herself from an impure world. Right-hand pathers also tend to value goodness and selflessness, using service to others as a way to demonstrate their generosity and kindness. This they believe will elevate their spirits high enough to break free of the cycle of reincarnation and allow them to join God. Another thing that differentiates right from left is a belief in karma. Most right-hand pathers believe in a system of rewards and punishments, or more accurately, a system of karmic return, where what you dish out comes back to you—in some cases, threefold.

Left-hand pathers, on the other hand, are very much anarchists and embrace taboo. Whereas those of the right-hand path view the physical world and human urges as impure, the left-hand pather see all these things as natural and worthy of pursuit. Many left-hand pathers reject the notion of any kind of union with God, believing instead that they can achieve godlike status themselves by becoming masters of their environment and the people in it. To substantiate this, they evidence the dominance that the powerful have over the weak and, for this reason, deny any notion of punishment or backlash for evil tactics they may employ to gain such power.

Somewhere between these two moral positions rests the middle path, or Path of the Serpent. Those of this path value spiritual perfection and understand karma, but also realize that the physical plane has a purpose, and acknowledge the need for power in the world. At the same time, those of the middle path value balance, because only by bringing these two forces (positive and negative) into balance can we see how they work together to create ideal physical, mental, and spiritual change. In order to orchestrate this balance, middle pathers must be free to move between shadow and light, pushing and pulling constructive and destructive forces in the right direction to create the most ideal situation for everyone. And this is why it's called the Path of the Serpent, because the middle pather weaves in and out of both domains in order to achieve his or her goal.

Which path you choose is up to you, but whatever the case, you will end up swinging left and right whether you intend to or not. Reality dictates that sometimes you need to bring down the hammer, while other times it is necessary to show generosity and kindness—the key is to know when!

KARMA AND THE PRINCIPLE OF CAUSE AND EFFECT

The word *karma* is actually Sanskrit for "action, work, or deed." What this is really referring to is the effect of Hermetic Principle of Cause and Effect on one's life. Everything we do causes something to happen, or more specifically, doing good deeds brings good things into our lives, while doing bad deeds brings negativity into our lives. For example, commit a crime, and you get arrested, or act like a bully, and people will rise up and put you down. It really doesn't take a lot of investigation or experimentation to determine whether this is true or not. In fact, most people can make this judgment based on life experience.

What might not be so apparent is the energetic-spiritual effect of having a good or bad attitude. In the world of spirit, like attracts like. Therefore, if you have a nasty attitude, you draw in nasty people, illness, and calamity, and if you have a positive attitude, you attract other positive people, health, and fortune. This has nothing to do with punishment, and everything to do with the fact that we shape reality with thought.

BEING THE AGENT OF KARMA

But who said you had to sit back and let nature take its course? No, no, no. You *are* the agent of karma—we all are. How do you think karma works anyway? When nature doesn't step in, somebody's got to dish it out—that would be you. But before you go out and set the world on fire by trying to purify it of all evil, keep in mind that the purpose of karma is not punishment: it's education.

Karma teaches us lessons, and above all, karma is fair. If you are a compulsive thief, you will eventually get caught and arrested. If you murder, it will eventually catch up with you, and you will be imprisoned for the rest of your mortal life or be executed, and if you punish your body by being gluttonous, you will go to your grave early—but no one deserves cruel punishment for a small infraction. It's as simple as that. Nature usually takes care of these kinds of karmic infractions, but when it doesn't you might be the right person to deliver it. This is an aspect of the middle path. But in order to make that determination, you have to do a little soul-searching.

The only reason I mention this is because if you intend to practice what you learn in this book, you will be more than capable of delivering dramatic change—the thing is, that kind of power is intoxicating. Being intoxicating means it takes control on your part to resist using it for selfish or petty reasons. When you fire off a spell at someone for negative reasons, you begin to resonate with negative energy. If the vibes are powerful enough, you will begin attracting all kinds of calamity into your life. Have no doubt: the law of attraction is real thing!

You should not only be concerned how your magick will affect you, but also how it will affect the world at large—remember: everything is connected. This is a tall order, though, because spells can manifest in an infinite number of ways. The good thing is there is a solution. You could either, one, divine the outcome of what could happen if you decided to take a certain course of action, or two, you can ask for moral guidance from a High Spirit. Trust me on this: it's worth it in the long run.

LEVEL OF CONSCIOUSNESS

As a Sorcerer or Sorceress, consciousness is the fabric that you weave—your consciousness, environmental consciousness, and the consciousness of others. So, seeing how important it is to your craft, it would behoove you to have a good understanding of its different levels.

Now please understand that I hold no official degree in psychology—I am self-taught in matters of the mind, and an astute observer. What I am about to say may sound degrading to others, or quite possibly to yourself, but don't make the mistake of translating my bluntness as a disrespect for creatures or people with a lower consciousness. In the end, there will always be someone or something that is more enlightened than you—and of course, I am not exempt from this rule.

Before I begin, let me say something about the human condition and its role in the development of conscious awareness. Taking care of basic needs has always come before higher cognition. That is, we cannot hope to think greater thoughts, or become more than what we are, unless we are able to take care of our basic needs first. This concept is best illustrated by Maslow's Hierarchy of Needs, which is represented as a pyramid.

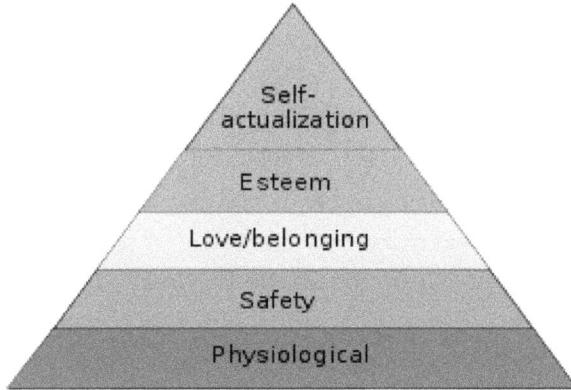

Abraham Maslow (1908–1970) was an American psychology professor at Alliant International University, Brandeis University, Brooklyn College, New School for Social Research, and Columbia University. In his 1943 paper "A Theory of Human Motivation" in *Psychological Review,* Maslow outlined four basic stages we pass through before we can self-actualize—self-actualization being the point where we are motivated to achieve or think about higher things—raising consciousness. He labels these stages as physiological, safety, love and belonging, and esteem.

A physiological need can be seen as a basic human desire or universal human need that will cause great discomfort or even death if not properly attended to. Such a need would be any threatening health issues, lack of food or water, insufficient shelter, sleep deprivation, or even the need to procreate. According to theory, one may overlook or disregard personal safety in order to fulfill a physiological need.

Safety can be challenged by things like war, physical, mental, and emotional abuse, health, as well as economic hardship. Once, and only once, safety is obtained can a person focus on the next step in the pyramid, Love and Belonging.

Love and Belonging can really be seen as social belonging. Only after one's physiological and safety needs are met can they can concentrate on interpersonal relationships such as friendship, intimate relationships, or family.

Next comes the need to fulfill one's ego, or what Maslow calls *esteem*. Esteem, or ego, can be seen as the need to be recognized, feel important, and be respected. This would also include the need to feel good about oneself, or what could be labeled as self-esteem or self-respect. At this stage, these feelings may lead a person to seek status or position.

Lastly, self-actualization is described as the drive to meet one's full potential or to be all that one can be. At this level of consciousness one may try to educate themselves or express themselves through art or inventions, or even begin to probe the depths of who they really are so they can move closer to their higher-selves.

Although this is a very good model, life doesn't always work this way. In many cases, tragedy and hardship will spawn sudden realizations that lead to mental ascension. For example, extreme poverty can teach us the absurdity of materialism, or life-threatening illness can cause us to appreciate the essentials of life or the value of friends and family. In such case, we can rise above the mundane and concentrate on what really matters.

Knowing this, we can identify at least five stages of consciousness, each influenced by what level of Maslow's pyramid one is passing through. It is also worthy to note that those of lower consciousness cannot be motivate by a higher purpose, because they are incapable of understanding higher concepts and are occupied by trying to fill more primal needs. So having said this, let's look at look at these different levels of consciousness.

Animal

Animals have a limited capacity to obtain and retain knowledge. Therefore, they are only concerned with procreating and taking care of their basic needs. To this end, they may use primitive tools to help accomplish goals, but rarely invent them. They tend to be only aware of their immediate environment, which is usually small.

Primal

A primal consciousness also has a limited capacity to obtain and retain knowledge. They are concerned with taking care of their basic needs, gratifying basic desires, and procreating. However, someone with this level of consciousness may look up every once in a while to wonder about the mysteries of the universe, but only as it concerns his or her ability to find food, water, shelter, and procreate.

Sleepers

This is the average person. They can be someone of low intelligence or high intelligence. They are also primarily concerned with taking care of their basic needs, gratifying their basic desires, and procreating. Such as person is only aware of their physical reality or a spiritual reality that has been defined by others. This type of person will consciously or unconsciously try to seek out ways to validate their ego by wearing the most fashionable clothes, mimic popular behavior, fashion, trends, or by seeking fame or status within their peer group or society.

Awakened

This is typically someone with a medium to high intelligence. Such a person seeks knowledge and practices personal development because they desire to have a better understanding of the universe and their place in it. Because such a person is grounded in the physical world, they understand the importance of taking care of their basic needs. However, they are aware of a higher reality and are oftentimes preoccupied with it. Even so, such a person still has hang-ups, or character flaws because they have not fully overcome the physical condition. On the other hand, this lifestyle of personal development and seeking knowledge oftentimes leads to great intuition and the emergence of natural psychic abilities.

Ascended

Because I am in no way shape or form ascended, I can only theorize about what it is like. I imagine an ascended person to be someone who has fully transcended their physical limitations and has therefore freed themselves from all mundane attachments. Whether such a person could be considered good or evil is debatable. I have read numerous stories about monks that have ascended only to isolate themselves from the suffering of humanity.

RAISING YOUR LEVEL OF CONSCIOUSNESS

No problem can be solved by the same level of consciousness
that created it."

—Albert Einstein

You already know that certain needs must be met before you can even
think about raising your level of consciousness. Unfortunately, we are so
wrapped up in the system that most of us don't have the time or energy
needed to escape the mind prison that has been imposed upon us by the
powers that be. So without the willingness to do what it takes to improve
our quality of thought—come what may—we can't expect ascend through
the ranks of consciousness.

So what is the solution? First, a person must be aware of their flawed
thinking. If they don't know there is a better way or are not convinced that
one exists, it is unlikely they will even make the effort. And this is where education comes in: the more informed you are, the more successful you can be.
Additionally, one must fearlessly tear down all the lies, misinformation, and
deception that has been programmed into us as a child and continues to be
programmed into us on a daily basis. For example, we have become willingly
enslaved because we have become convinced that this physical world is the
highest level of existence. And because of this, many of us have erroneously
devoted ourselves to mundane pursuits under the assumption that making
more money and having more things will make us more complete.

The second thing that will save us is understanding the value of constructive criticism, then being willing to adjust our thoughts and behaviors
when we are in error. Without the ability to criticize oneself or take criticism from others, we are doomed to repeat old mistakes. And this is tough,
because we all want to believe we are right and have it all figured out. To
overcome this mind-set, we can simply write down all the problems that have
occurred in our lives and then organize them by similarity—if a problem
repeats, we can consider it red flag. Those repeating problems are caused
by bad choices we make. Now unless we able to think outside the box, we
can't expect to come up with the best solution, but we can go to others we
trust (who are successful) and get advice.

The third quality we must possess is bravery. We must be able to overcome fear and take chances before we can expect to overcome our problems. That might involve being uncomfortable, being in pain, loss, and even facing death. Of course, that doesn't mean we have to take unnecessary risk or go through life haphazardly. But let's face it. Without bravery, we will remain enslaved.

PRACTICES FOR POSITIVE CHANGE

You are either all in or all out. That means if you want to be a powerful Sorcerer or Sorceress, then you need to live in accord with what you believe. If you accept that thought is constantly creating change in your life, and the world at large—for good or ill—then you had better devote yourself to perfecting your mind. And why not act on this knowledge to help create positive change? If you agree, then there are several things you can do.

Be Positive
Don't just think good thoughts, but genuinely desire and believe that things will turn out for the best. In this way, you will attract positive things to you.

Know Thy Self
Use the exercises in this book to identify your hang-ups and rectify them. By doing so, you will be able to overcome negative psychological influences and be pulled into a more positive frame of mind. When that happens, your life will become way better.

Focused Positive Intent
Use positively charged intent to imbue your surroundings with healthy energy. This means to bless the people you meet, the food you eat, your home, and your surroundings with energy that will cause positive transformation.

Educate and Help Others
Sometimes the best way to create change is to teach others how to do so themselves. This might involve sharing your knowledge by a giving class or

guiding those people who are open to wisdom by giving advice. On some occasions you may be called to directly help others. But be careful, though. Don't rob people of important karmic lessons.

Commune with Nature and Higher Spirits

You are not alone. Everything is alive and can be communicated with, including Nature itself. Not only this, but also there is a plethora of wise and powerful entities who are very much interested in helping you with your spiritual development. Use the techniques taught in this book to contact them and benefit from their wisdom.

The next few chapters will be dedicated to teaching you about the human mind, various states of consciousness, and the practice of meditation. These exercises are meant to be a part of your regular daily practice and can be extended by increasing their duration and complexity in order to sharpen your skills of focus and visualization to an even greater degree. As you incorporate these practices into your daily routine, you should also incorporate the Practices for Positive Change that I have suggested above—all of this will bring you to where you need to be in order to get better results using the techniques in this book.

The remainder of the chapters focus on the actual practice of magick, dealing with subjects like how to manifest things within reality, forms of magical protection, how to use entrancement, working with thought-forms, and how to evoke spirits. As this is a book on Sorcery, each practice will build on three main principles: science and technology, psychology, and magical techniques. That is, each practice will use a little bit of all of these ideas whenever necessary to create working techniques that are extremely powerful.

The Nature of Reality

Science does a great job explaining how the world works—so much so that scientific knowledge can be used to create working technology and make accurate predictions. However, none of this changes the fact that we still don't have a full understanding of what lay beneath physical reality.

But there are some things we do know. For example, we know that everything—be it you, me, your home, the earth, earth's atmosphere, and space itself—is actually nothing more than waves of energy organized into complex patterns. Science also knows that even though there are different types of energy, all of these different types of energy are made of the same stuff—and what that stuff is, no one can really agree on. What this means is, we, and everything else, are like waves in a giant immaterial sea.

So what does science know about this primordial wave energy that is at the core of everything? The first thing that we can say about this energy is that it exists beyond space and time. And that which exists at no particular point in time or space is not physical at all. The ancients knew this as the First Hermetic Principle of Mentalism, which states that everything originates from a mind or, more precisely, *is* thought—which leads to the next astounding traits of this rudimentary energy.

The fundamental energy of which everything is composed reacts to our thoughts, or is psychoreactive. The most mundane example of this would be the very real effect of placebo and nocebo. The placebo effect was initially meant to be a derogatory term used to describe a fake medicine or medical procedure used to trick the mind into healing itself. Used in medical trials all the time, this genuine practice gets significant results—people have been known to fully recover just by taking a fake pill. Again, this is nothing to turn your nose up at considering that a change has occurred in conformity with the patient's Will—see where I'm going with this? On the opposite end of the spectrum is the nocebo effect. The nocebo effect is the worsening of a condition caused by the anticipation of harm. This psychogenic effect can cause beneficial medicines to fail, pain, and even death. A good example of this is "voodoo death" and "the pointing of bones." The "pointing of bones" is a ritual performed by an Australian Aborigine called a Kurdaitcha (executioner). In this ritual, the Kurdaitcha creates a kundela (killing bone), then tracks down the condemned, and points the bone at him while uttering a curse. As a result, the cursed dies in a matter of days or weeks. Voodoo death is the same thing, because the target dies of psychosomatic shock due to belief in the power of the curse.

Another way to illustrate how the reality is affected by what we think is to mention the "observer effect." This observer effect was first demonstrated in 1972 when Davisson, and Germer performed the double-slit experiment. This experiment showed that light waves could be made to transform into particles by merely observing them. The goal was to shine light through two slits in a panel to see what kind of pattern it made. In this way, they would be able to settle the argument of whether light was a wave or a particle.

Basically, when the light was observed with the human eye, the photons acted like particles, but when that same light was being recorded by cameras only, it produced a wave-like pattern. Thus, after many experiments over a great deal of time, they were forced to accept that mere "observation" caused waves of light to collapse (transform) into particles of matter. This was not only true for photons but for other particles as well. However, not willing to admit that this was the result of anything other than observation, they called it "the observer effect" and left it at that.

To further support the fact that matter can be affected over great distances by mere thought, I must mention the very real phenomenon of quantum entanglement. Think of quantum entanglement as a sympathetic bond between two or more particles. When such particles are separated from one another, even over vast distances, a change to one results in a change to the others. To best understand this concept, think of a barrel of quantum-entangled blue golf balls. Now imagine taking one of those golf balls to a planet one thousand light years away. Next, imagine painting the blue golf ball you just transported red. Because it is quantum entangled with the others golf balls (one thousand light years away), they would instantaneously become red, like the one you just painted. Of course, this is an oversimplification, but still an actual aspect of nature that science is now taking advantage of—especially in quantum computers. Again, mainstream science only recognizes the "observer effect." However, this assumption was about to be challenged when a man named Dr. Dean Radin (chief scientist at Institute of Noetic Science) conducted an experiment to find out if this same changes could be affected over great distances by the directed intentions (thought) of meditators.

In his experiment, Dr. Radin set up a double-slit device concealed in a box so that it could not be directly observed by the human eye. Then he let both expert meditators (Tibetan monks) and novice meditators focus their attention on the double-slit apparatus using their imaginations and visualization. The original experiment had the meditators sitting only a few yards away. However, in later experiments, they locked their concealed double-slit device in a room and encouraged people to focus on it from thousands of miles away. What was discovered was shocking. Those proficient in meditation were able to collapse the waves into particles, and even produce them, while those not proficient in meditation had little effect. What this essentially proved was that the ability to cause the wave to collapse had nothing to do with being physically observed but was, in all actuality, a psychic effect.

So as you can see, reality really can be shaped by thought. Even though the examples above only show that the mind can be used to effect changes at a very small scale (atomic particles), is it possible to effect this kind of change on a larger scale? The simple answer is yes, but the more complicated answer is that most people these days lack the skills to make even the smallest changes. We are so used to having machines do things for us that we have forgotten how to focus and create with our minds—and furthermore, despite all evidence to the contrary, we just don't believe it's possible. But the fact is that we are all shaping reality all the time with thought, whether we are aware of it or not.

At this point, you may be wondering that if everyone is connected and everyone is shaping reality all the time, what are the implications? To answer this question, I must explain a concept called *consensual reality*. Think of consensual reality as a web of popular beliefs that make up all the things we think of as real. It is this web or matrix of beliefs that sets the rules by which everyone in the world operates and thus produces the reality we see. For example, most people believe that telekinesis (levitating objects with your mind) is impossible. Therefore, levitating something with your mind will be extremely difficult.

This means that, whenever someone tries to do something contrary to what others believe is real, that thing will be stopped, greatly hampered, or will happen in a way that fits into the belief system of others. This also means that even if you are a powerful psychic, you will not be dropping a bus out of thin air in Grand Central Station, because people don't believe that sort of thing is possible—unless of course your willpower and focus is godlike. This is also the reason why many mystics have trouble making big things happen. It's not because their belief isn't strong enough, it's because they are working against consensual reality, not with it. Do you recall the Sorcerer's credo in the last chapter—to know, to will, to dare, and then shut the hell up? Well, there is a reason for this. You want to keep silent about the changes you make. Otherwise, everyone else will focus their powers of disbelief on what you are doing, and shut whatever it is you are trying to manifest down.

But is there any scientific proof to support the claim that we are all part of a consensual reality? Of course, there is. I wouldn't have mentioned it otherwise. The experiments conducted by Dr. Cassandra Vieten, Dr. Dean Radin, and Dr. Arnaud Delorme answer this question. These experiments, collectively known as the Global Consciousness Project, was an international effort by scientists, engineers, artists, and others to collect data from physical random number generators called EEGS (named after the electroenceph-alogram used to measure brainwave patters). Unlike traditional random number generators, like those based on computations from a computer, physical systems like the EEG could read random numbers generated by nature using quantum static. The goal was basically to see if global events that gain worldwide attention have an effect on the quantum field, which is intimately tied to human thought. To accomplish this, sixty-five EEGS were placed throughout the world at different sites. Between the years 1998 and 2015, they captured over five hundred events impacting the quantum field, including the 9/11 terrorist attack, the funeral of Pope John Paul the II, the election of Barack Obama, and the Chilean-miners-found-alive event.

After fifteen years of research, and over 450 tests, statistics consistently showed that there is a link between major events and global awareness. But it is only fair to mention that mainstream science does not necessarily see correlation as causation, meaning you can't necessarily pin the cause of something on the events happening around it. But this statement alone cannot be used to dismiss *all* correlating data, because more often than not, there *is* an effect-to-cause relationship—and such is the case with the Global Consciousness Project. To drive this point home, they set up EEGS at a Burning Man festival in 2012 and 2013, and of course, they showed peeks at both the burning of the temple and the burning of the effigy. So the fact that the quantum field fluctuates in tangent with the thoughts of the masses during global events tends to validate the concept of consensual reality.

THE REVELATION OF ANKI

When I first sat down to write this chapter, I had major doubts about various aspects of these theories, but one evening during deep meditation, I had a vision that was so vivid and shocking it caused a major shift in the way I think about these things. In fact, it was so profound it took me nearly a month to assimilate it. It goes something like this:

The vision began with a comet rocketing through the backdrop of space, followed by a clear and very audible word, "Anki." Although I had heard this world before and knew it had something to do with the Sumerians, I had not studied it and was not sure what it meant. As the comet rocketed through space, my orientation swiveled, and I was now gazing from behind the comet and was able to see where it was heading—the target was a blue planet—Earth. Once the comet hit the atmosphere, the scene paused momentarily, as if to emphasize something. As the comet cut through the atmosphere, the friction caused it to roar and explode into a ball of flames. Following a path downward, an ocean made up of chaotic waves came into view. There was a great explosion of moisture as the burning comet hit the water, causing it to form giant waves that rippled out in all directions—once again the scene momentarily paused. Once the comet was swallowed by the ocean, it tunneled through the depths until it hit a floor teeming with volcanic activity, but instead of causing the earth to fracture, it was consumed by the lava.

I woke from the trance stunned, but more importantly, I left with the word *Anki* and the memory of a comet transitioning from space, through air, into water, and finally accepted by the earth. It is not very often that I hear words in my head so clearly, so I immediately looked up the word *Anki*. My research revealed that the word *An* meant "from Heaven," and *Ki* meant "to Earth" (from Heaven to Earth), and these two words were used by the Sumerians to describe how creation arose out of what called the Abzu, or the primeval sea. When we think of heaven, we tend to see it as some invisible realm on another plane of existence, but to the ancients, heaven was quite literally space.

So my conclusion was that the Elemental Model is not a model at all—it's literal. Now of course, ancient humans tended to simplify things into four basic elements, but these elements can easily be associated with the energies we know of today. For example, Spirit is the ether or quantum field, fire is plasma or electrical energy, air is any gaseous atmosphere that supports life, while water is any liquid that acts as a carrier, and finally, earth is any solid that acts as the foundation on which life exists in the physical plane. So we can quite literally see the spirit world, because the planet we live on is hanging in it. And the subatomic particles that make up the atoms that form our bodies hang in this ether to—in other words, the ether is in us and *is* our spiritual body.

In summation, what you see is not physical at all, and the mind has the power to make changes to this world, even from afar. Understanding this is the key to knowing how to shape the world in a positive way and avoid being the victim of negative mental influence. In the upcoming chapters, we will take these concepts and apply them to techniques that will enhance the belief, focus, and imagination necessary to cause that change.

What Is Magick

Any sufficiently advanced technology is indistinguishable from magic.

—Arthur C. Clarke

The word *magic* was borrowed from the Persian word *magi*, which was used to describe a priest of the religion Zoroastrianism (followers of Zoroaster), who entered the scene around the fifth century BCE. The word *magi* actually means "to be able to have power" and was a fitting title for the priests of Zoroaster, because they were known to be able to do miraculous things. The first point I want to make is that magic(k) has meant different things to different people throughout the ages. Today, "magick" with a *K*—the science, and art of causing change in conformity with one's will, according to Aleister Crowley—is seen as real magick and is used to differentiate itself from the word *magic*, ending in a *C*, which is considered sleight-of-hand tricks, stage magic, or illusions.

But magick is really just a "technique" used to shape the natural forces. That "technique" could involve using the mind only, or the Sorcerer's focus, and imagination enhanced by symbols, or even all that, plus worldly technology. The forces being shaped by magick are either forces that already exist with physical reality or the *very real* higher spiritual energies from which the physical world is based—either way, it is all natural. The reason why most people today don't believe in magick is because they really don't understand what it is. People have this idea that magick exists somewhere in the realm of fantasy, outside of science—it does not. What most people fail to realize is that yesterday's magick *became* today's science and that the scientists of the past were oftentimes practicing magicians. Galileo, for example, who was considered the father of science, was also an astrologer, Sir Isaac Newton, the inventor of classical mechanics, practiced alchemy, and Paracelsus, the inventor of toxicology, used natural magick to cure people. As a matter of fact, chemistry stems from alchemy, herbal medicine (witches' brews) became today's pharmaceutical industry, astronomy was born from astrology, and in many cases, today's quantum physics is a rediscovery of what the ancients already knew about the nature of reality.

The main difference between magick and science is the way in which they classify matter and higher energy. Both recognize phenomena that exist here in the physical world, and both understand that there is something happening on an even more subtle level, but whereas scientist tend to refer to this subtle energy as quantum, Sorcerers tend to use the words *spirit, ether,* or *quintessence.* And whereas science is very good at describing the physical world and telling us how to use the forces within it, its understanding of the spiritual forces that compose this world (quantum reality) is still in its infancy. But to be fair, many who practice magick have also lost touch with their spirit science and have no idea how these things really work.

So as you can see, magick, just like modern science, can be divided into different disciplines, each concerned with various aspects of nature. However, unlike science, magick can be used to take advantage of the already manifest properties of things that exist here on this plane as well as the higher spiritual properties from which it is based. That is, while modern science tends to focus only on what they can see and measure here in the physical world, Sorcerers are aware of and can manipulate the spiritual template of that thing.

Having said this, I will try to define the various branches of magick so that they can be understood within context. We will simply call magick that is concerned with the physical world "Natural Magick," because the word *natural* means "of physical reality," and we will call magick that deals with the mental and spiritual plane "Psychic Magick," because *psychic* actually means "relating to the soul or mind." Just understand that these branches deal with different manifestations of the same energy. Now let's divide both of these branches into specialties. Natural Magick would, of course, include all technology, Herbal Medicine, and Knowledge of Minerals and Crystals. Psychic Magick, on the other hand, is its own distinct branch, because it deals with energies that are not physical at all—things not yet manifest. In this branch would be the study and practice of things like precognition, divination, kinesis, the manipulation of probability, forms of psychic communication as well as abilities and techniques used to connect with the spirit world (mediumship, channeling, evocation, and theurgy).

It is worth noting that many of the words used above to describe phenomena are actually describing the same thing. For example, the term *precognition*—a word used by parapsychology to describe foreseeing the future—is nothing more than divination, a term used by practitioners of magick to describe the many techniques used for doing the same thing. The same is true of mediumship, channeling, evocation, and necromancy—all of these practices have the same aim, to contact incorporeal entities. It gets even more interesting when you realize how the field of psychology connects to all of this. Magick shapes a reality that is living and conscious. Therefore, that which is conscious also thinks and has a psychology. Also, the field of psychology has helped humanity understand different mental states accompanied by things like meditation, and trance—and these mental states are the *key* to making psychic magick work.

But when most people talk about magick, they are not really referring to chemistry, astronomy, or quantum physics—they mean spell casting. Is this what magick is? In a way, yes—practitioners of magick do cast spells, and perform rituals, but it's not cosplay. It is actually a type of science. The symbols, gestures, and incantations of a spell are outward expressions of the Magician's mental intent—and that intent is directed at the part of reality that is malleable—the quantum field. In summation, practitioners pull from the many disciplines, including science, psychology, and metaphysics to get magical results. Some of it comes from working with low-level energy that exists in the physical world (classical science), while other results are gained by working with high-level quantum energy that exists on a plane of probability (spirit science). Either way, *real* magick is not easy, and takes lots and lots of practice. It's not like you can just wave a wand and transform lead into gold, or say a few magick words and open up a portal to another world—but the reality is that real magick *absolutely* exists and is powerful.

An Unofficial History of Magick

Even though the word *magic* has its roots in fifth-century Persia, it can be traced even further back than that. Magick is actually a lost technology, one that was originally handed down to us by the old gods, or more precisely, the Anunnaki (those who from heaven to earth came). As unbelievable as this may seem, the history of the Anunnaki is well documented and can be found recorded on Sumerian cuneiform tablets and even represented in hieroglyphs on temple walls across this planet. As a matter of fact, the evidence is so overwhelming that, once you are aware of it, it would be extremely difficult to deny. I will cover their history in more detail later on in this book—but for now, all you need to know is that they created us and taught select humans an advanced mental science, which later became known as magick.

It is this science that was adopted by the Human-Anunnaki priesthood across the globe, and adapted to meet the needs of the specific cultures that used it. Although magick once played an integral part in the lives of our ancestors during a time when the Anunnaki ruled openly, once they lost their footing, it became necessary to repress and restrict the use of magick to a very small number of the elite ruling class who still worshiped them. In this way, knowledge of magick was virtually lost.

The main instigator of this moratorium on magick was the new religion—or the Catholic Church. People had always been very suspicious of men and woman who practiced magick, but not more so than after Christianity established itself as a religion and dominated the landscape. When this happened, it became necessary to make their subjects believe that only they held the keys to heaven. But in order to do that, they needed to get rid of the competition and make those they ruled over ignorant of any other path to enlightenment. And if you've ever studied history, it's pretty obvious how they did it—murder, mind control, and the destruction of knowledge.

So as you can imagine people like Witches, Magicians, and, in fact, anyone who was believed to have spiritual power were prime targets. In order to make this mission easier, they needed to make the common folk fear those who practiced the mystic arts. This campaign happened over many centuries as they had to try to kill off anyone practiced magick or any other form of opposing spirituality and "reeducate" or intimidate whole cultures into believing that magick was *bad*. It is important to understand that as this was happening, Catholic priests of the highest level were practicing magick themselves. Their goal was not to eradicate knowledge of magick entirely—only from the minds of the common folk so that they were the sole purveyor of that power. They could then use this power to take control over humankind under the influence of the forces of a certain faction of Anunnaki who wished to regain what they had lost.

To further this agenda, Christian priests made up stories of how Witches, Warlocks, and Sorcerers made pacts with the devil, cursed people to death, spoiled crops, and bewitched innocent men and women to cheat on their spouses. Then, once paranoia was in full swing, they encouraged people to hunt them down and turn them in to the authorities.

These victims were then brought in, tortured, and made to confess to contrived crimes. Not surprisingly, most of these people weren't even witches—many were just innocent women who turned down advances from lecherous men, or poor old ladies who had birthmarks or warts in the wrong places. Although most victims were women, many men were also rounded up as well—especially Christian priests of competing denominations. In many cases, those who were accused owned property that could be obtained by those making the accusations, and at one point, Witch hunting had become so profitable that it became a viable way to earn income. It is my guess that the actual practitioners of real magick were wise enough to disappear at that point.

But as far as the history of the practice of magick is concerned, the interesting outcome of all this was that these torture sessions created a type of Christian-centric fantasy magic based on the inquisitor's accusation that witches worshiped the devil. What is interesting is that in pre-Christian times witches couldn't have worshiped Satan, because the Christian idea of Satan did not exist within their pantheons. There were, of course, some Gods and Goddesses that were considered more mischievous or destructive than others, but they were no more monstrous than the God of the Bible. This development of devil magick happened because those accused were made to confess against fictitious allegations made up by Bible-believing accusers, then all of those confessions were meticulously recorded by the court. So with no real practitioners of magick around (or willing to reveal themselves to the public) and the destruction of any legitimate information on actual magick, the records of the inquisitors became the only available source of information on magick—thus, the new age of Satanic magick was born.

As this was happening, Christianity was waging war in the Middle East (the Crusades), and as they conquered nations, they collected their knowledge and stowed it away in their secret vaults, destroying everything else so others couldn't benefit from it—think Vatican. This kept most of the power centralized to the church and is why Christianity is so powerful to this day. But the church fathers were not the only people who were interested in taking advantage of this knowledge—the nobles were also. However, in those days, although nobility ruled over the masses, they were still very much controlled by the church. So whenever they had the opportunity, kings, queens, and other men and women of privilege collected old grimoires secretly, researched and practiced magick, had alchemy labs, and hired soothsayers against the wishes of the church. But during this age, the practice of magick had to be disguised as Christianity. Therefore, Ceremonial magick was born, which is just a derivation of very old pagan practices, decorated in the guise of Christianity.

Eventually, as time went by, and nations became more ambitious, those in power wanted to expand. In order to do this, it was necessary to invent new technologies, so nobility naturally turned to their magicians—who they referred to as natural philosophers—to create them. Therefore, a deal was brokered between the natural philosophers (magicians) and the church, which allowed them to work, albeit in secret, without being persecuted. This deal basically said, "We will allow you to use the natural forces of the material world to create technology. However, we claim dominion over the heavens and the human soul." And so it was that magicians were able to do their work as long as they didn't step over that physical/spiritual divide.

What is interesting is that the word *science*, which was taken from the Proto-Indo-European root *skei-* actually means "to cut or divide," but once it entered the Latin language, it became *scire*, which means "to know." Even more interesting is the similarity between the German word for science, *wissenschaft*, and the word *witchcraft—just an observation*. Moving on now. So eventually the research, and discoveries of these natural philosophers put them in conflict with the church, because what they discovered threatened to overturn the doctrine that was keeping people in check. And every time that happened the church intervened. This resulted in "natural philosophers" being tutored, imprisoned, or even executed. So needless to say, this not only caused resentment, but also created the need for philosophers to distance themselves from spirituality even more—or at least create the appearance of a separation. To do this, they began to call themselves "scientists" and omitted spirituality from their practice all together.

Eventually, this separation became fundamental to their practice, and *scientists* worldwide began to pride themselves on the fact that they could explain how the world worked without the need to insert God or spirit into the equation. As this magick without invoking spirituality idea took root, practices like alchemy and astrology got makeovers and became chemistry and astronomy. The end result of this distancing was that scientists began to fervently deny the existence of all things spiritual. Of course, this didn't happen overnight, but it did result in the final split between those who practiced magick (scientists who included spirituality in their practice) and mainstream scientists (magicians that deny spirituality).

Even so, real magical practitioners have not died off. It's only that spiritual science has developed separate from its physical counterpart. The problem, however, is the animosity that exists between those who practice science and those who practice magick, and the ignorance caused by suppressing valuable information about the spiritual world. The fear and disdain of all things spiritual that was initially caused by the church has been institutionalized for so long that it has become difficult, even for men and woman who have vowed to be seekers of the truth, to acknowledge the possibility that anything exists beyond their rigid view of reality.

In this day and age, those seeking to practice magick are met with books that contain little to no science. At the same time, those savvy enough to dig deeper by studying old grimoires (which are still available) find books that have been polluted with so much Christian dogma that they conceal and distort valuable magical knowledge. And while the spiritual seeker is trying to ascertain the truth, he or she is being inundated by a society that believes that magick is hogwash, or Hogwarts—either way. At that point, practitioners either become so deluded by nonsense or so discouraged that they give up all together. In the end, the only option for those who wish to learn real magick is to pry knowledge from many available sources and then spend the time experimenting with what they have learned in order to reclaim what has been lost.

Mind and Magick

I f what you think truly shapes reality, then what's going on in your head is really the only thing that matters. In this chapter, we will examine not only human consciousness and its connection to the greater consciousness, but also the tremendous power of the mind.

First and foremost, your power to affect the world is limited by what you know. In other words, if you don't know how to do something, you are not going to do it and, therefore, will have no impact. Secondly, your beliefs dictate your actions. So, if you don't believe you can do something, or it goes against your ideology, you probably won't try to do it—and thus gain no benefit. And lastly, if you are too lazy or afraid to take action, it's unlikely that anything will ever get done. Ultimately, your willingness to be ignorant or unwillingness to use what you know will make you helplessly dependent on others and easy to exploit by those who want to manipulate.

But this is only what is going on below the surface. Every time you make a conscious choice, your thoughts are literally building an image (thought-form) of what you are thinking in a higher dimension of reality. Once you decide what you *believe*, that belief causes a chain of events to occur, which causes that thing to take shape here in the physical world. This principle is at the core of every ability considered supernatural. Be it considered psychic or magick—consciousness is king!

WHAT IS CONSCIOUSNESS?

In order to be conscious, we must first be compelled to make choices and take actions. Because without that desire, there would be no movement and therefore no measurable life at all—so this means *will* is at the root of all consciousness. But where does this *will* come from? Most mystical traditions believe, as do I, that *will* is given to us by the Source. But because much of what is known about the Source is a big question mark, exactly what *will* is and how we are imbued with it is also unknown.

But what we do know is that *will* by nature is dualistic, that is, it dictates what we are repelled by or attracted to. And that dualism can be seen in every aspect of nature: creation and destruction, life and death, love and hate, and of course, the positive and negative magnetic forces. These two basic forces of push, and pull cause us to make choices that create a complex web of information that forms who we are.

Existing parallel to *will* is awareness or our abilities to acquire information about the outer and inner worlds through our physical and psychic senses. Without that awareness, we would have no way to acquire knowledge, and therefore, nothing to base our choices on.

And this brings us to the third aspect of consciousness—knowledge. We are compelled by will to obtain knowledge that we act upon, so everything we are exposed to, either voluntarily or involuntarily, dictates who we are. So by these three aspects (will, awareness, and knowledge) can we measure just how conscious we are.

This means that consciousness is limited by our willingness to investigate the universe, and our ability to perceive it. Ultimately, the things we know and decide to act upon become who we are. So when a mystic, or adept talks about raising your level of consciousness, what he or she is really talking about is acquiring knowledge through investigation, study, and understanding.

THE CONSCIOUS, SUBCONSCIOUS, UNCONSCIOUS

As Sorcerers and Sorceresses, our ability to effect change in the world using *will* rests on our understanding of how we and others process thoughts. In psychology, these different modes of thinking are divided among various levels of awareness commonly referred to as the conscious, subconscious, and unconscious mind.

Of these three, you are probably aware of the first—conscious awareness—because this where your attention is focused now. Conscious awareness or the conscious mind takes information received through your five physical senses and uses it to produce a picture of the physical world. When that information comes into conscious awareness, it is categorized according to its differences, and judged using logic and reasoning. And information filtered through conscious awareness is expressed as words, sentences, and nonverbal movements. But there is more going on than that. Before anything comes into conscious awareness, it passes through the unconscious and then the subconscious mind first.

The unconscious mind is in charge of your body's automatic processes such as the beat of your heart and breathing. And because of this, physiological changes can be registered using instruments well before they come into conscious awareness. Another important function of the unconscious mind is the role it plays in storing instinctual behaviors. Whenever a repetitive task becomes automatic, it gets stored away in the unconscious mind so that it can be recalled whenever needed. This is both good and bad. Good because some of those behaviors can save your life when you are in danger—such as the fight-or-flight response—however, automatic behaviors can impede us when triggered against our will through suggestion, subliminal messages, or covert hypnosis.

Another unfortunate aspect of the unconscious mind is dissociation, or the repression of memories. Dissociation occurs when an experience is so traumatic that it would interfere with normal life functioning. Traumas like being witness to a grisly murder, sexual abuse, or being involved in a horrible accident oftentimes get tucked away in the dark recesses of the unconscious mind so they can do no damage.

In the same sense, we bury things that can't be understood within the context of our normal view of reality. Such an event might be a mind-blowing fact about life, a flying saucer hovering over a field or an encounter with an entity. In fact, sometimes these memories don't get repressed. They get erroneously interpreted and stored away as something entirely different. For example, the flying saucer might become a plane or may be interpreted as a shadow or abstraction of lights.

The subconscious mind, on the other hand, is primarily about accessing stored memory—that is, we don't have access to it until we want to recall it. Unlike conscious awareness, the subconscious mind communicates by means of symbols, mental images, sensations, and emotions. All of these symbols are intricately tied together in related clusters of thought. For example, the simple smell of hot cocoa might invoke images of your grandmother, cold weather, and memories of your life as a child. You will learn later on how these memories can be purposely invoked using magick to help tap into their energy.

What must be understood, though, is that while we are consciously taking in information from whatever we are focusing on at the time, we are subconsciously absorbing information from our surroundings. As long as it's within the range of our senses, we are receiving and storing it. This means, with some effort that information can be recalled later on. However, if you choose to ignore what is going on around you, you could also end up being unconsciously motivated by something you picked up subconsciously.

Another important aspect of these levels of awareness is how they connect to higher dimensions of reality. In the chapter "The Nature of Reality," you learned that the physical world is a manifestation of thought. Mind creates matter, not the other way around. Of course, the Source is the primary creator of reality, but we are also participants in this process. Who we are, our souls or spirits, does not reside in the physical world, but exists in a plane of higher dimension, starting as a thought from that Source. Because we to are a mental reflection of this first thought, who has chosen to focus its attention in the physical world, who we are transcends multiple mental dimensions.

Each of these dimensions corresponds to a different level of awareness. For example, while conscious awareness is centered in the physical world, subconscious and unconscious awareness are focused on the higher spiritual dimensions. This means, by leaning how access your subconscious and unconscious mind, you can touch those higher plane and shape reality before it gets reflected into this plane. Being able to shift your awareness also means being able to gain access to your natural psychic intuitive abilities— the deeper you go, the more information you can access. Exciting, huh?

THE COLLECTIVE UNCONSCIOUSNESS

In the chapter "The Nature of Reality," I have already talk about how shared human beliefs create consensual realities, so now I will talk about how those consensual realities act as a type of hive mind. So, without invoking a supernatural cause, I can explain that most human beings are a part of a collective, because we as social creatures tend to work together in groups toward common goals. Using the law of attraction, we automatically know that each person within a group recognizes the same cultural symbols, share the same cultural practices, have the same attitudes and morals, and use the same language as every other individual within the group. In this sense, all such groups can be considered a collective consciousness. Even though that group is made up of individual people, with their own personalities, they act as a whole on society. Therefore, if you want to access their knowledge, take advantage of their resources, or influence them, you must mentally "resonate" with that group.

But the collective nature of these conscious groups runs much deeper than that—that is, they are connected on a much higher level and therefore act as a single entity. Whereas a single individual within a group may think he or she is acting independently, his or her thoughts and actions are actually being motivated by the collective nature of the mind which they are a part of.

Not only this, but also because consciousness does not originate from the physical brain, these collectives can be accessed through deep meditation and drawn upon for information or even aid. When drawn upon for aid, any individual who is a part of that collective becomes an agent for change. Therefore, any change would be carried out by a member of that group. For example, if I were to call upon my Cherokee ancestors using meditation as the means of connecting with this collective, that help may come in the form of another human being who also has Cherokee blood, and would most likely be wrapped in the symbolism and teachings of the Cherokee tribe.

Also, when you draw upon a collective for information, that information comes in the form of symbolic images called *Archetypes*. An Archetype is an iconic symbol that expresses a thought or idea within a particular collective. That iconic symbol would be laced with the morals and virtues of that particular group of people of which you are a part. Although many archetypes exist, there are four main ones that are shared by all of humanity: anima/animus, the shadow, and the self.

Anima/Animus

Anima and animus embodies the idea of polar opposites in gender, such as active versus receptive, logical versus intuitive, and brute strength versus grace, which are manifested as attitudes, behaviors, and traits over centuries.

The Shadow

The shadow is a mental construct or archetype that lives within the unconscious mind of all people. This construct is made up of the basic of animal instincts and repressed personality traits that have been quarantined from the ego, or conscious self-identity. A single person can have many shadows or dark-personality types hidden within the deep unconscious mind. According to Jungian psychology, the shadow doesn't necessarily have to be negative: for example, someone with self-esteem problems can benefit by calling forth their more aggressive/assertive shadow, or it could be greatly advantageous for someone who is chronically depressed to let their more happy-joyous shadow self move to the forefront. Shadows tend to project, meaning they tend to blame their problems on the moral shortcomings of others, when the moral shortcomings they are pointing out are actually their own. For example, a rude shadow may actually blame others for being rude when the flaw is with it. It is also worthy to note that Carl Jung believed that although the outer layer of the shadow is composed of personal negative archetypes, the inner layer of the shadow is actually made up of negative universal traits or archetypes that exist within the collective unconscious and are shared by all of humanity.

Some magicians and witches theorize that it is the shadow that is actually being called forth when someone conjures or performs an evocation. If this is so, then the Magician or Witch could be connecting with an aspect (negative or positive) of his or her own personality or even an aspect (negative or positive) of the universal unconscious mind. This conjecture might be a valid explanation of what most people call angels, demons, or even spirit guides—and you always wondered why angels and spirit guides always have your best interest at heart and demons seem to be aware of all those things you are afraid of and are ashamed off. One might think that the occurrence of physical phenomena, such as objects moving, lights turning on and off, and apparitions, might negate this theory, but even that can be explain by telekinetic forces created by the Witch or Magician doing the conjuring—in other words, he or she may be the source of all those things.

The Self

The self represents the unification of the ego with the collective unconscious of humankind. This self is depicted by a circle with a dot in the middle: the dot representing the ego, the circle collective traits of humankind, and the two together form the whole self. Jung understood that when born our identity is encompassed by the wholeness of the universal traits of the collective. Then, over time, we develop egos and must work to rediscover the true self by finding an equilibrium between our individual personalities and the traits of the collective whole—this, he thought, could be done through rites of passage and initiation.

DREAMING

Dreams have been important to most, if not all, cultures throughout history—after all, we all experience dreams at one time or another. The first dreams were recorded on clay tablets five thousand years ago in Mesopotamia. Ancient cultures understood the dream world to be the place where they could communicate with their ancestors, the gods, or even see the future. Thus, dreams have played an extremely important role in religion and the esoteric traditions for thousands of years.

Even so, Western culture has only been studying dreams for the last century. We have Sigmund Freud and Carl Jung to thank for our current understanding of this phenomenon from a psychological perspective. However, the study of dreams in the lab first began when Aserinsky and Kleitman discovered REM (rapid eye movement) in 1953. Many theories have been put forward to explain the phenomenon of dreaming: Freud thought dreams revealed hidden thoughts and emotions, Carl Jung believed dreams were a type of language expressed by the unconscious mind, while others believed that dreams were used to help form memories, solve problems, and heal. And lastly, some believe dreams hold no real meaning, because they are simply the product of random brain activation during sleep.

Despite what scientists think dreams are, they have been able to discover a few important facts. Everyone dreams, even if they can't recall them. Most people dream about the last thing they had on their minds before they fell asleep. People commonly have about three to five dreams a night, or even up to seven on rare occasions. Those dreams can last a few seconds or up to twenty to thirty minutes. Dreams tend to get longer as the night passes. Eighty percent of all dreams are recalled from the REM state. This state is similar to the waking state in the sense that the same waking brainwaves are being produced and the eyes can be seen darting back and forth as they are trying to focus on things in the field of vision. Most sleepers experience a type of paralysis during sleep. It is thought that the mind paralyzes the body to prevent a person from acting out dreams and hurting themselves or others. In fact, there is a sleep disorder called parasomnia where paralysis no longer happens. Without paralysis, those dreams are acted out, resulting in danger to the person sleeping and those near him or her—spouses have been assaulted, and crimes have been committed, all while totally unconscious.

Also, just as we shift from one state of consciousness to another during our waking hours, we do the same during our sleeping hours. In this sense, sleep can be divided into two different states: REM, and NREM. Whereas REM is known for producing fantasy-like scenarios, the NREM, or non-REM state is a time when the mind tries to learn by rehearses scenarios over and over again. It is also known that roughly 20 percent of all dreams are recalled from non-REM states (NREM). It is also worth noting the similarities between the dream state and heavy trance states. They both can produce vivid imagery, they both produce paralysis, and consequently, memory of what one experienced while in both these states seems to evaporate after one has shifted to a more conscious state.

But what do mystics think the dream state is? Those practicing the mystical arts typically believe that dreaming is a refocusing of attention from one plane to another—in this case, from the physical plane to the spiritual plane. That is, when you fall asleep, if you remain consciousness, or if you can gain consciousness while dreaming, you become aware that you are actually in the astral. If awareness is not attained, the fabric of the astral will morph into whatever the person is thinking at the time. Consequently, this is what most people studying the occult and parapsychology believe happens to many people when they die. In other words, when some people perish, they wake up in a dream of their own creation. And because what they think typically mimics what they knew when they were alive, they create similar settings and see no difference.

Just like trance, dream states can be extremely powerful, so powerful that if aware while dreaming, one can access their natural psychic abilities in the dream state. The reason for this is that psychic abilities are a function of the subconscious mind, and when you are dreaming, or in a deep trance, you are fully immersed within your subconscious. However, being lucid (conscious) while dreaming takes practice. Fortunately, this kind of awareness can be developed.

One such technique is to keep a dream journal. By recording what you dream about, you are able to consciously recognize common themes taking place in those dreams. You effectively train your mind to *know* that something is a product of dreaming while you are asleep, and therefore have a better chance to become aware that you are actually dreaming. This is typically recorded in book or audio archive record of your dreams. When making such a journal, you will not only want to record what you dream, but you will want to record the date, hour, and moon phases. Because dreams and deep-trance visions evaporate quickly, you will need to do this immediately after you wake or come out of trance.

Another good practice is to incorporate dream sharing into your life. If you have a good friend or partner, make it a point to tell that person about your dream immediately after you wake up. If you both practice doing this, you will both see better dream recall in the future.

Another simple method of developing in-dream awareness is something called a *reality check*. A reality check is checking for dreamlike phenomena, such as flying, distortion of time, and fantastical themes, while in the conscious state. For example, you may try willing yourself to levitate or check your watch to see time is running slow or fast. Therefore, not being able to levitate or lacking evidence of time distortion probably means you are awake. If you make a habit of doing this while you are awake, this habit will carry over into sleep, and you will eventually become conscious that you are dreaming. By the way, try not to do this around other people, or they will probably think you're a nut case. If you can manage to become conscious while dreaming, you can astral travel by willing yourself out of the dreamscape to a distant location.

It is also very possible to connect with entities while sleeping. Most spirits have the ability to communicate telepathically; this simply means they can mentally communicate with you by sending information in the form of symbols. This is particularly useful if you have managed to become lucid while dreaming, but if not, you can try to remember those messages once you have woken up, and record everything in your dream diary. It is important to understand that entities can influence and affect you while sleeping, so if you practice magick, evocation, are psychic, or live in a haunted location, you can draw the attention of negative spirits. Since the dream state is very similar to the heavy, coma state of trance, you are more vulnerable while in the nonlucid dream state.

To illustrate this danger, I will tell you two stores. When I was about eight years old living in Pennsylvania, I had a disturbing waking dreaming (lucid dream). I dreamed that I had woken up and walked into the living room to watch some television. After switching on the TV, I sat down on the couch, which was located just below a long window. As I relaxed on the couch watching *Hee-Haw*, I heard a muffled scream coming from outside on the patio. Although I was terrified, my curiosity inevitably drew me to the patio blinds. Upon opening them I was shocked to see a wicked half-man, half-goat figure, wearing tattered shorts and T-shirt, wielding a blood-drenched machete. On the patio laid a man and woman with severed arms and legs, who were flailing and screaming in torment. Upon beholding this goat man, he shot me an evil glance. So I locked the patio door and ran back to the couch, terrified. As a sat there in state of terror, wondering if all the doors and windows were locked, I heard something scratching at the window above me. Once it popped open, I screamed and ran into my parents' bedroom, trying to get their attention. At that point, I woke up in my bed, only to find my father and mother staring down at me. Needless to say, I slept with them that night. Was this a spirit or just a dream? Hard to know, but this is how a spiritual attack might occur during sleep state.

Dream Incubation

As mentioned above, a person will oftentimes dream about the last thing that was on his or her mind before falling asleep. This means, if you so wish, you can intentionally "incubate" or seed your dream with a question or suggestion before drifting off to sleep. This is what is known as dream incubation. In this way, you can prime yourself to receive specific information, or even to use your sleep cycle to manifest intentions. When done correctly this will oftentimes produce powerful results.

Step 1: Question or Intent

Decide if you will be asking a question or trying to manifest something. If you intend to ask a question, simplify it so you can easily remember it as you fall asleep—do the same with intentions.

Step 2: Meditate

Lie down as you usually do, and meditate on your question or intention. If it's a question, think about possible answers, and if it's an intention, see that intention already manifest. Trying holding these thoughts in your mind as long as you can, until you can no longer resist slipping off.

Step 3: Enjoy the Dream

This will most likely produce an extremely vivid dream, so be prepared to record it when you wake up. Also don't be surprised if your intentions manifest immediately or the very next day—dream incubation can be that powerful. Please note, the same rules that apply to manifesting intent by casting a spell, applies to manifesting things using dream incubation. But I will talk more about this under "Occult Magick."

TRANCE

The word *trance* is used to describe an altered state of consciousness where awareness is shifted away from the physical world to another point. This kind of shift can happen through meditation, hypnosis, drugs, and by listening to certain patterns of rhythmic sound. A shift from one state to another can be felt as a rising or falling sensation, a sudden burst of energy, or a sensation that is unique to the individual experiencing it.

Any number of phenomena can be experience while in a trance: visions, sounds, smells, a knowing, a feeling of bliss and oneness with the universe, among many others. Science tends to categorize these things as hallucinations because they cannot be represented in the physical world, but shamans, mystics, gurus, and mediums have been using trance to do things like tap into psychic abilities, enter other dimensions, collect information, and heal people from afar for thousands of years. In other words, even though some of these experiences don't take place on this plane of existence they do effect things here in the physical world, and serve an important function. Not only this but things such as objects moving by themselves (psychokinesis), apportation (teleportation of small objects), the distortion of time and space, and the manifestation of lights and apparitions (more physical phenomena) have all been observed occurring in the vicinity of those who are deep in trance.

It is also important to understand that mastering trance not only allows you to have an effect on yourself and the environment, but also gives you the ability to pull other people into a trance as well. This ability can be used for positive reasons or to create harmful psychosomatic effects and to dominate minds. Modern hypnotists do this to a lesser degree when they use induction to put people into a hypnotic trance, but most don't understand or acknowledge the tethering of energy fields or exchange of energy that goes on, like those who have mastered trance themselves.

The fact is, we are beings composed of thought energy. Even though those working in the fields of mainstream science may not agree to this assertion, they know that the brain produces electromagnetic waves that fire off across the cortex at a certain number of cycles per second or hertz—this, they were able to measure using what is called the EEG (electroencephalogram). Using both this tool and brain-imaging technology, scientists were able to measure changes in brainwaves not only in seizure patients, but also in those experiencing trance. What they discovered was that when someone experiences a trance, activity in the left hemisphere, the area of the brain responsible for logic, reasoning, and our senses of self, decreases, while activity in the right hemisphere, the area responsible for creativity and intuition, spikes. It was also discovered that those in trance state experience intermittent spikes of theta waves similar to those entering or coming out of a dream state. I just want to make it clear, a single type of brainwave pattern (alpha, beta, delta, theta, or gamma) cannot be associated with a particular trance state; many parts of the brain light up, all oscillating at different frequencies—so it's a little more complicated than saying this frequency is associated with this level of trance. Fortunately, you don't have to be able to measure brainwaves or own a EEG to experience a trance.

THE POWER OF TRANCE

The following information was garnered through my study and practice of hypnosis and meditation. It is relevant because a hypnotic trance is no different than a self-induced trance accomplished by any other means. It is also relevant because psychology has extensively studied and verified the power of trance. So anyone who enters a trance state, whether it be of their own accord or with the assistance of a hypnotist, can experience (or be subject to) all the phenomena listed below depending on the depth.

Scientifically Recognized Trance Phenomena

Anesthesia (Pain Killing)
The brain can be told to ignore pain, so much so that if one is in a deep enough trance, open-heart surgery can be performed without any anesthesia.

Amnesia (Forgetting Things)
People dissociate things they can't deal with all the time. Those things get pushed to the dark recesses of their mind and forgotten. This can happen due to shock or trauma and can be caused whenever a hypnotist suggests that you "forget" something.

Somnambulism (Triggered Actions)
Somnambulism is the Greek word for "sleepwalking." Somnambulism is used to describe the phenomenon of suggestibility during trance state. This means those who have placed themselves in a trance can modify their own behaviors, or those put into a trance by a hypnotist can be given suggestions that may be acted upon while entranced, or in a conscious state.

Paralysis (Immobilization)
Simply put, the mind can be told that a limb, part of the body, or the entire body has been paralyzed and cannot move, and thus that limb, part of the body, or entire body will be effectively paralyzed—this is sometimes referred to as *catalepsy*.

Hallucinations (Sensory Illusions)
People in a trance experience a vast array of sensory anomalies ranging from visions, auditory hallucinations, phantom smells, and even a sense of being touched. Those working in the field of psychology tend to write all this off as hallucinations. However, this is not always the case. Not only do our minds embellish what we experience with our own preferences and ideas while in trance, but also how we see things in the physical world while awake. So it doesn't necessarily mean that what we see, hear, smell, touch, and taste while in a trance is just an illusion. Anything we experience, whether it comes from a vision during a trance, or something we

experience while awake is extremely important, because those experience motivate our behavior. And when you are able to acquire valid information while in a trance—information that is outside of the scope of your current knowledge—that tends to blow the hallucination theory out of the water.

Having said this, suggestions given to those under a hypnotic trance by a hypnotist or skilled magician who knows how to entrance can trigger hallucinations, and those hallucinations can be extremely real to the person experiencing them. For example, a hypnotist or witch can suggest that he or she is invisible, and to everyone but the hypnotized (which I have personally done), that person will not be there. Any number of sensory illusions can be suggested to a person in a deep trance, and that person will most likely experience them as being real.

Scientifically Disavowed Trance Phenomena

Clairaudience
This is the ability to hear sounds coming from other dimensions such as the voices of spirits in existing the astral.

Claircognizance
This is the ability to simply know things by reading subtle energies off of an object or person or area.

Clairvoyance
This is the ability to see into other dimensions or see the entities existing in that same dimension.

Gremlins
This refers to the disruptive effect that psychokinetic energy can have on technology, such the charge being sucked out of voice recorders or cells phones during a séance or machinery breaking down whenever a psychic energy is prevalent.

Manifestations

This refers to the physical manifestation of phenomena that can be experienced by everyone within the vicinity, whether they are in a trance or not, such as orbs, apparitions, and the apportation of objects.

Psychic Communication

This refers to the ability to establish a telepathic link with another person or entity in the same location at a vast distance for the purpose of communication.

Past-Life Regression

This refers to the recall of memories from one's past lives.

Psychokinesis

This means moving things with the power of the mind. This includes levitation, and things seemingly moving on their own accord.

Trance Channeling

This is the ability to allow an entity to slip into your body, and use it to communicate with others, and perform tasks.

Trance States

A trance is just a state of altered consciousness. In fact, we naturally shift from one state to another throughout the day. States are defined by where our awareness is focused. During the waking hours, our attention is typically focused in the physical world, while during sleep or meditation, our attention is focused inward. Trance states can also be described by the way information is processed; full consciousness and light trances rely on logic and reason to interpret information, while medium, heavy, coma, and the sleep state rely on the subconscious intuition.

Light

A light trance is nothing more than a deep level of relaxation with a focus of attention. This can be managed by most people without any problem. Those achieving a light trance through meditation or induction can gain insight if they can sort through the mind chatter. People in a light trance will resist suggestion in the same way they would resist any suggestion made to them while fully conscious.

Symptoms
- Physical relaxation
- Eyelids may flutter or twitch
- Hearing is heightened
- The limbs feel heavy
- Breathing slows down and becomes deeper
- Physical sensations from the body begin to fade

Medium (Apparent Somnambulism)
Although a medium trance looks very similar to a heavy trance, it's not. Those entering this state may feel the shift as a sense of heaviness or lightness overtakes them. The person may continue to receive more insight as evaluation of stimuli is handed off to the subconscious mind, but their level of suggestibility remains pretty much the same, because their conscious mind has not entirely let go. Entering a medium trance state means that you are crossing the threshold, and you have just entered the astral, or spirit, realm.

Symptoms
- Breathing deepens
- The movement of internal energies can be felt
- Catalepsy begins to occur

Heavy (True Somnambulism)
The heavy trance state is marked by all the major symptoms of being in a trance—it is as if that person has fallen asleep. At this level, there is no interference from the conscious mind. Thus, the subconscious mind has fully engaged and that person is now open to experience psychic phenomena. Any suggestion given is taken with little to no resistance. Although this level allows for a great deal of suggestion, it is unlikely that any suggestion would be carried out if it goes against a person's moral character. If there is any fear or mental confusion, even suggestions that are beneficial to a

subject may be rejected. If used for its pain-killing/blocking benefits anesthesia can be strong enough to perform minor surgical procedures, such as tooth fillings or extractions, and if deepened, it can be powerful enough to perform things like a vasectomy, varicose vein stripping, or even open-heart surgery. If trained, the subject can control his or her involuntary body functions such as heart rate and blood pressure. All phenomena described as scientifically recognized trance phenomena and disavowed phenomena can be accessed in this state.

Symptoms
- Eyes cannot be opened without affecting the trance
- If the entranced opens their eyes, their pupils will be dilated, and they will appear to have a fixed stare
- Amnesia is likely to occur as that person exits the trance
- Rapid eye movement (REM)
- Intense feeling of falling, rising. or energy coursing through the body as you transition into deeper states

Coma (Esdaile State)

The coma state is blissful trance state denoted by a lack of concern for things going on in the outside environment. During this state, the subject can experience a "oneness" with the universe, along with a sense of great peace and joy. However, this feeling tends to fade once they have exited the trance—even so, the person can still awaken if their personal safety has been threatened. A very small segment of society can achieve the coma state. This is the perfect state for receiving information from the collective consciousness, or Akasha. While in this state, a person can benefit from the same depth of anesthesia as a heavy trance and thus be able to undergo major surgery, However, they are not very susceptible to suggestion because, like deep sleep, they tend to shut out all external stimuli.

Symptoms
- Loss of sensation to all external stimuli
- Catatonic
- Psychedelic experiences

Meditation

Being able to meditate is an extremely important aspect of psychic magick, because without it, you would not be able to achieve the right trance state to cast spells. On a very mundane level, meditation lowers blood pressure and helps unify the creative and logical sides of the brain. Therefore, meditation will help you think and process better. Meditation should be practiced ten to fifteen minutes a day at least three times a week, but for best results, on a daily basis. You should start to see the positive physical and psychological effects in about a week, but gaining a more controlled access to your natural psychic abilities can take up to a month or year to manifest—trust me: it is well worth it.

Meditation is taking focus off the external world and turning inward. This can be done by simply closing your eyes and focusing on your breathing, staring at a single fixed point for a duration, or even by concentrating on a word while repeating it over and over again like a mantra. Meditation will shift the frequency of your brainwaves and, thus, shift you into a different state of awareness, allowing you to access the powers of your right brain, or subconscious mind. Although these shifts occur naturally while drifting off to sleep, you want to know how to recognize them and consciously make the shift as you perform rituals or cast spells. Furthermore, you should be able to remain in these deep states during the entire operation.

On the most fundamental level meditation allows you to speak directly to your subconscious and unconscious mind. Why is this so important? Because the subconscious and unconscious mind is the seat of memory and behavior, and those memories and behaviors are what define who you are and set your limitations according to what you believe. Therefore gaining access to these sectors of the mind will allow you to identify the thoughts and behaviors that limit you and enable you to replace them with more constructive thought patterns. Once you have done that, you are well on your way to mastering sorcery.

As already mentioned, emerging from a trance is similar to waking up from a deep sleep, so much so that memory of what you have experienced while in a deep trance tends to quickly vanish as you become more conscious. The deeper the trance, the more fleeting your memories of it will be, and that is why you should immediately record what you have experienced after becoming conscious.

So how does meditation work? To meditate, you need to be able to focus and silence mental chatter. Silencing chatter means dismissing wandering thoughts, such as an argument you may have had with your spouse, worrying about finances, or internal dialogue about a project that you may be working on. These random thoughts are interference, acting as a barrier that separates you from what is going on in your subconscious. In some mystical traditions, this separation is referred to as *the veil*. Some believe the veil to be a literal ethereal membrane that physically separates you from the spiritual plane, while others believe it is more of a euphemism for distraction, illusions, or mental garbage—therefore, silencing this chatter is called *lifting the veil*. Most importantly, being able to control your thoughts and recognize these states is a fundamental keystone of magick—without this kind of mental control, you will not be able to give enough focus to your intent, move energy, or create thought-forms in a higher dimension.

RELAXATION

Relaxation is the first step in meditation and in any form of higher magick. Many times, knowing how to relax is enough to bring you into the right state. Becoming relaxed is extremely simple—in fact, you already know how to do it. There are so many ways, there is really no need to go into any lengthy discussion about it. To relax, try some of the methods listed below.

- Listen to some soothing music
- Take a bath, or shower
- Stretch
- Watch a movie
- Read a book
- Write
- Think about something relaxing
- Drink some mugwort tea

Simple as that!

POSITION AND BREATHING

Comfort is an important factor in meditation. Little things like sitting, lying, or standing in an uncomfortable position as well as breathing wrong can interfere with your concentration and therefore make it difficult for you to achieve a trance state. First and foremost, while meditating (as well as practicing magick), you should wear something that is comfortable, lose fitting, and appropriate to the climate.

Secondly, while meditating, choose a posture that is most relaxing to you. That is, if you are more comfortable sitting, then sit, and if you are more comfortable lying down, then by all means lie down. Just understand that if you are laying down, you will be more likely to fall asleep as you shift into deeper trance states, so you may want to sit instead. As you begin to master meditation, you will want to eventually attempt it while standing up and moving. This you need to be able to do, because you will be moving while performing spells and rituals, and as you move, you need to know how to maintain your trance.

Lastly, knowing how to breathe properly can aid in the achievement of a trance state. Even though your breath will automatically become more shallow as you slip into an altered state, if you know how to slow your breathing, you will be able to slip into that state quicker. To consciously slow down your breathing, try using the two-four breathing method described below.

Two-Four Breathing

Perform this method for one minute every time you meditate. Then move to simply trying to breathe comfortably. At first, breathing in this manner will seem quite odd, but if you add it to your routine, you will subconsciously do it without even making an effort, and likely drop right into trance because of it. To perform two-four breathing, breath through your nose for four seconds, then hold for two seconds, and breath out through your mouth for another four seconds. Cycle your breathing by simply repeating this process. Remember: consciously try it for at least one minute before giving up, and eventually you will do it naturally.

VISUALIZATION

Visualization and meditation go hand in hand. When you dream, what you see may be so vivid that you mistake it for waking reality. The reason for this is that when you close your eyes and fall asleep, your conscious mind shuts off, and you stop experiencing external stimuli. When that happens, your brain will begin to interpret internal thoughts as reality and therefore produce vivid imagery. Although meditation is not the same thing as sleep, it is very similar, so the deeper your trance state, the more your conscious mind begins to shut down those senses, and eventually you will have what is called a "mind-awake, body-asleep" experience. And when that happens, the images in your mind will become sharper, and more realistic.

As I see it, there are four levels of visualization; knowing and acknowledging, memory recall and mental tasking, phantom visualization, and virtual reality. Each of these levels can be experienced during different trance states.

Knowing and Acknowledging (Light)

This type of visualization is based on belief. You see no image, nor do you experience any sensations—you simply know that they are there and acknowledge that it is so. In order to pull this off, you must divorce yourself from the need to scrutinize what you are trying to know and acknowledge, give yourself permission to indulge in fantasy, and just believe. There is nothing wrong with this, because it opens the channels of imagination. This is where I started off, because I am very skeptical. One can still perform successful magick if they are truly able to know and acknowledge what has been done.

Memory Recall and Mental Tasking (Light to Medium)

We recall past events and play through scenarios in our heads all day long. During memory recall, people don't typically see events in full 3-D, high-definition color—if we did, it would screw with our abilities to operate in the physical world. However, when we do think of the past or play out what-if scenarios in our heads, those thoughts create shadowy images that are good enough to represent that memory—we might not actually *see* the look on our wife's face when we kissed her for the first time, but we can remember it, and that invokes emotion. And this type of visualization what most people are capable of—and that's great, because it invokes emotion, and is a step up from simply knowing and acknowledging. Memory recall and mental tasking is usually good enough for most magick.

Phantom Visualization (Medium to Heavy)

This is when we begin to experience true visualization. If you are seeing phantoms, then you are most likely in a medium or heavy trance. As a result of being in such a deep trance, it is likely you will be sluggish and blurry eyed. A phantom is something that seems semi real, shadowy, or transparent. Phantom images may even produce a physical sensation when you come into contact with them. This form of visualization is good enough for things like evocation, scrying, and remote viewing.

Virtual Reality (Heavy to Coma)

In this state, everything seems real. What you see is 3-D and in high definition. You will be able to touch it, taste it, hear it, see it, and smell it. If you are seeing things with such clarity, there are four possibilities: (1) it is real; (2) you are schizophrenic; (3) you are in an extremely deep trance, quite possibly the coma state; or (4) you are sleeping. Experiencing things in this way can be so real that it can be life changing. Unless you are an experienced meditator or have practice dream recall, you will forget what you have seen seconds after you have exited this kind of trance. Such vividness is not necessary for most magick, but is exceptional for evocation, scrying, remote viewing, astral travel, and experiencing higher spiritual planes.

The exercises below are intended to help you sharpen your powers of concentration and visualization. If you incorporate these into your daily routine, you will see a vast improvement in your ability to conceptualize thoughts and perform magick.

VISUALIZATION EXERCISES

Exercise 1: Dot, Dot, Dots

Step 1: Preparation
Buy some blank index cards and get a sharpie. Mark one dot in the middle of the first card, two dots in the middle of the second, three in the middle of the third, four on the forth card, and so on until you have marked six cards.

Step 2: Stare at a Card
Choose a card to stare at. If you are just beginning this exercise, start with the card marked with one dot. Otherwise, stare at the next one in sequence. Do this for approximately one minute.

Step 3: Imagine the Dot
Now, close your eyes and try to reproduce the image of the card with its dot in your mind. If that card has flaws, imagine those flaws also.

Step 4: Repeat
Repeat steps two through four until you have worked with all your cards.

Exercise 2: Object Recall

Step 1: Find an Object
Choose a simple object that is small, for example, an apple, pen, or crystal.

Step 2: Examine That Object
Pick up that object and examine it by feeling it, turning it over, smelling it, tasting it (if you are able), and finding out what kind of sound it makes.

Step 3: Imagine That Object
Put the object down, then close your eyes, and try to visualize every aspect of that object to the best of your ability.

Exercise 3: The Clock
Close your eyes and imagine an old-fashioned clock with an hour, minute, and second hand. Begin your visualization with all hands in the twelve o'clock position. Visualize the second hand clicking away until it does a full rotation. Then imagine the minute hand slightly moving. As the clock's second and minute hands continue their rotations, try to image the hour hand being slightly moved. Visualize ten to fifteen minutes passing in this way.

MEDITATION EXERCISES

Exercise 1: Body Awareness
There is more going on in our bodies than most are aware of—in fact, most of us don't give attention to our bodies unless we are sick, injured, or having sex. And because of this, we are oftentimes oblivious to what our body is telling us about the physical and spiritual environment that surrounds us. Therefore, this body awareness exercise is as much about recognizing feelings and sensations coming from within as it is about recognizing how our bodies feel while we pass through different environments. By paying closer attention to what your body is saying, you can heighten your psychic senses and overall awareness of your environment.

Step 1: Get Comfortable

Settle down somewhere that is comfortable and private.

Step 2: Overall Feeling

Take an overall inventory of how you feel both physically and mentally.

Step 3: Stimulate Your Body

Run your hands down your body from the top of your head, over each arm to the hands, down your torso, then over both legs, all the way to the tips of your toes. As you do this, pay attention to the sensations.

Step 4: Shift Body Focus

Move your attention to the toes of your left foot without actually touching them. Pay attention to how this makes you feel.

Slowly begin moving your attention up the left foot to your calf, over your knee, then to your upper leg until you get to your hip. Pay attention to how this makes you feel.

Repeat this process with your other leg.

Continue bring your attention up your body, through the abdomen, solar plexus, then chest. Pay attention to how this makes you feel.

Now concentrate on the fingers of your left hand, bringing your attention over/through your fingers, then over/into your hand.

Continue moving your attention up the hand, into your wrist, through the arm, and all the way up into the left shoulder.

Repeat this process with your other hand.

Move your attention from your shoulders into the neck, into the skull, and finally all the way up to the crown of your head. Make sure shift your attention to the ears, and all other parts of the face: lips, nose, facial muscles, forehead, and eyes.

Step 5: Record any unusual sensations in your journal.

Exercise 2: Flame Tratak

Many forms of meditation rely on the focusing of your attention on one thing with your eyes closed, but tratak is done with eyes open—in this case, you will be staring at the flame of a candle or lamp. Practicing this method not only will teach you how to maintain focus and a clear mind, but also will gradually open the third eye.

Step 1: Preparation

Position a candle or lamp at eye level about one to two feet away from the place you will be sitting. Shut off or dim the lights. Then sit comfortably with your back straight, facing the candle or lamp.

Step 2: Focus on the Flame

Gently stare at the flame without blinking. If your eyes tear, ignore it. If thoughts arise, acknowledge them and let them go. Do this for as long as you can.

Step 3: Breaking Point

When you get to point where you can stare no more, because the tears are flowing, close your eyes. Notice how the image of the flame remains in your mind's eye. At this point the image of the flame may begin to transform, growing dimmer, or brighter—perhaps even changing colors.

Step 4: Focus on the Third Eye

With eyes closed, bring your attention to your forehead, just between and above your eyes—this is your third eye. Pay attention to how you feel when you do this, because it is likely you will feel an overwhelming sense of bliss—let this feeling spread throughout your body.

Step 5: Open Your Eyes

Turn away from the candle and slowly open your eyes. Use eye drops to refresh your eyes if you must.

Exercise 3: ROY-G-BIV (Getting into Alpha)

This simple exercise can be used to get yourself into an alpha state. From this alpha state you can proceed to basic meditation, or mindful observation. ROY-G-BIV stands for red, orange, yellow, green, blue, indigo, and violet.

Step 1:

Sit or lay down, close your eyes, and begin two-four breathing.

Step 2:

Visualize the color Red flooding in from all sides of your peripheral vision until your vision is blanketed with nothing but red. Hold this in your mind for ten seconds.

Step 3:

Repeat the above visualization with orange, yellow, green, blue, indigo, and violet. Then when you are done, proceed to another form of meditation.

Tip: If an image comes to mind, try to see that image in the same color you are trying to visualize. If you can't manage that, continue with the visualizations and try again another time.

Note: Don't be surprised if your third eye begins to buzz when you get to blue or indigo. You may even feel your crown chakra activate when you visualize violet.

Exercise 4: Clear the Mind

Find a quiet place where you will not be disturbed for at least ten minutes. Make yourself comfortable by sitting or standing. Don't lie down. Otherwise, you might fall asleep. If you have never mediated before, start by closing your eyes. This way you will not be visually distracted. If you decide to keep your eyes open, I suggest dimming the lights and staring at a fixed point. Begin by taking deeper, slower breaths.

As you do this, focus on the sensation of your chest moving up and down. That is all—think of nothing else. Yes, not easy, I know. Other thoughts will inevitably creep into your head. When this happens, mentally say, *Stop!* acknowledge those thoughts, and go back to concentrating on your breath.

Practice this for at least ten minutes a day, working up to a good fifteen minutes. If you do this on a daily basis, the chatter from your little monkey mind will fade away and eventually be replaced with nothing. At first, the silence may seem foreign and eerie, but eventually you will see it as a tranquil oasis. With the chatter gone, you will become more aware of the subtle energies running through your body and will have the control you need to sharpen your imagination.

Exercise 5: Mindful Observation

Perhaps one of best forms of meditation for developing an awareness of the subtle energies running through your body and a recognition of different states of consciousness is what I call mindful observation. In this type of meditation, your anchor, meaning that which keeps you from falling asleep, is the observation of thoughts, waves of vibrations that occur spontaneously as you shift from one state of consciousness to another. If you can master this, then you can enter a deep trance while remaining conscious and in control.

Step 1: Everything Is Thought

Begin this meditation by acknowledging, and dismissing any external and internal distractions that may arise. External distractions might be things like the sound of your air-conditioner kicking on and off or the feeling of the breeze from an open window hitting your body. Internal distractions would be things such as the itch on your big toe or the slight throbbing of a headache you are trying to get over. Acknowledge all of this by saying, "The sound of the air-conditioner kicking on and off is thought. The itch in my big toe is thought. My body and the air that surrounds me are nothing but thought. My thought is thought. It is all a natural part of my conscious state."

This may seem silly, but what you are doing is realizing that everything around you, the sensations, and what you are thinking cannot interfere with slipping into a trance state, by acknowledging that they are a part of it. This takes practice, but once you have acknowledged this, your mind will eventually filter all of those things out like white noise.

Step 2: Breath

Initiate two-four breathing; remember: do this for at least a minute. After that point, move to breathing naturally and do not fixate on your breathing pattern. You will eventually drop into alpha.

Step 3: Observe

This is the point where you become the observer. Don't move, breath naturally, and pay attention to the feelings and sensations coming over your body. Notice how relaxed your body is. Your body may feel warm and heavy. If you feel yourself being pulled away from this observation by mind chatter, take note of it. Say to yourself, "OK, I'm beginning to drift. What was I thinking about at the time? How nice. It's time to refocus."

Step 4: Desensitization

Don't be surprised if you encounter some strange sensations while doing this. Such sensations may include things like your body being bathed in a fuzzy static charge, phantom sounds, shadowy images, the feeling of movement, such as lifting or falling—you may encounter all of these things and more.

Don't worry. None of these things will kill you—it's all natural. These sensations arise as a result of trying to shift your awareness from the physical world into the world spirit while in a fully conscious state. Although this shift occurs during sleep, most people are not prepared to experience these sensations while conscious. If for some reason you lose focus, you will simply fall asleep and wake up at the end of your sleep cycle.

Because you usually don't pay attention to such things as you are drifting off to sleep, when they happen during conscious observation, they are likely to jar you and throw you out of deep trance. Trust me: knowing about these sensations beforehand does not help—it's still quite shocking. Don't be surprised if your heart races. This doesn't mean you are having a heart attack. It just means you have been spooked.

If experiencing one of these sensations causes you to lose your trance state, note what that sensation was like so next time you will be prepared for it. It is always easier to adjust to something once you have experienced it—and that is one of the purposes of this exercise. Eventually these sensations will lessen, and you will be able to move into a deep trance with full consciousness.

Step 4: Experimentation

Once you have experienced some of these odd sensations, are used to them, and have mastered not falling asleep, it is time to experiment. The first thing you should do is see how close you can get to the edge of sleep before losing the ability to pull back. To do this, allow yourself to drift. Then when you sense yourself falling asleep, let yourself coast a little bit closer to dream land before commanding your consciousness back. If you fall asleep, just try again another day.

Another thing you should try is focusing on some of these sensations and trying to enhance them. For example, if you are hearing phantom sounds, focus in until they become louder and more distinct. If you are seeing images, turn your attention to that image and study it closer. Reach out with your mind and see if you can feel your surroundings as if you are feeling around in the dark with your hands. Because the array of sensations that arise from such meditation are so vast, virtually any type of worldly or unworldly sensory input can be felt. At this point, what you are doing is reaching into the astral and seeing, hearing, smelling, touching, and tasting it with your spiritual senses. Make note of everything you sense in your dream diary.

Exercise 6: External Awareness

Exercise 1 taught you how to shift your awareness throughout your body— but did you know you can also shift your awareness to points outside of your body? By outside, I don't mean merely experiencing things right in front of you with your ordinary five senses, I actually mean is moving your awareness into an object and experiencing what it feels like to be that object. To understand how this works, consider what I have told you about reality; not only are we all connected, but also the position of an object is all in the head. So what you are actually doing here is choosing to access information with intent—this is a psychic operation.

Step 1: Location
Find a location, such as a park, public place, or large building and take a seat somewhere.

Step 2: Center Yourself
Bring yourself into alpha by performing ROY-G-BIV, meditating on a single sound, or stilling the mind.

Step 3: Find a Distant Object

Scan the area for a distant object such as a tree, piece of furniture, person, or animal. Once you have located that object, focus on it.

Step 4: Focus on That Object

Focus on that object with the intent of experiencing what it what it would be like to be that object and experience what it is experiencing. If at any time you receive negative vibes, stop focusing in on that object and choose another.

Step 5: Remain Open

Pay attention to incoming sensations as you focus on the object, and be open to the experience. When you do this, you want to run through the gambit of sensations by asking the following questions.

1. What does the object look like up close?
2. How does that object sound up close?
3. What is the texture of that object?
4. How does that object taste?
5. How does that object smell?
6. What is that object's emotional state?
7. What might that object be thinking?

Don't write off any feelings just because you think you might be imagining them—that is not the point of this exercise.

Step 6: Check for Accuracy

If you have the chance, get up, walk over to the object, and experience it through your physical senses. When you do this, go down your list of questions and make comparisons—you might be surprised how accurate you are. If that object is a human or animal just be mindful of its private space. As you repeat this exercise, choose objects that are further away—it doesn't matter if they are blurry or just look like a dot on the horizon—all the better.

Exercise 7: Know Thy Self

Who are you? What are your goals and aspirations? What do you fear? These may seem like irrelevant questions, but what you will discover is that knowing who you truly are will not only make you a more powerful Sorcerer, but also make you a better and more fulfilled person.

To really understand what this exercise is all about and just how important it is, you must understand that all your habits, fears, the limitations you place on yourself, attitudes about life, and your expectations are hidden away in your unconscious mind. These were things you learned when you were younger, especially during early childhood. And just because they are hidden doesn't mean they don't affect you. We form survival strategies based on this early programming, and those strategies get acted on automatically without out us even thinking about it—that's just how the human mind works.

Consequently, this exercise will allow you to ascertain your true motives before you waste your time casting the wrong spell. Oftentimes after one casts a spell, they act against the very thing they profess to want, or make poor decisions based on unrealistic expectations. What good is a love spell when cast to gain the affection of an incompetent lover? Why cast that spell to find the perfect job if you are lazy and unwilling to work, or you wouldn't be happy doing that job anyway? And lastly, why go through the effort to uncross yourself if you are just going to destroy your life by making the same poor choices again. My point here is how can you even begin to help yourself, if you lack the ability to tell the difference between a bad choice and a good one. No amount of magick will help you, if you lack enough intellectual honesty to own up to all of the crap you have brought upon yourself.

Not only this, all magick puts you in an altered state. In the process of trying to achieve such a state, you are bound to be confronted by your dreams, aspirations, and nightmares. Being in this state is much like being in a dream. When life is going grand and everything is OK, those dreams can be exciting and fun, but when your life is in turmoil, and you've succumb to depression or anxiety, those dreams can be horrifying. In such a case, it becomes necessary to know yourself—and only then will you be able to change your life. So what this exercise does is allow you to reach into your unconscious mind, examine that programming and change it.

Phase I: Collect Memories

Step 1: Buy a Journal
Buy or make a journal and label it "Know Thy Self." Consider this book private—so keep it away from prying eyes. Try to make a journal entry once a week.

Step 2: Achieve a Light Trance
Use whatever method of meditation you wish to enter alpha.

Step 3: Observe Your Thoughts
Let go of whatever method you used to enter a light trance and turn inward— that means, no longer concentrate on your breath if you are focusing on your breath, or no longer concern yourself with the fixed point you are staring at. Now, simply let your mind wander, and observe your thoughts. This will send you into an even deeper trance. Try not to get sucked too far into any particular chain of thoughts—by chain of thoughts, I mean long series of related thoughts.

Example:

.oO "Man, that spaghetti today was delicious. Maybe I should make another plate."

.oO (Thinking about eating spaghetti.)

.oO (This causes you to remember going on a date with your ex-wife at an Italian restaurant.)

.oO (This reminds you of your ex-wife and all the problems you had with her.)

.oO (This brings up a particular argument.)

You notice that you are obsessing over this argument, and it keeps repeating in your head, because you can't resolve it.

At this point, you want to pull yourself back. Otherwise, you will continue obsessing over this argument. To pull yourself back, think the word Stop! then refocus and let your mind wander again. Go through this process until you have collected several of these deep rooted thoughts.

Step 4: End the Session

Open your eyes, get up, stretch, then immediately write down the deep rooted thoughts you have collected, before they vanish from your mind. Make sure and write down everything you remember.

Example:

> Argument with Ex-Wife.
> Having dinner with my ex-wife and got into an argument about money. The whole night was ruined. We went home, and I slept on the couch. The next morning, she told me she wanted a divorce.

> Cottage in the Woods
> I keep thinking about a cottage in the woods. It is so beautiful. I have solitude, and feel connected to nature—no sounds of traffic, a simple life.

> Enjoying Time with My Kids
> I recalled a time when I taught my young son and daughter to swim, how afraid they were, how much I loved them, the trust they had in me, and finally how they had so much fun and laughed. This made me think of my ex-wife again.

Phase II: Analyze a Memory

Step 1:

Reflect on the thoughts you have collected and choose the most important one. In this case, it would be the Argument with your Ex-Wife, because

Enjoying Time with My Kids pulled you back to this event. Grab your journal and make an entry. Write down the title and date.
Example:

Argument with Ex-Wife (2-12-2016)

Next begin asking questions about this event. Write down each question and try to answer it.
Example:

Q: Why did I have this argument?
A: My wife was upset because we didn't have enough money to throw a party for her friends.

Q: How did it make me feel?
A: I felt angry because she never seemed to appreciate what she had, and I felt like she had to spend more money to impress her friends. I felt like a bad husband because I couldn't provide what she needed.

Next ask questions about your answers.
Example:

Q: Why didn't you have enough money to throw a party for her friends?
A: Because she kept spending all her money and my money.

Q: Why do you think she never appreciated what she had?
A: Because she is a materialistic bitch.

Q: Does the ability to fund your all of your wife's social exploits make you a bad husband?
A: I don't know—yes maybe.

I'm sure you can see where this is going. Notice that the last question couldn't be answered honestly. This is a sign of a deeper block. We will choose to mediate on this answer in our next step.

Step 2: Go Deeper
Choose one of the questions you were unable to answer, and mediate on it. To do this, repeat phase one, but instead of letting your thoughts drift, meditate on the question you chose. Once you have held that question in your mind for one or two minutes, let your mind drift. This should start a chain of thoughts centered around that question. Collect those thoughts and repeat the steps in stage II.

By performing this exercise, you will be able to peel back the layers of your subconscious mind, and discover all the hidden things that motivate you. This process will allow you to confront your fears, discover those things that really matter to you, and thus change your life—just be gentle—this is not an easy task. You may encounter aspects of yourself that you have forgotten about. Some of those aspect you may wish to change with the help of theurgy, or spellwork. Last note—please don't underestimate the life-altering power of this meditation—it is so important.

Exercise 8: Gaining Spiritual Insight
In the beginning of this chapter, I mentioned that you could use trance to tap into the collective consciousness and uncover valuable information— but what I didn't mention was just how powerful this technique really is. The collective consciousness, oftentimes referred to as Akashic records, is a global consciousness that forms the blueprints and thus the collective knowledge of humankind. Highly creative people and those who are aware, tap into this energy to draw inspiration, and ideas. Many of those ideas have inspired great works and scientific innovations that would have otherwise taken thousands of years to produce. As farfetched as this may seem, tapping into this source of information is an easy thing to do.

Step 1: The Subject
Choose a subject that is important to you; this could be a problem, a hard question, or any general topic you want to understand better. Once you have

come up with the subject of your meditation, make sure you know what you want to get out of the session. For example, let's say you interested in answering the question, "Is time travel possible?" However, before you can even answer that question, you need to know exactly what time is. So this is where you start.

Step 2: Plant the Seed

Before meditating on the question at hand, do some research on your topic and use your creativity to try to come up answers on your own. Now, review everything that you have learned and any solutions you might have come up with—consider this step a form of purging. Only by acknowledging what you already know can you purge that information from conscious thought, and make yourself open to receive unique information from the universal conscious.

Step 3: Meditate

Bring yourself in to a trance by using a simple meditation. When you feel you are deep enough, bring that question to bear in your mind. Again, review what you already know, and go over any solutions you might have come up with in mind. Next, open yourself up to inspiration by allowing your mind to wander around the subject. If you begin thinking about something else, pull your attention back to the topic of the meditation. If you are in a deep enough state, new unique ideas will begin to form. Don't scrutinize or dismiss anything. Just let your thoughts flow. When you are no longer receiving information or you feel like you have received all of the information you can, cease meditating. Just keep in mind the deeper your trance, the better your connection will be with collective consciousness. This means you may have to stay in meditation for quite a while.

Step 4: Record It

Once you come out of the trance, immediately record what you have seen. Otherwise, like a dream, it will quickly fade. It is also likely that your mind will continue receiving information after you have become lucid, in such a case, pay attention to any new ideas that may come, and quickly add them to your records.

Exercise 9: Auto-Suggestion

Auto-suggestion is a form of self-brainwashing using repetition. The idea is that something becomes a habit if it is repeated enough, and when that happens, it becomes a behavior that is stored in the unconscious mind and automatically recalled whenever needed. And of course, there is no question that this works—repetition does breed habit, and things get unconsciously pounded into our head all the time. This type of behavioral self-programming is called an *affirmation*.

For example, if you didn't like the fact that you were timid and wanted to be more brave, you might say, "I am not afraid to speak my mind and stand up for myself," and if you decided that you cared too much about other people's opinions, you might say something like, "My opinions are just as valid as others."

So how do affirmations or auto-suggestions work? Typically, an affirmation is programmed by exposing oneself to it over and over again over a period of weeks, months, or even years—but there is a quicker way. But before you decide to brainwash yourself with an auto-suggestion, use the "Know Thyself" exercise in this chapter to trace any bad thoughts or behaviors back to their true sources. Once you have determined what the bad thought is, then you can proceed to replace it with a healthier, more constructive thought. To do this think of an appropriate affirmation, then go about setting it using deep meditation. As far as the meditation technique goes, use whatever method works best for you to achieve the deepest trance that you can manage. Once your attention has been directed to what is in your unconscious mind, repeat your affirmation over and over again, for about ten minutes. Do this each day until you see results—this will cut programming time down tremendously.

Working with Energy

Most critics of magick deny the existence of "magical" energy on the grounds that practitioners who claim use it cannot seem to define it. And this easy to understand when you consider that most contemporary magicians don't really care enough about the science behind their practice to learn it, and therefore can't explain these concepts to outsiders. This does two things: one, it stifles the development of magick as a science by failing to investigate the why and how; and two, it makes the entire practice look silly, because oftentimes new age garbage is accepted without question, without any kind of proof.

In reality, a true magician or witch utilize many different kinds of energy—some that can be currently measured by scientific instruments, and others that cannot. But even though we are unable to measure something with a piece of technology, that doesn't mean it doesn't exist, because of the effect that it has on the environment and the people in it. There is in fact a common form of energy that is recognized by both scientists and magicians alike. The only difference is its label. Having said this, I shall try to define what energy *really* is, starting with its most subtle form.

From the first emanation of the Source comes a very subtle layer of energy that could be called quintessence. The word *quintessence* stems from the Latin words *quinta essentia* and refers to the fifth element, the purest essence of anything—or simply spirit. Quintessence is the very same thing as quanta. And the word *quanta* is used by quantum physicists to describe quantum wave particles, or the smallest element that science can measure at this moment. Both quintessence and quanta have the same qualities—they are both described as psychoreactive, nontemporal, and nonspatial by nature.

That is, this energy reacts to and can be manipulated by thought (because it is a type of thought), and does not occupy any particular point in space or time, and is therefore not restricted by distance or sequence of time.

This means you do not need to move quintessence as you would lower forms of energy. Quintessence is used by impressing your will upon it. Once you have done that, it will manifest naturally. But in order to impress your will upon quintessence, you must be able to hold a thought or idea in your head long enough to be able to imagine the outcome you want—and this is where magick comes in. Magick is a collection of techniques that takes advantage of a symbolic language meant to enhance your focus, and visualization. These techniques will be discussed later in the chapter entitled "Occult Magick."

A step down from quintessence is an energy called ether. Ether can be understood as a field of energy—referred to as "radiant energy" by Nikola Tesla. Although it still exists within the physical realm, it is fluid, and less solid than matter. Ether is said to contain the blueprint for all things in the physical universe—this means humans, animals, and plants, as well as noncorporeal entities such as those living on the lower planes. Although mainstream science does not believe this form of energy exists, we can infer its existence through logic. We do know that everything is made up of atoms, and those atoms are made up of electrons and protons. We also know that those electrons and protons orbit around the atom's core, called a neutron, and that orbit, or spin creates an electromagnetic force, in the shape of a toroid that envelopes the atom. Since all things are made up of atoms, all things have a magnetic field—albeit some much weaker than others. And such is the case with the human body. The human heart emits an electromagnetic field that can be measured up to three feet away using sensitive scientific instruments—it is second only to the field generated by the brain.

In the book *Linked and Communiqué*, physicist John E. Best (PhD) communicates with Margerie, his fiancée (a physicist also), through a medium. During these conversations, his wife, who has passed on, describes the etheric body and how it works. She explains that the etheric body is made up of electrons and positrons that are held together by consciousness itself. She goes on to explain that after life leaves the physical body, this field of energy, which she calls the electric body, loses cohesion and dissolves. But the conscious part of the person, or mind-body continues to exist in a higher realm.

And this makes perfect sense because everything dies, degrades, or breaks down after death—this is called entropy. And when that entropy is complete, that magnetic force no longer holds that thing together, and that energy is released back into the universe to be used. So if ether is related to electromagnetic force (which I believe it is), then this would explain things like poltergeist activity, and psychokinesis. It would also make sense that this "energy" could be affected by other fields of energy to heal or even cause harm—everything, after all, is made up of resonant waves that produce an electromagnetic force. So this means if you want to develop psychokinesis or energy healing, you need to learn how to increase your ether field and become sensitive to electromagnetic energy.

The next and lowest category of energy would be considered physical energy. When I say physical energy, I am talking about the type of energy that can currently be measured by science, such as light, sound, kinetic force, and so on. Such energy would come from the sun, the wind, hydroelectric systems, lightning, and the earth itself. What must be understood, though, is that all these lower forms of energy are also composed of ether, and quintessence, which is constantly being generated by the Source—they would not manifest here on this plane otherwise.

To learn how to manipulate these lower forms of energy, all you have to do is take a course at your local collage, do some research on the internet, or find a good book on the type of energy you are trying to harness. Therefore, the remainder of this book will be dedicated to the use of quintessence and ether.

CHAKRAS

The word *chakra* means disc or wheel in Sanskrit. The chakras are considered to be energy centers of the subtle body that control various aspects of our well-being. The idea of chakras was developed by the Yogi between the years 600 and 1300 CE, and was picked up by Western Yogis around the sixteenth century. Today, we are taught that there are seven Chakras, but the fact is that not even the Yogis could agree. The reality, depending on which ancient text you read, is that there can be over twenty.

Also, the idea that the chakras occupy a particular part of the body, and are somehow tied to a particular organ or nerve bundle doesn't seem to be true. The Yogis believed that because the subtle body or etheric body is fluid, and changing the location of a chakra can also change. In fact, it was believed that the number of chakras could change according to the type of Yoga a person was practicing. There really are only three chakras that exist within all systems: the chakra located in the lower belly (Sacral), the one at the heart (Heart Chakra) and the one at the crown (Crown Chakra). Consequently, these three chakra locations are where most people report feeling physical sensations associated with emotions. It is also worthy to note that the association of chakras to colors, or the rainbow scheme was not originally taught by the Yogi—that came about in California, sometime during the late twentieth century. Another interesting fact is that none of the ancient texts ever mention a particular emotional or psychological state associated with a chakra. Instead, when a chakra was envisioned as a lotus, each petal had an emotional/psychological association with each peddle. Also the association of herbs, minerals, stones, angels, or tarot cards were never a part of the system. These associations seem to begin with Carl Jung. The main purpose of a chakra was to activate a specific mantra for a particular purpose within a certain part of the body.

By saying these things, I am not trying to invalidate the use of chakras as we know them today, I am only trying to make you realize the chakra system is symbolic. And that is OK because the intent carried by those symbols can be used to imprint quintessence and move ether. Nonetheless, you are still working with very real forms of energy when you work with the modern chakra system. Although the number of chakras vary from system to system, most Western systems recognize seven. It is also thought that besides the seven primary chakras, there are a multitude of secondary chakras in both the hands, feet, and throughout the entire body. All of these chakras are thought to move energy through the body's channels as we go about our daily lives.

For those hoping to develop their psychic abilities and work with magick, working with the chakra system can be highly beneficial—just don't get too caught up on which system is correct, because like I said it's symbolic. Not only this, but also remember that the chakra system is not the only way of moving energy or imprinting quintessence. So without further ado, let's take a look at the basic correspondence of each of the seven main chakras below.

Seven Primary Chakras

Root (Red)

Thought to be located at the base of the spine or tailbone. Seen as vermilion red, yellow, and gold. The root chakra is responsible for keeping us grounded and controls aspects of our survival, and material well-being. This Chakra is also called upon to help us ground, and can be used to draw energy from the Earth up into the body.

Signs of Imbalance

- Negativity and distrust of others
- Overeating or undereating
- Greed
- A distorted view or reality
- Living in survival mode

Sacral (Orange)

Thought to be located in the lower part of the abdomen: two inches from the navel and two inches into the body, also associated with the lymphatic system. Seen as orange or white at higher vibrations. This controls our contentedness and sexual pleasure as well as our ability to relate to others and be comfortable with new experiences. It is also connected with creativity and emotion. Certain psychic sensations said to be felt in the stomach are also sensed though this Chakra.

Signs of Imbalance

- A dependency or codependency on others
- Drug and alcohol addiction
- Lack of emotional control, being hung up in one particular emotion, or being emotionally detached

- Flights of fantasy
- An obsession with sex or lack of sexual desire or sexual satisfaction

Solar Plexus (Yellow)

Thought to be located in the upper abdomen in the area of the stomach. Seen as yellow or at higher vibrations golden yellow. Is tied to self-esteem, worth, confidence, discipline, intellect, and most importantly, Will.

Signs of Imbalance

- A dominant attitude or passivity
- Obsessive planning or being scatterbrained
- Applying logic to things when empathy is needed
- Manipulative, power hungry, psychopathic behavior
- Lack of clear direction, lack of purpose, or ambition
- Starting too many projects at one time, or jumping from one project to another

Heart (Green)

Thought to be located in the center of the chest but is also associated with the thymus gland which is responsible for hormone production and the regulation of the immune system. Not only is the heart Chakra connected to the heart, but also the lungs. Seen as green or at higher vibrations pink. Is responsible for our capacity to love ourselves and others, joy and inner peace. It is also associated with compassion and the ability to forgive and accept. Known to be our center of awareness.

Signs of Imbalance

- Defensiveness
- Emotional detachment
- Jealousy; fear of intimacy
- Codependency
- Always placing other people's wants, needs and desires above yours
- Always trying to save the world, or seeing oneself as the victim
- Antisocial behavior or isolation
- Holding grudges, or the inability to forgive

- Respiratory ailments, such as lung infection, bronchitis
- Circulatory or heart-related issues

Throat (Blue)
Thought to be located in the throat and is associated with the thyroid, which regulates the processing of energy in the body through temperature and growth. Controls self-expression, feelings and all forms of communication. Is connected to the World of Spirit and governs your ability to project things into the material plane using psychic and worldly communication. Because it is a bridge between the etheric body and the Spirit World, it wants nothing more than to express the true you. This Chakra also gives us our sense of timing.

Signs of Imbalance
- Saying inappropriate things, saying too much, or not speaking up
- Overtalking others
- Fear of communication
- Uncontrolled clairaudient abilities; hearing voices
- Lying, or bragging
- Inability to keep secrets, or excessive secretiveness
- Not being able to identify your purpose in life

Third Eye (Indigo)
Thought to be located at the forehead, just between the eyes. Is responsible for insight, imagination, wisdom as well as mundane and psychic perception. Our third eye is associated with the pineal gland that regulates our sleep cycle.

Signs of Imbalance
- Overactive clairvoyant ability: may see spirits or thoughts manifesting on the astral
- Inability to see beyond the physical world
- Problems visualizing
- Feeling disconnected from the Source
- A rejection of the spiritual realm

Crown (Violet, White, or Gold)

Located at the top of the head. Although the crown Chakra is linked with the brain and entire nervous system it is associated with the pituitary gland, the pineal and hypothalamus. Both hypothalamus and pituitary gland work in tangent to regulate the endocrine system. Represents our connection to our higher spiritual self, the collective consciousness and Source. Can affect how content we are in life and with the spiritual forces around us.

Signs of Imbalance

- A disconnection from Spirit
- Difficulty seeing the connectedness in all things, therefore feeling isolated
- Being close-minded
- Not being grounded, neglecting the worldly
- Obsession with the spiritual

Ether-Moving Exercises

In addition to the meditation exercises you are currently doing, you can incorporate Chakra and energy work into your regiment. These exercises are intended to help you move energy that you have been sensing as the result of meditation (ether). By practicing the exercises in this chapter, not only will you be able to move this energy, but also you will increase the amount of electromagnet force you can produce, and extend its range.

Three exercises will be your mainstay; the Middle Pillar, the Circulation of the Body of Light, and the Psi Wheel. The Middle Pillar will help you open your Chakras, and keep them balanced, while the Circulation of the Body of Light will help you move and increase the amount of energy you can produce. Using the psi wheel will allow you to see the energy movement by producing psychokinetic effects, and help you gain control over this force.

Middle-Pillar Ritual

The middle pillar is an energy raising ritual created by the Hermetic Order of the Golden Down and is the mainstay of most Ceremonial Magicians. The original ritual calls upon the divine names of God at each Chakra points.

Although these correspondence are meaningful to Ceremonial Magicians, we are not practicing Ritual Magick, so we will not be using them.

Instead, we will be creating energy at the chakra points by resonating the traditional vowels associated with them—doh, reh, mi, fah, sol, la, and ti. It is thought that these notes are the same resonant frequencies used by the Source to manifest reality. Resonating at a particular note creates a vibration that truly stimulates those chakra points in a very spiritually powerful way. When you perform this ritual vibrate each vowel at the suggested note using the diametric scale. The vibrations of these intonations should be directed inside the visualized spheres to actually cause that chakra vibrate and open. After you do this for a while you will see how intoning each vowel, while visualizing actually creates a vibration in that area of the body—and that is the entire point.

Step 1: Facing
Stand facing the direction of the rising sun resting your arms comfortably to your sides. The sun is the first emanation of divine essence in our solar system. Therefore, by facing East you are drawing energy from the Source.

Step 2: Crown Chakra (Ti)
Envision a ball of white-light energy manifesting halfway inside the top portion of your skull. Know that this energy connects you to the All. See this ball of white light pulse and rotate in a clockwise direction. Intone the vowel at the keynote of ti. Sense this vibration resonating from with this brilliant white orb invigorating it.

Step 3: Third-Eye Chakra (La)
See a line of energy come down through the skull, stopping right above and between the eyes. Envision a ball of indigo-light energy about the size of a small dinner plate manifesting within right above and between the eyes. Know that this energy is the center of your psychic awareness and gives you both heightened physical and spiritual senses. See this ball of indigo light pulse and rotate in a clockwise direction. Intone the vowel at the key note of La. Sense this vibration resonating from within this brilliant indigo orb and invigorating it.

Step 4: Throat Chakra (Sol)

See a line of energy come down your third-eye chakra to the middle of your chest. Envision a ball of green-light energy about the size of a basketball manifesting in the center of your chest. Know that this energy connects you with your ability to feel compassion and empathy and gives you the ability to heal. See this ball of green light pulse and rotate in a clockwise direction. Intone the vowel at the keynote of Sol. Sense this vibration resonating from with this brilliant green orb and invigorating it.

Step 5: Heart Chakra (Fah)

See a line of energy come down through the skull, down the neck, and into the chest cavity. Envision a ball of green-light energy about the size of a basketball manifesting within the chest cavity. Know that this energy connects you to the World of Spirit and gives you the capacity to manifest your will into this reality. See this ball of green light pulse and rotate in a clockwise direction. Intone the vowel at the keynote of La. Sense this vibration resonating from with this brilliant green orb invigorating it.

Step 6: Solar Plexus Chakra (Mi)

See a line of energy come down through the middle of the chest, and end right between the peak of your rib cage. Envision a ball of gold-light energy about the size of a plate manifesting at that same location. Feel this chakra fill you with courage and willpower. See this ball of gold-light pulse and rotate in a clockwise direction. Intone the vowel at the keynote of Mi. Sense this vibration resonating from with this brilliant gold orb invigorating it.

Step 6: Sacral Chakra (Reh)

See a line of energy come down your Solar Plexus chakra and end in your stomach region. Envision a ball of orange-light energy about the size of a baseball manifesting at that same location. Feel this chakra fill you confidence and charisma. See this ball of orange light pulse and rotate in a clockwise direction. Intone the vowel at the keynote of Reh. Sense this vibration resonating from with this brilliant orange orb invigorating it.

Step 7: Root Chakra (Doh)

See a line of energy come down your Sacral chakra and end in genital area between your legs. Envision a ball of red-light energy about the size of a baseball manifesting at that same location. Feel this chakra fill you sense of well-being and grounding. See this ball of red-light pulse and rotate in a clockwise direction. Intone the vowel at the keynote of Doh. Sense this vibration resonating from with this brilliant red orb invigorating it.

Step 8: Ground

Extend a line of energy from the Root Chakra down to your feet. At this point, form a sphere of energy. Let that energy run into the Earth and ground you.

Chakras and Sigil Invocation

As mentioned above, some Yogis spoke chanted God Names inside each chakra in order to invoke the power or essence of that God or Goddess inside a particular energy center. Although you don't need to invoke deities, you can take advantage of this method also. Instead of using a God Name as a mantra to invoke the power of that God, create a sigil and sigilized charm. A sigil is a symbol that represents intent, while a sigilized charm is a fabricated word that represents intent. The making of sigils and sigilized charms is fully detailed in the chapter entitled Occult Magick. If you want to create them, I give you permission to jump forward to learn how to make them. Once you have created the sigil and sigilized charm, they can be invoked at any chakra point by chanting the word at the appropriate key and visualizing the actual sigil symbol inside the chakra itself. Repeat the sigilized charm like a mantra, over and over until you mentally resonate with it.

Circulation of the Body of Light

The Circulation of the Body of Light is another ritual designed by the Hermetic Order of the Golden Dawn. Its purpose is to help the student to learn how to move Kundalini from the base of the spine (the Root Chakra) to the crown Chakra. Kundalini which means "the coiled one" in Sanskrit describes a toroid of energy that resides at the base of the spine. As it is released, it moves up the spine by traveling the channels, and passes through the centers (chakras). This is also sometimes referred to as the "path of the serpent" because the energy, which resembles a snake, actually travels upward in a spiraling motion, forming a coil.

Performing the Middle Pillar

Left-to-Right Circulation

Focus on your crown chakra and visualize it as a sphere of bright white light rotating in a clockwise direction. Repeating the "Ti" mantra visualizing the sound vibrating that sphere. Next, as you breathe out, visualize this energy flowing down your left shoulder all the way down to the sphere at your left foot. As you breathe in, visualize this energy moving from the left foot to the right, then up the right side of your body all the way up to the crown chakra again. Do this for about three to five minutes. As you cycle this energy visualize it extending outward about five feet from the body, but if you wish, take it out as far as you want.

Front-to-Back Circulation

Now instead of cycling this energy from left to right, cycle it from front-to-back. Do this for another three to five minutes, expanding that energy as far as you wish.

The Mummy

Concentrate at the sphere of energy at the base of your feet. See and feel it become energized. Once you have done this, visualize a coil of energy extending from the right side of the sphere and wrapping around your left leg. Bring that coil of energy around the back of the left leg, making it wrap tightly around the front of your right leg. Continue this wrapping visualization until you have completely wrapped your body all the way to the crown chakra. Once you have connected with the crown chakra see this energy explode like a fountain and fall like rain to the sphere at your feet. Reabsorb this energy and continue cycling this energy in the same manner. Keep that up for about five minutes. Please be cautious when performing this exercise. It creates a rocking motion, and has been known to make people very dizzy or even fall over.

The Psi Wheel

The Psi Wheel is essentially a piece of aluminum foil folded into a pyramidal shape that rests on a pin. This simple tool is used to practice psychokinesis. Some of you may get movement right off the bat, while for others movement may take fifteen minutes to an hour. You may in fact get no movement at all—in such case, just keep trying and eventually you will. So even if you are just sitting there like an idiot staring at the Psi Wheel trying to get it to move with no action, make this a part of your exercises. Psychokinesis can sometimes take weeks and months to manifest, so don't give up.

Step 1: Create a Psi Wheel

Find a large mason jar and clean and dry it thoroughly. Remove the cap and glue a small Styrofoam or balsa-wood block onto it. Take a large needle and stick it into the center of the block. Get some aluminum foil and cut out a small, square piece large enough to be seen, but small enough to fit inside the glass mason jar. Once you have cut the aluminum square, fold it into a pyramid. Open the pyramid, turn it point up and rest it gently on the pin. Next, carefully screw the upside down jar onto the lid and place it on an even surface where you can't knock it over and it can be clearly seen.

Step 2: Connect with The Pyramid

Spend as much time as you need connecting with the pyramid, using tratak meditation.

Step 3: Move It

When you feel that you have entered a deep enough trance (theta-gamma is best) use visualization to spin the pyramid. How you visualize this happening is not important, only that it is clear and intentional. You could visualize a phantom arm reaching out and tapping it, or you could simply visualize the pyramid moving. You could see a current of air pushing it, or even it being moved by your own magnetic force.

QUINTESSENCE EXERCISE

The purpose of this exercise is to practice effecting the energy of chance (quintessence) using your mind. Dr. Joseph Banks Rhine of Duke University, North Carolina, was the first-person experiment with controlling chance by testing the effects of intention on dice rolls during the 1930s. We will be doing exactly this, because this same experiment affords you the opportunity to develop your ability to tap into and control quintessence.

Really all you need for this experiment is a single six-sided die. However, you can practice your control over multiple objects by rolling more than one at a time. First, make a record in your magick journal. In this record write down date and time as well as your physical/emotional condition. Next, choose what number you want to manifest (one to six), how many rolls you will make, and the number of dice you will roll at one time. For scoring purposes write down the number of rolls you decided to make, and draw a line over it—this will be your fraction. Next make your rolls (with eyes open). For the best accuracy, relax, breath normally, and focus on your target number without straining. Record all hits as ones and all misses as zeros, and then when finished, add up your hits and write them down above the line of your number-of-rolls fraction.

Take note. You can also practice on other random systems, such as traffic lights, lightning strikes, and encounters with people. If you decide to do this however, please be mindful of the people you will affect when making these changes. For example, changing all the traffic lights from home to work will affect the flow of traffic for everyone else, and messing with the weather can cause floods, fires, and other natural disasters. I flooded out my own apartment trying to manifest rain one night—no joke, instant karma!

Other Ways of Raising Energy

Raising energy is actually an easy thing to do—as a matter of fact, anything that puts you in a highly charged emotional state will raise energy. But no matter how you decide to raise this energy, you should open a circle to contain it or have a vessel to store it in, else that energy will bleed out into the environment and dissipate. A circle or container is just another immaterial idea given the power to contain energy by *will*. So let's talk about some traditional ways to "raise" energy.

One very common method is song and dance. If you are the type of person who likes to do this, choose a song that embodies the type of energy you wish to raise, and dance to it. To accomplish this, sing or play music. Drumming is another very common form of energy raising. It is used all the time in Wiccan, Voodoo, and Santeria circles. If you decide to drum choose a rhythm that is between 4 and 4.5 beats per second because this will help you achieve trance much quicker. Some people raise energy by just walk a circle as they meditate on the intent of their spell or ritual, while others simply rock or sway back and forth—the point is some kind of movement. Energy can also be raised by storytelling, watching a movie, chanting, shouting, or stomping—in fact, anything that causes a vibration will create energy.

So let's now talk about the two most controversial but also most powerful ways of raising energy: sex and bloodletting. The reason why these two methods constitute the most powerful forms of energy raising is because they invoke primal instincts. The desire to have sex is genetically built into the human condition—most people like to have sex. So if you are going to use this method, make sure you open a circle and end your lovemaking by casting a spell or drawing the energy into a vessel—sex energy falls more into the positive spectrum.

The latter method, bloodletting, invokes a primal fear response and therefore generates negative energy. This type of energy is induced by our desire to protect ourselves, and feeds off of the shock of being injured. I think most people would agree that not being harmed is better than being harmed. Consequently, the power generated by bloodletting is not actually in the blood itself, but generated by the shock and trauma caused from being hurt. Bloodletting does not mean something has to die. It simply means it is generated through physical trauma. Therefore, it can be raised by any action which causes pain or injury, such as flagellation (ritualistically flogging or beating oneself), sticking yourself with a needle, or slapping oneself in the face. As a matter of fact, just the mere belief that harm might occur will generate this kind of energy. Do note, if you decide to use any of these methods, it is unnecessary to actually injure yourself; pain can be induced without doing great bodily harm.

Collecting and Storing Energy

If you have been practicing meditation and the energy-work exercises above, you may already be aware of what lingers about in the environment. If that is the case, now all you need to know is how to collect it, add to it, and program that energy with purpose. To collect energy means to tap into it, capture it, and store it in something. Doing this is an act of will that utilizes visualization. To prevent yourself contaminating your own field of energy and causing a drastic shift in your mood you can store this energy in a stone, Witch's Ball, sigil, or any other literal sealed vessel. Remember: It is not the physical object that holds the energy. It's the symbolic intent that does—the energy is held, nonetheless.

Another good thing to know is that some physical objects hold energy better than others. That is, certain objects glow (albeit lightly) with a stronger aura than others. This is a good sign that an object will actually hold energy. If you can't see auras, try holding an object for a few minutes to sense its vibes. It will either feel cold, indicating that it is a good negative energy container, or warm, indicating it is a good positive energy container. Charged objects may also generate a specific emotional response, which is another sign.

Such energy can be collected from just about anywhere or anything, including living things like animals or humans. Collecting energy from an object, place, or plant is just considered collecting energy, but collecting energy from an animal or human is considered psychic vampirism. Whenever you take energy from a living thing, you are in fact taking its life force. Thus, most practitioners consider it an act of black magick. To collect energy from an area, stand in that area, quiet your mind, and become open to it until you can actually sense it. Once you can, begin pulling this energy in through your crown Chakra by visualizing it being sucked in like a whirlpool. Temporarily bring this energy down to your sacral chakra and continue the process until you feel full or can't take in any more.

In the same way, if you intend to leach energy off of a person, stand next to that person or visualize him or her and then quiet your mind and become receptive. Concentrate until you begin to feel that person's mood. Then visualize a cord or tether attached to them, and see or feel that energy being transferred to you. Just know that when you do this, they will be weakened and quite possibly become ill. That is why I suggest only doing this to people who make worthy targets for curses, for example, someone who has harmed you or means to harm you or a loved one. Using this method on an innocent person just makes you a psychopath.

Taking in this energy will undoubtedly cause you to sense it on a more profound level. If it is dark energy, you may feel uncomfortable; if it is light energy, you may get a positive high.

Now it is time to strip this energy of its former programming and give it a more generic purpose. For example, if you want to use this energy for white or black magick, you would focus on the attributes of these two types of energy; white-light energy is loving, caring, compassionate, generous, and healing, while dark or abyssal energy is destructive, full of fear, and hate. You could also associate this energy with the elemental properties of air, fire, water, and earth. To actually program the energy, all you need to do is meditate on the properties you wish to imbue it with; light, abyssal, elemental, and so on. There is no need to do any fancy visualizations during this process. Just think about the properties of the energy type you wish to create, until the energy you have taken in strongly resonates with those properties. Once you have impressed your collected energy with those properties, you are ready to transfer it to your vessel.

Visualization with the intent is the method you will use to transfer and store this energy. How you visualize this happening is entirely up to you. You could visualize this energy being packed into a suitcase and then emptied into the vessel by a little guy in a business suit, or you could visualize your vessel suddenly lighting up because the energy has been instantaneously transferred—it really doesn't matter. Don't make the visualizations too elaborate or complicated, or it will actually impede your ability to transfer it.

So let me make a few suggestions. If you are using the chakra system, remember that energy is stored in your Sacral Chakra. Your chakras spins, so as it spins, visualize this spinning motion causing the energy to compact into a dense ball about the size of an orange. Once you have your orange-sized ball of energy bring it up through your Solar Plexus Chakra, then to your

Heart Chakra, and down through your primary arm into your hand and release it through your palm into the vessel. If you are storing the energy in a tool, hold that tool in your hand and see, feel, or just know that tool is being filled and charged. Continue this process until you don't feel the energy's emotional state anymore.

Energy and Intent

The way you choose to raise energy will imbue that energy with an emotional charge as well as with information. This is why it is important to keep your intent in mind while raising energy. This means that if you are performing a wealth spell and singing and dancing to raise that energy, you should also be thinking of getting that money you want. On the same note, if you are casting a love spell and are raising energy by sexually gratifying yourself, you should be thinking about attracting a lover at the same time.

It is also possible to raise energy and charge it with intent afterward—in fact, that is what you would have to do when using energy that you have stored. If you decide to go this route, the stored energy you choose to use is easier to program if its emotional charge is similar to what you intend to use it for. Let's say, for example, you've been saving up all your hate in a jar—yes, it can be done. Now you want to use that hate energy to cast a massive curse on someone. That would be the perfect use for that particular type of stored energy. However, it would take more effort than it would be worth to try to change hate energy into love energy to use it in a love spell. The process by which you program stored energy is simple; you hold the object and meditate on your intention until that energy resonates with that emotion—no complicated ritual needed.

Science as Magick

We are living in an age of technology, so why shouldn't we use it? Before you scoff at making yourself seem superhuman by taking advantage of science, medicine, or technology, consider the fact that most of us already do this. We don't need telepathy to communicate with people over vast distances—we have cell phones. We don't need to produce fire with our minds, because we can build a flame thrower. Nor do we need to levitate things with telekinesis; we can use electromagnets!

Is this cheating because it involves technologies we already know about, or is it just foolish to avoid using these things because we want to imagine we are Merlin or Magneto? I am not saying that things like telepathy, pyrokinesis, and telekinesis don't work, but why expend a lot of energy trying to start a fire with your mind when you could simply whip out your Zippo and set something a blaze? Seriously, guys, think this through logically. Of course, no one is going to see you as superhuman for using a cell phone, pulling out a lighter, or setting up electromagnets to levitate something, but if you really want to make yourself look like Dr. Strange, with a little bit of sleight-of-hand magick, and science, you can damn well make the common homo sapiens believe you are—trust me: idiots are born every day!

Additionally, science, medicine, and technology can be used to measure, perfect, and enhance occult magick and psychic abilities as well. Not many people incorporate this into their practice, because they simply overlook it. If you are smart, with a little bit of study and persistence you can develop your own tech to help you achieve your goals.

If you want to understand how things work, or if your ultimate goal is to develop new technologies that will enable you to go where no one has gone before, then your studies, experiments and methods should be grounded in science. As I have mentioned before, mainstream science and mystical teaching is beginning to merge, so don't discount either one, instead, consider both of these teachings before you form a hypothesis.

Always keep in mind that both science and mysticism are plagued by people with close-minded, rigid, and unwavering beliefs that are based more in faith than logic. For this reason, don't discount something just because it sounds impossible, silly or considered fringe—test it! It would be a tragedy if you passed something up just because you lacked imagination or you gave into to an assertion that something was not true just because some authority figure told you so.

With this said, also know that people are greedy and love to entertain fantastical beliefs. If you are going to buy a piece of technology, make sure you do your research. There are a lot of people out there selling bogus devices that can allegedly produce supernatural effects. Psychic fairs and online websites are littered with crap that does nothing but produce dazzling light shows and look pretty—so don't get sucked in.

THE SCIENTIFIC METHOD

Most practitioners of magick don't consider what they practice as a type of science, but that can't be further from the truth. Research has shown that one's intentions can have a measurable effect on the environment, so why not put your craft to the test to make sure you are being effective? The purpose of performing experiments is not necessarily to prove to you or someone else that magick works (although when you do get confirmation, that acts to solidify your belief and therefore makes you a more powerful practitioner). No—it's to improve your ability to perform magick and perhaps discover something new. But in order to do that, you must be objective, and have an open mind at the same time.

To understand why, you must understand the *observer effect*. The observer effect states that whenever you try to observe something (or focus on it with intention), it shapes reality in conformity with your will. This means the expectations of scientists performing experiments can affect the outcome of the experiments they are conducting. If they expect to get a particular result, they will probably get it, unless it balks against consensual reality—so in a way, even science is prone to subjectivity.

So how do you test magick? The answer is to use the scientific method like any good scientist and to be as honest as you can about the results you get. Anything less than honesty makes you vulnerable to building a practice based on fantasy, and when that happens, the magick you practice becomes useless. The scientific method represents definitive steps to helping you confirm or discount the results of an experiment.

The steps of the scientific method are thus:

1. Ask a question.
2. Do research.
3. Come up with a hypothesis.
4. Perform an experiment to test that hypothesis.
5. Determine if the experiment is effective, or ineffective.
6. Analyze the data and draw a conclusion.

Scientific Method Details

Step 1: Ask a question.
Come up with a question about something that you can measure. A measurement doesn't have to be something measurable with a piece of technology—it can be a mental state, a mood change, or the occurrence of an event. Ask questions like how, what, who, when, where, and why.

Step 2: Do research.
Become knowledgeable about the subject you are experimenting on. Find out if other people have conducted the same or similar experiments. If so, what did they do, and what results did they get?

Step 3: Come up with a hypothesis.
A hypothesis is an educated guess concerning the expected outcome of the experiment.

For example:

If I do A, B, and C, then I expect X, Y, and Z to happen.

Step 4: Perform an experiment.
An experiment should be a fair test. This could involve tests under controlled or uncontrolled conditions. Consider using the blind and double-blind method as well as instituting multiple controls. But if you alter elements within your experiment, make sure you do it one element at a time. Repeat this experiment several times to make sure that results are not random.

Step 5: Determine if the experiment is effective or ineffective.
If the experiment seemed to be effective, move on to step 6, or modify the experiment and conduct it again.

Step 6: Analyze the data and draw a conclusion.
Take a good look at the data to see how it lines up with or doesn't line up with your hypothesis. Did it prove the hypothesis true or false? If your hypothesis turned out to be false, create a new hypothesis based on the results of your data and conduct more experiments.

The Control
A control is used to minimize or negate outside influences on an experiment, or to provide comparative data when assessing variables. For example, if we wanted to look for anomalous electromagnet activity in a house that is purportedly haunted, we would sweep the entire home using an EMF reader looking for naturally occurring electromagnet fields or those produced by large electronic devices. Doing this would allow us to dismiss fields that are obviously not of paranormal origin so we don't mistake them as supernatural. Another example would be if we were trying to find out if we could induce genuine clairvoyant abilities in a group of ten individuals by hypnotizing them. If we wanted to include a control, we would recruit ten other people to participate who we would not bring into a hypnotic trance. This would allow us to make some judgments: If those who were induced did better than those who were not induced, then we might conclude that clairvoyance is improved under hypnotic conditions. If those not under hypnosis did better, then this would lead us to believe that entrancement is

not conducive to clairvoyance. If neither did well, then that might indicate entrancement has nothing to do with clairvoyance at all.

Blind and Double-Blind

An experiment is considered blind when information about the subject of the experiment is hidden from the participant(s) in order to reduce bias, and is considered double-blind when that information is kept from both the researcher and the subject(s) for the same reason. For example, if we wanted to test the legitimacy of remote viewing, we might give the viewer a target number or sigil of an undisclosed location and have her view it. In this way, positive results (correct information gleaned about the target) are more credible, because the remote viewer had no prior knowledge of the target. If you wanted to use double-blinding to add even more credibility to your experiment, make sure the target is unknown to both the researcher and the person remote viewing.

VALUABLE TECHNOLOGY

The items listed below includes technology that I have personally found useful. Most of these items are inexpensive to buy or make, but some do require technical skills to craft. As a matter of fact, I suggest you invest in multiple sets of tools such as those used for electronics, carpentry, mechanics, sound equipment, and so on. Of course you don't need to collect all this stuff at once, but if you collect a little at a time, you will eventually have what you need. These tools can be bought online, your local hardware or electronics store, found at a yard sale, pawn shop, or even your local thrift store, so there is no reason you should have to go broke. In addition to this you will need a good work space with adequate light.

Computer

This is a given. Computers are useful tools when doing research. And you can plug in all kinds of other devices to a computer to help you capture data to be analyze that data using any number of programs.

Microscope

You may not be able to afford a fancy microscope that will allow you to see things on an atomic level, but microscopes that allow you to view things on a microscopic level are relatively cheap now. You can use this tool to help measure small-scale changes in materials you are trying to effect in an experiment.

EMF Reader

Used to pick up electromagnetic fields, this device can be used to detect electromagnetic changes in the environment due to the presence spirits or your own energy field. Not only this, but also by knowing what is producing an electromagnetic field, you can choose to shut those things off so they don't affect the psychic operation or magical working you are trying to perform.

Tesla Spirit Radio

> My first observations positively terrified me as there was present in them something mysterious, not to say supernatural, and I was alone in my laboratory at night.
>
> —Nikola Tesla, 1901 article,
> "Talking with the Planets"

The Tesla Spirit Radio is a highly sensitive crystal radio that can be used to pick up electromagnetic fields or light sources in real time. Although parts such as the rotating nickel detectors and sensory relays have been replaced by 1N34A crystal germanium diode and a basic LC (inductor-capacitor), it still uses similar schematics. This design also allows you to create something that can be plugged into a computer to record sessions or speakers simply to listen. Not only does it make for a unique looking radio that picks up AM broadcasts, but also it can be used to register voices from the ether during evocations or spirit communication sessions. For full instructions on how to create this device go to http://www.instructables.com/id/Spooky-Tesla-Spirit-Radio/.

Digital Recorder

EVP, or electronic voice phenomenon, is the art of recording the voices of spirits on an electronic recording device. Such voices have been found both when played forward and backward. When voices are not apparent or clear they can be cleared up using a program that can perform a spectral analysis.

Random Number Generator

A true random number generator generates numbers based off of quantum-level static in the environment. That information can be recorded and fed into a computer to show statistics. The reason why this is so important is because intentions or Will cause that quantum static to become uniform during times of intense concentration—in other words quantum random number generators can be used to measure how much of an effect you and those you are working with are having on the quantum field (the ether). Such an effect was proven by Dr. Radin when he set up many such devices worldwide in his International Observer Effect experiment held in the early 2000s.

Cameras and Video Recording Devices

With advancements in technology such as tablets and cell phones, most people have the ability to record video. That's great because having a visual record of any experiment or session you do, whether it be a spell or spirit communication, can be extremely valuable. These devices are really not that expensive, and now video captured by even the cheapest of cell phones can be run through an infrared filter to expose energies not seen by the naked eye.

The Dream Machine

The dream machine is a stroboscope flicker device that produces bright, elaborate colors meant to be viewed from behind closed eyelids. These colors have been said to produce visions by sending the viewer into a hypnagogic state. The original Dream Machine was made out of a cylinder with slits cut in the sides, and a light bulb hanging at its center. This cylinder was placed on a record turntable, where it could be rotated at seventy-eight or forty-five revolutions per minute. When turned on light comes out of the holes at a constant frequency of eight to thirteen pulses per second, the same frequency range that corresponds to alpha waves experienced during relaxation. This device is said to cause seizures in adults with photosensitive epilepsy, which is about one out of ten thousand, and twice that number in children.

HOW TO RESEARCH

Most people who want to learn magick believe they can just buy the latest, most popular book on magick, and trust that it will teach them everything they need to know—but I'm sorry: it really doesn't work that way. There are some major problems here. Number one, most magical practices are based on very ancient techniques whose true meanings have been lost to antiquity. Because magick starts in the mind, and text does not always accurately capture what went on in the mind of the Magician who performed a ritual or spell, instructions found in such books can easily be confused and misinterpreted. You must also understand that much of what we know about magick comes from civilizations that are long gone. We were not there to witness the original rites, nor can we assume that what we have is anything close to what it originally was—we could very well be wrong. You should also know that real magick in the wrong hands can be dangerous, and it is for this very reason that many traditions, both living and dead, obscure their teachings to prevent those practices from falling into the hands of people who might want to abuse them. On the flip side, malevolent groups like mainstream religious orders, government agencies, secret societies, and small, but powerful cabals of dark magicians prefer to hoard powerful magical knowledge in order to keep their competition ignorant. At the same time, various cliques of scientists who make a lot of money off of the theories they develop do not want those theories proven wrong by people of dissenting belief—especially if they are true. Therefore, in order to protect their cash cows and their reputations, they deny the existence of magick and promote their world view as being the ultimate truth while ridiculing what threatens to overturn their theories. In the same way, mainstream religion uses scare tactics to maintain control over their flocks by demonizing practices that bring about spiritual enlightenment. And that in turn causes many entering the mysteries, to begin their practice thinking that magick is tied to an evil force. So as you can see, there are a lot of things standing between those wishing to know the truth and the truth of what magick really is.

Although I have already revealed much of what I have pieced together as the result of my own research, study, and practice, don't think for a second that this book is the pentacle of all magical knowledge—there is plenty more out there. So then, how should *you* go about uncovering more. First, you should give up any notion of settling on any one system. Study all magical systems, even the dark ones. You may not want to become a dark Magician, but even so, you really should look into the left-hand path, and black magick because they hide some of the most profound truths—truths you need to know, even if just to protect yourself from them. And just as I have done here in this book, you should make it a point to learn just as much about all fields outside of magick—especially science and psychology. Science *is* magick, and magick *is* science—get used to it. Once you realize this, you can move past the silly pop-magick books and start getting results. Also, no matter how bothered you are by the atrocities committed in the name of religion, or a particular religious world view, don't overlook religion. Because even though you may not agree with a belief system, there are treasures of knowledge and pieces of the puzzle in each of them.

The same goes for what might seem to be outrageous conspiracy theories that might threaten to rock your view of reality—sometimes they are true. When I began to uncover the truth, I was blinded by my subconscious belief in mainstream, scientific, materialistic world view, because that is what society had taught me. Even though I outwardly professed to have an open mind, on a deep unconscious level, I chose to dismiss certain information because it didn't jibe with what I had been taught about the world. Just remember those who don't want you to know will purposely denounce truth by crying, "Conspiracy theory!" in hopes that you will ignore it. The point is, sometimes you *must* go down the rabbit hole in order to find the truth. Sure, most of the holes you explore will probably dead ends, but if you explore enough of them, you may unearth the keys to true spiritual awakening.

If you are wondering where to begin your search, I can offer some suggestions. Truth has been written into the nature of reality. This means, all you have to do is look to nature and study it to uncover the things you need to know. These secrets hide in plain sight out in the open for all to see—all you have to do is study them and experiment. For example, studying how insects fly can reveal levitation, or by studying natural cymatics one can discover new healing techniques. The movements of the planets and stars also have much to reveal—don't limit yourself.

But if you want to get a head start, you may want to look into some of the things that are already being studied by the government, military, and powerful corporations—trust me: they don't want to waste their time on things that don't work. They want to get results. The key to uncovering important secrets in this way is to realize that *smart* people **love** to brag. Apparently, being smart doesn't prevent people from keeping secrets. This of course could be that those people (the ones making the discoveries) actually want to help society. However, those who fund such research are doing it for selfish reasons. What will happen is that, once profound discoveries are made, they are quickly secreted away and discredited by the mainstream so that the common folk wouldn't consider looking into them. Sometimes this information is left in plain sight (in books or on the web) the midst a sea of official statements by "skeptics" and doubters renouncing it. The reason for this is simple—Why would anyone leave anything worthwhile out in the open to be taken advantage of by you and I if it were worth anything? If they are not protecting it, it must be bogus right? No—wrong!

So, it is your job as a Sorcerer to take this information and experiment with it. Just remember, when you do your research, to pull your information from many sources—this will give you a more realistic overview of what is happening. Look for holes in information and look for misinformation. In the end, try to find something in the natural world that mimics the same phenomenon produced by the science you are researching—if you do find something, then it's likely what you have found is legit. But by all means, please be careful where you poke around. If what you find is real, you may end up drawing unwanted attention.

Occult Magick

Occult: Secret knowledge. Supernatural, magical, mystical
beliefs or phenomena.
— Merriam-Webster Dictionary

As I have already said, Sorcery is a synthesis of science, technology, psychology, and occult practices, brought together for the purpose of producing the most powerful results the quickest. In "The Nature of Reality," I talked about how modern scientific understanding of reality is beginning to line up with what the ancients believed, and I have outlined what steps are necessary in order to produce the best results using magick. In chapters "Mind and Magick, Trance, and Meditation," I revealed what the powers of the mind are and exactly how to hone your ability to focus, and visualize through meditation. I have also covered the scientific method, the importance of experimentation, and how technology can be a valuable part of your magical practice. So in this chapter, I will talk about the art, and science of what is typically known as "occult magick."

When people think of magick, they typically think of an old guy wearing a ritual robe standing in a circle speaking incantations that summon powerful forces or a wise old woman wearing a cloak and an earthy dress, stirring a cauldron. So when most people encounter someone who claims to practice magick, they are quick to assume that person is either deluded or crazy—not many people believe in this kind of magick anymore. In fact, this disbelief also extends into the magical community. Practitioners and nonpractitioners alike have such a difficult time wrapping their minds around the fact that speaking words, making gestures, and drawing symbols can have a real effect on reality that they try to redefine magick in a way that makes it more believable to them—this is why there are two models of magick.

The first model of magick constitutes literal belief in supernatural forces. In this model, magick is the result spiritual forces that are not yet understood by modern science. Those who believe in this model, have no problems believing in God(s), angels, demons, fairies, teleportation, or any number of things that would seem ludicrous to anyone who considers themselves a rational person. A belief in literal magick means you acknowledge that there is a spiritual layer to things.

The second model of magick is the psychological model, which tries to normalize the magical experience by explaining it away using psychology—in other words, it works not because anything spiritual is going on, but because you are changing your internal psychology to make it happen. For example, while someone who subscribes to the supernatural model would claim that their money spell worked because it caused a series of events to occur that brought their will into reality, someone subscribing to the psychological model would say they became richer because the spell cast subconsciously gave them keen awareness of opportunities to make that money—opportunities that already existed in the real world. In other words, the first person thinks he accomplishing his goal by changing reality, and the other person believes he is accomplishing his goal by changing his own psychology.

So which is true? The truth is, reality is more miraculous than we think, and what we *see* is contingent on what we want to see. The bottom line is, if you want to practice powerful magick, you must believe that matter arises from thought—and that means, what you think, you create—in other words, magick. This also means that the literal model and the psychological model are the same thing. What you experience happening in the physical world, the one you consider to be *real*, has a direct effect on your psychology, and what is happening in your head has a direct effect on the real world—there is no separation. Both get results, because both are one.

This is why as Sorcerers—who want beyond anything else to get results—must strive to look at all possibilities without prejudice. Otherwise, we might chalk everything up to the imagination and overlook something very important. Don't always assume a concept is the thing of fantasy just because it doesn't fit into your rigid world view. Instead, look at how it could be an actual phenomenon that is part of the natural universe.

Besides apparent differences in magical philosophy, there exists hundreds of magical traditions each professing to be better than the next while borrowing ideas from one another. And with so many different traditions it becomes difficult for a practitioner to determine which system is worth spending the time to learn. But in truth, as you will come to see, it does not matter which system you use, it only matters whether or not you believe in what you are doing. All of these systems draw upon gnosis from antiquity and copy from one another.

For example, Wicca, which was invented by Gerald Gardner and Doreen Valiente sometime between 1940 and 1950, models many of its rituals from rituals taken from ceremonial magick. On the other hand, both ceremonial magick traditions and Wicca incorporate many ideas from spiritual teaching common to India, the mystery schools of ancient Greece and Egypt, Jewish Kabalism as well as early Gnostic Christianity. Not only this, once the catholic church rose to power, most magical traditions had to go underground and adopt a Christian disguise in order to keep practicing. Even the magical practices common to African religions had to take the form of Christianity in order to survive—this is where you get Voodoo, and Santeria. So don't think for a minute that the secret to ultimate magical power lies in the teachings of one particular magical system. It is for this reason that I encourage you to take what you need from each system, discard what you don't like, and use it to create a system that work best for you. So having said this, let's move on to what occult magick really is.

Occult magick is a type of mental technology. The outward expression of casting a spell or performing a ritual—that is, the incantations, gestures, and symbols—are only there to help strengthen and direct your thoughts and intentions. In other words, if you really wanted to, you could dispense with the trappings and perform magick all in your mind. And such is the case with practitioners of magick who have been at it for a long time.

However, if you are just starting off, performing a ritual or casting a spell can really help. I personally love working traditional magick, because it can be beautiful and awe inspiring. Having said this, there are some aspects of magick that are not just used symbolically. For example, herbs, stones, and even some tools have power of their own and practical functions.

So how does magick work? Do things materialize out of thin air? Yes and no—magick may cause things to happen so dramatically it may seem like something supernatural has occurred. However, everything that can happen will always happen through a series of naturally occurring events. The more unshakable your belief, the better your focus, and the more vivid your imagination, the quicker changes will happen, and the more stunning they will be.

A good example of this process would be the money spell. Let's say that you are just a fledgling Sorcerer, and you needed a quick influx of money to help you with a car repair bill—for this example, we'll use one thousand dollars. So, after going through the process of casting your spell, you wait. The first, second, and third day nothing happens—but on the third day, you miraculously receive a check for $996.32 for taxes you have overpaid over the last four years! Now let's say you have been practicing magick for a while—same scenario, same one thousand dollars, but this time, a couple of hours later, you get a knock on the door. After opening the door, you are greeted by a man in a suit, who wants to give you a thousand-dollar reward for a contest you won—sounds like fantasy, but this is how magick works. If you were Merlin, you might have cast the spell, closed your circle, then snuggled down in your recliner to read that old book you inherited from your deceased grandfather, only to open the pages to find a mysterious envelope that contained the money you needed.

This tendency of things to manifest in very explainable ways is the reason why most people never get past step one (belief) in magick—because most of the time, magick is not blatant. However, the more you work with mental energy, the more obvious it becomes that your spells are actually changing reality. The trick is to measure your successes by keeping a good record of the spells you cast, rituals you perform, and the results that have come about—but we will talk more about your magical journal in another chapter.

But no matter how natural or unnatural the results of your magick may appear, what you must understand is that everything that manifest—events, physical objects, and so on—is nothing more than waves of thought energy translated by your mind into the appropriate event or object. According to the first Hermetic Principle of Mentalism, everything is mind—or thought. Nothing is actually physical—it's all data. Science also backs this up with quantum physics. Of course, this does not mean that *all* thought energy is so malleable that it can be shaped by anyone at any time. If that were the case, then the physical world be constantly shifting, because everyone would be shaping it into what they wanted it to be. Thought has cohesive structure—it's just that some thought-forms are more cohesive than others—either way, all thought is susceptible to change by the right mind under the right conditions.

In the physical world, anything you try to manifest is subject to the Natural Laws established by the Source as well as the fervent beliefs of the many (laws of the consensual reality). Both of these influences (Source and consensual realities) fix things in place, give them structure, and cause things to take form. Everyone, including the Source—the supreme influencer—is pushing and pulling with their intentions to shape reality. This means all manifestations are subject to the flow of probability, and that probability is the result of things being thought about and "decided upon." It also means that the mind or minds who are most invested in seeing that thing happen will tip the balance and make that thing manifest.

You should also know that everyone is manifesting reality all the time, whether they are conscious of it or not. You don't have to be a Witch or Magician to make things happen; all anyone has to do is want it really bad and believe it will happen. Fortunately, not many people these days believe they can bring something into existence by thinking about it. Therefore, they don't have the skills necessary to do it. However, you are not alone. There are others like us who do believe and consciously manipulate reality—though they are rare.

Many practitioners of magick, especially Witches, will snub their noses at all this technical speak, because they know it's not necessary to know how magick works in order to make it work—and of course, they are absolutely right. But the purpose of letting you in on the mechanics of this stuff is not to prove that magick requires a Masters in Meta-Science—it serves to make you aware of all the factors that influence magical operations so that you can tweak your spells to get better results. Also, some of you, like myself, may be very technically oriented or will be reading this book from a skeptic's point of view. In such case, it will benefit you to know that all this relates to real science—and once you realize that, you can start getting results. Having said this, let's talk about metaphysics.

THE TRIANGLE OF MANIFESTATION

One of the primary purposes of magick is to cause manifestation—that is, to cause the *will* of the Sorcerer to become reality here in the physical plane. The Sorcerer's will may be to manifest a physical object or to cause something to happen—either way, magick directs this will using spellwork. However, even though the gestures, symbols, and other linguistic elements are fueling the intent, it is the mind that is doing the work. This means great mental control is paramount to the success of any spell or ritual. To this end, there are three things that must be developed before you can expect to manifest anything: belief, focus, and imagination. These three things form what is known as the Triangle of Manifestation.

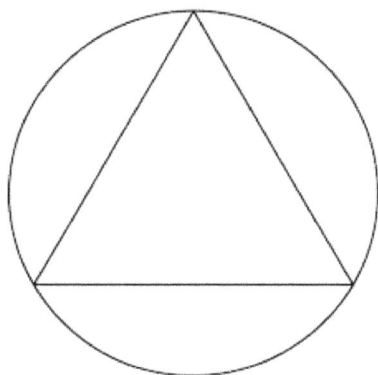

Belief

At the very top of the triangle is belief—because without it, nothing can be built. This means, the more you consciously or unconsciously believe a thing is possible, the more likely it is that it will happen. If you don't believe at all, or don't have enough belief, then that idea (thought-form) may appear in the higher dimension, then quickly dissipate—never to enter reality. But if you firmly believe something will happen, a series of events will occur that will eventually bring that thing into existence—sometimes dramatically, but more often than not, in an unimpressive seemingly natural way. If the object of your desire is something that goes unchallenged by belief—as is the case with many unconscious thoughts or things we take for granted—the likelihood that it will manifest becomes governed different factors: focus and imagination (the two bottom points of the triangle).

As you practice magick, you will eventually get to a point where you realize it is not fake, but before you get there, you must know how to bypass those mental walls so you can eventually see results. To this end, I have provided several tricks below.

Trick 1: Gnosis

Study magick and science—no, don't limit yourself to pop-magick books you might find in some online store. Actually start studying real science— especially quantum physics, biophysics, parapsychology, psychology, and astronomy. Once you have done that, you will know how magical the universe is, and know anything is possible.

Trick 2: Be a Willing Participant in the Fantasy

If you've ever entertained yourself by watching a movie, reading a work of fiction, or by playing a game based on fantasy or science fiction, then you've most likely been a willingly participant in that fantasy. That means you became so engrossed in the fantasy that your critical mind could care less if it were real of fake.

So, if you are an unbeliever who is trying to practice magick, do not concern yourself with its validity during the process of performing a ritual or spell. Instead, enjoy immersion process, and become a willing participant in the fantasy. Do that in the same way an actor would by playing a role. *You* may not believe, but the character you are playing—that of a Sorcerer—does. And that person will enjoy the experience and put his or her whole heart into it. For that moment, relinquish your critical thought and speak, think, and act as a Sorcerer. Save criticism for outside of the Sacred Space!

Trick 3: Immersion

Know the ritual or spell you are casting. Be an expert on its every aspect. Know all the steps, be able to pronounce all the words, and know what they mean. Know what all of the symbols represent. Delve into the history or belief system surrounding all the customs, traditions, and entities you are calling upon. Prepare for the casting of the spell or ritual hours or even days before you intend to perform it. Perform that spell or ritual on the appropriate planetary day and hour. If you haven't already, personalize the spell or ritual to your liking—become emotionally involved!

Trick 4: Auto-suggestion

Use the auto-suggestion exercise provided in the Meditation chapter to implant a suggestion that is most appropriate to your own psychology. For example, if you don't believe in magick, but believe in science, implant "Magick is science. All things are possible through science!," or if you lack confidence in your own ability, you might try, "I am a powerful Sorcerer/Sorceress, and can do anything," or if you are morally conflicted about magick, because you come from an oppressive religious background, you might say, "Magick is my natural God-given right." Ultimately, you will know what is best for you.

Focus

The bottom-left point of the triangle is governed by the principle of focus. Think of focus as how much attention you give an idea. This means that if you are the type of person who is easily distracted, you must make sure to kill those distractions before you go about doing any kind of magical working—otherwise, your efforts will be thwarted. It also means, if you like to chatter, you need to learn how to shut up, drop whatever you are thinking, and focus on the task at hand.

Focus can be developed by adamantly practicing the meditation exercises in this book. If can meditate for ten minutes, try extending it to fifteen, then twenty, and so on. Try meditating while walking. When something enters your mind, dismiss it, and continue to concentrate.

Another way to help you focus is to prepare a head of time. Standard preparation involves cleaning your area, taking a ritual bath or shower, getting dressed in your magical attire, and/or anointing yourself. These practices are described in the chapter entitled "Binding, Banishing, and Protection." Think of preparation as a way of putting the worries of the day behind you and reminding yourself that you are about to perform magick.

Imagination & Intent

The third principle, or lower right-hand point, is occupied by imagination. You must be able to visualize your desire or intent before you can expect it to manifest. The more detailed the mental image, the more likely it is that your desire or intent will manifest precisely how you imagined it. Not only this, but also you must be able to imagine that thing as if it has already has happened, and you are enjoying the benefits. If it's rain you are calling for, then you must be able to feel the rain on your skin. If it's money, you must be able to see yourself spending that money on the things you want or need, and if it's the perfect lover, then you should be able to see yourself with that person, enjoying the relationship.

Let me pause for a moment and talk about purity of intent—and here, I am not referring to purity from a moralistic standpoint. When I talk about purity, I am talking about a genuine unfettered desire to really want that thing to happen. It matters not if your will is considered evil or good by social standards, only that you honestly want it and wouldn't feel guilty if it were to come to pass. As far as magical intent is concerned, the only thing that matters is if you can live with the results. This means that what you manifest must be in perfect alignment with your sense and understanding of right and wrong. Therefore, if you use magick to get all your friends to give you their money, you had better not care about making them poor, or if you throw a death curse on your neighbor, you had better not shed any tears when he or she dies. Of course, I am not condoning this kind of behavior. All I am saying is know how you truly feel about things before you cast.

Another important aspect of asserting your will is clear intent. You can't expect your magick to work if you don't have a well-formed goal. Intent asks, "What do you want to happen?" Are you casting this spell to draw in success, attract love, or to bar someone from your life? Know exactly what it is you want, and when deciding on a spell's purpose, try to be specific. A vague and muddled intent produces vague and muddled results. Oftentimes when people make their intentions too broad, they are doing so because they are afraid of failure and unconsciously don't believe it will work in the first place. A spell that is too broad will bear results, because anything can fulfill its purpose—in fact, it would probably occur whether you used magick or not. In other words, a result from that kind of spell is tantamount to luck. A good example would be if you were to cast a spell to bring joy into your life. How hard would it be for that to happen without the intervention of magick? The first time you happen to go out and do something that makes you happy, you can claim that the spell worked! Sounds nice, but such results won't help you much, are not a good test of your power, and will not exercise your magical abilities in any way shape or form.

At the same time, you don't want to narrow your intent too much. Doing this restricts the avenues your energy could take to accomplish your will. You want to allow that energy to naturally travel along all available paths to find the results that are best for you. Suppose I were to cast a spell to obtain the love of my coworker Julie—she is everything I ever wanted—pretty, successful, and single! Let's say that the spell went off without a hitch, and she falls madly in love with me—in fact, we end up getting married. Great, right? At first, everything seems wonderful, but lo and behold, three months later the relationship turns out to be a nightmare! What now? Maybe I should have made the focus of my spell a little bit broader? If I would have made my intent a little broader, I might have attracted someone who I could actually get along with.

Another aspect of deciding on the purpose of your spell is to focus on one thing at a time. Your focus should not be split between two or more intentions. Focusing on one purpose at a time always works best. If you want to do more than one thing, save it for another day. You must allow yourself to regenerate, so you will be clear and ready to crystallize your next intention. The best intents are those that you really, truly want. If the object of your desire or the thing or situation you want to change is something that invokes deep emotion, visualization will follow suit, and you will see it clearly.

For this reason, you must create a clear image of what you want in your mind so that it will manifest on the mental plane. You should be able to close your eyes (or keep them open—doesn't matter), and literally *see* the object of your desire. By *see*, I don't mean a static image, but a fully immersive dream that engages all of your senses. Please understand: it is unlikely that you will be able to see these images as if they were real. That will only happen while dreaming or in the heavy, or coma-trance, state. But either way, you should allow yourself to imagine what it would be like to already have that which you desire. It should be so real that you can see yourself taking advantage of all its benefits.

The best example I can give is obsession. When you are obsessed with something, it is all you can think about or talk about. Everything revolves around the object of your obsession. Mental images produced by obsessive thoughts are some of the strongest and most vivid. I am not saying that I want you to become clinically obsessed. You want to be able to pull away from it at the end of the spell, not be trapped by it, but you do need to ruminate over your focus. Furthermore, you must adopt the attitude of certainty and believe that it will come to be. Fortunately, if you are able to achieve that obsessive state, certainty and belief will follow suit.

This is where the actual spell work comes into play. Every aspect of your spell should reflect something about your intent; that is, your candles should be a certain color, the ritual gestures you make should reinforce it, the incense you burn should remind you of its purpose, and the words you speak should be affirmative. In other words, all of the ritualistic components of your spell will reinforce what you are thinking, and help create a vivid enough image on the astral that it will begin to manifest.

For this reason, your spell should have components that can be repeated or be long enough to give you enough time to play out your vision in its entirety. During this process visual, audible and sensory cues such as incantations, ritualistic gestures, and symbolism will reinforce the intent. You should remain in this state for as long as it takes to completely visualize your desires, then when you are near to exhaustion, end the spell and disconnect.

To disconnect, you should make an abrupt noise such as a loud clap or bell ring. What this does is force you out of your trance, preventing the astral form you have created from being tainted by unrelated thoughts. What I mean by this is it distances you from that energy before it can be injected with doubt—if that is still a problem. This is important because if you are performing the spell as an actor, then your tendency will be to question whether the spell will even work as you emerge from your trance. Once you have slipped back into Beta, you will naturally stop playing the role, and your logical mind will begin to scrutinize your working. A jarring noise can be used to shock you out of this trance quick enough to sever the link before your rational mind has a chance to program that astral form with any contrary thought. Once the spell has been cast, you'll need to put it out of your mind.

Grounding

Whenever you perform magick, there is always some kind of residual energy. The more spells and rituals you perform in an area, the more this energy will accumulate. As this energy builds, several things can happen; one, it will begin to effect the emotions of the people residing in that area; two, it will attract unwanted entities who want to feed off of that power; and three, it may cause funky space/time anomalies that screw with your head. Like the mass of a planet, this buildup of energy will begin pulling on nearby energy lines, causing these lay lines to connect and form a nexus point in your ritual chamber—that all seems really cool, until you have to deal with the spiritual interlopers.

The point being is this: get rid of that excess energy by grounding it. Having said this, the process is very simple. Once again, it is intent based— *will* that energy back into the earth using both visualization and the language of magick. By *will* I don't mean stand in the middle of the circle and say, "Energy be gone!" I mean actually make a point to visualize, feel, know, and acknowledge that the excess energy has been sent back to the earth. To help you visualize, use some of these very simple magical methods listed below.

- Cast a pinch of salt to the four corners of your circle.
- Walk around the room holding a magick tool, visualizing the energy going into it.
- Perform the Banishment by Air and Fire, Water and Earth again.
- Stand in the middle of the circle, visualizing this energy flowing into you, then see that energy flow down your body, into your legs, and being sent back into the earth to be reintegrated by nature.

The Seven Hermetic Principles

The first body of knowledge we are about to cover not only is very ancient, but also was so influential it gave rise to the Italian Renaissance, sparked the Age of Enlightenment, and kick-started modern science. This gnosis (knowledge) is taken from the Corpus Hermeticum, a series of letters thought to be handed down by Hermes Trismegistus (aka Thoth, the Egyptian God of wisdom, mathematics, science, and magick). As for whether or not this wisdom issued from the lips of an Egyptian God, or a mere mortal, it matters not, these truths stand on their own merit. Of these truths, there are seven in total, forming what is known as the Seven Hermetic Principles. They are mentalism, correspondence, vibration, polarity, rhythm, cause and effect, and gender. Each one of these principles plays an important role in how reality operates. For now, let's examine each. Then I will move onto how they relate to what is currently known and how they can be applied to magick.

Mentalism

The first principle states that everything is Mind. That is, reality itself is composed entirely of mental energy, which is infinite, all powerful, all knowing, ever present, and most importantly, conscious. Not only does this mean that everything is governed by thought, but it also means that we are all connected to this Ultimate Mind, because we are a product of it. Understanding of this principle means that we must acknowledge that thought is the prime creative force in the universe.

Correspondence

This principle teaches us that there is a relationship between what exists in the physical world and what exists in the world of spirit. With this principle, we can draw conclusions about certain states or invisible levels of reality by examining what precedes or follows it. This is because that state or level of reality is a reflection of what came before it. In this way, we cannot only say that what is below is like that which is above, but also that which is without is similar to that which is within. For example, the very thing that makes up the human body, the atom, is similar to that which is above it—the solar system and spiral galaxy. And from a psychological standpoint, we can say that people's appearances and behaviors are reflected by their internal thoughts and personalities.

Vibration

This truth reveals that nothing, be it matter, energy, thought, or spirit, is ever at rest—everything is, in fact, in a constant moving wave of vibration. This truth really shouldn't be too hard to swallow once you realize that atomic particles—the stuff everything is made of—are nothing more than waves of energy vibrating at different frequencies.

Polarity

The law of polarity states that all things have a dual nature; hot, cold, constructive, destructive, positive, negative, attracting, and detracting. The most profound revelation of this truth however is that these dualistic states are just manifestations of the same thing, just at varying degrees. For example, both good, and evil are aspects of morality, hot, and cold are just different degrees of temperature, and night, and day are environmental conditions dictated by more or less light. Being familiar with this principle, teaches us how we can cause one thing to change into another by pushing a condition a certain number of degrees to the left or right. This is not only true for physical manifestations, but also mental states.

Rhythm

> For every action, there is an equal, and opposite reaction.
> —NEWTON'S THIRD LAW

Because all things are in motion, all things are subject to the rise and fall of rhythm. Like a pendulum, when something swings one way, it must swing in the opposite direction the same amount.

Cause and Effect

Everything that has happened and is happening is the result of everything that came before it. In other words, nothing happens for absolutely no reason. This simple rule teaches us that we can know the cause of something by observing its effect, or can predict the outcome of a thing based on similar instances, and can even cause an effect by creating a condition.

Gender

In conformity with all other laws, everything has a masculine and feminine nature—not just biologically but also psychologically. These two forces are responsible for the creation of all things. Whereas the masculine force in nature is the exploratory and penetrating aspect that initiates the creative process, the feminine force is the receptive-nourishing aspect that is responsible for birth. When these two forces work together to create balance, they manifest healthy relationships, environments, and ecosystems, but when they are imbalanced, they lead to degradation, destruction, and death.

FACTORS THAT INFLUENCE THE SUCCESS OF SPELLS

Your personal level of belief, ability to focus, and imagination are not the only things that contribute to the success or failure of a spell—outside influences can change the effect magick. So let's examine these elements one by one and see how they play into magick.

Health & Diet

Physical injury, sickness, disease, stress, anxiety, depression, and fatigue can all contribute to magick failure. When we are unhealthy, our attentions are drawn to whatever ails us, and we lose focus and the ability to concentrate. The same is true for eating large meals before performing rituals or casting spells. Being too full can make you uncomfortable and therefore pull your focus away from what you are doing. My advice to anyone thinking about performing magick while sick, injured, or under a great deal of stress is to take care of source of that ailment before proceeding. Magick can definitely be used for the purpose of physical and psychological healing, but if you are too sick to concentrate, seek professional medical or psychological attention as well as healing from an outside spiritual practitioner. If you are interested in recovering some of that lost energy, consider following the advice I outline in the chapter "Binding, Banishing, and Protection."

Probability

Some people erroneously believe that they can cast a spell and make anything happen. Unfortunately, this is not true, because some things are more likely to happen than others. In order to cause the changes you intend, you must first plant those intentions in fertile soil. That is, if what you are asking for is improbable according to the laws of nature, then it is highly unlikely that you will be able to make it happen using magic. For example, you shouldn't really expect to be able to manifest rain in a desert or cause someone who hates your guts to love you. Magick does not suspend the laws of nature. Magick works best if you know how to work with the forces of nature, instead of against them. So if you want to manifest rain, make sure the precipitation already exists, and if you want to draw someone's love, make sure they already like you.

Because of this magick is often times a process of creating the right conditions in order to manifest a greater goal. For example, before making that person who hate you, love you, you would have to make yourself more tolerable, then finally more likable—then and only then can you expect to be able to use magick to draw their love. All of this may take weeks, months, or even years.

It is also worth noting, that the laws of probability are often times determined by the version of reality that society submits to. This is why it is necessary for the magician to familiarize him or herself with what society thinks is plausible. Because of this it would make no sense for him or her to try and cast a spell or ritual in order to try and bend reality in a way contrary to everyone else's beliefs. This is just inviting failure. Instead it would make more sense for the sorcerer to try and change those consensual beliefs before trying to push or pool reality in a way that is not seemingly natural. This will increase the likelihood of the sorcerer to manifest more extraordinary things.

Magick and Timing

Although you can perform a spell or ritual anytime you wish, there are certain times when magick can happen unabated. For example, you obviously don't want to perform magick when you are ill, anxious, or depressed, because this will affect your concentration, and focus. But besides this, what other factors are there? Time of day can also play an important role in the success of your magick. For example, when people are awake, their thoughts are pushing, and pulling at physical reality to shape it. Therefore, if you want to reduce this effect, you should perform magick at nighttime—especially between the hours of three and five in the morning—when most people are asleep. Furthermore, people are more susceptible to suggestion when they are asleep, so if your target is a person, find out what their sleep pattern is and perform your spell or ritual two to three hours after they have slipped off into dream land.

Another thing to consider is the very real effect that the moon and other celestial objects have on the atoms that make up our bodies. According to the Laws of Atomic Gravitational Fluctuation, the nucleus of an atom shifts according to the central gravitational point of massive nearby bodies, such as the sun and moon. Remember that all atoms spin, creating their own electromagnetic fields, and that our brains, and therefore moods and behaviors, are affected whenever we are exposed to any kind of electromagnetic change. This means every time a celestial body causes the nucleus of our atoms to shift, it is also causing a disturbance in our electromagnetic fields. The end result is a shift in mood and change in behavior. This is most likely why certain operations of magick correspond to certain lunar cycles. Even so, this mood/behavior change is probably different for everyone. In such case, you should monitor the way you feel during the waxing and waning moons—especially on new and full moons—and learn how to use these cycles to benefit you.

Immersion

Immersion is the process by which one gets psychologically and emotionally involved in a particular project. In this case we are talking about casting spells and performing rituals. Immersion involves educating yourself about a subject and engaging your senses of sight, sound, taste, smell, and touch over a duration. This process causes our conscious and unconscious minds to build a thought-form in the astral or to become quantum entangled with a thought-form that already exists. This could take minutes, hours, or even days, depending on the type of spell you are trying to cast, the magical operation you are trying to perform, and your degree of belief.

If you are not actually thinking about the intention of your spell or taking the steps to bring that thing into existence, your subconscious mind will not be fully devoted to the creation of that energy. This means you not only do you need to psychologically prepare yourself for the coming of that thing (make plans), but also make worldly preparations. So by immersing yourself ahead of time, you begin building that thought-form, then when it actually comes time to cast your spell, half the work is already done. Unless you are an Arch Magi, you will not be able to imprint your intent on astral in a single spell casting.

Repetition

Oftentimes, it is not enough to cast a spell or perform a ritual just once and expect it to have an effect. Most of the time, you will have to repeat your magical operation over and over again in order to thoroughly imprint your will upon the astral so it will manifest. As a rule of thumb, the weaker your intent, the less confident you are and the less likely it is that that thing *can* actually happen, the more you will have to repeat your spell in order to really make it come to fruition. Therefore, if you know yourself, and you are familiar with the Seven Hermetic Principles, you should be able to determine whether you should cast a spell repeatedly.

The Power of Many

If a single person's thoughts have an impact on reality, then the unified thoughts of many can have an even greater impact. The key word here is *unified*, meaning all participants must be focused on the same intent, else they will not have any effect. This means when working in groups, choose people who are disciplined, know how to focus, and share the same goals. This means, if even one participant lacks the right skills to perform magick, or has different plans, they will stymie the spell—at best, it will have no effect, and at worse, it will have opposite or chaotic effects. For this reason, if you intend to work as a group, you need to choose those you work with very carefully and also train with them.

On the other hand, people don't necessarily have to be a part of your group in order to harness their willed intent. If you can draw their attention long enough, then get them to think about *your* goals and *your* intentions, then their thoughts will be shaping those intentions—it doesn't matter if they are aware of what you are doing or not.

However, doing this can be risky, because what other people are thinking is not always what you will be thinking. If what they are thinking is not in alignment with what you are thinking, then their attention and thoughts can shape things in ways you could never expect. Of course, this doesn't matter if your intentions are extremely general. For example, if your intention is to manifest a great feast, it doesn't matter if every person focused on your intent is thinking about a different type of food—the end result will be a feast with a variety of food. Perhaps the biggest risk would be trying to borrow focus and intent from someone who understands what you are actually doing. But honestly, that is rare, because most people are just not that aware.

The Language of Magick

The language of magick is more than just the verbal recitation of words. It uses the outward expression of symbols to communicate with the subconscious mind. By doing this, it creates thought-forms on a higher dimension so they will manifest here in the physical world. In this way, magick is both an inner and outer discipline—a kind of moving mediation that invokes the powers of the mind by "physically" stimulating the senses. These symbolic expressions can take many forms: mystical gestures or sigils (symbols) that represent complex ideas, fragrances that invoke memories, colors that generate emotional energy, and of course incantations that help project the Sorcerer's will through voice. In a sense, when the Sorcerer, or Sorceress uses the magical language, he or she is performing a magical act—and that is simply action backed up with strong intentions.

The point that I am trying to make here is that the key to magick is not some kind of secret formula, but in the power that esoteric language has to communicate vast amounts of information to the subconscious mind. This of course is significant because the subconscious mind is the bridge to the plane of spirit where things begin to manifest. Once this is understood the power of magick can be increased one hundred fold.

Having said this, the magical language can be found throughout all spiritual traditions, including mainstream religions and rural shamanic cultures. However, this language is so expansive that it would be impossible to detail it in its entirety here in this book, so you should take it upon yourself to explore the symbolism found in all things. Even so, let's start by exploring symbolic concepts that are common to all forms of magick.

THE ELEMENTAL MODEL

One of the oldest ways of representing creative forces of nature, and also thought, is the Elemental Model—in fact, it is still in use today. Before we had high-powered microscopes and atom smashers, the ancients tried to explain reality by observing nature and going inward through meditation. To explain what they had learned, they used the classical elements. The elemental model is a system that uses the five elements in nature to explain the movement of natural forces within the physical world, the mental plane, and within the world of spirit. This system is so widespread that it can be found in almost all cultures across the globe. To the Greeks it was air, earth, fire, water, and ether. The Egyptians, Babylonians, Japanese, Tibetans, and people of India replaced air with "wind" and the ether with "the void"—even the Native Americans have their own version.

Now atomic theory recognizes over one hundred chemical elements that can adopt different physical states under varying temperatures, and pressures. So the classical elements of earth, water, air, and fire have simply been replaced by the solid, liquid, gas, and plasma states of atomic theory—the only thing missing is the fifth element ether, or spirit. In fact, science once recognized the spiritual realm as ether, but this fell out of popularity because scientists did not want to recognize evidence supporting it. Ether was thought to be the medium by which electromagnetic energy, and gravitational waves were propagated, and transmitted throughout the universe—but now the runner-up is dark matter. This is a theoretical dark substance is supposed to emit no light, have no electrical charge, and no strong pull on regular particles of matter. It is said to permeate everything and make up 80 percent of matter in the universe. If this is so, then dark matter is nothing more than another physical manifestation that originates from what we in the mystical arts refer to as "Spirit."

As suggested above in Sympathetic Links to Modern and Ancient Thought-Forms, a thought-form is only as powerful as its popularity. Considering that this Elemental Model is still in wide use today, it is worth understanding, because it will allow you to tap into the quintessential/spiritual quality of these forces. Besides this, you will eventually get your hands on ancient texts of magick that describe things in terms of these elements.

Therefore, you will need to know how to put what you read into perspective. So let's look at this elemental model and its applications one by one.

The Four Worlds

Correspondence

Element		Behavior	World
Spirit	–	Omnipotent, Omnipresent, Omniscient	Not a World
Fire	–	Creative, Volatile	The Emotive Plane
Air	–	Logical, Probabilistic	The Mental Plane
Water	–	Empathic, Reflective	The Etheric Plane
Earth	–	Stable, Cohesive	The Physical Plane

The four worlds model is based off the idea that matter arises from thought, and that all of existence began with a first emanation from the Source. Needless to say, according to this model entities existing in the higher planes would be more archetypal energy forms and less solid than those living in the lower planes.

It is also believed that entities traveling from one plane to another must do so by either creating or shedding a body suitable for the plane they are going to. In other words, if a spirit existing in the Emotive Plane (Fire) wanted to visit the Etheric Plane (Water), it would need to create a emotive body, as well as an etheric one. Therefore, one could assume that anything existing on the lowest plane (the physical universe) would have a total of four bodies (physical, etheric, mental, and emotive).

Another common belief is that we are tied to this physical reality because we are dependent on and yearn for stimulation (good or bad) that we can only find in the material realm—that would explain why some spirits choose not to move on. Part of this due to the fact that humankind as a whole knows nothing about the higher planes or the benefits that could be gained if they were to raise their level of consciousness high enough to travel to them—so it is ignorance and attachment to physical things keeps us grounded. Therefore, the ability to travel to other planes requires one to first be aware they exist and then be able to relinquish materialistic attitudes and/or attachments that hold our attention here in this plane.

Spirit

This is the Source; thus, it is not a world at all. Now, of course, we all have a seed of that divine spark in us, and therefore are tapped into the Source to some degree, but most of us can only hope to experience brief moments of alignment with this being (our true nature). This alignment usually comes with a sense of piece and true understanding of things, but like a dream, those experiences can be lost once our attention is drawn back to the physical world.

Fire (The Emotive Plane)

The Emotive Plane is perhaps the first state of existence that constitutes a real plane. In this plane, the creative process becomes possible, because ideas and concepts begin to manifest in a dualistic way—light is given meaning by the existence of darkness, good by evil, and creation by destruction. These polar opposites create a firestorm of possibilities that desire to be worked out, and when that happens, action occurs and begins to build itself in a complex matrix of energy that will eventually appear as a "probability" within the Mental Plane of Air. As a plane, the Emotive Plane is not physical at all—instead, it is governed by pure primal forces. By primal, I mean archetypal thought-forms made of elementary ideas. Such beings would be immaterial currents of consciousness—having no body, no ego, and motivated only by the very powerful emotional-intelligence that drives them.

Air (Mental Plane)

This is the world of logical decisions. Therefore, it is associated with probability and choices. Although basic concepts and ideas exist here, they are not yet permanent, because they have not been fully realized or decided upon. Those things that are more likely to happen will be composed of more data, and thus have a stronger vibration. This building up of data will eventually cause those thought-forms to shift into the world of Water. Those focused on this world, or beings existing within it, can sense the likelihood or eminence of things to come. All things on the Mental Plane are in constant flux.

Water (Etheric Plane)

This is the World of Akasha. Although it has not been fully realized and is not entirely permanent, you can pretty much rely on the fact that what you see exist. When focused on, perceivers can experience being in an actual world that seems to have a physical landscape. Most beings living there have a physical representation. Because this is a pool of data, when tapped into, you can shift from one region to another in order to experience any-place at any time that has ever existed. One could say, the World of Water encompasses the higher levels of the astral.

Earth (Physical Plane)

This is our world, the physical world we can see, hear, smell, touch, and taste—but it also includes many things we are incapable of sensing. Things existing in this world have physical form or energy and are bound by the laws of time and space.

Part of this world that many are not aware of includes the lower planes of the ethereal. Beings existing on this level are still made of energies grounded in physical forces, but exist outside of the range of our perception. Such beings would include ghosts, elementals, and other life forms. We can however train ourselves to perceive these things.

The Transmutation of Thought to Matter

Correspondence

Element		State
Spirit	–	Consciousness
Fire	–	Will
Air	–	Intellect
Water	–	Memory
Earth	–	Matter

The table above uses the elemental model to explain how thought energy goes through a process of transformation until it manifests here in physical reality for all to see. Because this is such a complicated subject, I will try to make it as simple as possible—please forgive me if you are already familiar with this concept.

To understand this model we have to assume a few things.

Something caused everything—that is, the Source.

That Source is an immaterial conscious being.

This Source is not only the most powerful thing in existence, but *is* existence itself, and that means it is omnipresent (in everything).

And this is why we associate the Source with Spirit, because Spirit is the most basic element and therefore has infinite potential.

We must also assume that the process by which the Source caused existence was thought—in other words, it *Willed* things into existence.

And this leads us to Fire. Fire has always been seen as a manifestation of Will—and so it was the Will of the Source that ignited the spark of creation. Will is also a powerful force that drives action, and so energy in its fire state is all about the desire to act.

Once this Source energy has been infused with Will, it enters the realm of Air and turns into Thought. This state is associated with air because ancients viewed Thought as having an airy quality. Unlike the Will of fire, Thought tries to answer logical questions. It is about reason, structure, and order. Once this airy energy has decided how it will manifest, it enters the world of Water.

The World of Water is about memory or the matrix of reality itself. It is also emotional and receptive. This energy like water has the ability to reflect and therefore, by reflection, creates an image of itself that becomes what we see as the material existence.

So finally we have Earth, which is associated with material existence. Although it is still composed of thought energy, it has the most cohesive structure of all the elements.

To put it in the simplest terms, everything you see including yourself began as a thought from the Source. As this thought was realized, it transformed into more complicated information until it manifested into what we see here as physical reality.

Nature Spirits

Correspondence

Element		Spirit Type
Spirit	–	High Spirits, Daemons
Fire	–	Salamander
Air	–	Sylphs
Water	–	Undine
Earth	–	Gnome

Ancient cultures saw everything as being composed of at least four elements: air, earth, fire, and water, with spirit being the binding factor of all matter. Because of this, they believed in something called *elementals*. An elemental was thought to be the spiritual aspect of the literal element, in the same way that the human soul inhabits the physical body. At the level of Spirit were higher spiritual beings called daemons, or what we now know as angels and demons. These beings were thought of as being above the existence of the material world.

Below that, existing right above the realm of the material, were the elementals. A fire elemental became known as a Salamander, an air elemental became known as a Sylph, water elementals were called Undine, and earth elementals were known as Gnomes—and all of these elementals had personality traits based on how the ancients perceived that element.

This philosophy was first adopted by a Hermetic Magician, an Alchemist named Paracelsus who existed during the thirteenth century. He was known for his observational methods of study, and the way he applied those methods to magick and the occult. Some of his followers even believed him to be Hermes Trismegistus, or Thoth (one and the same). He was also the father of toxicology, and consequently the one who named Zinc. It is thought that he probably got his ideas from studying the Hindu God of Creation Brahma.

Paracelsus, and many other ancient Magicians and Alchemists, taught that the energy composition of an elemental was somewhere between the matter of the material world and the ethereal substance astral. That is, elementals vibrate at a higher rate than the element they reside in, yet have a slower vibratory rate than the astral realm, making them composed of something in between. As a result, it was believed their movements were more akin to that of a spirit, and that is why it was thought that most humans could not see them or that they could only be seen under certain conditions.

Elementary Psychology

Correspondence

Element		Behavior
Spirit	–	Oneness
Fire	–	Passion, will, aggressive or chaotic energy, lust
Air	–	Thought, intellect, logic, reasoning, learning
Water	–	Emotion, empathy, divination, childbirth, love
Earth	–	Reliability, grounding, wealth, bounty, structure

The elemental system can also be used to understand human psychology on a more individualistic level. Since mental states do indeed elicit energy programmed with a particular emotion and intent, it is beneficial to understand what those elements are supposed to represent, so a mental correspondence can be created between the symbolism of the element and the actual emotion or mental state. Let take a look at the basic elements that make up human psychology.

Spirit (Oneness)

We are all connected to a universal consciousness that is spiritual in nature, so Spirit represents our awareness of this connection. Unfortunately, most of us have been taught that we are separate from our environment and therefore have little awareness outside of ourselves, the people around us and the small communities we live in. The more we learn, the more we know, the more we can see how everything is part of everything else and, moreover, how it is conscious.

Therefore those who are more spiritually connected, or more in touch with their higher selves tend to be aware of the connectedness of all things which leads to in appreciation for nature and the welfare of humankind. On the other hand those who lack a connection to their higher spiritual nature tend to be more materialistic, selfish and lack any kind of spiritual practice.

Fire (Will)

Without will and determination, we would not be motivated to anything! A wise man once told me, "Sometimes the people who win are not the really the best, but just the ones that decided to show up." Although this statement is simplistic, it is quite profound and, moreover, true. It doesn't matter how much you know or how skilled you are, if you are unwilling try, you will get nowhere. In the same sense, you need to be aware of what motivates other people. A lot of power is to be gained by knowing what makes people do what they do—so you should pay attention. But *Will* without reason and empathy spells calamity. You should always know when to quit or at least know when it's a good time to choose another path. Chasing after a dream that will not pan out is a big waste of time.

Air (Intellect)

In order to get the most out of life, you must be able to draw logical conclusions about the world around you. And the more you know, the more informed your decisions will be. By using logic to form conclusions based on the things you know, you will be able to shape the world in a way that is real and beneficial to you and those you love. Not only this, but also knowledge can be used to motivate those around you. Intellect is king!

On the other hand, the most intelligent people have the ability to reason themselves into believing the silliest things, this is why it is so important to follow the evidence where it leads, and be willing to see things for the way they truly are.

Water (Empathy)

Empathy is what connects us to other people, it is our ability to care, our morals, values, and capacity to love. Without empathy, we would all be sociopaths! The more empathic you are, the more you will be able to read others and discover what motivates them. And people are generally sympathetic to those who can sympathize with them.

The dark side of empathy is being overemotional—I'm sure you know what I'm talking about! This leads to things like depression, anxiety, and hysteria. Someone who is led by their emotions tends put too much emphasis on their feelings and disregard logic. Yes, you should listen to empathy when making choices, but if you are always basing your decisions on feelings, you will become trapped in fantasy—again, a big waste of time.

Earth (Practicality)

Without physical, mental, and spiritual stability one would not be balanced—or grounded. When one is not well grounded, forces in that person's life are always trying to find equilibrium to balance themselves out. This is sometimes chaotic and painful. Earth typically represents structure and being grounded. It also represents things in our lives that are mundane and earthly, but are entirely necessary: our wealth, being mentally well grounded, health, and so on. So if you want to bring this kind of stability to your life, you want to work with earth energy.

A person who is too earthy is someone who lives a mundane existence. They are typically unaware of their connection with nature, and thus do not have a strong connection to spirit. Because of this, they can oftentimes be shallow, materialistic, and obsessed with wanting to fit in at the expense of not being able to find their own individuality.

SEASONS & SABBATS

Another aspect of the magical language are the Sabbats of the agrarian cultures and the influence these high tides have upon the minds of the practitioners who pay attention to them, and other people living on this planet. Regardless of whether a Sabbat is the correctly appointed time to pay tribute to a particular pagan deity, we do know that the seasons have an effect on human physiology as well as all of nature, so it would be foolish to think they have no practical use in magick.. As a matter of fact, if you intend to use magick to influence the minds of society then it would be a good idea for you to familiarize yourself with the moods and attitudes elicited during each one of these seasons. This is why I suggest you observe how you're and other peoples attitudes and behaviors change over the course of the seasons and keep a record of this in one of your diaries. Do this over the course of many years and you will be able to recognize trends that will become useful when constructing more powerful magick. For example, you may find that it is best to cast spells meant to materialize things you need during Yule (Christmas) and spells intended to draw love during the spring.

As for the changing of the seasons, there are eight major holidays called Sabbats, which correspond to the equinoxes and solstices. It is also worth noting that each of the Sabbats are celebrated in some way shape or form everywhere around the globe by most major religions. Not only this but as paganism becomes ever more popular, more and more people are beginning to gather to recognize these special times of the year. Although I will only be discussing the eight major Sabbats, there are in fact twelve holidays, so if you really get obsessive about it, you can find a reason to celebrate twelve times a year. In pagan religion, these holidays have religious significance, but they also represent important shifts in the energy of the season that can affect the magick in various ways.

Without overcomplicating things, all you really need to understand about the seasons is that the hot seasons represent a positive life-giving energy, while the cold seasons represent a negative, but necessary, death-bringing energy. Because of this, summer can be related to conscious mind, practical pursuits, and more primal energies like reproduction, and winter can be related to more subconscious energy dealing with the underworld and ancestry. You should also know that the celebration dates of these holidays are flexible, and that as these dates are moved to a day that corresponds to closest full moon or new moon, they become more powerful. Because the purpose of this book is not to indoctrinate you into a particular religion, I will not be covering how these holidays relate to a particular pagan deity, but instead will describe corresponding magical significance.

Midwinter (Yule)

Date: December 20, 21, 22, or 23

Midwinter is important because it signifies the coming of spring and summer—this is a time when day begins to dominate night. In this sense, it signifies the rebirth of all solar deities.

Imbolc

Date: February 1 or 2

Representing the first cross-quarter day, leading to spring, this day is often-times used as a day to perform purification and banishment rites.

Vernal Equinox (Ostara)

Date: Mid to late March

The Vernal Equinox is the time when the heat of the day begins to move northward from the equator. This means, the end of winter and the beginning of spring for those in the north, but the beginning of autumn and the end of summer for those in the south.

Beltane

Date: April 30 or May 1

This is the first day of summer.

Midsummer (Litha)

Date: June 20, 21, 22, or 23

This marks the height of summer, when the sun shines the longest during the day.

Lammas, Lughnasadh, or August Eve

Date: August 1

The name Lammas itself translates to "loaf mass," which insinuates a celebration of the fist harvest.

Mabon (Autumnal Equinox)

Date: September 20, 21, 22, or 23

This holiday corresponds to Thanksgiving, and is the second of the harvest festivals, after which comes Samhain.

Samhain

Date: October 31, or November 1

This represents the third harvest festival, but more significantly, it is a time to honor the dead because it is believed that the vial between the words (physical world and spiritual world) is the thinnest.

THE SYMBOLIC LANGUAGE OF SPELLS AND RITUALS

As mentioned at the beginning of this chapter, the language of magick is symbolic. This means that spells and rituals are made up of various components that each serve to represent aspects of the magician's intention in someway—when combined they spell out a complete concept.

You should also understand that the symbolic value of any of these components can vary from magical tradition to magical tradition. Therefore, don't be deceived by anyone who tells you that something has only one particular meaning, because the more books read on magick the more you will discover that each book says something different. Below is a detailed description of each of these components and how they are used in spells or rituals to represent an idea.

Incantation and Chants

As you might already know, words are extremely powerful. Everything you say or hear has the potential to trigger off a series of thoughts, which leads to some kind of action. And once you realize that words are a form of energy imbued with power, you can use that knowledge to make everything you say count by infusing those words with intent.

Simply decide what you need to say and say it in a way that is meaningful to you or your target. This can be done dramatically or uttered in a solemn tone. You can do this poetically, melodically, rhythmically, or stated in a simple or direct manor. Such incantations can be long or short, cryptic, or detailed.

Short incantations are easy to remember and build energy through repetition, while long incantations take more effort to memorize and raise energy by building urgency through progressively stronger words. Both short and long incantations can be chanted melodically or by using a sincere and earnest tone. Use a method that suits you. Take a look at these examples below.

Short and simple → "Bring me money; bring me wealth."

This one is catchier → "Bills of tens, hundreds and twenties, come to me in quantities plenty."

Forceful, commanding, wordy, but said with emotion → "I command the forces of nature to materialize that which I desire. Like thunder, I call thee. By the forces of the sun and the moon do I pull down thy power. Come now and manifest my desire with speed and urgency."

How to Speak Your Incantations

Another aspect of saying an incantation is the way you say it. Although there is really no inappropriate way to say an incantation, the method used should drive your mood and be in alignment with your intent. With that being said, if the way you speak an incantation feels silly or if what you are saying sounds ridiculous, don't say it that way—this will cause a distraction that will kill any energy you raise—find a method that works best for you. There are several very popular and ancient methods of intoning an incantation; these are called the Great Voice, the Secret Voice, Rhyme, and Babblogue.

The Great Voice

The Great voice uses a controlled vibratory tone. It would sound something like a Tibetan monk chanting a mantra or Catholic priest citing a prayer—the idea is that this vibratory tone creates sound energy that resonates into the astral. If you think about it, many spiritual traditions believe that it was sound that created the universe, so it is only natural to think that speaking an incantation at a certain pitch would help shape your intent. A primary example of this would be the Solfeggio frequency, composed of six tones. These frequencies are said to balance energy between the mind and body. They are also thought to have the ability to heal and produce miracles. The Solfeggio frequencies were discovered by Dr. Joseph Puleo during a vision, while studying the Pythagorean method of numerical reduction. Using this method, he discovered the pattern of six repeating codes in the Book of Numbers, Chapter 7, verses 12 through 83. I highly encourage you to play around with these tones when speaking incantations. The exact frequencies are found in Correspondences Tables at the end of this book.

The Secret Voice

The Secret Voice taps into energy in a very different way. It is essentially a whisper. It accesses the part of the mind that understands you are calling upon a force that is so ancient and so powerful that it should not be heard by the uninitiated masses. It lulls the energy into existence. Imagine a coven of witches standing in a circle, whispering an ancient chant. The Secret Voice is great for baneful magick. It cannot fail!

Rhyme

Another great method of vocalizing your incantation is the art of rhyme. Rhyme works so well because it can be easily memorized and is extremely catchy. Witches use this all the time, and it works.

Babblogue

Yet another great method is Babblogue. Babblogue is a nonsensical pattern of syllables or words used to create the sense that one is speaking in another language. This method speaks to the deep mind and has meaning to the speaker. This method actually works very well, especially when you are having trouble finding the right words. It is the same method used by some branches of Christianity when they speak in tongues. If you use this method long enough, you could end up creating an entire babble language.

Babblogue can be used spontaneously or can be constructed beforehand. Personally, what I like to do when using this method is to decide what I am trying to say, then write it out in plain English. After I do this, I meditate on those words and begin writing down the Babblogue. What usually comes out is more akin to automatic writing, meaning the spirits help me find the words. What appears is usually inspiring and powerful. You can also do the opposite by the way. In other words, think about the intent of the incantation, then let your mind babble off nonwords, syllables, and sounds. Take what you have written and translate it according to how it feels.

Examples:

Babblogue → "Ex nil Noxis"
English → "The light banishes the darkness."

Babblogue → Alt les ne tep so est alm."
English → "The Gods have lent me their power, and I will it to be."

Babblogue → "Resh zul vos."
English → "I pour forth my voice!"

Mathematics

Most esoteric traditions recognize the magical significance of numbers. In fact, the Jews, and to a lesser degree the Assyrians, Babylonians, and Greeks, assigned numeric values to the letters of their alphabet and found relationships between words that added up the same—this was called Gematria.

But Gematria does not use ordinary math. The "sum" is not only created by adding the numeric value of each letter, but also each individual number within the total is added together until the result is a number between one and nine. For example, the Gematria table below shows how each letter in the English alphabet lines up with number.

Western Gematria								
1	2	3	4	5	6	7	8	9
A	B	C	D	E	F	G	H	I
J	K	L	M	N	O	P	Q	R
S	T	U	V	W	X	Y	Z	

Therefore, by reducing a word, sentence, or phrase to its numeric value and performing "occult math," one can reduce that idea down to a single number. For example, the numbers for "happy" are 8, 1, 7, 7, and 7. So, by adding 8 + 1 + 7 + 7 + 7 to get 30, you can then add 3 + 0 to come up with 3. Such numbers are oftentimes associated with the planetary forces—in this case, "happy" would somehow be related to Saturn. Hint: try this with your full legal name and magical name if you have one.

But the idea that math is magical also comes from the discovery of what is called the Fibonacci sequence. The Fibonacci sequence is a pattern of numbers, where each number in sequence is the sum of the two numbers before it—for example, 0, 1, 1, 2, 3, 5, 8, 13, and so on. As this sequence mounts up into infinity, it is said to approach the golden ratio, which forms a logarithmic spiral—a pattern that naturally occurs in nature.

The study of math and magick runs very deep and, therefore, is beyond the scope of this book. However, a lot of data has been published in books and can be found freely on the web. But for now, understand that any mathematical expression can be used as a sympathetic link to an idea. For example, zero can represent the Source, because it forms an infinite look and is nothing, or "no thing," we can understand. One can represent singularity of thought; two, cooperation between two people or a union. The number three forms a triangle or trinity such as the Father, the Son, and the Holy Spirit, or the Wiccan Maiden, Mother, and Crone. Consequently, it can also stand for the cycle of life, death, and rebirth, or be represented in nature by the planting season, the growing season, and the reaping season. Four is the number of the material plane; it provides structure and foundation with its four dimensions—and it just goes on and on—whole lectures have been written about the significance of numbers.

Sigils

Have you ever heard the saying "a picture is worth a thousand words"? This is true with symbols. A sigil is a symbol that is thought to have magical significance. The symbolism of sigils speaks to us on a subconscious level and helps us invoke or channel the energies needed to make magick work—this is why spells and ritual are chalked full of them. Some sigils, such as the pentagram, have been around for a very long time. Using universal or collective sigils allows the Sorcerer to tap into that very ancient energy. If you do the research, you will find plenty of books that list and detail these sigils. Just like anything else in the magick language, you must be able to connect with it in order to tap into it. If you cannot identify with a particular sigil or can't seem to find the right one, you can always create your own. Because sigils are a type of magick unto itself, we will cover how to make sigils under its own heading in the chapter "Common Forms of Magick."

Sigilized Charm

A charm can be an object or act that is believed to have magical power—but in this case, we are talking about a word or phrase. This kind of charm is a type of specialized word crafted from an extremely long winded intent—because sometimes when you need to say a lot and you can't simplify it down to a few words, you need to cheat. Fortunately, a sigilized charm that is well crafted and well linked to your subconscious mind is as powerful as a visual sigil. Here's how you do it.

Example, Long Intent:

"Gods and Goddess of light and dark, we invite you to our circle. Bless us with your presence, protect us from harm, guide us with your wisdom, and aid us in our endeavors. Come if you will, go if you please. We ask this with eternal gratitude."

Step I
Take your overblown, wordy intent and scrap all extra letters, keeping at least one of each. Also remove all punctuation, commas, and other symbols.

Reduced Intent: G O D S A N E F L I H T R K W V T Y U C R B P M

Step II
Now take what's left over and begin creating words. As you do this, keep your intent in mind. Just let your hand do the work as you mediate on the original incantation. If a word jumps out at you while you are staring at the letters, just accept it and use it. When creating words, don't feel restricted—feel free to use any letter, any number of times, arranging them in any way you see fit. If a word looks like it needs to be changed or completed, but that letter does not exist, add the letter you think belongs there. Feel free to use real words when it seems appropriate—rhyme and repeat words if you have to. Do not ignore any powerful words or phrases that pop into your head. Continue this process until what have sounds and feels powerful.

Words →	Gods flight light know nefli tarku
Revision →	Lit-fli-targs
Revision →	Flight of targos ow en light
Final →	The light of targos flies by night!

Step III

Read your initial intent and stare at it for a good ten to fifteen minutes, then mediate on this charm phrase. Stay in meditation for another fifteen minutes, then when you come out, write down what you remember of the charm phrase—that is your final charm. Remember: it doesn't matter if it makes sense, because it will make sense to your mind.

Result: Light of Targos!

If you don't have one yet, make a book of correspondences, then write down that phrase in the book along with what it means, this way if you ever forget it, you can go back and repeat step III.

Gestures

Gestures are movements and signs made by the body. Religion and mystical orders have been using gestures from the dawn of time. Christians clasp their hands together when they pray to connect with the divine. Buddhists sit quietly with their hands in their lap, palms up, with their index finger touching their thumb during meditation. These gestures help reinforce intent because thought follows action. This is why using the right gestures in your spells and rituals can be a powerful tool in your magical arsenal.

Common Gestures

- *The process of moving in a clockwise direction, or diocel, signifies drawing energies in, while moving in a counterclockwise direction (widdershins) is a gesture of banishment or sending energies away.*
- *To direct energy, thrust your hands forward or place your hands above an object that you want to imbue it with and feel that energy move in your mind. See it flow; envision it lighting up the Astral.*
- *When you call to a solar or lunar deity, raise your hands to the sky as if beckoning them to come.*
- *Kneeling is a sign of respect.*
- *When calling upon a liminal deity or deity of the underworld, make an X across your chest using your arms to form the Sign of Death. This signifies a call to the Spirit world and can signify physical death.*

- *Many practitioners evoke the elements by using elemental hand gestures. To call air, hold your arms out to the side with your fingers spread; to call fire, form a triangle above your head by putting your index fingers and thumbs together; to call water, cup your hands together in front of you; and to summon earth, make a fist. You can, of course, create your own gestures that resonate with you.*

Herbs

Medicine men and women, Witches, and Shamans have been using herbs for thousands of years to heal, alter consciousness, and cause death. Herbs can be smoked, made into teas, and used to create incense and magical oils. Although I will not be extensively covering the natural properties of all herbs here in this book, because it would take up volumes, I do believe that every Sorcerer should make it a point to study herbology. Just as a cautionary note: some herbs are extremely dangerous or deadly when ingested or even handled, so this is why you should be extremely careful when dealing with them.

There is a magick properties correspondence table at the end of this book for herbs—and what you will discover, if you do some research, is that many of those properties correspond to that herb's actual use in medicine—this is why things like Mugwort Tea will actually relax you—mugwort is a muscle relaxant. Other properties—such as, this herb will bring you good luck and that herb draws money or even attracts love—are nothing more than belief associations—in other words, what people believed those herbs were capable of.

Before you write such associations off as unimportant and insignificant, understand that our beliefs matter. Medical science administers pills and other so-called cures that have absolutely no pharmaceutical value, but do in fact heal those who receive them—this is called the placebo effect. Sometimes, those placebos heal better than the real thing. Furthermore, consider that every herb has an appearance, texture, taste, and smell—these are the very senses we are trying to engage in the language of magick. Therefore, if you are not using an herb for its medical value, sympathetically link that herb with a state of mind, or idea, so it will be magically viable.

Incense

The word incense literally means "to burn." As mentioned above, incense creates a fragrance that engages your sense of smell. Incense can contain one or more blend of herbs to create unique fragrance. Herbs can be used by burning them whole or ground directly over coals, or by making balls, cones, or sticks. I myself prefer to make powdered incense and burn them over coals because it's easier. However, I will provide the recipe to make your own balls, cones, and sticks in another chapter.

So how do you use incense to impart a magical charge or add energy to a spell? First of all, the act of making and burning the incense follows the rule of immersion, thus getting you into state. Secondly, the incense combination itself, depending on the herbs you chose, may have mind-altering properties—again, helping you get into the right state. Third, the idea of burning incense releases smoke, which adds to energy into the air, and because you are in a circle, that energy is captured and can be directed to your magick. Fourth, you can charge items with the smoke by passing those items through the smoke three times, thus enforcing your intent. And lastly, but just as important, the smell of that incense is reminding you of your intent, thus encouraging the formation of your will.

Oils

Oil is another great substance to use in spellwork. Oil is typically created by adding one or more herbs to what is called a carrier. A carrier oil makes up the majority of the finished products content. Because that oil is infused with herbs that have real medical or mind-altering properties or both, it can be applied to the skin to react with your chemistry. Using an oil in magick has the same benefits as burning incense, except that magick items are imparted with energy of the oil by applying it to them. Oils are oftentimes applied to the forehead in a process called anointing, in order to symbolically bless oneself in the name of a deity—this usually involves some kind of a prayer. Anointing would be considered a form of purification by theurgy. Different oils can be applied to each Chakra to stimulate them.

Candles

What can I say? Magick and candles go together like peas and carrots. Candles are a great alternative to electrical lights when high EMF is a concern, also illuminating your ritual chamber with the soft glow of candle light can really help to create the right mood. Not only this but also different color candles can be used to represent different thoughts and ideas. And if your candle is scented, by oil or otherwise, it can satisfy the olfactory sense.

Stones and Crystals

It has always been a hot debate between magick and science, whether stones or crystals have any kind of "magical" effect. Again, this depends on how you define magick. Science does know that all crystals are piezoelectric—that is, when mechanical stress is applied (impact, or friction), electricity is generated. And sending a pulse of electricity through a crystal will cause it to vibrate at a certain frequency. Add to this that stones are high in certain minerals like iron, copper, silver, and gold make good conductors of electricity and that there exists stones that are magnetic, it is hard to throw out the idea of "magical" minerals and crystals.

Pair this knowledge with the understanding that biological matter, such as bones and other proteins, are also piezoelectric, and one can see crystals very well could affect the body and mind. Now, whether or not a crystal or stone is good for, say, attracting money, love, or warding off evil spirits, that has yet to be proven. However, a sympathetic links that reinforce one's intentions can be made with anything—be it an herb, sigil, stones, or crystals.

Music

You are already using sound when speaking an incantation, but you can also use song, chant, or music during spells and rituals. Sound creates a resonance that raises energy. However, if you decide to employ the use of sound, make sure it's not distracting. Remember you must remain in alpha while casting your spell. Also, when using song or playing music, make sure the words, if any, relate to the spell you are casting—you don't want your mind to be pulled in another direction. For this reason, it is best to choose ambient music without words, rather than music with words. Another interesting fact is that sound can even be used to shift your brain wave patterns and elevate you to a higher level of consciousness.

Representation

A representation is anything that represents your intent or the target of your intent. This could be fake money, if you are trying to cast a wealth spell, or it could be a picture of a person you are trying to heal, or a curse. The better you represent something, the more energy you give it, and the more quantum entangled it becomes with the real thing. You can reinforce your intent by representing that intent with something that embodies that idea—in other words, like attracts like. Therefore, if you were casting a spell to ensure the security of your home, you may want to include a lock in your spell, of if you wanted to create a spell to contain energy, you may use a bottle or box. Just remember it's the idea behind the object not the object itself that gives the spell its power. Furthermore, if you can get a tag-lock from your target that contains its genetic code, this will vastly improve your chances of success. Also realize that your involvement in the creation of this representation utilizes the principle of immersion, again improving your chances of success.

Magical Times

It is believed by many practitioners that performing a spell or ritual on a particular Holiday, day, or hour can augment their magick. This is true for a number of reasons. As already mentioned, the ether is more pliable during the night than it is during the day. Also, historically speaking, certain entities are best contacted during specific days and hours. This has less to do with physics and more to do with the ideas and beliefs built up around those ancient thought-forms. However, there is logical reason to believe that the cycle of the moon and perhaps the orbits of the planets do have an effect on our psyches. Not to get too sciencey, but the moon and the planets exert gravity on the atoms of our bodies, affecting a polar shift. When that happens mood can change. Needless to say, one may feel different during the summer than one does during the winter—so it goes without saying, the holidays that occur during those seasons have an effect on our psychology. So if you are interested in incorporating magical times into your spell or ritual, take a look at the correspondence tables at the end of this book.

Color

Color, like sound and other forms of energy, are nothing but the same type of energy existing between a certain band of frequency. This band, which is somewhere between infrared and ultraviolet (430–770 THz), represents the range of the electromagnetic spectrum that our eyes are capable of receiving. The higher frequencies are interpreted by our brains as blue, while the lower range is more in the red spectrum.

The important thing to take away from all this is that color is a form of electromagnetic radiation and that electromagnetic radiation has an effect on brainwaves. Therefore, color changes the way we think. Now, that doesn't mean that a certain color will have the same effect on every individual—certainly everyone reacts differently to different stimuli. This only means that color does have an effect and should be taken into consideration.

Just like any other sense, when used in magick, color should be tied to certain thoughts and emotions. But, more generally, you will want to gauge the way you feel when exposed to different frequencies of light and record the mood change so you will be aware of their effect.

Pain and Pleasure

Pain and pleasure obviously elicits emotions: pain invokes negative thoughts in most of us, while pleasure invokes positive or intoxicating thoughts. The more intense the sensation, the more our mind is focused and drawn into narrower state. That is, during intense pain, or orgasm, we can usually think of nothing else but the experience. Pair these feelings with any other stimuli (an image, sound, smell, touch, or taste) and like Pavlov's dogs, exposure to that same stimuli will recall similar feelings of ecstasy or pain—and that can be a powerful tool for magicians, because that level of energy supercharges magick. The only problem with the pain/pleasure technique is that its effect can be highly chaotic, because the emotions they invoke are primal in nature.

So how do you use pain and pleasure in magick? The obvious solution is to inflict pain upon yourself, someone else, masturbate, or engage in sex. As vulgar as all of these things may sound to the prude, their use in the esoteric arts is nothing new. Flagellation—ritualistic flogging or beating—has been a practiced by many religions, including Christianity, even in recent times. Sex as a ritualistic act is also not uncommon. Although ritualized sex is not found in mainstream Christianity (resist making cruel jokes), it has and still is a part of many pagan and Eastern religious traditions. Having said this, sex is natural, so there is nothing wrong or perverted about having consensual sex with someone of legal age. In any case, if you choose to adopt these practices, you will want to do them safely (nonlethal pain-inducing tools and contraceptives).

Potions and Tinctures

Tinctures and potions are practically the same thing—some form of medicine contained within a solution. The only real difference is that a potion is specifically seen as being magical. Again, today's medicine was oftentimes yesterday's magick—so it's really just a matter of how you define magick and medicine. With that being said, any potion that contains any herb, for whatever use—be it purely symbolic, medicinal, or mind-altering—can be used in ritual. I would only forewarn: if you are going to use herbs in a potion, make sure you damn well know those herbs won't kill you—herbs are dangerous to the ignorant! If you are not an expert of herbal medicine, go find one and have him or her teach you. You could also take a course at your local college or buy a good book—just be careful experimenting, I am not responsible for your death.

Theurgy

Theurgy is a technique used to call upon powerful spirits tap into your own divine authority—this you will learn about later on in this book. In short various spirits, diamons, angels, and gods, who rule over various forces can be called for their direct intervention aid in spell and rituals.

Magical Tools

Magical tools can serve three main functions: they can be practical (used only as a tool), be a sacred symbol in divine practices, or be used to hold, channel, and imbue other items with the elemental energy (fire, air, water, and earth) that tool represents. Although there are many such tools, four magical tools seem to be common among most systems. These are the wand, athame, chalice, and pentagram.

But where do these tools come from and how were they adopted into the practice of magick. If you haven't noticed, all these tools have practical use. The wand is actually a shortened version of a staff, which was used as a weapon or to aid in walking. The athame, a knife, is just a smaller version of a sword, which was also used as a weapon or for cutting herbs or any number of things. The chalice, being a cup, was used for drinking or holding liquids for the purpose of mixing potions and brews. And finally the pentagram, which was a plate bearing the symbol of a five-pointed-star, was used for holding food or offerings.

It could also be said that the elemental associations of each tools follow naturally; the wand or staff, even though a symbol of earth, because it was taken from a tree, is actually associated with fire. Why is that? Simple— trees oftentimes get struck by lightning, which was categorized as fire from the Gods—this is why wands or staffs made of wood struck by lightning are thought the most powerful magical tools of all. The athame, on the other hand, is not so obvious. It is a knife and therefore used for cutting. In magick, the knife is seldom used for cutting physical things, but instead it's used for slicing through the air to make symbols—and this is where the association comes from. The chalice, being a cup, is the most obvious symbol of all— cups hold water, and therefore water is its association. The last symbol is the pentagram, a plate that holds food. The fact that it holds a bounty that has been harvested from the earth (usually bread made of wheat) gives it the association of the same element.

When you use these tools in ritual and spell, they transform your state of mind according to the ideas they represent, but ultimately they are extensions of what is going on in your head—you do not need tools to practice magick. Having said this, tools are a part of magick, which is a system based on sym- bolizing things externally—so they can be of useful when actualizing your intent. If you decide to use them, make sure the design of the tool embodies the ideas they are meant to represent,. Otherwise, they will just be pretty bobbles resting on your altar.

As each tool is unique, each tool is used differently, but what is for sure is that your tools should be protected and concealed so the energy they represent is not diminished and depleted. Therefore, once you have bought or crafted your tools, and after you have cleansed, consecrated, and charged them, they should be wrapped in the finest of natural cloth and put away somewhere where they cannot be seen by the general public—your tools are sacred to the practice of magick.

Wand (Fire)

The wand is basically a shortened staff that can be held in one hand. It can be made of wood, metal, or a solid piece of crystal. Wands can be plain or adorned with feathers, stones, or any other type of natural material. The wand represents the element of fire, and is used to direct energy. It is associated with aggressive energies such as passion, offensive, and defensive forces. It is most often used for channeling energy and opening your sacred space.

Athame (Air)

An athame is a ceremonial knife. Although an athame can be made out of just about anything, cold iron is the best because it has the property of banishment. Adorned or unadorned it represents logic, reason, intellectual pursuits, and the attainment of knowledge. It is seen as having a masculine quality because of its obvious phallic shape. The athame is used in the same manner as the wand, to draw symbols in the air.

Chalice (Water)

Chalice is another word for an ornate cup. On a very primal level it represents the mother's womb which all life is born. It is a holy item used in theurgy as well as a practical item used for mixing magical liquids. Although a chalice can be made of anything, I suggest that it be cast of silver, for silver is the metal typically associated with the feminine energies of the cosmos. As such, it should be adorned with a water symbol, and the names of Goddess associated with the birth (if you practice theurgy).

Pentagram & Pentacle (Earth)

In magick, a Pentagram is a special disc-shaped tool about six to nine inches in circumference which bears the symbol of a five pointed stare within a circle. A pentacle, on the other hand, is the very same symbol except in the form of a talisman or amulet that is worn around the neck. As an altar tool, this plate-like item is used to place other items on when consecrating them, because it is thought to help draw down those elemental forces and channel them into the item you are trying to charge. The same tool can be used in various forms of magick to reflect any elemental energy and as a protective symbol to ward off unwanted spirits. When worn as an amulet or talisman, the pentacle can be charged for just about any purpose. For this reason, it is perfectly acceptable to choose to use both, one, or the other because they are interchangeable. You may even choose to disregard pentagram or pentacle all together and replace it with a different symbol, but if you decide to go that route, consider that you would be choosing to lock yourself out of power connected to a very ancient thought-form.

THE SYMPATHETIC LINK

In sorcery a sympathetic link represents a link between one of the linguistic elements of magick, as mentioned above, and an idea or concept. Unlike the idea of sympathetic magic, which describes the ability of objects to have an effect on one another from a far, the purpose of a sympathetic link is to help the Sorcerer or Sorceress actualize his or her intent by invoking concepts and ideas using elements of a spell or ritual that are deeply linked to his or her subconscious mind. For example, if the sorcerer or sorceress wanted to use a green candle to invoke healing powers, he or she would spend time mentally associating the candle and it's green color with healing energies. Then anytime the sorcerer or sorceress wished to invoke healing he or she would simply grab the green candle and use it in a spell or ritual. Without this link, the practitioner would have to rely on their mental acuities alone in order to cause change in accordance with their will—which is what most of us who have been practicing magick for a long time do.

This symbol-to-idea link can be one that has been developed naturally over the course of one's life, or something that must be developed over the course of one's practice. For example, you might already associate the color of pink with love, the symbol of the medical caduceus with healing, or even the sign of the cross with calling the divine aspect. However, you might not be familiar with what a pentagram or hexagram means. Therefore, you would have to create that link in your mind in order for it to have any effect.

These associations, or correspondences can be created between just about anything: a particular time (day, and hour), the phase of the moon (waxing, and waning), or even made up words and symbols (a sigil). Then, once a powerful enough link has been established between the symbol and idea, that symbol can be used in spell and ritual to "call up" that idea so that it can be used to create the needed change. Witches and Magicians have been doing this since time immemorial. As a matter of fact, these ancient thought-forms create their own mini-consensual realities.

Finding and Making Sympathetic Links

One of the most important aspects of magick is knowing what symbols best communicate the right messages to your subconscious mind. For this very reason, you can't just pick a book of popular symbology and expect to find the right symbol to convey your intent—because none of us associate the same meanings to the same symbols. For this reason, you must either discover these symbol-to-meaning links or develop them. Doing this is really another method of personal development, because discovering links is the same as discovering subconscious triggers and creating a link is a chance to craft new, more positive triggers.

To take advantage of this process, you need to find a quiet place where you won't be disturbed for at least thirty minutes—make sure you will be able to dim the lights and sit or lie comfortably. You will basically be exposing yourself to the "symbol" of your choice. If that symbol is a visible symbol, you need to create an image of it; if it is a sound, you need some way of playing that sound continuously or in a loop; if it is a fragrance, such as incense, you will need enough to burn for the duration; if it's a gesture, you will simply be making that gesture using your body or hands: and if it's an incantation, you will be speaking it like a mantra.

But before you assign any meaning to a symbol using this method, try to find out if that symbol is already subconsciously linked to any meanings. To do this, get comfortable, and make your symbol "present" by looking at it (visual symbol or color), playing it (sound), burning it (incense), forming it (gesture), or saying it like a mantra (incantation). Continue soaking in the symbol through your natural senses for a good five minutes while consciously contemplating what that symbol means to you. Once about five minutes has passed, close your eyes and continue to visualize or concentrate on (in the case of a sound, or fragrance) every aspect of the symbol—spend another five minutes doing this. At this point, stop intentionally trying to analyze the meaning of the symbol. Instead, just remain open to any images, sounds, sensations, or ideas that pop into your mind as you meditate. Pay close attention to any sensations, visions, feelings, or knowledge that seems to come out of nowhere. When nothing else seems to be coming, exit the trance, and immediately record everything you have experienced in your correspondence journal under the right symbol heading. Review what you received, and highlight or underline any sensations or ideas that seem to go beyond the meanings you ascribed to the symbol while in the conscious state—those sensations/ideas are more likely to be the more powerful ones.

If after trying the above method, you still draw a blank, it probably means that symbol is not linked to any meaning. In such case, you can link it with whatever meaning(s) you want. Although a symbol can be assigned any meaning you want, you may want to connect the actual traditional meaning to that symbol. The actually process of forging a symbol-to-meaning link is twofold: conscious memorization of the symbol and the linking of that information with the symbol in your deep subconscious mind. The first part is simple—study, memorize, and understand the meaning of your chosen symbol. When you are ready to do subconscious linking, go to the same quiet place you went to before in the last method, and dim the lights. Next, make that symbol "present" to your senses; this means, if it's an image, display it where it can be clearly seen; if it's a sound, play it; if it's a fragrance, burn it; and so on. Once the symbol is present to your senses, spend the next fifteen to thirty minutes meditating on the meaning of your symbol while experiencing it through your physical senses. The point here is to associate a feeling (emotional energy) with that symbol, so if necessary, conjure an animated scene in your mind. As you do this, take time to actually experience that symbol through your physical senses—in other words, if that symbol is meant to be seen, look at it; if you are supposed to hear it, try to focus on the sound as you visualize; and if you are supposed to smell it, take some time to appreciate the smell as you conjure the animated scene in your mind.

Please note that it may be necessary to perform both of these exercises more than once in order to discover every single hidden meaning, or reinforce the meanings that you assign, so don't just use a method once and expect to accomplish what you want. You will know that you have mined all the information from a symbol when you come up with nothing more while in a deep trance, and you will know that a symbol is linked to an idea when the appropriate thoughts and emotions are invoked every time you see, hear, or smell it.

Sympathetic Links to Modern and Ancient Thought-Forms

Thought is a thing or type of energy that can become structured and sticks around for a very long time, especially if a group of people are constantly giving it their attention. As I have mentioned above, the ancients have been building associations between symbols and ideas for a very long time. Modern Magicians have even contributed to these correspondences by incorporating them into their practice. Because of this, these thoughts have created a type of thought-form that can be tapped into and taken advantage of. This thought-form acts as a type of consensual reality that coexists with the global one. These subrealities operate under different rules than the more restrictive global reality we are used to, and by aligning yourself with such a thought-form, you can create changes that are not otherwise possible.

If I had to divide these thought-forms into two distinct categories, I would probably separate them into living and dead traditions. A living tradition would be one that is still being practiced, such as Wicca, Voodoo, Satanism, Golden Dawn, Zoroastrianism, and of course Catholicism, and a dead tradition would be those that are practiced by no one, or perhaps only a handful of people. Do dead traditions hold more untapped power because they are ancient? It's hard to say. I would argue that the most popular living ones hold the greatest power, because the sheer number of followers create the largest, most influential consensual realities.

You could also look at it this way. At the time this book was written (2018), roughly 90 percent of the world's population claims some form of spirituality. Eighty percent of that number, actually claim a religion, while 10 percent, consider themselves spiritual but nonreligious—leaving about 7 percent as atheists. In order to hypothesize about how much of an influence religious or spiritual people actually have over reality, we must consider what percentage of those people actually practice, then we must make an educated guess about how many of those practicing believers actually have the ability to effect the world with their belief.

To make this simple, I am going to use the 80 percent BS rule—in this case meaning 80 percent of those people who claim to practice some form of religion or spiritual belief are really just lying, and don't. According to that rule, this means about 20 percent of the world's population could possibly have the skills needed to intentionally change reality—but we are not through. Not all of those people know how to effectively manipulate reality. Of that 20 percent, only about 4 percent are actually aware or believe that they can bring change about through prayer, magick, or focused intent.

But what you must realize is, even though only 4 percent of the population can and probably do manipulate reality, they are still forced to do it by working within the reality matrices (consensual reality) that are the most popular. That means, if they want to tap into and manipulate existing realities in the most effective way, they must do it by tapping into existing thought-forms—and at this time, those thought-forms can be best accessed through Christian, Islamic, and Hindu names, and symbolism.

So what does this mean for you? Does this mean that you have to subscribe to one of these religions to get anything done? No, but what is does mean is, if you want to more effectively move and manipulate this energy, you must alter your rituals and spells to take advantage of popular religious/ spiritual concepts—especially when it comes to influencing those people who are a part of them. It also means that you must determine what people realistically believe. For example, the concept of fairies (nature spirits), as ridiculous as it may sound, is actually very possible—however, not many people believe in fairies anymore. What they do believe in are demons and aliens—it really depends on your country of origin and the community you live in. This blanket of belief, or disbelief not only governs the people within an area, but the energies within that area.

Having said this, you must understand these forces, in order to be able to resonate with them. Thus, the more you study the beliefs and gods of your local community, the more you will sense their energy, and the better your chances will be to effectively call them. Either way, you don't have to be Christian to call upon the God, or Satan of the Bible, nor do you have to be Hindu to call upon one of the many Hindu Gods or even Hindu demons (called a Rakshasa). Every single one of these thought-forms are tied together to the Source. I would even argue that the Gods of old are embodied within the names and idea of these newer religions—the only difference is that they can now be more effectively accessed through new religious iconography.

Performing Rituals and Spells

If one has sufficiently mastered the Triangle of Manifestation (belief, focus, and imagination), casting a spell, or performing a ritual becomes a matter of representing your will by using the right linguistic elements of magick. As a result, the elements you use determine how the spell must be performed. For example, candles must be burned, sigils are meant to be created, then incinerated, or put away, amulets and talismans should be worn, oils applied, bags carried and incantations recited—so forth and so on. As you will see, it doesn't really matter what order you perform these actions as long as the objective is realistic, it's cast at the right time, you are in the right state, and your will is clearly expressed.

All and all, it takes time to get into the right state, invoke those emotions, and project the right thoughts, so you will want to keep this in mind while you craft your ritual or spell. Some elements, like meditation on symbols, circumambulation, and incantation can naturally be extended to allow for more time to introspect. With that being said, you must not overextend your mind by making your spell or ritual too long, and you must not allow your state to be shifted back into conscious thought by making your spell or ritual too complicated. At the same time, you must give the process enough time to work—allow for enough time to become emotionally engaged, shift into the right state, and actualize your thoughts into form. So if your spell is too short, you need to extend it. The closest analogy I can make to performing a spell is singing. You can learn a song, then sing it, but you can't really drive it home until you can belt it with emotion. This is art we are talking about here, not an equation.

Last but not least, most practitioners of magick cast their spells within a Circle or their Scared Space—remember: doing so is meant to protect the sanctity of the spell and augment its power. Even so, this is only as necessary as you make it. Unless you have good reason—you are concerned about the thoughts of others impinging upon your will, or you are trying to create a controlled environment for spirits to manifest—it is entirely unnecessary to work within a space. This means that as long as you have the right tools, you can perform a ritual or cast a spell anytime you want. However, doing so within a Sacred Space is safer and can magnify the results.

Theurgy

The word *theurgy* is a combination of the Greek words *theou*, meaning "God," and *ergos*, meaning "working," which together can be translated as "to work with God." Theurgy is considered high magick as opposed to low, low magick being any magick that calls upon forces within the physical world (or lower dimensions) and high magick being magick that calls upon forces existing at the very root of everything (or higher spiritual dimensions). In the classical sense, theurgy is seen as a way to ascend to God by freeing one's self of mortal imperfections. This ascension is said to give the Magician power over nature and the forces of darkness. The theory is, once a Magician achieves a sufficient amount of divine authority, by becoming pure like God, he would then have the ability to bind and control lower beings in the name of the Almighty.

This idea was introduced to Western magick sometime during the seventeenth century through the Ars Goetia, the first section of the Lessor Key of Solomon, which featured the legend of the Biblical King. As the legend goes, Solomon the Wise was given power by God to control seventy-two demons for the purpose of building his temple, after which he bound them all in a magically sealed brass vessel and cast them into the Dead Sea. In fact, many such books appeared during this era, all based on a system of Christian mysticism—and all sketchy. The reason why I consider them sketchy is because most practicing this form of magick were not really practicing theurgy for the purpose of becoming spiritually enlightened. They were practicing it to satisfy their own selfish desire to gain wealth, murder, and even to get laid. It is laughable to think that any of this worked, due to the fact that in order to gain authority by God to control the demons they were trying to summon, they had to become authentically pure, or godlike themselves—the greedy, selfish, or unclean nature of their goals kind of ruled this out.

But this system dates back further than that. The Greek Magical Papyri (100 BC–AD 400) was a collection Greco-Roman Egyptian spells and rituals, written on parchment, that provided a sorted number of charms that could be used for healing, protection, victory over one's enemies, attracting a mate, and speaking to the dead, among many other things. So as you can see, the idea that one can petition God or the gods for favors or to gain wisdom is a very ancient concept that has carried over even to this day.

In lieu of all this, do I think that theurgy is a type of magick worthy of being practiced? Yes, *but* not without understanding what theurgy really is. One, theurgy is about understanding what God is and our relationship to It. Therefore, there is nothing wrong with using theurgy to learn more about our connection to the Source—this is something we can all benefit from. Two, theurgy is about understanding all other manifestations of the Source, be that nature, lower spirits, or higher spirits. There is nothing innately wrong with using magick to do this. However, it's just asinine to try to accomplish this by trying to beat powerful spirits over the head with the name of God. Besides these things, I have only two other issues with this philosophy; one, the assumption that God is something that must be reached, and two, that one needs to be pure in order to tap into God's power—I don't find either one of these assumptions true—here is why.

There is no need to become one with God, because you already are. All you need to do to affirm this connection is to become intimately familiar with yourself, and the universe. The more you realize this connection, the more mysteries will be unlocked to you, and eventually you will achieve your full spiritual potential. All the knowledge, wisdom, and power you seek is already within you waiting to be discovered and called upon—all you need to do is just be aware of it. In my opinion, this is what true theurgy is all about. Now let me explain why.

God is all powerful! The God which created this universe and everything in it also created you. Because of this, everything created by the Source is connected, and that means that the power and knowledge that is intrinsic to the Source is also available to you. Just as the cells of your body form organs that serve a specific function, so too are you a functioning part of the Source, created for a purpose. Such a powerful being would not create another life form just to see it fail. That means what you are doing now or may be doing in the future is exactly what you were meant to do. It also means that who you are and who you might become will never be in conflict with God's divine plan. This doesn't mean you have no free will or that you shouldn't work on becoming a better person. No—it just means what you do in this life, and how you go about doing it, is not only up to you, but also in line with God's will.

This brings us to morality. If you are a despicable person who loves to perpetrate evil for the sheer pleasure of seeing people suffer, does this mean that your lifestyle is still in alignment with God's plan? Yes—and I'll tell you why. If God is truly the creator of all things—which It is—then God created both good and evil. In such case, we must assume that both good and evil serve a purpose. All we would have to do to prove this is to cite all the instances when God has allowed innocent, men, women, and children to be killed by earthquakes, tsunamis, famines, diseases, and wars. Then to support the claim of benevolence, all we would have to do is acknowledge that we have been blessed by the life-giving illumination of the Sun, the birth of new progeny, and all the gifts given by nature. This quote from verse 31 of the Poemandres, the first book of the Corpus Hermeticum sums up this idea the best.

> Holy art Thou, Lord of the universe.
> Holy art Thou, whom nature hath not formed.
> Holy art Thou, The Vast and Almighty One.
> Lord of the Light, and of the Darkness.

But why, *why* does God seem so bipolar? This is one of the great unanswered mysteries. Allow me to offer you some theories. It could be that enlightenment is only possible when the challenges of good and evil exist side by side. To know love, there must be hate; to be motivated to live, we must be aware that we will eventually die; and to have light, there must also be darkness. And all this makes sense until you realize that God is all powerful. Couldn't a being with unlimited power, simply create an existence where nothing bad ever happens?

It could also be that morality is subjective—that is, what is right for one is wrong for another and vice versa. For example, in one country, it may be OK to get married as age sixteen, while in another you must be at least eighteen. Otherwise, it would be considered wrong. Or in one society, thievery is considered a mortal sin punishable by death, while in another, it will only land you in jail. Now, of course, I would argue that in any case it would be plain evil to kick a baby or push an old lady down a flight of stairs. However, if I'm to be honest, I must admit that those things could be subjective to. It all boils down to this: if morality is subjective, then it's a personal choice. I choose good over evil. What about you?

But this doesn't really answer the question. Evil may exist in the world because there may be other Gods, with other agendas, who are just as powerful—a true struggle between light and darkness. In such case, it would be very important to choose a side. This would also mean that God is not all powerful or all knowing. Sacrilege, right? I don't think so. Who or what created God? It would be easy to assume that God had no beginning and has no end—that God is eternal—but that's kind of a cop out. We just don't know, so why assume. In such case, God must be learning, and if that's true, our lives, our incarnations, may be a part of its learning process. After all, human beings are capable of learning by running numerous scenarios through our heads to determine the best course of action. Also, if you believe, as many scientists do, that the universe arose from consciousness itself, then you must entertain the possibility that our lives may be the product of the Source role-playing out scenarios by thinking or dreaming about them.

All of these questions are things we're trying to answer by practicing theurgy. Unfortunately, no one can wave a magic wand and make you instantly know the answers—that requires work and personal experience. None of these questions are simple, or have clear-cut answers, but the rewards that come from trying to understand these mysteries are great. Discovering the answers to these questions can be mind-blowing, freeing, frightening, depressing, and even seductive—in fact, this whole journey can be an emotional roller-coaster ride.

These experiences often time lead to a period known as the "dark night of the soul," which is a time of spiritual crisis, resulting from mental conflict with a spiritual principle, idea, or aspect of reality. For example, those who have always believed that God is love may suffer from a dark period as they try to reconcile God's light and dark aspects, or those who believe in one God might have a dark-night-of-the-soul experience after contemplating the possibility of multiple Gods. This troubling period can last for one week, or years, but *if* you successfully find the end of this dark tunnel and emerge into the light, you will have spiritually grown and be forever changed.

This is why I always suggest that anyone practicing theurgy, or any other spiritual pursuit for that matter, take a break after any kind of mind-blowing spiritual experience. You *must* have time to process this new information. For the true spiritual seeker, these experiences are unavoidable. However, if you take time to assimilate what you have learned, you may reduce your time of suffering. For this reason, I advise you to share what you have discovered with a trusted friend, especially one who has already taken the journey—he or she may be able to help you along the path and put things into perspective.

GETTING IN TOUCH WITH YOUR HIGHER SPIRITUAL ASPECT

I have used the term Higher Spiritual Aspect numerous times in this chapter, to describe the Source, and its other manifestations, the gods (with a lowercase G), but now I want to talk about *you* as a Higher Spiritual Aspect. Just as Higher Beings are expressions of the Source, so you are too. Your Higher Spiritual Aspect is that part of you that is connected to the Ultimate Divine Power—the Source. And like the Source, it has limitless potential and power. So it isn't as if you need to discover a way to become connected; you only need to realize that you already are. Everyone will move toward this realization, and eventually come to recognize their Higher Spiritual Aspect, whether they are trying to or not—this is the natural progression of life. Just as energy is neither created nor destroyed, we are refined through the cycle of life and death until we achieve perfect understanding—that process of understanding is called Gnosis.

Gnosis is the Greek word for "knowledge," but not just any kind of knowledge—knowledge of how the Universe works on a deep spiritual level. Fortunately, achieving gnosis does not require faith. But what it does require is lots and lots of research, study, and learning through trial and error. The deeper you dig, the more you study, and the more you apply that knowledge, the more illuminated the truth will become to you, until finally things like ignorance, deception, and self-delusion fall away.

This will do several things for you. By studying all manner of things, you will come to understand that matter *really* does arise from thought. Once you finally accept this, you may begin to notice little synchronicities happening in your life—something appears when you need it, or someone will call when you think about them. When that happens, you may decide to use what you have learned to intentionally manifest reality the way you want it. At that point, you will either succeed, have partial success, or fail. If you fail, you may dismiss the whole idea of manifesting reality as bunch of nonsense, and give up entirely, or you might simply adjust your method and try again. But if you are anything like me, failure may cause you to walk away and not look back for years.

If that happens, you may simply rejoin society and try to make the best of life according to how you think reality works. That may take the form of working a nine-to-five job, joining a religion, or following a carrier path. If that is the case, then it means there are important life lessons you *must* learn before you are ready to learn higher truths. Once—and only once—you have learned those lessons will you be ready to step back on the path.

However, if you succeed, this will cause a mind-blowing experience. If you don't fall prey to cognitive dissonance and chalk it all up to coincidence, this mind-blowing experience will reaffirm what you have learned, and replace your old view of reality with a new one. This will elevate you to an entirely new level and cause you to ask many other questions. Those questions may be, "If I can change reality, then can others do the same thing? If so, what are the moral implications? Can I cause havoc by tampering with reality, and if so, how can I do it safely?" and lastly, "Is there anything more to life, than just manifesting whatever the hell I want?"

It is also very likely that you will experience an instantaneous knowing of information. This means, when asking difficult questions, the answer may appear in your mind in a very clear and detailed fashion. In this way, you will gain the information that you are *ready to assimilate and understand.* Oftentimes, this instant knowledge will contain information that can be verified through other sources, has practical application, and can be backed up by science. If you continue to probe this mystery, you will soon realize that you are pulling information from the Akashic records or being handed information by spirits.

This is the natural progression of spiritual evolution. This doesn't happen by casting spells or performing complicated rituals. All of these things and more are the results of seeking gnosis—and as I have said, gnosis is attained by studying the mysteries. Gnostic mysteries can found within all disciplines—they hide out in books of science and ancient esoteric texts, and they can even be drawn from the direct observation of nature itself. Gnosis is not only the main focus of Theurgy, but is also considered "The Great Work," because life itself is driven by our desire to know. Even though you can consider this book a gnostic text, do not end your studies with it. Instead, branch out and study all things. So without further ado, here is the secret to achieving gnosis.

- Research Everything
- Study What You Have Learned
- Experiment with What You Have Learned and Use It in Everyday Life
- Ask Your Higher Spiritual Aspect for Clarification
- Meditate
- Repeat Daily

Research Everything
Begin by reading this book, then branch out into books of science, psychology, magick, religious texts, and any other subject that might pique your interest.

Study What You Have Learned
Once you have found a subject that really interests you, spend some time thoroughly studying it.

Experiment with What You Have Learned and Use It in Everyday Life

Run experiments on those things that require it. Much can be gained by working with the knowledge you have acquired. Determine how you can use this knowledge in everyday life, and apply it to make yourself a better person.

Ask your Higher Spiritual Aspect for Clarification

Many times, you will encounter information that is difficult to understand or needs clarification. If you can't find an expert to teach you, or if there is no one around who is knowledgeable about this subject, ask for your Higher Spiritual Aspect to enlighten you. This can take the form of constructing a specific question or simply intensely focusing on that same question.

Meditate

Once you have formulated your question, meditate on it—Exercise 8: Gaining Spiritual Insight, in the chapter on meditation is perfect for this.

Repeat Daily

Never stop learning. The more you know, the more enlightened you will become. Achieving gnosis is an ongoing process. I suggest setting aside time on a daily basis to research and study. However, your lifestyle may not allow for it. If you can't do this every day, make it a point to learn something every week. When you get tired, stop. If you become inspired, let that inspiration lead you.

OTHER MANIFESTATIONS OF THE SOURCE

We are not the only intelligent beings created by the Source. In fact, there are many others. Knowing what these other beings are, what motivates them, and how to properly interact with them is just as much a part of the practice of theurgy as getting to know your own Divine Aspect. Perhaps the greatest concern to us as Sorcerers are those beings that have been commonly referred to by society as gods, demons, and angels.

The word *god* with a little *G,* can be used to describe any being that is at the apex of its spiritual development, has supreme mastery over the elemental forces of nature, and likes to interfere in human affairs. This is most likely referring to the gods of legend, written about by the ancients—like Enki, Marduk, Thor, Mars, Quetzalcoatl, Shiva, or Hecate. An angel or demon is usually considered a subordinate or emissary of a more powerful deity, such as the ones mentioned above. The first question perhaps should be, did these gods really exist, and if so, why should we care?

The truth is, there is a *hell of a lot* of evidence that points to the possibility that they actually did exist. Nearly every culture across the globe has a legend about powerful beings that came from the heavens to inhabit and rule over the Earth. Not only do these cultures, which were separated by thousands of miles, have strikingly similar stories, but also archaeological evidence has been left behind to back those stories up. I, of course, am talking about megalithic structures like the Stonehenge of England, the pyramids of Egypt, the Parthenon of Greece, and the Moai of Easter Island—just to name a few. Not only can these structures be found aboveground, but also they can be found underground as well. Kaymakli and Derinkuyu in Cappadocia, Turkey, are two great examples. Honestly, there is so much evidence to support the belief that we have been visited by *gods* (aliens) from the *heavens* (space), it would be ridiculous or simply ignorant to ignore or deny it.

So what do these stories actually say about these godlike visitors? To answer this question, I will have to explain by summarizing the account of the Anunnaki (a name that roughly translates to "those from heaven to earth came"), which was recorded on clay tablets in cuneiform thousands of years ago by the Sumerians. The story goes something like this:

> There once existed a powerful race of transcendent beings called the Anunnaki, who visited Earth for the purpose of mining gold. After becoming weary of doing the work themselves, they decided to create a new race called Humans, to do it for them. To these humans, they taught language, mathematics, science, agriculture, and the arts. But some Anunnaki were conflicted about creating a slave race, and so a war erupted between the two factions causing a great flood—this not only made mining impossible but also killed most of the Earth's population. So eventually, the Anunnaki abandoned their temple bases and

left humanity to fend for themselves. And so it was that after many years of abandonment, knowledge of the Anunnaki fell into obscurity and became a thing of legend.

Many other accounts across the globe can be found that describe a similar scenario; each telling of extremely advanced beings that came from the stars to civilize humanity—teaching them things like agriculture, science, and language, and each telling of a great flood of apocalyptic proportions. There are even similarities in the building styles—temple architecture—for example—such as the shape chosen (pyramidal), the massiveness of the construction, the fact that temples were lined up with constellations, and increased electromagnetic emanations coming from the stones. You will of course find entire books, websites, and videos debunking this ancient-aliens theory, but where you find anything that seems incredible, there will always be a campaign to debunk it. The only thing you can really do is to do the research yourself and make up your own mind. You have to realize that religion is highly motivated to keep such information repressed. Otherwise, they would lose control—which is already happening.

In all actuality, the new religions such as Judaism, Christianity, and Islam, which are celebrated by their devotees as religions of peace and goodness, were actually based on the legends of the Anunnaki. The only thing one really has to do to prove this is to compare the stories of the Old Testament to the Sumerian accounts—keep in mind the foundation of Judaism, Christianity, and Islam is the Torah (Old Testament). And it's not as if they (Judaism, Christianity, and Islam) borrowed just a little—they pretty much copied verbatim—they just changed names and inverted certain concepts to fit their own political and ideological agendas. In many ways, the new religions only repeated the sins of their predecessors (the Anunnaki, who inspired the original stories) by exalting oppression, slavery, and the quest for gold over truth and actual spiritual development. And this kind of behavior makes sense because, after all, we were created (genetically engineered) in the image of our gods to be a slave workforce. As a matter of fact, the word *worship* is a derivative of the Middle English word *woer*, "to work," and of course *ship*, "a sea, air, or space vessel"—in other words, a vessel where you work.

But as much as one might hate an alien species for meddling in human affairs, we must not be too judgmental, because according to the legend, we would not exist if they did not create us. And the legends say that they created us in their image, which most likely means they spliced their DNA with ours. If that is true, then it means that we have advanced alien blood in us. And if that is the case, they gave us power. Another important thing to realize is not all aliens saw us a tool for labor, slaves, or even livestock (yes, there are accounts of us being used as a food source)—according to legend, some wanted to free us and help us evolve beyond a primitive species—that was part of the conflict between Enki and Enlil.

Another thing you must realize is that the Earth is millions of years old. In that span of time, countless global disasters have buried evidence and wiped out entire civilizations. What I am trying to say here is that the Anunnaki were probably not the first to visit Earth. There have probably been many gods (species of aliens) that have set foot on this planet. Each of those visitors may have created new species or might have even remained to become us. Although some of those visitors might have simply wanted to create a workforce; others may have wanted to help us.

The reason why you should care is because our history was most likely affected by the presence and direct interaction of these beings. They have influenced not only our religion, but also our culture by passing on their knowledge. We don't hear anything about them now because most people aren't looking—but this doesn't mean they are gone. After doing your own research, you will understand that these beings had insanely long life spans. This means they may still be around. In such case, we should be aware and try to understand what motivates them. Otherwise, we may become victims of their foolishness or even pass up the opportunity to learn more from them.

But communication with these beings is an enigma. Many theugic practices deal with this by incorporating prayer to the old ones into spells and rituals in the form of evocation and invocation. But, honestly, we do not know if we are communicating with what we are calling. Spirits by nature are invisible to those who have not developed the sight. Not only this, but also many spirits can take on any form they want. This means, even if you could see them, there would be no guarantee that you are actually communicating with the entity you called—in other words, you could be talking to a run-of-the-mill shade posing as an Egyptian god, or think you are talking to an angelic spirit, when in fact, you are having a conversation with a malevolent force. On the other hand, humans can be extremely imaginative. Casting a spell or performing a ritual effectively puts you in a trance, hypnotizing you. Once in this deep altered state, your subconscious mind is capable of hallucinating anything it wants. If you want to see a Greek god, you will, or if you are afraid you will encounter a demon, your mind may conjure it.

At the same time, the majority of the world prays, and praying is just another form of evocation and invocation. Prayer helps many, despite any chances of inadvertently being manipulated by evil forces, or the very real possibility it could be a fabrication of the mind. This practice could also be the reason why so many people suffer mental illness, such as schizophrenia and DID (dissociative identity disorder). What is clear, though, is something happens when you call upon a force you assume is greater than yourself. People have been miraculously healed, blessed with new jobs, relationship have been mended, and all kinds of other problems have been rectified. An easy explanation for these occurrences could be the placebo effect. By calling upon a force greater than themselves, they are actually calling upon their own personal power to affect reality—in such case, no god or goddess is needed. This is one of the problems of calling upon an invisible force—how would you ever know if you made the change or if a god was responsible?

I am really not trying to cause you to become disenchanted with the idea of communicating with a god or goddess by mentioning the Anunnaki, spirits, and placebo—I am only trying to make you aware of the possibilities. We as Sorcerers and Sorceresses must have a high level of intellectual honesty if we want to discover the best way to change ourselves and the world around us. This means that we should examine all possibilities in order to come to an understanding of how the world really works. Having said this, we may never find the answers to these problems. In the end, what really matters is the quality of information gained through these practices as well as the changes you can make when using these techniques. If we can discover why it works as we practice it, then great, but don't get too frustrated if you can't find the answer.

Contacting the Old Ones

Having said this, there is a procedure for working with these gods. In my experience, the Old Gods want to be communicated with and are waiting for people to reach out to them and make contact. Yes, some of them may have been responsible for the creation and enslavement of the human race and have little interest in our well-being. But there are also those who wish to help us, and see us evolve to our full potential. So, if you wish to call upon these gods and goddess, which I recommend, you must first reach out to them. The procedure described below is actually quite simple and meant to establish light contact. A heavier, more direct contact can be made using the art and science of Evocation, but that is an advanced practice. Whether you make indirect connection or direct connection, it doesn't matter—the quality of the relationships and the benefits are the same—the difference is really in the style of communication.

Working Relationships verses Worship

You probably remember me saying that Sorcerers do not worship. So, if this is true, why do I even suggest calling upon the gods? To answer this question, I must first distinguish between worship as a form of ass-kissing and a magician or sorcerer's working relationship with a higher being. Most of you are already very familiar with the Judeo-Christian version of worship, which involves groveling on hands and knees, with a sense of self-loathing—this is not what I am talking about. Worship is actually meant to establish and strengthen your connection to deity, whether that be the Source or some other higher being.

With that being said, you never want to venerate or worship any being that requires you to hate yourself, do harm to yourself or others, or otherwise dwell on negative things—unless that being is actually trying to help you overcome your own demons. Another thing you should realize is that these higher beings are not there to satisfy your every need. Yes—most wish to help, but they understand karma, and for that reason, they understand that *you* must do the work in order to earn enlightenment.

Procedure for Connecting with a Deity

Step 1: Research
Before making contact with any god or goddess, I recommend you do lots of research. Plain and simple, you want to know who and what you are connecting with before you reach out. This research will give you an idea of what the ancients thought about a certain deity and how it was worshiped or called upon. Just realize that human beings have a tendency to exaggerate and embellish and that this information has most likely been distorted over its many centuries of existence. To help you in this endeavor, answer the questions in the checklist below, as you discover them.

Deity Research Checklist
- God/Goddess Name?
- What culture is this god/goddess from?
- Can this god or goddess be traced back to another culture? If so, what did that culture call him or her?
- What other god/goddesses is this god or goddess related to? Family tree?
- What does the god or goddess look like? How has he or she been depicted?
- What is this god's personality like, and how has it been described by followers in the past? Does he or she have a positive and negative side, or maybe even threefold nature (multiple personalities)?
- What is this god/goddesses domains? For example, is he or she a god/goddess of the moon, thunder, love, death, birth, and so on?
- Does this god/goddess have any symbols associated with him/her?
- What plants, animals, minerals, places, days, hours, directions, planets, and so on are sacred to this god or goddess?
- What are the legends or tales associated with this god or goddess?
- How was this god or goddess worshiped in the past?

Step 2: Setting Up Your Altar
Altars are extremely important to the practice of theurgy. Think of an altar as a type of foci that is used to draw your attention to a specific entity—remember

to connect with other minds (in this case, that of a god or goddess) requires intense focus—the altar accomplishes just this. Altar setups are individually unique, that is, they are oftentimes specific to the culture, deity, or even practitioner of magick that creates them. Therefore, in order to successfully set up your altar, you need to draw upon the information you have gathered above. In addition to an altar set up, you will need to pay attention to any particular customs used to establish that connection. In any case, your information may be lacking. It may be that a deity is so old or obscure that the customs that surround it have faded into antiquity and been lost. In such case, you will want to go with a simple altar setup, then make contact via deep meditation, drawing upon the Akashic records and/or inspiration from the god or goddess that you have called to fill in any lost information—trust me: if a high spirit is interested in speaking to you, they will send visions.

Step 3: Open a Circle or Sacred Space

Although I have not covered it yet, opening a Sacred Space is necessarily in first contact with such a high-level being. So before moving on to the next step, skip to the next chapter, "Concerning Magick Circles and Sacred Spaces," and learn how to create a sacred space or open a circle.

Step 4: Inviting the Deity

Set aside at least fifteen minutes in a quiet place (preferable your ritual chamber) to establish communication. Begin fulfilling any requirements of custom before the next step—this might involve burning a particular type of incense, saying a specific prayer or even taking a certain divine posture. If that custom is a form of meditation, use the customary meditation instead of what I suggest next. After you have fulfilled customs, or if there are no customs at all, take a good long look at the altar, keeping in mind its purpose—to draw the attention of that deity. Once you have soaked in every aspect of the altar, officially invite the deity to your sacred space using a simple prayer.

For example:

> GOD or GODDESS NAME, I invite you to this circle (sacred space). Please honor me with your presence.

Although you can be poetic, it's not necessary. The only thing that really matters is strong intent. Communicating what you want by saying it invokes the intent in your mind.

Step 5: Communicating with the Deity

Now, close your eyes. If you are not already in alpha, use whatever meditation technique you wish to get into that state. Once in this alpha state, you are free to introduce yourself, or if you are already acquainted with the deity, ask questions.

Keep in mind that communication with a deity happens just as described in Psychic Communication. Therefore, you should expect to see visions, feel sensations, and even hear things (perhaps a voice), all according to your own talents. Also keep in mind that these entities can be quite powerful. When they arrive their energy may subtle, strong, or even dizzying. If that energy causes discomfort, try to allow yourself enough time to get used to it. But if you feel like you are going to pass out, or you become sick, end communication immediately!

In any case, be respectful and keep dialogue polite. Once you have accomplished what you set out to do, received the answers you were looking for, or feel like it's the right time to end, close the conversation with a simple thank you, then open your eyes. Lastly, pick your dream diary or voice recorder and record everything you saw, heard, felt, smelled, and so on. Otherwise, it will disappear like waking from a dream.

Step 6: Close the Circle or Sacred Space

After you have made this record and closed your circle or sacred space, then do some kind of activity, like going for a walk or making yourself a snack—this will help you disconnect from that energy.

Prayer

Connecting with a deity or relaying a request to one does not always require one to open a full circle or set up an altar. Prayer can be done anywhere at any time. Even so, it is always best to pray to a deity that you have already made contact with and developed a relationship with, because this is when they have the most impact.

You must also realize that the attention of such entities is divided between many followers. Yes, they are powerful, but they are not always going to appear every time you cry for help. Instead of moving their full consciousness to your location, they may instead choose to help you by granting your request—that means sending their energy remotely. I have been told by many spirits on many occasions that traveling from one plane to another—in their case, from a place of higher vibration, to a lower one—requires a lot of effort. Because of this, it's much easier for them to just send their power, and communicate mind to mind—these beings can and will even communicate through other people, synchronicities, your dreams, and signs. For example, you may ask *Hypnos* (God of Dreams) a question and get your answer in a dream that night, or you may ask *Hades* to deliver a message to your dead grandmother, and he may send one of your long-lost living relatives to relay a response (without his knowledge, of course).

In conclusion, remember that developing a relationship to your chosen deity (or one who chooses you) will become an important aspect of your work with occult magick. No, you don't need to do it, but I definitely wouldn't neglect it, because it is great for spiritual development and adds an enormous amount of power to everything you do. In any case, whenever you pray, make it heartfelt, keep it simple, and say what you mean.

CALLING ARCHETYPES VERSUS CALLING GODS

If the idea of calling upon an invisible foreign god or goddess bothers you, don't. You can still incorporate theurgic energy into your works without uttering the name of a deity by invoking an archetypal force instead. As a matter of fact, everything in the universe, including yourself is an archetypal thought-form anyways. That is, every god and goddess is nothing more than a manifestation of a specific type of primal energy that, in and of itself, is a manifestation of the Source. From this perspective, you can call upon the divine power of healing without calling upon Hermes, and in the same sense, you can call upon a powerful force of destruction without uttering the names Satan or Kali. In a way, calling out to a force can be more powerful than invoking a specific god, because you are connecting to that unfiltered energy.

DEVELOPING DIVINE AUTHORITY

Divine authority is calling upon the power of the Source, a God, Goddess, Daimon, or High Spirit to cause change. Although we all have some amount of Divine Authority, those who have a better connection to deity have more. Divine authority is attained by being aware of, *understanding,* and *acknowledging* your connection to the divine. And it is further enhanced by aligning yourself with the deities you call. Notice how none of this stuff involves things that you can just proclaim or profess; all of these things must be genuinely authentic. In other words, you really must be aware of your connection to the divine, and you really must understand it, not just be able to spout off philosophy you have heard somewhere—and lastly, you must fully *accept* and *acknowledge* your connection with this divine current. Without all of this, any expression of Divine Authority is meaningless. Without divine authority, any magick you perform is fueled by your own energy and perhaps the lower elemental forces.

So how do you get there? How does one gain divine authority? Let's first talk about being aware your connection to the divine. If you cannot imagine that the universe was created by a higher force that is conscious, then you cannot fulfill this requirement. In such case, you need to do some more soul-searching and work with these forces through meditation and the lower magical arts. If you are adamant enough, you will eventually be exposed to these higher forces and become aware of them—also, you may, through your exposure, accept your connection to these forces and come to understand them.

Once you have become aware of these higher forces, you can then go about studying them. However, oftentimes, if you can establish communication with a deity using meditation and magical technique, you can simply ask for wisdom. If your request is honest, and if they feel you are capable of understanding it, they will hit you with that wisdom, and you will instantaneously understand. When this happens, it's like being brought up to a new level. This kind of event not only makes you wiser, but also causes a personality change—it's that powerful!

But this wisdom and connection can fade over time due to our exposure to the lower planes, and at that point, we may deny our relation to the divine in favor of what we think is more real. In such case, if we wish to maintain our connection, we must seek to commune with the Gods on a regular basis and incorporate the use of Divine Magick into our spells and rituals.

ASSUMING THE GOD/GODDESS FORM

Another way to gain wisdom and add power to a ritual or spell is to assume a God or Goddess form. Assuming a God form is a type of invocation, meaning, you are inviting the spirit of a God or Goddess to possess you for the purpose of creating a connection to the realm of the divine or the world of fire. When you do this, you are acting as a representative of that God or Goddess, and borrowing their power, so to speak. Doing this requires a good relationship with that entity and must only be done if you have developed explicit trust. Once you have assumed the God or Goddess form, your magick will become supercharged.

Which God or Goddess form you chose to assume will be wholly dependent on the nature of operation you are doing at that moment; for example, when healing, you may choose to assume the form of Isis, but when cursing someone, you may choose to take on the visage of Anubis. In order to do this successfully, you must be well familiar and connected with the God or Goddess you are trying to assume the form of—in other words, don't just pick a random God out of a hat one day, one you've never worked with, and try to assume its form.

The first step in Assuming a God form is to say a prayer inviting that deity to use you as a vessel. This prayer should be said with reverence and should come from the heart. For example, if you wanted to assume the form of Hecate, you might say,

> "Goddess of the Underworld, dark lady who works from
> afar, cast your energy down upon me. With much respect

and reverence, I ask that you use me as a vessel to enact your will. I invoke your presence in me."

With your eyes closed or open, visualize the energy of the God or Goddess manifesting over your head. For Gods or Goddess in their positive aspect, this energy should be seen as bright and awe-inspiring light, but for Gods and Goddesses in their negative aspect, this energy should be visualized as shadowy, abyssal, dark, and disturbing. Positive energy could be visualized as an orb of bright light or brilliant sun, while negative energy could be visualized as a dark tempest, or shadow hovering overhead.

Once you have this image actualized, see this energy enter you through your crown chakra. Feel it fill your body, causing you to either glow with the same light or radiate darkness. Notice how the merger makes you feel. Sense the change in attitude and personality happening within you as its presence grows.

Once you have taken in every ounce of this energy and are bursting with it, feel it integrate with and merge with your etheric body. As it integrates, visualize it taking on the physical appearance of that deity and mold it into the image of that God or Goddess you are assuming. Start by shape shifting this energy into a vague or anthropomorphic shape, then visualize clothing and accessories. Finish this with skin color, facial features, hair color, eye color, and skin texture until you have visualized every aspect of "being" that God or Goddess. Once the transformation is complete, finish with an affirmative invocation.

For example, for Hecate, you might say something like,

> "I am the keeper of the keys.
> "I am the worker from afar.
> "I am the Goddess of the Underworld and Queen of the Dead.
> "I am Hecate."

Cleansing, Consecrating, and Charging Items

There is this concept within magick that items like magical tools and components, such as herbs, stones, and other things, need to be cleansed, consecrated, and charged for a specific purpose—but does this actually change the item in any way?

Yes—although everything is made up of a type of nonphysical energy (quintessence), here in the material world, most objects are made up of a stable matrix of well-defined information that gives them their physical unchanging appearance. Having said this, not only can items be physically altered in a direct way by physically modifying them in the real world, but also they can be altered in a subtler way through a process of mental impression. In this way, this modification of the items quantum matrix (the matrix of information that defines it) can affect the item's energetic field (etheric energy), which can in turn affect the auric field of the person wearing or otherwise handling that item. Furthermore, these changes may be so subtle that they would not be visible to the untrained eye. However, if someone trained to see auras were to look at that item or if that item was to be viewed using Kirilian photography (photography of electrical coronal discharges), those changes would be apparent.

With that being said, it is unlikely, unless you are extremely powerful, that your thoughts will change an object so much that its physical appearance will be changed, because even though that physical object is nothing but a wave-form, its physical makeup is extremely stable. If things in the physical world were that easy to change, this world would be an ever-changing landscape, and nothing could be relied upon to exist. Despite this, mind *can* change the appearance of living and nonliving things in very subtle ways on a microscopic/subatomic level. And in the long run, those changes can usually be seen as the item takes on a healthier or sicker/dingier appearance, depending on the type of energy received.

It is also worth knowing that some objects are easier to change than others—according to the elements they are made up of and density. Water, for example, accepts charged thought extremely well, especially if that water is high in electrolytes (salt water). Harder objects, such as metals and crystals, are also very capable of accepting and keeping mental charges— consequently, sound travels through denser objects better than less dense objects like water. Other materials, such as plant matter (wood, fresh herbs) and the human body, contain a certain amount of water, and therefore are ideal for charging.

The question is, "Is there any science behind all this?" The answer is, actually, "Yes, there is." Dr. Masaru Emoto, doctor of alternative medicine from the Open International University for Alternative Medicine in India, has demonstrated that water can in fact be affected by intention. Dr. Masaru Emoto spent years collecting water from around the world and examining it by freezing it and looking at it under a dark field microscope to compare crystallized structures. He discovered that water from clear mountain springs and rivers formed beautiful crystalline structures, while water from polluted sources was deformed. He also demonstrated that exposing water with malformed structure to classical music would change it, giving it a more well-formed structure. In his experiments, he even went as far as labeling bottles of distilled water with the words "Thank You," "Love," and "You Make Me Sick, I Want to Kill You," then focusing his intentions (according to label) on the water over time. After examining them, he found that the water labeled with positive messages had beautiful, well-formed structures, while the water labeled with negative messages had deformed crystalline structures.

MASARU EMOTO RICE-WATER EXPERIMENT

If you don't own a microscope or have access to one, you can confirm the effects of intention on water by performing a similar experiment. To perform this experiment, you will need some distilled water, three glass mason jars of the same type with lids, three cups of the same type of rice, sticky labels, and a pen to write with.

Step 1: Sterilize the Jars
Thoroughly wash each jar and lid with soap water, then clean them once more with rubbing alcohol, and let them dry.

Step 2: Fill Jars
Fill each jar with one cup of rice, then pour in an equal amount of water. Make sure each jar contains the same amount of rice and water. Seal each jar tightly with the lid.

Step 3: Label
Using the sticky labels and pen, label the first jar with the word *Love*, the second with *Hate*, and the third with nothing.

Step 4: Store
Store all jars in the same place so that all jars will be exposed to the same environmental conditions.

Step 5: Send Intentions
Every day, at approximately the same time, for the next month, pick up the first two jars, and focus your intentions on them. For example, pick up the jar labeled "Love" and send loving intentions to it. Tell the jar, "I love you and appreciate you." Do this for a good five minutes. Next, pick up the "Hate" jar and send hateful intentions to it and say hateful things to it. For example, "I hate you and wish you would die!" Make sure to actually conjure those feelings when sending emotions to the jar—this may actually involve shedding a tear or yelling and screaming.

Lastly, leave the third jar alone—it is a control. At the end of the month, note how the rice in each of the jars looks. Open them up and smell. Then record the results in your magical journal.

Another important example comes from France, where Nobel Prize laureate (received for discovering HIV) Luc Montagnier, experimented with something he called water memory. In a lab, Dr. Montagnier took water that was contaminated with the diluted HIV virus (diluted millions of times) and made a digital recording of its electromagnetic signal. According to classical biology, water diluted that much should not contain any signal whatsoever. After making the digital file, he emailed it one thousand miles away to a lab in Italy run by Dr. Giuseppe Vitiello. Dr. Vitiello then took a vile of sterile solution—protecting it from EMF, by placing it in a metal cylinder—and infused it with the building blocks of DNA. Once that water had been impregnated with nucleotides, he then played the digital recording of the virus into the solution. Amazingly, the result was the reconstitution of the virus in the new vial.

What we must remember is water is vital to life. We are born in a sack of amniotic fluid, and our bodies are 80 percent water. Practically everything contains a certain amount of water. Therefore, we can draw the conclusion that water can be charged through sound and intent, and that charge (intention) can be transferred to other systems via proximity, and ingestion. This means the idea of charging an item through the magical process is not really fantastical. So what does the cleansing, consecrating, and charging process actually do?

First, the cleansing process negates foreign energies that may have been impressed on the auric field of the item, returning it to its natural energetic state. Secondly, the consecration process gives outside spiritual influences (spirits, elementals, or deities, or some combination of these) the opportunity to impress their energy upon the item in the form of their intentions. And lastly, charging the item allows you to do the same thing. So with all this in mind, let's talk about how to charge items using everything we've learned.

The Cleansing, Concentrating, and Charging Process

Preparation

Shut off all electrical appliances, including cell phones and other wireless devices. Do not let those who do not believe in magick or those who may have contrary intentions to observe the ritual. Perform cleansing, consecrating, and charging within a Sacred Space. If you are using theurgy, call spirits or deities that are pertinent to the way you want your item consecrated.

Step 1: Cleanse the Item

This is a very important step in charging—you must rid the item of previous mental charges before you can successfully imprint its quantum matrix with new information. There are several ways of doing this; you can use sound, visualization, a cleansing gesture, or cleanse it in the most traditional way, by fire and air, and water and earth.

Method A: Smoke each item with sage or some other cleansing incense, then sprinkle each item with consecrated water.

Method B: Place the items in a box, totally submerged in sea salt overnight. The sea salt will absorb negative energy.

Method C: Use your fingers to symbolically scrape at the item as if you are tearing away negative energy. Do this until the item feels clean.

Method D: Build a phylactery (see: magical tools), then place whatever it is that you wish to cleanse in the phylactery along with a small speaker connected to a player (can be a cellphone). If you are using a player of some sort, you will need to record the frequency you wish to transmit. However, if you are using a cell phone, you can simply download a tone generator from your app store. I suggest you play a Solfeggio frequency that corresponds to the type of charge you intend to imbue the item with. For example, if you are creating a ring that will be used help you in your personal development, you might use 417 Hz, or, if you are making a talisman of healing, you might use 285 Hz. Once you have everything set up, shut the lid of the phylactery and play your tone—leave the item in there for about thirty minutes.

Step 2: Consecration

The next thing you need to do is ask for the blessing of the spirits or gods. To do this, pick up the item, turn and face the altar of the spirit or god you are asking to bless the item, and say a simple prayer. Keep in mind that no visualization is required on your part, because these are independent entities and they are doing the work. Remember: prayers have to be specific, so you should tell the deity exactly what you want that item to be blessed for—if it will be used to magnify elemental energy, tell them you want them to bless it so that it will magnify elemental energy, and if it is an amulet of protection, tell them you want it blessed for protection.

Step 3: Charge the Item

The point of charging an item is to imprint its quantum matrix with functional energy. Because all "energy" is conscious, this energy is a type of sentient thought-form that has the ability to affect you or the environment or both, according to the type of programming that is bestowed upon it. For example, if you were making a talisman of sex appeal, then once that item is programmed, it will make the wearer more attractive to potential mates. In the same sense, if you were to charge your wand to magnify energy sent through it threefold, then that is what it will do whenever held.

But, I must stress, the power of any charged item is only effective as the person who charged it. Therefore, if you are a beginning Sorcerer, you cannot expect to create items that will produce miracles. On the other hand, if a Sorcerer who is more powerful than you charges an item for your use, you can expect it to work better. Having said this, how do you charge an item? This can be done in two ways: pure visualization and ritual.

Method A: Visualization. Shift into a deep state by meditating upon the purpose of the charge—the intent. Once you have it clearly visualized, see those thoughts transform into a glowing ball of light (any color that corresponds to your intent) that rests in your head. If you wish to draw energy from your chakras, see that energy moving up from the corresponding chakra, through the meridians, and into the glowing ball resting in your skull. Once you have fully empowered this ball of energy, reach out and take the item in your hand. Otherwise, if your item is resting on your altar and you want to use your wand, take your wand. You now want to visualize this ball of energy moving through your body, into your sending arm, up that arm, and into the item through your hand. If you are using a wand, hold that wand over the item and channel the energy into the item through it. You might visualize this like an electrical charge that jumps from the tip of the wand to the item itself. Either way, see the item being filled with light until it seems to burst with energy. When you can't make it any brighter, stop. At that point, see the glowing light conform to the item and begin to harden like crystal. As it hardens, hear it crackle and feel it become solid.

Method B: Charging Spell In the next chapter, you will be introduced to spellcraft. Use what you learn there to create a spell that empowers the item you wish to charge you want. Personally, I suggest you create a pentagram or physical triangle of manifestation with a circle around it large enough to hold all the items you wish to charge. Once you create that, you can set the items in it, adding any other item that will contribute to the charge, such as incense, stones, crystals, sigils. To further solidify the intent, use a charging incantation of your design.

Phylactery

> Definition: A container, usually a box used to guard or ward
> off negative influences.

If you wish to protect the energy or charge of any important magical item, you can do so with a phylactery. A phylactery is a container used to prevent an item from being contaminated by negative or unwanted energies. The use of such an item is based both in science, and the occult. All magick items are imbued with both the energy of ether and quintessence. A etheric charge can be affected by outside electromagnetic fields, while quintessence can be altered or contaminated by intention (ill or otherwise) through direct observation—even from afar.

The task of making your phylactery unassailable to outside electro-magnet fields is an easy one—simply make your container out of any kind of conductive metal—the best metals for the job are aluminum, iron, copper, silver, or gold. If you wish to make your phylactery out of stone, choose a mineral that is high in iron or copper, such as black tourmaline, chalcopyrite, epidote, goethite, hematite, lazulite, lepidocrocite, limonite, marcasite, pyrite, rhodonite, serpentine, staurolite, or sugilite. When adding electromagnet-field-blocking properties to your phylactery, choose a shape that is conducive to blocking such as a box, sphere, or tube. Whatever the case, make sure this container is fully covered and that the lid fits securely—water tight containers can be filled with charged elixirs.

Protecting the content of your phylactery from negative attention is an altogether different task. Although it is already protected because it is sealed and the item inside is not visible (if it can't be seen, it can't be focused on), further protection can be had by adding wards. Like all magick, this must be done through ritual and spell casting. In such case, you can to ward your phylactery with an existing banishing symbol or by creating one yourself—you can do this by studying the chapter on Occult Magick and Talismanic and Amulet Magick.

Lastly, you will want to store your phylactery somewhere safe and out of sight. If not, it will draw attention, and that would be counterproductive—yes, it should be able to take the assault, but hiding it adds another layer of protection.

How to Detect Charges

All items have an electromagnetic field created by the spinning atoms that can be picked up by very sensitive equipment. Powerful electromagnet fields can be detected using a regular EMF reader. However, detecting really subtle fields, like those produced by the brain or heart, requires special equipment. Unfortunately for us, we do not have a lab, so we cannot scientifically verify that our item has actually been charged. However, we can pick up this charge by other means. The sensory organs of our body, including the skin, have the ability to feel these fields. The problem is, we are surrounded by so much EMF interference that it is difficult to distinguish one field from another. Even still, you must be sensitive to those energies in order to be aware of them—so it is unlikely you will be able to pick up the charge unless you meditate on a regular basis or have been practicing the exercises in this book. If you have developed this skill, congratulations—you can use it by holding your hand over that item to see if it feels hot or cold.

If not, there are other ways to gauge a charge that don't involve buying expensive machines. Tools, such as dowsing rods and pendulums can help interpret sensations traveling through the body via the ideomotor effect. For a full explanation of how this works, read the chapter on divination. To do this, first program your ideomotor device. If you are using dowsing rods, tell the dowsing rods that the more charged the item is, the more the rods will open. If you are using a pendulum, tell the pendulum that the more charged the item is, the more it will spin. Then hold your pendulum or dowsing rods over the charged item and see what it does—if nothing happens, just keep practicing. It takes time to learn how to effectively use both of these items.

Concerning Magick Circles
and Sacred Spaces

Ａll sacred spaces, be they circles or some other shape, are gateways to higher dimensions. Being a gateway does not mean that a physical portal will be opened, but that the space itself will augment the Sorcerer's ability to shift his state from the physical world to the spiritual so he or she can affect energy at a quantum level. By creating the right atmosphere using the symbolism of magick, fragrance, sound, and the proper illumination, the Sorcerer's mind can be pulled into the right state in order to touch the realm of Spirit. The second most important purpose of a sacred space is to provide an area for working magick that is free of energetic clutter. When created properly, that area is wiped of all unrelated energy so that new energy can be raised and applied to the work at hand. Protection from harmful energies can also be afforded by making sure you reduce the amount of EMF (electromagnet field) in your ritual chamber. The reason is not because EMF can directly affect quintessence, but because exposure to high levels of EMF have been known to alter mood and thought. To reduce EMF, simply turn off electronics (including wireless devices like cell phones) or perform your spells and rituals outside, away from power lines and cell phone towers. If illumination is needed, use candles instead of electric lights—they produce less EMF.

The last and most controversial purpose of any sacred space is its function as a barrier of protection against negative entities that might wish to invade. There are two problems here: one, if you enter your sacred space with the fear of being attacked by evil spirits, you will draw them; and two, because the Sorcerer *is* the gateway, any spirit who wishes to enter will do so through you. Therefore, the idea that a protective barrier will somehow keep invading entities out is simply false—protection comes from authentic divine authority and keeping your own energy field in a high state of vibration (positive).

Although a sacred space can be any shape, the most common shape used is the circle. The circle is the perfect symbol for containment because it represents the idea that what is outside is separate from what is inside—a closed loop. But simply drawing a circle upon the ground will not empower it. Only when the caster truly understands that he is invoking the highest power by casting an infinite loop (a symbol of the Source) will that circle be charged with divine energy. At that point, anytime the Sorcerer steps inside the circle, he or she is invoking the power of the Source and practicing truly powerful magick.

The circle itself is actually considered to be a large sphere of energy that surrounds your work space, and it is for that reason that many practitioners will tell you that it is necessary to visualize yourself being fully enclosed in order to be protected. This is actually nonsense, not only for the reasons mentioned above, but also because when most people draw a circle, they automatically assume they are being protected from all angles—and it is that assumption or *intent* that helps imbue the circle with its power. But if this is not the case for you, by all means, go ahead and visualize a spherical shape—it won't hurt. And this brings up the issue of physically drawing a circle versus imagining it.

There is an ongoing debate over whether one should actually draw their circle upon the ground or just visualize it using their mind's eyes. In my own opinion, both methods can be just as powerful, but if your visualization skills are not developed yet, I feel it's best to have some kind of physical representation. This is kind of what magick is all about anyways—externalizing our thoughts through the use of symbols and empowering them by doing so.

There are many ways you can physically create a circle; the easiest is to lay down a cord. The good thing about using a cord is that it will not damage your floor, and can be picked up when you finished. The bad thing about a cord is that it's difficult to lay down in a perfect circle. The next method involves using chalk. If you have a bare surface, you can mark your circle out on the floor by taking a length of cord, tying chalk to one end and a stick to the other. Once you have determined where you want your circle, hold the tip stick down in the center of the floor, pull the cord to length, and begin marking the floor with the chalk until you have a complete circle. Another good alternative is to get a large cloth and permanently mark out your circle upon it. Then lay that cloth down anytime you want to open a circle. When you are done, you can just roll it back up and put it away.

The next thing to consider is fragrance; any herb, candle, or oil can be burned as long as its scent reinforces the purpose of the circle. Just keep in mind that if the aroma is distracting, choose something else. I personally prefer to burn Palo Santo or Frankincense and Myrrh for general magical workings and Copal for evocations/conjurings—your choices should be very personal to you. When trying to create the appropriate atmosphere using sound, play music that incorporates a Solfeggio Frequency that corresponds to the intent of your ritual or spell, or play the pure tone using a tone generator.

Light can also be used to create mind-altering effects that add to the power of any sacred space. Light is a type of electromagnetic radiation that has wave properties. Human beings are capable of seeing only a narrow spectrum of light—between 380 to 730 nanometers—which falls between ultraviolet and infrared. Because different colors resonate at different frequencies, certain frequencies can be used to entrain the mind, and shift it into an altered state. Because of the subtle nature of light energy, it is capable of immobilizing and blocking the other energy forms, such as spirits that may be potentially dangerous. Not only this, but also because light resonates at a higher frequency than matter, it is rooted in a higher plane of existence and visible to beings on those planes of existence. Illumination close to the infrared spectrum is suitable for negative spirits, while repelling higher vibrational entities, while light radiating closer to the ultraviolet spectrum, such as blue, indigo, and violet, are suitable for positive spirits.

Light can also be used to help induce trance by highlighting other colors within your ritual space. In *The 21 Lessons of Merlyn*, Douglas Monroe explains that the Druids burned black candles in glass globes (called a Pelen Tan, meaning "fire globe") of deep cobalt blue in order to highlight the white robes they wore to set themselves apart from the rest of the world. In

the same manner, Witches burned candles within globes made of red glass,
because it brought out the black in traditional black robes they wore. This
whole idea of light play can be taken a
step further by actually using light to
project your circle upon the floor.

Sacred spaces can also be enhanced
by adding symbols of power, names of
gods, or meaningful runes—especially
those for binding and banishing of negative energies. These symbols, names,
and runes are usually drawn within a double circle and in a direction of the
specific to the entity or power that is being called. The symbols you choose
to add will be totally dependent on your personal belief system and symbol correspondences you have developed. For example, because I venerate
Hecate, I sometimes draw a cross in the middle of the circle to represent
the crossroads, and therefore when in the circle, I know I am standing at
the crossroads between the physical dimension, and Spirit World. Many
of these details can be worked out by researching esoteric symbolism.
Consequently, if you choose to communicate with a divine force, that entity
may simply reveal symbols to you—the gods and goddesses tend to make
that information known. With all that being said, take a look at the "Fully
Qualified Circle Opening" ritual I have created—and by all means, feel free
to adjust it to your liking or even throw it out in favor of your own creation.

FULLY QUALIFIED CIRCLE OPENING

Note that this ritual does not call the "elements" in the typical way. Instead,
the elements are used to create a connection from one dimension (the element of plane of Spirit) to another (the elemental plane of Earth).

Components
- Altar
- Black or White Altar Cloth

- 4 Quadrant Candles (Yellow, Red, Blue, and Brown/Black)
- Goddess Candle (Black Pillar Candle)
- God Candle (White Pillar Candle)
- Illumination Candles
- 4-Tools (Athame, Wand, Chalice, and Pentacle)

Altar Setup
- Place altar facing east.
- Place the altar cloth over the altar.
- Place black pillar candle in the left rear.
- Place the white pillar candle in the right rear.
- Place your athame in the center rear of the altar arranged vertically with its blade facing toward the center.
- Place your chalice in the western quadrant.
- Place your wand on the altar in the southern quadrant, horizontally with point facing inward.
- Place your salt bowl in the northern quadrant.
- Arrange everything else where it will be aesthetically pleasing.

The purpose of this ritual is to create a sacred space suitable for any magical operation. This circle acts as a containment field for raised energies, a consecrated area suitable for higher beings, and a portal between the worlds. This ritual is intended to be fully immersive.

Preparation

Physically Clean Area
The first thing you should do is physically clean your space. Remember everything is energy, so even by physically cleaning your space, you are in fact creating more positive "vibes." Once your area is clean, if you wish, play some soothing music, then perform Banishment by Water and Earth, Air and Fire.

Banishment by Air, Fire, Water, and Earth

Many people believe in the awesome power of sage and holy water to banish evil spirits and negative influences and purify living spaces. That's fine, because it is indeed a wonderful technique. This tradition is so old that it has rooted itself as deep in our subconscious as holy and almighty power of God.

So how do you use it? It's really quite simple. First, you will need to acquire a few items: sage, purified water, and sea salt. Sage can be harvested in the wild, if you know where it grows, or can be bought at your local metaphysical store. Purified water can usually be bought at your local grocery store, or you can simply purify tap water if you have a filter—and sea salt can be found just about anywhere.

This next part is important: take these items and set them on a clean table. If you have set up an altar, place them there instead. Now place your hands over the top of these items and bless them by saying,

> "Great and powerful source of all things, bless this sage, salt,
> and water so that no negative force can stand in its presence."

If you don't believe in a higher power, don't force it. Just know that these items have been endowed with divine power from the universe itself, and nothing negative can exist in their presence. These items represent the ancient concept of the elements created by the divine to shape our existence. The prayer or blessing represents the fifth element, spirit, which gives these elements the ability to take shape in the first place. Specifically, the smoke of the sage represents air, and the smoldering tip represents fire. Water and earth are represented by the purified water and salt. Feel free to change the words of this prayer to something more meaningful to you.

Once you have blessed these items, pour about a cup of water into a small dish and add three pinches of sea salt, then dissolve the salt into the water by stirring it with a utensil. Before you light your sage, make sure you have something that can catch the ashes as you carry it around the room and a burn-safe surface to place it on after you are done with it.

Now, light the sage and wave in a spiral motion from the center of your ritual area in a counterclockwise direction. Continue walking in a counterclockwise direction around the room, from the center to the perimeter of your ritual chamber until you have carried the smoke everywhere. Know and acknowledge that the sage has been blessed and the area is clean. In the same manner, pick up your bowl of holy water and dip your finger in it. Sprinkling from the center of the room to the perimeter in the same fashion as the sage. Know and acknowledge that the water has been blessed and the area is clean.

Cleanse and Anoint Yourself

Take a ritual bath or shower.

Anoint yourself and say,

> "I invoke the divine within me to empower all my works."

Spend some time in meditation envisioning divine light pouring down upon you from your crown chakra and filling your entire body. Know that you are connected to the Source and any divine energy you use will be replenished.

Creating the Circle

Draw a physical circle in the middle of the room, large enough for everyone to stand in it, then place your altar inside the circle arranged according to the "Altar Setup" above. Once everything is set up, move to the eastern edge of the circle, point your Athame or Sword at the circle's edge and begin to walk in a clockwise direction while vibrating the words, "Vaci Esona." (Reduction is shown below.) See the circle become alive with a white energy, forming a sphere around the entire area if you wish. It is important that you know exactly what these words mean so that the energy you put out is charged with the proper intent.

Formulation of Circle Incantation

The Intent

This circle represents our connection to Source. This Circle acts as a shield against anything that wishes to harm us. This Circle enhances magical energy raised within it. This Circle contains raised energy.

Simplified Intent

Circle is Source, a Shield against evil, enhances Power, and is a Container.

Sigilized Intent (all double letters reduced)

C I R L E – S O U A – H D G I – T V N P – W

Reduced to Babblogue (Intuited with letters above)
VACI ESONA

Creating a Portal
Pick up your wand, go to the South, light the Red candle and say,

"Light is born from darkness, and given will!"

Now walk clockwise around the circle while pointing your wand to the ground. See or feel Red energy charging the entire sphere. Know that this energy represents the Divine Spark and that you have made a connection with the World of Fire by lighting the candle and saying the evocation.
     Next, pick up your athame, go to the East, light the Yellow candle, and say,

"Will contemplates all paths."

Now walk clockwise around the circle while pointing your athame to the ground. See or feel Yellow energy charging the entire sphere. Know that this energy represents the Divine Spark entering the World of Air and being transformed into the energy of Fate. The Connection has been made.
     Next, pick up your Chalice, go to the West, light the Blue candle, and hold the Chalice on high, saying,

"Will becomes Fate when its path is chosen."

Now walk clockwise around the circle while holding the Chalice on high as if you are making a toast. See or feel Blue energy charging the entire sphere. Know that this energy represents the Divine Spark entering the World of Water, being given the qualities of time, and form. The Connection has been made.

Next, pick up the Pentacle, go to the north, walk up to the Green candle and light it saying,

"What is Fated is fully realized, and can be clearly seen by all."

Now walk clockwise around the circle while holding the Pentacle on high as if you are displaying it with honor. See or feel Green energy charging the entire sphere. Know that this energy represents the Divine Spark entering the World of Earth, where it is fully manifest and connected to the physical circle you have drawn upon the ground.

Finally, walk back to your altar, pick up the wand in your left hand, the athame in the other, and point to the pentacle on your altar, saying,

"As above, so below. The Gate between the Worlds is open."

Calling of the Old Gods

At this point, you may evoke the old Gods. To do this, use whatever rite is specific to the deity or deities you are calling.

[[**Perform Spellwork Here**]]

Close the Circle

When you have completed your magick, thank and dismiss any entities (Gods, Goddesses, Angels, Daemons, and other spirits) you have called. You can do this by simply saying,

"We thank all spirits that have aided us in our works, and now close this circle."

Next, extinguish each candle in the opposite order you lit them (green, yellow, blue, red) imagining those connections being closed. Finally, erase the physical circle in opposite direction you drew it also imagining that energy dissipating.

Ground any excess energy.

ALTERNATIVES SACRED SPACE OPENING METHODS

Erecting a Sacred Space is not the only way of achieving what a Sacred Space does. As a matter of fact, at some point in time, you may be comfortable and experienced enough to dispense with all the trappings and use one of the methods below.

Force of Will

Note: Cleanse the area with sage, and consecrated water as described in House Blessing in the previous chapter.

This method works well for experienced practitioners that are very spiritually grounded. It's simple—*know* and *acknowledge* that your area is clean and protected, and it will be. Warning: do not rely on this method if you are not an expert at shifting into the right state, lack the visualization skills, or have no divine authority.

Summon the Divine Light

Note: Cleanse the area with sage, and consecrated water as described in House Blessing in the previous chapter.

Summon the image of divine light (bright like the sun, darkness banishing, peace inducing, healing) at your heart chakra (alternatively, you can summon it at the crown chakra). See and feel the light grow as you breathe, until it fills your entire body. Let the light continue to grow until it fills the entire room creating a sphere that encompasses your ritual space. Once the sphere is large enough, envision the edges of the sphere becoming hard and impenetrable like a crystal shield. Visualize this as sharply as you can: its appearance, the sound of the crystal crackling as it hardens, the smell of rock, the feeling of peace, and rejuvenation.

Incantation, Mantra, or Song

Note: Cleanse the area with sage and consecrated water as described in House Blessing in the previous chapter.

Invoke your patron deity or your own divine authority to give you the power to create a sacred space. Write an incantation or song that states your intentions. Make it powerful and inspirational. If you choose to speak a mantra, choose or make one that embodies the intentions of creating a sacred space. If you are not a singer and wish to play an instrument instead, create or choose a musical piece that represent all the elements of Sacred Space creation, and sympathetically link those ideas to the piece of music—this can even be drum beat. Remember your intentions should include clearing the area of unwanted energy, setting up a field of protection, calling the correct spirits or gods. The act of speaking the incantation, singing the song, or repeating the mantra over and over should draw you into the right state.

Wards

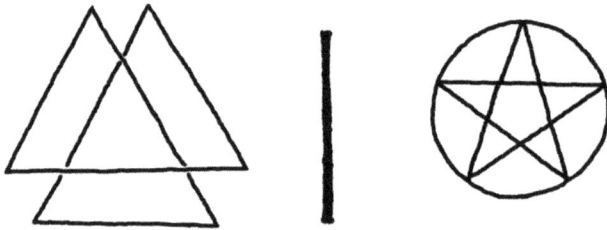

A ward is a type of protective sigil that is drawn, etched, or painted upon a surface such as a box, wall, column, or door. Just as any other act of magick, the power of the ward comes from one's intent, and the bestowed blessings of a called deity. Beyond this, special protective minerals can be added to paint in order to magnify the ward's protective energy.

Step 1:

Choose or create a warding symbol that has been sympathetically linked to you.

Step 2:

If you are painting the symbol and decide to enhance that paint with protective minerals, choose those minerals (according to your own correspondence), grind them as needed, then mix them with the paint.

Step 3:

Cleanse, consecrate, and charge all components.

Step 4:

Paint the chosen ward on the chosen surface with intent.

Amulets and Talismans

And amulets or talismans constitutes any object that has been magically charged, and worn. Amulets technically "protect," while talismans can hold any kind of power. This means either one of these items can be created and imbued with the same power called when opening a Sacred Space. Once created, these items can be worn, and that power goes with you. The procedure for creating such an item can be found in the next chapter under "Magick Items."

The Art of Ritual and Spell Craft

Before talking about how to create spells and rituals I want to reiterate something. You don't have to cast a spell or perform a ritual to manifest your will. So then, why would anyone want to use a spell or ritual? In simplest terms, a spell or ritual is a way to enhance your imagination and focus by getting you into the proper state. Therefore, spells and rituals can be a powerful tool for acolytes and seasoned practitioners alike.

Having said this, you will not see a lot of spells and rituals in this book. The reason for this is twofold: first, because there are already thousands of good books out there covering spell-work, and secondly, because I ardently believe that all spells and rituals should be personal. Allow me to elaborate.

Spells and rituals that are ancient or that have been written by an accredited magician or witch are not inherently powerful. They are powerful only if they use symbols that can speak directly to the unconscious mind of the person who casts them. Also, no generic spell or ritual can effectively communicate your personal intentions and goals. Therefore, in order for a spell or ritual to be powerful, it must not only express the caster's exact intent, but also invoke the deepest and most powerful of emotions. Simply put, you can only accomplish those two things if you write the spell or ritual yourself. Therefore, spells and rituals that lack personal message or an emotional charge are no more than a stage performance.

With that being said, a spell or ritual is no more powerful than the witch or magician who casts it. Therefore, if you don't believe in what you are doing, can't focus, or lack you the ability to visualize your goal clearly, it doesn't matter how loud your incantations are, or how complex or beautiful your ritual is, you will not manifest anything. We all set limitations by deciding what we think are realistic, or possible. This is why when you create a spell or ritual, you must be realistic about what you want to accomplish.

Another thing to consider is already established magical systems. Many of these systems have been used for so long that the thought-forms supporting them are extremely powerful. For this reason, I suggest that all magicians and witches become familiar with various traditions of magick. Once you have done this, you can choose to adopt that tradition, or take the elements you like from each one and put it together to create your own style. But if you decide to merge many different traditions, make sure that the finished product works well together. It will of course take you time to find your footing, but once you have, you can begin to tap in to the symbolism of those traditions and your magick will be all the more powerful.

Lastly, I have provided a description of various common magical techniques in the following chapter. Please understand that this is not intended to be a comprehensive list, but should act as a starting point until you can explore the various styles of magick yourself. Feel free to use these methods as a template. However, for the reasons I have already mentioned, I want to discourage you from copying them verbatim. So without further ado let's talk about the basic format of spells and rituals.

The Difference Between Spells and Rituals

There really is not a whole lot of difference between a spell and a ritual—both are intended to produce change in conformity with Will. However, a spell is a piece of magick that is performed to get a specific result. For example, you might choose to create a spell to manifest $5000, the love of a specific mate, or perhaps even the ruin of an adversary—these are all very specific intentions.

On the other hand, a ritual is a common set of magical instructions that are used on a repeated basis. A common Wiccan circle opening ritual or even evocation rites are good examples. A ritual is generally intended to help bring the sorcerer into the right trance state to cast a spell, where as a spell is intended to help the sorcerer reinforce his or her intent by sharp visual imagery and strong emotions—in other words, energy raising.

The Intent

Before crafting any spell or ritual you must be absolutely sure without a shadow of a doubt what you want to accomplish—this is your spells intent. Remember, if you are creating a spell then it will most likely be for the purpose of accomplishing one specific thing, but if you are creating a ritual its purpose will be more general and utilitarian. Because the process of crafting a spell or ritual is an observation of the rule of immersion it is extremely important to write your intention in the most emotional language that you can. By doing this what you are affectively doing is starting the process of creating a viable thought-form on the plane of spirit and polarizing it with emotional energy. Remember to be as descriptive as possible without reducing the probability that your intention will manifest.

Archetypes

Once you have thoroughly mapped out your intention using emotional language, begin looking for archetypes. Remember an archetype is a cluster of ideas, symbols, and beliefs that are common to human culture. Such an archetype might be something like love, wealth, well being, or even death and destruction. These are the same archetypal energies that you have been mapping out in your correspondence journal as sympathetic links. If you are new to the practice of magick, then you may have to go through this linking process with each new archetype.

Choose the Linguistic Elements

At this point you should have a list of all of the archetypes found within your written intention. Now is the time to consider which elements or components of the magical language that you will use to create your spell or ritual. Again, if you have already started the process of creating sympathetic links, then you may have already linked certain colors, fragrances, frequencies, herbs, crystals, planets or even sigilized charms to these energy forms. In such case, it is just a matter of choosing the elements that best represents the archetypes of your spell and ritual and create the highest emotional charge. Also keep in mind that if your spell or ritual is intended to be performed as a group, all participants must have made the same sympathetic links.

Spell or Ritual Structure

Now is the time to consider how your spell or ritual will be structured. By structure I am referring to how and when each element will be used, and in what order. The main thing to remember is that each element will need to be used long enough to crystallize your intention, but not used for so long that it causes mental fatigue. When deciding what order you will use each component keep in mind that you are trying to tell a story—something must happen in the beginning, middle, and end. Keep in mind that it literally does not matter what order each component is used, as long as it makes sense to you and elicits the right emotional response.

As a last note, if the spell or ritual is to be cast by multiple people, each person should be given a role to perform during the casting process. These roles should be assigned according to the skills and preferences of the individuals participating. For example, if one of your group members is more adept at creating art, then let him or her create any sigils that you will be using. And if one of your members is a talented speaker or singer, let that person recite incantation or sing if appropriate.

Ending Spells or Rituals

Obviously, how you end a spell or ritual will be unique to the magical working and its intent. Even so, here are some things to consider. First, any spells or rituals that involve calling upon spirits, diamons, angels, or gods should also dismiss them. Dismissal is not intended to be rude, but to thank entities for their assistance and to let them know that the spell or ritual is over. Without such a dismissal some entities may feel compelled to stick around. This does not necessarily mean that such entities will cause trouble, but not dismissing them will not negate the possibility of that happening. If a spell or ritual is powerful enough, or you are constantly performing magick in a particular place, that energy will draw entities regardless of whether they were called or not.

Another technique used to negate energies during the closing of spells and rituals is reversal. Reversing a procedure is symbolic act that reinforces the intentions of negating a particular energy. Therefore, circles can be closed by walking or drawing them in reverse, and "powers" conjured by drawing sigils can be dismissed or dispelled by tracing them in reverse—this of course should not be used on energies that were sent out for the purpose of manifesting your intentions. In the same sense the sorcerer, if his or her powers of focus and visualization are developed enough, can simply envision the symbols and their corresponding energies fading from the astral until they have dissipated completely.

EXAMPLES

Wealth Spell

The intent of this spell is continually manifest money and material things over time.

Archetypes: Physical manifestation, abundance, money, and material needs.

Physical Manifestation

I have chosen to use the pentagram to represent physical manifestation because each point represents one of the primordial forces that brings things into existence. Therefore, I will get a large sheet of poster-board and draw a pentagram on it large enough to place other items in. I will then draw a double circle around this pentagram in order to scribe runes and sigils in. Finally after consulting my grimoire of sympathetic links, I decide I will chant my personal mantra of manifestation (wowa) to raise energy.

Abundance

I have chosen to represent abundance in several ways: first, I will scribe the formula 3x3x3 around the full circumference in between the double circle. Also, because I have associated quartz crystal with the magnification of energy, I will place my collection of quartz crystals inside the pentagram with the other objects that I intend to put there. I also remember that I have a special wealth herbal blend in my sympathetic links grimoire which includes five finger grass, bay leaves, patchouli, high john the conqueror root, and nutmeg, so I will burn this over coals during the spell.

Money

I will place representations of the type and amount of money that I wish to receive inside the pentagram. For this I decide to use monopoly money, and a fake check filled out for the amount of $2000.

Material Things

I need a new car, so I find a toy matchbox car and use it to represent the type of vehicle that I want. Also, because I like to go out and have fun once in a while, I collect company logos of all the places that I like to visit—this includes the logo of my local movie theater, and my favorite restaurants. All of these items I will place inside of the pentagram.

When it comes time to cast the spell I bring all my materials to my ritual chamber and open a sacred space. I then use a smudging technique to cleanse all of the items, including the herbs for the purpose of manifesting wealth. After I throw my incense on the coals, I draw the pentagram on the poster-board, and scribe the symbols between the double circle. Understanding that all magick is an intentional act, I empower the symbols as I draw them by knowing what they mean, and acknowledging their power.

Next I place all items that represent the things that I want inside the center of the pentagram. This includes the toy money, the fake check, the matchbox car, and all of the printed logos I have collected. After doing this I stare at the pentagram and the items in it and I visualize myself spending the money I have received, driving the new car, and going out for a night on the town. As I stare at the pentagram and the items I extend my right hand over the pentagram and begin to move it in a clockwise direction as if generating energy. As I move my hand I chant the mantra "Wowa," which to me has been sympathetically linked to the meaning, "By my divine will it shall come to pass."

Storm Summoning Ritual

I am sure that all witches and magicians at some point have thought about changing the weather. So in order to for fill this goal I have decided to create a simple shamanistic ritual to summon thunderstorms. Because I feel that not all rituals have to be complicated, I have tried to keep it as simple as possible.

Archetypes: summoning music, water elemental

Summoning Music
Music is a fantastic way to get into state and to communicate one's intentions. This is why I have chosen to create a chant, as well as a special drum beat to bring myself into a trance and instruct my subconscious/unconscious mind that I want to summon a thunderstorm.

Water Elemental
As you have already learned, a water elemental is the considered to be the living essence of water. As both a practitioner of ceremonial magic, and shamanic mystic arts, I believe that we can tap into the consciousness of the elements around us and communicate with them. In this case, I want to tap into any developing or pre-existing storms in the region and pull them to my location. If you are not already aware, with a little bit of study you will discover that elementals are thought to have kings or rulers. In many magical traditions the or lord or elemental king of water is called Nicksa, which translates to "the hidden one." Therefore I will incorporate this name into my ritual as part of the chant.

My ritual will have a simple structure: first, I will take a ritual bath, then, I will move to a dedicated ritual space outside and begin drumming and chanting my evocation . Then, when I feel like I have achieved the right to trance state, and have sufficiently communicated my intentions, I will abruptly quit and close the ritual.

My evocation chant will be a sigilized charm. This charm will be composed using the following sentence,

"Nicks-a great king of water bring me storms."
Then reduced to, "Ofwea Nicksa"

I will sympathetically link this evocation to the idea of manifesting storms in the name of Nicksa. As for my music, it will consist of a four drum beat per second rhythm. My first strike will be to its center, followed by three strikes to its edge—in African notation this would be gun, rest, pa, ta, pa.

Common Forms of Magick

The aim of this chapter is not to provide extensive lessons on how to cast spells and rituals, because there are literally thousands of books that teach that. Instead, the purpose of this chapter will be to introduce you to common forms of magick so that you can use them as a template for your own personal spells and rituals. So instead of copying these spells and rituals verbatim, try to come up with your own unique style of magick. Remember magick is not about following recipes or formulas, magick is about finding and using symbols that invoke the most powerful emotions and thoughts. Lastly, remember that none of these spells will work for you if the elements are not properly sympathetically link to ideas in your mind.

CANDLE MAGICK

Burning a candle has deep significance in magick. By lighting the wick, you are igniting your will and by snuffing it out or letting it burn out, you are making a statement about completion. Candle magick in its most basic form involves simply making a wish (intention) and lighting it. However, more power can be added to the process by following a few steps to the ritual process.

Different Candle Magick Techniques

Quality
Most candles these days are made of an artificial wax. Although this works, actual paraffin wax candles hold more power. Make the candle yourself, and you become more quantum entangled with it.

Color
Candles are available is a vast array of colors. These colors can be used to represent the emotional energy of your spell. Perhaps red for love, black for banishment, and yellow for spells involving children—what thoughts and emotions each color corresponds to will be unique to your own psychology.

Anointing
Choose or make an oil that best suits your intention, then anoint your candle with that oil according to whether you want to banish something (send someone or something away) or manifest something (bring someone or something to you). For banishment, massage the oil in from the base of the candle to the wick in a counterclockwise spiral motion, and for manifestation, massage the oil in from the wick to the base in a clockwise spiral motion.

Written Intent
Write your intention out on a piece of virgin paper, then you can then sit the candle on top of the written intent, or when you are ready, read the intent and burn it to release it.

Candle Marking
If your candle is large enough, etch or scribe your intent or sigil on it using a hot nail or pen. When etching, you can rub magical herbs or minerals into the engraved letters or symbols to make them stand out.

SIGIL MAGICK

The word *sigil* comes from the Latin word *sigillum*, meaning "seal." A sigil is a symbol with magical power that represents a simple or complex idea—that idea is usually the intent of the Sorcerer. Sigils can be used by themselves or included as a part of a spell to augment its power. When done correctly, sigil magick is one of the most powerful forms of magick available in your arsenal. The reason for this is because symbols speak directly to the subconscious mind.

There are many ways to create a sigil; sigils can be created by combining symbols that already exist or by reducing a written intent down to its consonants only and then arranging those consonants together to form an artistic symbol. Sigils can also be created by tracing out the letters over a magick square or Sigil Mandala.

Creating a Sigil

Step I

The first step in creating a sigil is to formulate your intent. To do this, write it out in every emotional detail—if that means writing five pages, do so. Once the intent has been written out in full, summarize it using no more than five words—make sure you keep the most emotionally provocative words. Once you have summarized your intent down to five words or less, decide what method you will use to actually create the sigil.

Artistic Symbolism

Consult your correspondence table to determine what symbols represent your intent the best. If you can find none, spend some time meditating on what symbols are the most meaningful to you and best represent your intent. Take any number of those symbols and sketch them on a scrap piece of paper, combining them or positioning them around one another to create a unique symbol.

Combining Consonants

Take your three-to-five-word reduced intent and scratch out all vowels, then remove all extra consonants, making sure to keep at least one of each. Next take what's left and arrange those into something that looks like a mystic symbol. To do this merge letters, flip them upside down, right side up, or even reverse them—if you can create two or three letters by combining one or more consonants all the better. Letters can be lowercase or uppercase—it doesn't matter.

Magick Square

Reduce your intent to consonants as described above, then find a magick square that embodies the same energy as your intent. Next, use Gematria (see: Correspondence) to convert the remaining consonants into numbers. Now take your numbers and begin tracing your chosen magick square. Start with the first number (which used to be your first consonant) and end with your last number (which used to be your last consonant). When you have finished, highlight the beginning and ending points of your draw sigil with a special symbol (arrowhead, cross-through, pitchfork, and so on.)

Sigil Mandala

The word *mandala* is a Sanskrit word that literally means "circle." Most notably found in the Hindu and Buddhist religions, they are used by many cultures, including Native American cultures and Mesoamerican cultures. Different mandalas are used to represent different divine forces or archetypal powers, so for this reason, they are a perfect aid for sigil construction. One can even create their own mandala to represent an archetype.

A mandala is usually a circular shape formed from combined geometric or fractal patterns. Oftentimes a mandala will resemble a flower, with open areas that look like petals, which is perfect for assigning letters to. Needless to say, there must be enough petals to assign all the letters of the alphabet—or at least the consonants.

Once letters have been assigned to the peddles of the mandala, a piece of tracing paper can be placed over it and your reduced intent can be traced—letter by letter—to form a unique sigil. The result is a sigil empowered by the archetypal energy that the mandala represents. As an example, take a look at the Triangle of Manifestation Mandala below.

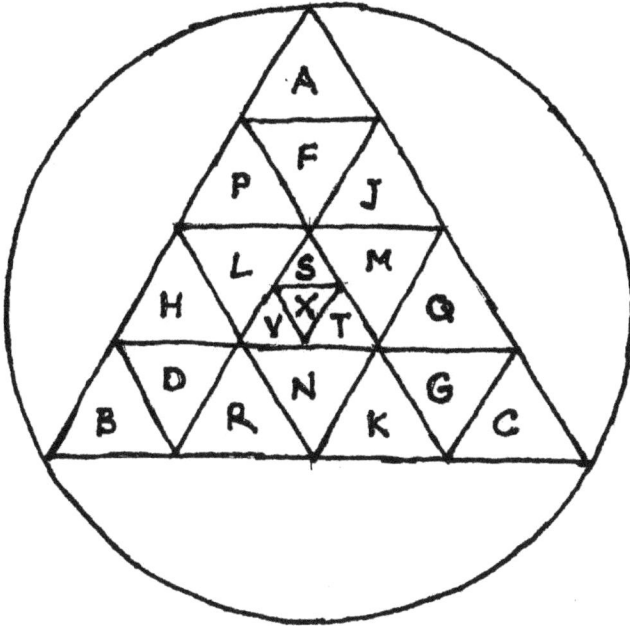

Triangle of Manifestation Mandala

Step II

Just like any other magical operation, you need to imprint the intent into the object, while actually scribing the symbol in order for it to be magically activated. The rule of immersion can be adhered to by inscribing the sigil on a piece of virgin paper of the same color that corresponds to the intent of the spell—this can be determined by consulting your personal correspondence tables. To further follow this rule, special inks can be made or bought for the actual inscription.

Once the basic sigil has been sketched out using one of the above methods, you should grab another scratch sheet of paper and freehand it over and over again. As you do this, you need to meditate on the intent, allowing your hand to be led by your subconscious mind so that the final sigil can take shape—do this until it feels right. During this process, resist becoming logically involved—perfection is not necessary. The only thing that matters is that you allow your subconscious mind to guide your hand (ideomotor effect) to produce the symbol.

Step III

Once the final sigil has been created, it needs to be etched on the metal or wood or sketched on paper using the special ink or a charged pen. While doing this, you must hold the intent in your mind. When the symbol has been transferred, you can begin officially charging it. To accomplish this, use one of the methods described in the chapter, "Cleansing, Consecrating, and Charging." Then, after the intent of the sigil has manifested, destroy it by burning it or put it away for future use.

MAGICK ITEMS

I considered writing a different section for how to create amulets, talismans, magick bag, bottles and boxes, tools, and so on. However, they are all the same thing—magically enchanted items. An enchanted item would be any item that has been programmed with some kind of intent (to protect, to bring wealth, to attract love, and so on). Some examples would be an amulet (worn to protect), a talisman (worn for any magick purpose), a mojo bag, a dream catcher (to protect from bad dreams), a wand (used for directing intentions), or a witch bottle (use for capturing spirits).

So how do they work, and what is the best way to make a magick item? These magick items work the same way any other spell works—they help the Sorcerer shape reality by focusing their intentions upon the quantum matrix. Therefore, the best magick item will serve to remind the Sorcerer what it was made for, by clearly representing the intention. That is, if it is meant to entrap something, it may take the form of a net or container. If it is meant to protect, it would bear a protective symbol, and if it were to bring good luck, it would incorporate stones, crystals, herbs, and colors to represent luck.

If those intentions are meant to affect another person, the opposite is true. Not only does the purpose of item have to be understood by the Sorcerer, but also by the person or people it is intended to affect. Now of course, like a good subliminal message, the symbolism displayed by magick item can be directed at the unconscious mind of the onlooker—this way, the intention can be understood without the onlooker consciously knowing why.

Furthermore, magick items can incorporate materials that give off special frequencies, such as crystals, magnets, herbs, and so on, and in this way, they can affect the energy field of the wearer or those next to him or her. Such additions can be meant to magnify the power of the wearers intentions or diminish the ill intentions of others.

Magick Item Creation

Step 1: Intent

Write an intent—use emotion! Remember: *if the intention of the magick item is meant to affect others, it must be understood by them.* Reduce that intent.

Step 2: Form

Decide what form your magick item will take: Is it a piece of jewelry, a bag, wand, statue, bottle, or box? Once you know what it will be, collect the items necessary to craft that item—this may be wood, metal, clay, herbs, stones, salt, or just about anything. These materials may be used to craft the body of the item, or even placed inside it if it is a box, bottle, or bag. It is also worthy to note that if you do not possess the skills or tools to craft your item, it is perfectly OK buy an item that has already been crafted, or have someone else make it for you, but if you go that route, you still have to cleanse that item.

Step 3: Sigilize or Archetype

You should now do one of two things according the item's form. If it is something that will bear a symbol, then you need to find the right symbols or create them according to "Sigil Magick" as described in this chapter. Otherwise, you will need to break your intent down into archetypes, as described in the last "Spellcraft" chapter. Either way, whether you use a sigil or materials that represent the intent of the item, *that intent must be clear to you or the people or both viewing it.*

If you decide to combine both methods and craft your amulet or talisman with symbolic material like clay, wood, copper, silver, or gold, then engrave or emboss a sigil upon it, you will need to consult your correspondence tables or use the sympathetic linking process described in "Occult Magick" to make sure the materials are linked with the intent. Nonetheless, you will need to cleanse all materials before you use them to craft with.

Step 4: Craft the Item

Now is the time to craft your item. How you do this, depends entirely upon the item you are crafting. If this is a particularly intensive project, you may have to work on this item over a period of days—either way, you must do it within your Sacred Space.

Step 5: Consecrate and Charge

Once you have cleansed and crafted your item, it's ready to be consecrated and charged. This of course is done within a Sacred Space. If you decide to consecrate using theurgy, you will need to call gods and goddesses that correspond to your intent. That means you may even have to perform your ritual on a specific day and hour. To charge your item, use the same method described in Cleansing, Consecrating and Charging. When concentrating an item, I would suggest that you add a user constraint, meaning, add "This item will only work for NAME OF PERSON(S)." Once you have done this, your item is ready to be used.

POPPET MAGICK

A poppet is a magically enchanted doll used to affect change in a target from a distance. If you're still not sure what a poppet is, just think Voodoo doll. Contrary to how poppets (Voodoo dolls) are portrayed in movies and literature, they don't have to be used for torturing victims or delivering hexes. In fact, poppets can be used to perform beneficial energy work and healing on the person that doll represents. The purpose of the poppet is to provide a sympathetic link to a target. Once that "sympathy" has been created by incorporating a tag-lock and other magical components, it is then cleansed, consecrated and charged and can be used for a multitude of purposes. The reason why poppets are so popular is because, once they have been linked with a target, any energy work or magick performed with them is as good as if worked on a person who was right there in front of you—simply put, poppets are great foci!

Poppet Creation and Use

Making a Poppet

Poppets can be made out of just about anything, but the easiest way to create a poppet is cut out a paper doll. Once the paper doll has been cut, you can use your pen to give it the characteristics of the person it represents. The problem with a paper poppet is that all components; the tag-lock, herbs, stones, and other materials must be glued or attached using some sort of adhesive. I personally like to attach such things by placing them on the paper doll and dripping the wax of a magically charged candle over them until they are covered.

The next best choice would be to go out and buy an actual toy doll—you can find these at your local toy store and even thrift stores. Just remember: the closer that doll represents your target, the more powerful that poppet will be—of course, the appearance of these dolls can be modified by anyone who is crafty. The advantage of using a toy doll is that most of them can be opened up so you can place things in them. A good example of this would be a plastic Barbie doll.

But if you are the crafty type, you might choose to sew your doll or make it out of bound straw. In order to this, you will need to have the tools necessary to craft it. There are literally hundreds of way you could make your poppet—all you need to do is use your imagination. The thing to remember is this—any effort put into acquiring the doll or actually crafting it yourself raises energy through the process of immersion, which gives the doll even more power.

What to Put into the Poppet

If you went the paper route, then you will not actually be putting anything into your poppet; you will be attaching them. But if you chose to buy a doll or sew one, it will need to be stuffed. Besides ordinary stuffing used to give the doll shape, I suggest that you add magical components such as herbs, stones, your intent, sigils, minerals, and whatever else is pertinent to the magick you are trying to work inside the poppet. In any case, those things will have to be chosen by you after considering the purpose of the poppet. If poppet is for healing, you may want to include agate, bittersweet, coriander, and eucalyptus. If it is for banishment, you may want to include aquamarine, agrimony, black willow, and coffee. At a minimum, though, I would include a cleansed, consecrated and charged piece of paper with their name, date of birth, and your intent written on it. Lastly, cleanse, consecrate and charge all tools and items, except any tag-lock that contains your target's DNA.

Amping Up the Power

Items such as herbs, stones, and other materials can be placed in/at the Chakra points that are most influential to the intent of your spell or energy work to create a more potent effect. For example, if you have created the poppet for the purpose of causing that person to lust you, you will want to place herbs such Witch's grass, vanilla, and violet in the part of the doll where the Root Chakra would be. If you wanted that person to dream peacefully, you might add the herb hibiscus and a stone of Jade where the Third-Eye Chakra should be.

Because the Chakra points on the poppet correspond to and are linked with the target, you can target those particular areas with your energy work—this is depicted in horror movies when the Voodoo Priestess sticks her victim in the head with a needle—but like I said, poppets don't have to be used in this way.

Charging the Poppet

To charge your poppet, place the completed doll on your altar and open a circle. If you used theurgy during your opening, make sure to call spirits with whom you have built a rapport, who are particular to intentions of the magick and willing to help. Once they have been called, ask them to put their energy toward the intent of the spell—that request can be made in your own words. Remember to be very specific with your requests.

Now pick up the poppet and being to walk a circle. As you walk, repeat your targets name while thinking about him or her—this will naturally bring you into a trance. Once you can feel your target's thoughts, you are ready to charge the poppet. Stop and carefully place the poppet back on your altar without losing your trance state, then pick up your wand. With wand in hand, accumulate this raised energy within yourself and send it through the wand into the poppet—then say your binding incantation. Although I have provided one for you below, you can use one you've written, as long as it expresses that the target's soul is now bound to the poppet.

> "Force of Spirit, breath of life, bind this soul to doll alike and when magick is worked upon this doll, on X it shall come to call."

> End with "So mote it be" or "So be it."

What Now?

Now that you have a poppet, you can perform energy work on it or cast spells upon it. Any magick or energy work you do on that poppet will be three times more powerful than if you were to use the tag-lock alone. So if you're going to heal then heal, if you're going to bind and banish do so, but if you intend to curse, just make sure that target really deserves it.

CORD MAGICK

Another type of popular magick is cord magick. Cord magick has been around for as long as people have known how to create cord. Interestingly enough, cords vibrate when sound passes through them, and cords can carry messages—even the three Greek Fates were said to operate a loom to that wove people's destinies. The repetitive process of ritualistically braiding ribbons or cords together or tying them into knots promotes meditation and helps symbolically represent the intent of a spell. These cords can then be worn as a type of talisman or amulet, or included in other spellwork to empower another working.

How to Transform a Cord into a Symbolic Magick Item

- Cords can be used to represent the idea of binding when used to restrain, or to strengthen or connect when used to tie things together.
- Choosing a cord of a particular type of material is magically significant.
- Color can signify a particular kind of power.
- The numeric length of the cord can be a magical indicator.
- The type of knot you tie into a cord can have a magical correspondence.
- Other items such as a tag-lock, herbs, stones, crystals, sigils, scrolls, and so on can be tied into the knots to add to the power of the spell.
- Knots can also be used to symbolize an oath or union.
- A cord can be coated with oil, have herbs or other materials tied into them to add magical charge.
- Adding a knot to a cord symbolically stores energy, while untying that knot is said to release it.

Tip: Seal the ends of the cord with wax so it won't unravel.

TAROT MAGICK

This is perhaps one of my most favorite types of magick because it relies on an ancient and highly symbolic system. Tarot cards can not only be used to divine the possible future and describe magical philosophy, but they can also be used to perfectly represent one's intent in spells.

The tarot embodies most of life's lessons, the elements and the planetary forces, divine forces and the mysteries. Not only this, but also the thought-form that comprises this collective knowledge and their beliefs are so well known that people are still familiar with it today. It is extremely powerful because that power is reinforced by books, movies, radio, television, and word of mouth—everyone knows what Tarot is.

Anyone practicing magick should do some kind of divination to get an idea what the repercussion of that spell might be before they decide to cast it. Tarot magick takes this a little further, helping to build a powerful thought-form, while allowing the reading to shape a more ideal outcome. The concept of tarot magick is rather simple, pose your intent as a question—in other words, say something like, "What would happen if I cast a spell for X?" Then, evaluate the reading and consult your higher self or deity to shape a more realistic outcome if need be. Needless to say, you must study and understand tarot before you can use this type of magick—the good thing is, if you use tarot magick often, you will become extremely familiar with it.

In order to successfully work with tarot magick, you need a good set of cards, and they need to be cleansed, consecrated, and charged. And you will need at least two magical journals to record card and spell data in. At this point, if you want to maximize your results, you need to consider incorporating theurgy into your tarot magick routine. If you decide to call upon a deity to help you interpret a reading or affect the outcome of your intent when using tarot magick, then you should consider developing a relationship with and calling upon some of the deities listed below.

Gods and Goddesses or Prophecy and Fate

Name	Culture	Sphere
Cerridwin	Celtic, Welsh	Goddess of Dark Prophecy
Eriu	Celtic, Irish	Goddess of Fate
Fata-Morgana	Celtic, Irish	Goddess of Fate
Sulis	Celtic	Goddess of Prophesy
Odin	Norse	Is knowledgeable about the future
The Fates	Greek	The spinners and weavers of Fate
Alphito	Greek	Goddess of Destiny
Arachne	Greek	Weaver of Destiny
Morpheus	Greek	God of Dreams
Oneiros	Greek	God of Dreams
Philyra	Greek	Goddess of Divination
Picus	Roman	Prophet
Vortumna	Roman	Goddess of Destiny
Rozanica	Slavic	Prophecy of children's Fate

Echidne	Libyan	Goddess of Prophecy
Shamash	Sumerian	God of Fate
Fatima	Syrian, Arabic	Goddess of Fate
Enlil	Assyrian, Sumerian	Determines Fate
Zurvan	Medes, Iran	God of Time and Destiny
Ataentsic	Iroquois	Goddess who counsels in Dreams
Tahit	Tlingit	God of Fate
Camxtli	Aztec, Mayan	God of Fate
Ifa	African	God of Divination

Using Tarot to Find a Better Solution

This process assumes you are using the Cross Spread mentioned under Tarot in the Divination Section in this chapter.

Step 1:

Begin by making your intent a question, then do a reading on that question. If the cards are acceptable and show the manifestation of your will, then move on with the actual spell. Otherwise, continue to the next step.

Step 2:

Pick up the Influence card and take a really good look at it. Remember: this card shapes your Expectations, which have an effect on what will manifest in your Future. Take time to study this card closely—understanding how this card shapes your Expectations is extremely important. Ask yourself how these Influences, caused you to have that Expectation and how that Expectation formed your future. Remove the Influence card and set it aside, then remove the Expectation card and the Future card and place them back in the deck. Remember: you can't change the Center card because it represents you and your current situation—nor can you change the past.

Step 3:

At this point, ask yourself, "What changes do I need to make in myself, my setting, or the people I associate with in order to achieve the Future I want?" If you are using theurgy, say a prayer to any Gods or Goddesses you have invoked. Then close your eyes and on meditate on the possible changes you could make to your attitude, setting, and social interactions that might lead to the manifesting your desired Future as you shuffle the cards. When you've exhausted your imagination, continue shuffling the cards, but remain open. At this point, stop trying to actively solve your problem, but instead become receptive—let the answer arise from your subconscious. If these scenarios continue to replay over and over again, let them—don't interfere; just observe—at some point, the answers will come as insight. This is when you begin pulling cards from the deck and laying them down into the missing positions. Begin with the Influence card, then Expectation and Lastly the future.

Step 4:

Open your eyes and take a look. Do the cards lead to an acceptable outcome? Examine the Influence card and see how it has affected your Expectations. Ask yourself, if that Influence and Exception is healthy. If so, then you know these cards represent the thought-form you want to manifest. If that's the case, continue on to Casting the Tarot Spell. Otherwise, go back to steps 2 through 4.

The Tarot Spell

Components
- Tarot Deck
- Pen and Ink of Art
- Virgin Paper
- Candle
- Oil
- Incense

Up until now, your goal has been to find an acceptable future by reading the cards and consulting a higher power. Now you want to reinforce the thought-form (your intent) and speed up its manifestation by doing a little spell work.

Preparation

You will need to make or buy several items before you cast this spell: spell-specific candle, oil, and incense.

- Candle: Make a candle out of paraffin wax in a color associated with the intent of your spell. Make this candle large enough to be burned over a period of at least three days.
- Oil: Make an oil using a specific blend of herbs associated with the intent of your spell.
- Incense: Make incense using a specific blend of herbs associated with the intent of your spell.

Performance

Step 1:

Simplify the reading down to its most basic form as you would a charm. For such a large body of text, first start by rewriting it in its simplest terms, then remove all repeating words. From that create a charm. Write this simplified intent down in your book of charms and place the record of your divination back into your divination journal. Now create a sigil out of your charm.

Step 2:

Lay your cards into position on your altar according to the resulting spread.

Step 3:

Anoint your pillar candle with your special oil blend and place it on the altar as well. Remember: if you are trying to cause that thought-form to manifest, you will want to message the oil in from stem to base in a clockwise fashion. Otherwise, if the purpose is to banish, or bind, you will want to message in a counterclockwise direction from base to stem.

Step 4:

Light the special candle and incense blend that you have created specifically for this spell.

Step 5:

Hold the sigil in hand as you walk clockwise or counterclockwise direction (depending on your intentions) around the circle to raise energy. As you do this, repeat the charm over and over again like a mantra, while thinking about the future it represents.

Step 6

Once you have raised all the energy you can, stop, burn the sigil over the candle, and end with "So mote it be!" or "So be it!"

Step 7:

Snuff out the candle and repeat steps 4 through 6 on the next days until the entire candle has burned down. You won't have a sigil to burn any more, but you can repeat the mantra and walk the circle.

PLANETARY MAGICK

Remember I mentioned everything is alive and conscious? Well, the planets have been around longer than we have, so they are extremely powerful. Planetary magick is working with the power and intelligences of the planets. All planets are associated with a seal and magical square. The magical seal is used to break the influence of the power which a planet represents, while a square is used to call upon the power of that planetary force to bring something into manifestation.

A magical square, also called a *kamea*, is a representation of a magical force using mathematics. They are arranged so that that sum of any row is adds up to and is equal to the sum of any column. While there are many magical squares, the most popular ones are those of the seven planets; the Moon, Sun, Jupiter, Venus, Saturn, Mercury, and Mars.

When working with planetary forces, you must be mindful that your intentions are in alignment with that planet. Each force is associated with an intelligence and a spirit; the intelligence being a guiding/informative force while the spirit a neutral force. Each Magick Square represents a matrix of planetary energy. Magick squares are based on the original work done by ancient mathematicians in their description of numbers. Magical practitioners expanded on this to carry over the correlation between a number and its corresponding planet, therefore representing that planetary energy in a mathematical format.

Therefore, each Magick Square is a direct link to the thought-form or spirit of that particular planet. The number associated with the planet and the corresponding numbers within each square was calculated long ago by ancient mathematicians, then expounded upon by ancient Magicians.

You will oftentimes read that each planet has an intelligence and a spirit. However, this overcomplication is unnecessary. All you need to know is that they are one and the same and that despite any attempt to tap into a planet's intelligence or spirit, you are in fact connecting with its life force.

A square lends manifesting energy to a spell that is governed by the correspondence of a ruling planet. For example, if you wanted to cast a spell to improve your health, you would use the planetary square of the Sun, while if your objective was to attract a lovely female, you would employ the square of Venus.

Notice also that each square has a corresponding Seal. Unlike the square, which builds these energies—using a Seal will reduce, degrade, bind, banish, or destroy those same powers. So using the same example, if you wanted to harm someone, you would include the seal of the Sun, or if your goal was to dissolve or break up a relationship, you might consider using the Seal of Venus. At this point, take a look at the correspondences for each planet.

Planetary Squares and Correspondence

Sun

Day:	Sunday
Color:	Yellow
Number:	7, 49, 175 and 1225
Sign:	Leo
Correspondences:	health, vitality, ego, power, success, advancement, leadership, and growth

Square   *Seal*

6	32	3	34	35	1
7	11	27	28	8	30
19	14	16	15	23	24
18	20	22	21	17	13
25	29	10	9	26	12
36	5	33	4	2	31

Moon

Day:	Monday
Color:	Silver
Number:	9, 81, 369, and 3,321
Sign:	Cancer
Correspondences:	Clairvoyance, sleep, emotions, astral travel, imagination, women, birth and reincarnation

Square   Seal

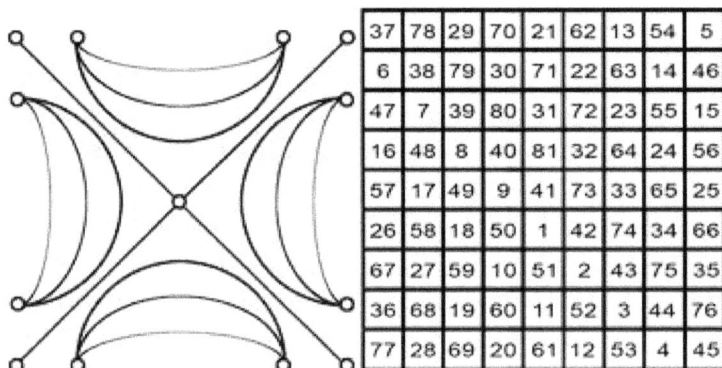

37	78	29	70	21	62	13	54	5
6	38	79	30	71	22	63	14	46
47	7	39	80	31	72	23	55	15
16	48	8	40	81	32	64	24	56
57	17	49	9	41	73	33	65	25
26	58	18	50	1	42	74	34	66
67	27	59	10	51	2	43	75	35
36	68	19	60	11	52	3	44	76
77	28	69	20	61	12	53	4	45

Mars

Day:	Tuesday
Color:	Red
Number:	5, 25, 65, and 325
Sign:	Aries, Scorpio
Correspondence:	Male sexuality, strength, lust, anger, destruction, medical issues

Square   Seal

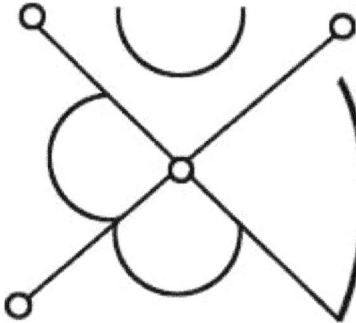

11	24	7	20	3
4	12	25	8	16
17	5	13	21	9
10	18	1	14	22
23	6	19	2	15

Mercury

Day: Wednesday
Color: Purple
Number: 8, 64, 260, and 2,080
Sign: Virgo, Gemini
Correspondences: Communication, intellect, writing, contracts, information, wisdom, science, memory

Square   *Seal*

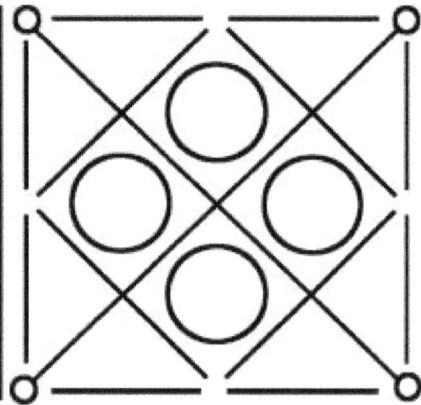

8	58	59	5	4	62	63	1
49	15	14	52	53	11	10	56
41	23	22	44	45	19	18	48
32	34	35	29	28	38	39	25
40	26	27	37	36	30	31	33
17	47	46	20	21	43	42	24
9	55	54	12	13	51	50	16
64	2	3	61	60	6	7	57

Jupiter

Day:	Thursday
Color:	Blue
Number:	4, 16, 34 and 136
Sign:	Sagittarius
Correspondence:	Success, abundance, money, court cases, growth, gambling.

Square	*Seal*

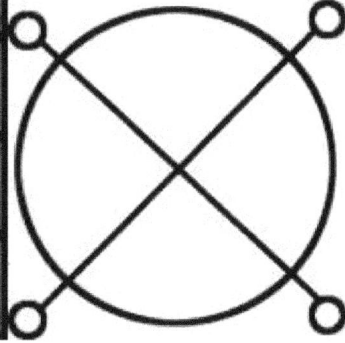

Venus

Day:	Friday
Color:	Green
Number:	8, 64, 260, and 2,080
Sign:	Taurus, Libra
Correspondences:	Love, pleasure, female sexuality, arts, music, beauty, luxury, social affairs

Square   *Seal*

22	47	16	41	10	35	4
5	23	48	17	42	11	29
30	6	24	49	18	36	12
13	31	7	25	43	19	37
38	14	32	1	26	44	20
21	39	8	33	2	27	45
46	15	40	9	34	3	28

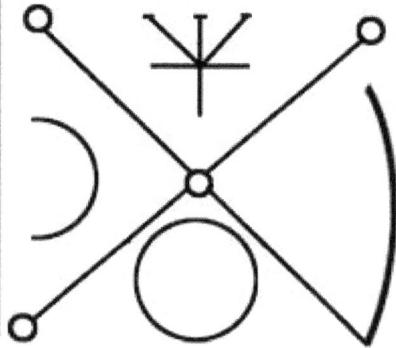

Saturn

Day:	Saturday
Color:	Black
Number:	3, 9, 15, and 45
Sign:	Capricorn
Correspondences:	Real estate, banks, debt, obstacles, binding, knowledge, time, discipline

Square   *Sigil*

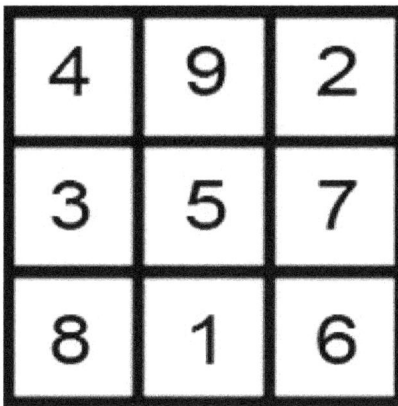
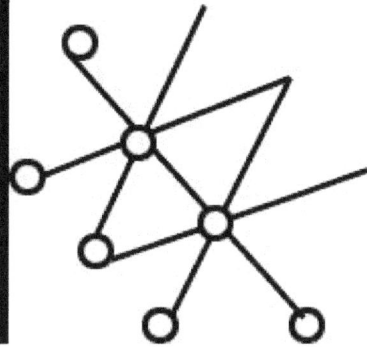

Sigil Magick Using Squares

The word *sigil* is derived from the Latin word *sigillum*, which means "sign" or "signature." A sigil can be created by using a planetary square that corresponds to the intent of your magick. This is done by choosing a word that represents your intent, then finding the numbers that relate to each letter of that word using the Gematria of your choice. After this, lines are traced from square to square, beginning with the first number of the word and ending with the last. Once this is done that sigil has been tied into the power of that planetary force.

You should also know that the meaning of this kind of sigil can be deciphered by someone if they know what Gematria you used to create it. All they have to do is simply trace from the end point back to the beginning.

To create a sigil using the planets, first, reduce your intent down to a single word. Next, find the numeric value of each of its letters using the Gematria of your choice below.

Western Gematria								
1	2	3	4	5	6	7	8	9
A	B	C	D	E	F	G	H	I
J	K	L	M	N	O	P	Q	R
S	T	U	V	W	X	Y	Z	

For example, let's say your intent was to acquire a car. In this case, *car* would be your key word. If you were to use Western Gematria, your corresponding numbers would be,

C	A	R
3	1	9

Lastly, to create the sigil trace the numbers over the square of Jupiter starting with three, then one, and lastly nine. To complete the sigil mark the beginning point with a small circle, and terminate with a cross. Charge this as you would any other sigil.

Binding, Banishing
and Protection

B anishings and bindings are methods that can be used to protect
yourself from negative spiritual influences. In fact, the Fully Qualified
Circle Opening Ritual, detailed under Concerning Magical Circles
and Sacred Spaces, provides a certain amount of banishment and protection.
The word *banish* means "to send away," and *to bind* means "to immobilize
and bring under your control."

WHAT DOES IT MEAN TO BE A VICTIM
OF NEGATIVE SPIRITUAL INFLUENCE?

Negative spiritual influence can result from the buildup of negative energies
caused by you, exposure to a negative environment, a curse, or being taken
advantage of by a negative entity. What I am about to discuss assumes that
you understand that your thoughts create your reality. From a scientific
standpoint, we know that everything in existence is made of information
and that all this information is connected at some level. This means, like
the butterfly effect, everything you do, say, and think ripples out into the
universe and not only affects you, but also affects the environment and the
people around you.

If the fact that thought can have this effect seems ludicrous, consider
that modern medical science has proven that anxiety, expectation, and
the belief in something negative can cause one to become physically ill or

even dead—the nocebo effect. So at this point, it doesn't matter whether you believe everything in universe is thought—bad thoughts can have a negative effect on your psyche and health. Having said this, let's explore the various ways negative energy can affect people.

Being Crossed

To be crossed means that you have been infected by a negative mind-set. This could simply happen because of the way you choose to live your life, or it can be the result of living in a toxic environment and on rare occasions it can happen when you've become the target of negative or baneful for magick.

How you became crossed can be determined by examining your life. For example, if bad things have been happening for a very long time, there is a good chance that you have crossed yourself. However, if you have suddenly run into bad luck, there may be a chance that you have been crossed by a practitioner of magick. Before assuming someone has cursed you, take a look at the people in your life and ask yourself what kind of influence they have on you—constantly being around negative people can cause you to be infected by this kind of energy.

Either way, all negative patterns of thought tend to muddle our judgment, causing us to make bad choices that can be harmful or even detrimental to ourselves and others. To make things even worse we as humans tend to surround ourselves with others who hold similar attitudes, habits, and perspectives—and when that happens, those attitudes, habits, and perspectives tend to reinforce themselves and multiply their potency. Also, because we are creatures of habit, we tend to seek comfort in familiar surroundings. When this happens, we can convince ourselves that we are living in a normal healthy environment, even if it's not—so it is a good idea to be familiar with the stages of the crossed condition.

Stages of the Crossed Condition

Psychologically speaking, there are three stages of the crossed condition. The first stage is denoted by low energy, anxiety, general depression, and bad luck. Oftentimes, the crossed person will not even be aware of it. They are so used to their bad habits, living under bad conditions, and the negative people that surround them that it all seems normal. If you are able to catch someone in this stage, they are easier to help because they are more apt to listen to reason.

The second stage is a little more serious. In this stage, the person's psyche becomes malformed. They are usually delusional about themselves and those around them. Such people tend to blame others for their misfortune, have very low self-esteem, or might have even developed a grandiose attitude. In this stage bad psychological hygiene begins to manifest in terms of physical illness and disease. They may appear gaunt, obese, or generally unhealthy. Dealing with persons in this stage is possible, but difficult. Helping them requires months or even years of counseling and spell work.

Stage three is where everything begins to come down like a hammer. Delusion can turn into serious mental illness such as psychosis or schizophrenia. More often than not, people in this stage are unable to operate in the physical world; they are usually homeless, cannot hold down a job, or on the verge of being locked up. The physical damage that can be done to a person from illness, while in this stage can be detrimental. This is the hardest stage to work in and may require work over a lifetime.

It is worthwhile to note that people can move back and forth between stages. The key to helping those who are crossed is working with them to identify bad habits, delusions, and other influences that might be contributing to their condition. In addition to this, you must use magick to help dissipate the negative energy that has built up around them—in other words, take a holistic approach. If you are the one who is crossed, then you must be brutally honest with yourself and be willing to change your lifestyle. If you are in stage II or III, then it may be time to employ the help of a professional healer or practitioner of magick. In all cases I suggest seeking out therapy, or psychiatric help.

What You Can Do

The first thing that you must do is to get the cooperation of that person. Whether that person is you or someone else, they must accept they have been crossed and be willing to do something about it—that can be difficult to do, especially if that person is in stage two or three. But once you have their acceptance and cooperation, you can move on to changing that person's life.

It is more than likely that person is living in a negative environment. In such case, they need to get out of it—and yes, I'm talking about moving. If they can't move, then you should suggest they spend as much time away from that environment as they possibly can—this will reduce exposure to that energy. It is also very possible that the crossed person is the one creating their own negative environment. In such case moving to a more positive setting where they can be exposed to healthy energy can greatly help them.

Just like the first step of casting a circle is to clean your ritual chamber, you need to suggest that this person clean their living quarters and make a good effort to keep personal hygiene—by doing this, they can eradicate some of that negative energy.

The next step involves the use of magick. Either create a spell yourself or employ one of the methods described below to get rid of that negative energy. Once you have done that, you need to use another spell to charge the person with positive energy. This spell should be personalized and adapted to incorporate any positive spiritual influences that person may believe in—if that person is Christian, use Jesus; if that person believes his ancestors can help him, call upon his ancestors; and if that person is pagan, then call upon the old Gods. What you must realize here is that magick is the pushing of intent (thought) and that affecting another person is easier when they believe in what you are doing. Of course, that is not to say that belief in yourself doesn't matter, but if the person doesn't believe in the forces you are calling, your chances of affecting them in a positive way will be diminished.

Another thing that is worth noting is you can't just cast one spell and expect that person to get well—this means it is more than likely that you will have to perform many spells. You must understand that it takes a long time to uncross someone, because you are dealing with energies that are continually building up or have built up over a lifetime. Healing manifests gradually and the crossed person must be tended to over this period. Things may seem to get worse before they get better—this is just the forces balking against the uncrossing.

Lastly, during this process you will need to talk with this person, give them guidance and listen to their problems—and by doing that, you will be able to adjust your tactics. Knowing this and understanding how contagious this kind of energy is, you need to cleanse your space as well as yourself after every session. If you feel like you can't help your client, encourage them to seek out a professional psychiatric help—just realize you can't help everyone.

Being Hexed

To be hexed means that you are the target of baneful magick or intense malicious thought—this is something that happens suddenly. Technically, a hex is harmful spell that has been cast from afar and a curse is harmful magick that has been delivered in person. Delivery can happen in one of three ways; it can be spoken, psychically impinged upon the mind, or delivered by a glance. When a curse is delivered by eye contact, it's called the *evil eye*. The evil eye can be seen as any social interaction with a highly negative person, usually someone who exudes foul energies that pin-points you with hateful intent by giving you a dirty look. This type of attack can cause a chill that instantaneously infects your auric field in a sickening way. Both of these attacks can be done as ritualized magick as performed by a black Magician or by the uninitiated using strong and persistent thought—in other words, they don't have to know how to cast spells.

The results of a hex can be varied; it just depends on the intentional or unintentional thought of the person delivering the hex—it could range from something as general as bad luck to your house catching fire or even a sudden and tragic death. Either way, bad luck will seem to happen spontaneously and can continue to escalate over time until the intention of the energy has fulfilled itself. If the practitioner of magick is powerful enough and if the target of the hex ignores the fact that he or she has been hexed, that hex can become generational—in other words, passed down from parent to child from one life to another.

What You Can Do

If you have been hexed, you need to break it. If you don't disconnect from that energy, it will just keep building until it ruins your life or outright kills you. Breaking a curse or hex could be a matter of simply cleansing yourself of the negative energy by taking a ritual bath, or require you to cast a more powerful hex-breaking spell—either way, you should put up permanent protection in the form of a psychic shield or talisman. If you know who sent this baneful energy, you may even choose to send it back to them by incorporating reversal into your protection. Either way, you will need to create a spell or adapt and perform one found in this chapter.

Negative Spirits

Even though most people don't have the ability to "see" spirits, negative spirits are a real threat nonetheless. They have a tendency to attach themselves to an individual and feed off of them causing mental distress, psychosis, and even sickness. Just as any carnivorous animal can develop a taste for a particular type of prey, negative spirits can develop a taste for a specific type of emotion—that could be anger, depression, fear, or even lust. In Western cultures, such spirits are called demons, but have names in other cultures that roughly translate to the same concept—evil spirit. They have been seen as devils, shadow people, Djinn, poltergeists, and alien abductors—just to name a few.

Also, due to the law of attraction, negative entities tend to have a negative appearance. For example, a shade will probably look like a dark shadowy figure; a demon may appear as an atypical being with horns, claws and a tail or even a disturbing combination of animal/human forms; a Djinn or genie may appear as a dark and terrible storm; a poltergeist as an invisible force that wreaks havoc; and an alien as a short, gray, humanoid figure with a big head, spindly limbs, and a cold gaze. But even if you can't see them, you will undoubtedly feel their dark presence.

If you have not developed your psychic senses, any of these beings may try to befriend you in an attempt to gain your trust—and if that happens, then they may try to take up residence in your body. Of this, I have firsthand experience. My near-possession experience came after my first attempt at spirit evocation. At that time, I was just novice practitioner in my early twenties living in a shotgun home in New Orleans, primed to experience something new. The prior occupants of the home were obviously practitioners of voodoo, because there were voodoo symbols scrawled in hidden locations everywhere around the house. The place was also very haunted! We had a resident spirit that would pace back and forth at night, almost three times a week. The method I used to evoke this spirit was based on the Goetia, a seventeenth-century grimoire used to summon demons, or daemon for the purpose of getting information or doing your bidding. After studying the process and preparing for a week, I set up my ritual chamber and began the long process calling the spirit. Unfortunately, nothing happened, so I assumed it was rubbish and walked off without properly closing the circle. At that point, I went to bed. This is where the fun began!

After a period of sound sleep, I woke up paralyzed. Even though I seemed fully conscious and could feel my body, I could not move. But to my surprise, I sat up, face contorted into a sadistic grimace and glanced down at my lover. As I glanced down, the most intense emotion of hate arose within me, and out of my mouth issued the word, "Murder!" This shook me to the core, because I loved my partner, and the thought of hurting him would have never crossed my mind. As this was happening, my nose filled with the smell of smoke, and out of the corner of my eye I could see flames roaring within the open closet. At this point, I knew that I was under spiritual attack—something had hijacked my body and was trying to possess me. Struggling to regain control over my body didn't seem to help, so instead, I imagined myself outside of my body performing a banishing ritual. This caused the spirit to cease action, and soon I was able to regain full control. After regaining control, I glanced over to the closet, only to see a lonely rack of clothes hanging there—no smoke, no fire. So I returned to my ritual chamber, immediately closed my circle, and repeated the banishment ritual.

Also note that some entities are attracted to people who use various forms of ideomotor spirit communication tools like spirit boards, pendulum, and divining rods. The reason for this is simple: such people really haven't developed their spiritual senses, and because of that, the entity is invisible and can use deception. At that point, they may choose to pose as a deceased relative or claim to be the devil himself in order to terrify the victim. Entities that use terror can usually read the surface thoughts of their victims without them even knowing it, then know exactly what to say in order to illicit the right emotions from the victim. Once this has happened, the entity feeds and becomes more powerful and can then use that energy to produce telekinetic effects to terrify the victim even more. This is why you always hear stories about children and teenagers summoning the devil after playing around with Ouija boards. One, they are primed for fear before they even touch the board; two, they are impressionable; and three, they don't put up any kind of protection—positive-minded spirit communication groups rarely have those problems.

What You Can Do

Negative spirits can be dealt with in the same way you deal with hexes and curses. First, you remove the effected person or people from the haunted dwelling, then the place must be physically cleaned and spiritually cleansed—make sure to remove any tools or items related to the haunting. Use the house blessing ritual described below, then have the occupants of the house take a cleansing bath. Once the house has been both physically and spiritually cleaned, place spirit traps and talismans at the windows, doors, and other problem areas to prevent any further incursion.

If the victim(s) were responsible for intentionally bring the spirit in using some form of spirit communication, counsel them against contacting the world of spirit anymore. If they persist in wanting to do this, encourage them to take protective measures and to always connect with the spirit world in a positive light. If the victims are open to instruction, teach them how to take these measures.

If the victim(s) unintentionally drew the spirit or the house was haunted before they moved in, inform them that they must work on keeping a positive attitude. At this point, instruct them on how to bless their home so that they can do this in the future—spirits have been known to come back when they feel they can slip in under the radar.

Basic Psychic Defense

Psychic defense can be done on the fly because it involves no rituals or spells. Most psychic defenses involve putting up what is called a *shield*. A shield is a semipermanent spherical or egg-shaped field of energy that surrounds the body. Shields are made functional when created with a particular type of intent. When creating a shield, raise energy using the Circulation of the Body of Light, then visualize that energy taking the color you associate with a particular type of function. To reinforce the shield, make sure to visualize that energy solidifying into a crystalline structure about your body—it's really that simple. Please note that you can program a shield with any number of abilities.

Absorption Shield

This type of shield is generally visualized as white light. Its purpose is to absorb negative energies and either feed that energy back into the body or back into the shield to reinforce it or make it stronger.

Banishment Shield

Usually visualized with blue light, this type of shield is programmed with the intent to throw or push the aggressor into the abyss or very far away.

Reflective Shield

Usually visualized as a black energy with a reflective property or simply a spherical energy with a reflective surface. The purpose of this shield is to reflect energy back at the source of the attack.

Weaponized Shield

This can be visualized as a black- or red-energy form surrounding your body. The point of weaponizing a shield is to visualize some sort of attack happening anytime a malicious entity tries to pass through it. It could be programmed with the intent of lancing the target with a spike, burning the interloper with flames, or some other creative attack.

Healing Shield

This shield would be visualized as white-light energy. Not only is it programmed with the intent to repel attacks, but also to absorb negative energy, convert it into positive healing energy and send it back to the attacker. In this way, the more the aggressor attacks, the more he, she, or it is inundated with positive healing energy and eventually becomes so positively charged that they will lose their desire to attack.

BINDING AND BANISHING VIA MAGICK

There are an infinite number of spells and rituals that allow you to bind, banish, and protect against negative energies and entities. Ritual baths, anointing, and purification by light are perfect for cleansing the body's auric field. This is done for the same reason you would cleanse any component or tool before you use actually use it in a magical operation—to get rid of energies contrary to the work you are doing. You should also smudge, or take a ritual bath anytime you feel you have come in contact with negative people, or negative environments—otherwise, this energy could build up, affect your mood and make you ill.

Ritual Bath

Components
- Water
- Sea Salt
- Other Herbs
- Other Stones or Minerals
- Cheesecloth, or Muslin

As you already know, water is a natural carrier of energies and salt has natural banishment qualities. So, draw a tub of hot water and add one-third cup of sea salt, three times (total one cup) to your water, then stirring in a counterclockwise direction (signifies banishment) until it has been dissolved. If your practice theurgy, say a prayer to the deities you venerate asking them to bless the water for the purpose of banishing all negative energy from your auric field. It can sound something like this:

> "Gods and Goddesses of light, bless this water for the purpose
> of banishing all negative energies from my auric field."

Notice that "other herbs" is a part of the list of components. This is because you can charge your field with the magical properties of other plants by adding them to the water—just make sure those plants are not poisonous. These herbs should be added to a pouch created of cheesecloth or muslin, then tied off so they spill out into the water—if you don't have that, you can use a coffee filter. To find the right herbs for your mixture, consult your personal correspondence table or examine the herbal correspondence table at the end of this book. The same thing can be done with stones and other minerals—they too have vibrations that can add to positively charge your field with unique properties.

If you decide to add herbs, let your bundle soak in the water for a good ten minutes, stirring occasionally so it combines with the water. Once this mixture has integrated, remove the bundle (or leave it) and hop in. Soak in the tub for at least ten to fifteen minutes before draining and getting out. Finally, drain the tub, imagining all the foul energies going down that drain with the water to be reabsorbed back into the environment where nature will sort it out.

Purification by Light

The simplest way to purge an area of negative energy is by invoking the light and using it to push out unwanted energy. If you practice theurgy, start by saying a verbal prayer. Use any words you wish, but whatever words you choose, make them meaningful and heartfelt. An example might be, "I call upon the powers of Light to enter me and purify my soul." Now concentrate on your breathing. As you breathe in, visualize a bright point of light appearing at the crown of your head. When you breathe out, see the light grow like a fire being stoked by strong jet of air. With each breath, watch the light grow and spread throughout your body. As it spreads feel it dissolve any negative thoughts that may have affected you throughout the day. Keep breathing and visualizing. Imagine this energy soothing your body as it purifies. Allow the light to radiate out of you and fill your ritual space. See it push everything negative out of that environment. Breath and visualize until you have filled your entire space, then stop when you have accomplished that.

Anointing

It will not always be practical for you to take a bath before every spell or ritual, especially if you have to perform one on the fly; instead, you can dab yourself with a special oil blend. An anointing oil is a magical oil that has been specifically cleanse, consecrated, and charged for the purpose of either cleansing the auric field or charging the auric field of the recipient with other magical properties. Anointing oils can be bought or made, but it's always best to make them yourself. If you are interested in making your own oil, which you should be, then consult the oil making guide at the end of this book.

At a minimum, you should have some kind of carrier oil—the best is Jojoba, of course. Then you will need to pick your herbs according to their properties. If you are making an anointing oil, you should consider incorporating Sage, or Palo Santo into the mix. Other good choices are Frankincense and Myrrh as well as Dragon's Blood because it enhances the powers of all herbs. If you are trying to make an oil used for theurgy, then you will want to research that deity and find out what herbs are associated with Him or Her.

To apply the oil, dab your finger and place a dot on your forehead where your third eye should be located. To follow ritualistic immersion, invoke the powers of banishment and purification in your own words. You might say something like the following:

> "By this oil all the negative energies are banished from my body, and I am purified."

If this oil is related to a deity, you will want to invoke that deity's name.

> "In the name of DEITY, all negative energies are banished, and I am purified"

Lastly, treat your oils as you would treat any magically charged item and keep them out of the eyeshot of others. Place them all in a box or special holder for this purpose.

Typical House Blessing

Components
- Lighter/Matches
- Burn-Safe Dish
- Sage
- Sea Salt
- Water

A house blessing is common ritual used to cleanse a home of negative energy. This ritual can be repeated periodically as needed.

Step I: Physically Clean

Begin by reordering the energy in the room by physically cleaning what needs to be cleaned in the entire house.

Step II: Prepare All Components

Create a babblogue charm that embodies the below statement.
Example:

> "I call upon the almighty source to purge this quarter of negative energy and replace it with divine light. May it dwell here always."

Consonants Only: C L P N T H M G T S R F V D W
Create Babblogue: Clypanth Magdivi Sif Tsarwa
Reduce: Lythagtsuwa
Reduce Again: Lysua

Take a moment to learn how to pronounce this word, then meditate on that word for about five minutes to create a mental link between the word and the statement it was drawn from.

Lay your components upon your altar, take a moment to summon divine authority, lift your left hand above your head, place the palm of your right hand just above the components, and command that those components be blessed.

"I call upon the divine within me to bless and charge this sage, water and salt for the purpose of vanquishing negative energy."

See it, feel it, know it, and acknowledge that it has been done! Now take three pinches of salt and add it to the water, stirring the mixture until it has been dissolved.

Finish with, "So it is done," or "So mote it be."

Step III: Open the House Up

Expose all hidden places by opening all windows, doors, drawers, and so on.

Step IV: Sage

Cense the entire home using sage, Palo Santo, or some other form of incense, starting from the middle of each room, to the perimeter of each room, moving in a counterclockwise fashion—this symbolizes banishment and will effectively push negative energy out. As you cense, repeat the charm "Lysua." Know and acknowledge that it is doing what it's supposed to.

Step V: Asperge

Asperge (sprinkle) the holy water from the center of the room to its perimeter. Make sure to do this at least once in each of the four quarters and once in each open space. With each sprinkle repeat the charm "Lysua." Know and acknowledge that it is doing what it's supposed to.

Caution: Protect electrical devices, art, and television screens from splash—water and electricity does not mix.

Step VI: You're done! Close your doors, windows, and drawers.

Uncrossing (Candle Magick)

Components

- 1 White Candle
- 1 Black Candle
- 1 Green Candle
- Higher Ascension Oil:
  2 part Yucca, 1 part Master Wort, 1 part Echinacea,
- 1 Quartz Crystal Pebble
- Holistic Healing Oil:
  2 parts Coriander , 1 part Gardenia
- Uncrossing Oil:
  2 parts Rue, 1 part Balm of Gilead, Clove of Garlic,
- Pinch of Black Pepper, 1 Hematite Pebble

This spell is used to break up and banish negative energies tormenting those who are crossed. It actually follows a three-step process that, one, calls to positive divine influences to heal the victim and encourage a balanced mind-set; two, uses candle magick banish those energies from the person's field and environment; and three, calls upon the power of the earth to physically and emotionally heal the victim. The power of this spell is a cumulative and should be repeated as needed.

Gather your components, then bring them into your Sacred Space, cleansing, consecrating, and charging them with smoke and water while call upon the spiritual forces to empower your efforts. Make this call a lengthy one and request help from as many positive spiritual influences you work with. Remember that the client should be able to identify with the spirits or gods being called, therefore incorporate his or her beliefs into the spell. If this means calling upon the name of Jesus, then do it because this will have the strongest affect for the client.

> "Oh, Source of all, who is mighty and powerful, be with me in my time of need, aid my efforts, and purify me. Watch over me and help me see clearly. Give me the strength to endure and overcome all adversity."
>
> "Wise Goddess of the Underworld, who knows the inner workings of my soul, be with me. Make me wise and give me the courage to confront my fears. Lend me your power so I am able to throw down illusion and find my true path. Thank you, Hecate."
>
> "Mighty Rah! Change my life! I call on you: purify me with your awesome light! Be with me; give me strength!"
>
> "I call upon my ancestors—[name them]! You are wise! I am your prodigy! Be with me; help me through this!"
>
> And so forth and so on.

Apply the Higher Ascension Oil to the White Candle by massaging it from stem to base. As you do this, imagine the candle being imbued with powers to attract higher spiritual forces and aid. The intention should be to strengthen the recipient's connection with positive divine influence and for those influences to work at that victim to make him or her more mentally stable and physically well. See the candle bursting with magical intent of divine intervention—know and acknowledge that it has been done.

Apply the Uncrossing Oil to the Black candle by massaging it into the candle from base to stem. See this candle taking on a charge that will break deeply ingrained negative behaviors and influences and banish them into eternity, while replacing this negativity with strength, understanding, and the courage to change. Know and acknowledge that it has been done.

Lastly, pick up the Green candle and the Holistic Healing Oil and massage it into the candle from stem to base. Imagine impregnating the candle with powerful healing of the earth and a calming force that creates clarity. Specifically call upon the power of the Earth and/or Earth deities to do this. Do this until the candle has accepted all the charge it can.

If the uncrossing is for you, then imagine these positive changes happening in your life. Otherwise, imagine the target of the uncrossing and see the change for him or her. To complete the spell, place each candle on your altar next to one another (left to right: white, black, and green) and burn them over three days. If these candles have been created for someone else, instruct them to display them in a prominent place where there is no clutter so that they can be plainly seen.

Burn the white candle first in the hour of Saturn (sunset), burn the Black Candle in the hour of Jupiter (midafternoon) and burn the Green Candle in the hour of Mars (sunrise.) These candles must be burned until they are totally incapable of being lit again. This process can be repeated if necessarily, but what one must understand is that even though this spell dissipates negative energies created by the crossed condition, the crossed person and his or her environment can still become tainted if he or she does not change the habits or attitude that caused it in the first place. Furthermore, if the crossed person remains in a toxic environment or chooses keep the same company, this negative energy can become replenished. In such a case, you may be just spinning your wheels, so to speak, by casting this spell, but by casting it, you are clearing negative from the person and area temporarily, and it may allow them the clarity they need in order to make better decisions.

Black Tourmaline and Quartz Crystal Amulet

Components
- Black Tourmaline
- Quartz Crystal
- Other crafting tools and materials
- Any tool you will use for Cleansing, Consecrating and Charging

Black tourmaline by itself is a powerful stone that is able to absorb all negative energies, especially those conjured by a black magick. Furthermore, when combined with a quartz crystal, that energy can then be transformed into positive energy that rejuvenates the person holding or wearing it.

If you are a crafty person, I suggest creating an amulet that combines these two stones; if not, then it's good enough to carry these two stones in a pouch and wear it around your neck. Either way, cleanse, consecrate, and charge your stones for the purpose of absorbing energy and feeding it back into the wearer before you actually craft the amulet—it really is that simple.

Mirror Reversal

Components
- Black Salt
- 2 Bowls
- Link
- Mirror

This spell is intended to reflect the curse back to the person who originally cast it. Before casting this spell, you need to identify the person who sent the negative energy. To discover this, ask yourself if you know anyone who is a practitioner whom you may have pissed off—they will likely be the culprit. If you are still not sure, use divination to verify your suspicion. Also remember that it may not be a practitioner at all—it could be someone who just hates you so much they have sent out an intentional or unintentional attack.

Once you have identified the caster, you must collect some kind of tag-lock. This can be a personal item such as a lock of hair, clothing item, or fingernail clipping—or if you don't have any of this, simply write the person's name down on a small sliver of paper.

If you want the spell to be more powerful, create a poppet. Use the small piece of paper or personal item(s) in this creation. If you are not sure how to create a poppet, you can find that information in the spells section of the book under Poppets.

Next fill the bottom of one of the bowls with black salt. Consecrate and charge your mirror for the purpose of reflecting magick back at targets, then place it in the center of the bowl of black salt facing upright. After you have done this, place the personal item of the caster, or his poppet in the other bowl. Finally, point the mirror at the bowl that holds the personal item or poppet. From this point on, any magick that is cast in your direction by the person who cursed you will be reflected back to him and enhanced by the power of the black salt.

Binding and Banishing via Poppet

Components
- Wax Poppet
- Cotton Cord
- Glue
- Black Tourmaline Powder
- Black Salt

This spell is used to bind a highly negative target from doing harm to others, then expel him or her from your presence or a premises. The cord, which has been coated with black tourmaline, is meant to feed off of any negative energies the target generate, which is then used to strengthen the binding power of the cord. This will make it virtually impossible to break.

Creation of the Poppet
Before performing this ritual, melt some wax by double boiling it. Take a large pot and fill it with about an inch or two of water. As you are creating this poppet, know that it will become a direct link to the individual it represents. Fill a glass bowl with enough wax to form your poppet. Place the

glass bowl in the water. If you think the glass bowl may become unstable when the water is boiled, pour out the excess water until the bottom of the glass bowl almost rests on the bottom of the pot. Bring the water to a boil, then lower the temperature to a simmer.

Monitor the wax while as it melts and reduce heat if water is boiling too rapidly or if it is melting too quick. Do not walk away until the melting is complete. Once the wax has melted, turn the heat off, remove from heat, and carefully remove the bowl from the water using a pot holder.

If you have made or bought a mold of human form, carefully pour the hot wax into it, then set it somewhere to cool. If you will be forming the mold by hand, then set the wax somewhere to cool. As it cools, expose the hot core of the wax by stirring it occasionally. Allow the wax to lower to a temperature that is suitable enough to be picked up and molded like clay—you can use a cooking thermometer for this. Once the wax is cool enough, pick it up and begin shaping it with your hands. Because wax sometimes flakes, you may want to put down some wax paper. By doing this, you can simply recover the wax by picking up the wax paper and pouring it back into the bowl so that you can use it for another project.

Using a probing device about the width of a pencil, create four holes; one in the head, chest, stomach, and groin. These holes will be used to fill with your tag-locks, herbs, and any other components you want to incorporate. With the remaining wax, form four tiny balls, large enough to plug those holes. Finally, set the poppet and plugs to the side.

Creation of the Black Salt of Banishment

Components
- 2 parts Sea Salt
- 1 part Black Pepper
- 1 part Ash

Remember: as you create this black salt, know that it is being created for the purpose of banishing. You will of course want to cleanse, consecrate, and charge all these things within your circle, for the purpose of binding and banishing. Place the black pepper and cauldron scrapings in a mortar and pastel and thoroughly grind. Finally, add the salt and blend—set the black salt aside.

Creation of the Cord of Binding

Take a small piece of black tourmaline, place it in a paper sack (or leather), and pulverize it on a solid surface using a hammer until it becomes powder. Place a piece of wax paper on a flat surface and pour the black tourmaline powder onto it. Spread the powder out until it covers a large enough area. Squirt enough glue to soak the cotton cord in a small paper cup. Cut enough cord to sufficiently entwine your poppet from head to toe. Coat the cord with glue, remove it from the cup, and place it in the black tourmaline powder. Coat the cord with the powder by rolling or sprinkling, then remove the cord and hang it somewhere to dry.

Performance

Although this spell can be performed at any time, it is ideally performed on the dark moon in the hour of Mars (God of War).

Place the poppet, cord, tag-locks, and all other components on your altar and cleanse each one using holy water and sage. As you cleanse these items, lay them on your pentagram.

Take a moment to connect with any spirits or deities that you have called, then ask them to bless all items for this work. You might say something like this:

> "All spirits, elementals, divine ones (and so on) present, put your power toward binding and banishing NAME by blessings these items from this purpose."

Take up your athame.

Charge the Black Salt of Banishing with Intent

Taking energy from the environment, channel it through the crown chakra, down your spine, through your arm, through athame, and into the salt. Once you feel the salt has been complete charged with energy, focus your intent in the same manner with your athame and impress the salt with the idea of banishment. This salt will cause this person to flee.

Charge the Cord with Intent

Draw energy from your natural environment, allowing it to pass through your crown chakra into your head, down your spine, through your arm, into your athame, and connect with the cord. Once the cord is absolutely bursting with energy, program it with intent. Know that the cord with bind your target from doing any harm, while the black tourmaline powder will suck negative energy from that person and empower the cord's ability to bind. Stop once you know that the intent is firmly fixed in the cord.

You may want to say some words like the following:

> "With this cord entwined, I give it the power to banish and bind."

Charge the Poppet with Intent

Pick up the tag-lock and stuff it into the hole formed in its head. Draw the natural energies from your surroundings through your crown chakra. Allowing it to pass through your head, down your spine, into your arm, through the athame, and finally into the poppet. Once the poppet is fully charged, visualize the person you are trying bind and banish and send this idea to the charged poppet. When you have completely imagined that person, finish by saying,

> "Force of Spirit, breath of life, bind this soul to doll alike, and when magick is worked upon this doll, on X shall it come to call."

///

Say something in the manner of this:

"With this salt, you are banished. Flee from my sight and return no more."

Sprinkle the salt in each cavity and seal with wax plugs.

Finally, read this babblogue passage. The power key unlocks abyssal energies that finalize the spell and set it into motion. I have provided both the babblogue as well as its translation. To make it easier to read, I have spelled it out for you phonetically.

Babblogue:

EH-NOED EP TETH-HEP!
AJNORAM, AL TEMPEST QUAL!
MOR-GAN-OOM ES DOCH NEL SIN-TET!

Translation:

Behold, I tap into the living darkness!
Almighty lord of air, bringer of terrible storms!
Morgana in her fullness is the bringer of stillness complete!

Finishing by saying, "So mote it be."

HOW TO TRAP A SPIRITS

When casting any spell, you want to make use of items that embody the purpose of that spell, this is why a jar, box, Witch ball, or any other vessel that can be sealed serves as the perfect tool to capture and contain a spirit. It is not the physical vessel that holds the spirit, but the idea that it can contain and trap that gives it its power.

The most common type of vessel used to trap spirits is a Witch ball. This is typically an intricately threaded colorful ball of blown glass that was hung at an entryway outside of one's home. Witch balls are still produced today and can be found in a great array of colors. When you purchase a

Witch ball, you need to cleanse, consecrate, and charge it for the purpose of binding in order to make it truly effective.

Spell to Charge Spirit Vessel

Components
- Vessel
- Wand
- PentagramA Spool of Fine Black Thread
- Black Tourmaline

Cleanse, Consecrate, and Charge for the purpose of binding.

Sage, then asperge the vessel with holy water.

Next, call upon the deity Odin to bless the vessel with the power to attract and trap evil spirits.

Next, draw a Valknut, on the South, East, West, Top, and Bottom of the jar or ball. The word *Valknut* stems from two old Norse words *valr*, meaning "slain warriors," and *knut*, meaning "knot." The symbol itself is thought to mean, "Knot of those who have fallen in battle." This symbol was oftentimes found on stones, long ships and urns, along with statues of Odin where men had been buried or entombed. According to historian H. R. Ellis Davidson, "Odin had the power to lay bonds upon the mind so that men became helpless in battle and he could also loosen the tensions of fear and strain by his gifts of battle-madness, intoxication and inspiration." So this symbol is most likely is a sigilized representation of that power. Keep this in mind while painting the Valknut on your vessel.

Unwind the black thread, then tangle it into a rat's nest. As you do this tangle, the thread say,

"With this thread I entwine, so the spirits it shall bind."

The intent you hold in mind should be that this thread is being charged with the power to entangle and bind spirits. If this spell is being cast by more than one person, you should pass the thread around and everyone should chant. This process should both raise enough energy and charge the thread for the purpose of binding.

Within the bottle, you may place an assortment of items. Make sure and cleanse, consecrate, and charge each item for the purpose of binding before adding them to the bottle. My direct experience with black tourmaline has convinced me that it is great for the purpose of binding spirits. I once made an amulet of protection for a former lover. After breaking up with me, I decided to astral project to his home to spy on him. Incidentally, he had the amulet hanging on a bookshelf. Being a novice at projection at the time, I decided I wanted to know what the amulet looked like in spirit, so I floated over to it to take a look. After taking a good long look at it and seeing nothing unusual, I became disinterested and went on my way. As I turned I found myself back facing it once more. Thinking that this was just a trick of the mind, I turned away from it again and coasted to a different part of the room. Once again, I was draw back to the black tourmaline amulet—eyes locked in place. At that point, I became annoyed and whisked into another room. Again, I found myself facing the amulet. It was only after a long struggle that I was able to unlock from it and come back to my body. For this reason, do include black tourmaline.

Once you have placed all items in the bottle, seal it and sit or hang it near a door or window. Let it remain there until a spirit has been captured, then dispose of it by burying it in the earth far from your home or opening the vessel and tossing the contents in a river.

How Do You Know If You've Trapped A Spirit?

I'm sure a lot of you are wondering, how can you really know if you've trapped a spirit or not. I'll answer this question using magical theory, paranormal theory and logic. If there is a spirit in the jar, then it may be putting off an electromagnetic field—however if the spirit is bound (hopefully), it might be incapable of doing anything and therefore may be unable to create a field. If it can produce an electromagnetic field, that also means it can draw electrical energy from outside sources and the jar will be cooler than its surrounding environment. This means you could use a thermometer to gauge the temperature of the jar against its temperature of the surrounding environment. Like I said, if this is the case, you need to get rid of that jar ASAP because it means that spirit is drawing power and could possibly escape.

The next method of determining whether a spirit has been entrapped is a psychic one. If you have followed the exercises in this book, you should have developed your psychic senses. But if you are not quite there, you can use an ideomotor motor device, such as a pendulum, or divining rods to answer the question, "Is a spirit trapped in the jar?"

Another thing to keep in mind is the maxim "As Above, So Below" or "As Within, So Without." This means that negative energy may affect the jar, or its contents and this will be reflected in its color, or condition. In other words, the glass of the jar may be fractured, the lid may be warped, or the contents might be awry.

Divination

The art or practice that seeks to foresee or foretell future events or discover hidden knowledge usually by the interpretation of omens or by the aid of supernatural powers.

DEFINITION BY MERRIAM-WEBSTER DICTIONARY,

A s you might have guessed from reading the definition above, divination includes any technique used by a psychic or practitioners of magick to gather information about a person, place, or thing that resides somewhere in the past, present, or future. This means not only can divination be used to read people who are sitting right in front of you, but also it can be used to connect with spiritual forces not present within the physical world.

Of these techniques, there are many. So many in fact, that I cannot possibly cover all of them here in this book—however, I will cover those methods I feel are better than others. All of these techniques seem to fall into one of two categories: systems based on interpreting seemingly random patterns and systems that rely on insight or extrasensory perception.

What makes each one of these systems work? Well, everyone has their own opinion. There are those who believe that nothing is truly random, so when you ask a question, then lay down random tarot card or rune you can "read" a pattern that has been predestined. There are also those who believe that there is a spiritual influence involved—that is, the spirits or gods are responsible for changing the order of the cards by some act of fate in order to reflect the correct answers. Still others believe that no valuable information can be garnered by drawing random cards or runes. Therefore, they use those symbols as a type of foci to direct their own natural psychic intuitive ability to a particular subject.

But no matter what you believe, one thing is true: you cannot accurately glean information using divination without drawing upon your intuition. Simply put, without good extrasensory perception, your readings will end up being so general that the results can be applied to just about anyone under any circumstances. At best, this kind of reading will get a few lucky hits, or worst, be totally off base and waste your time or your client's time. But before we get into these methods, let's talk about the nature of reading itself, or what I call the Prediction Paradox.

THE PREDICTION PARADOX

As you have read earlier, thoughts shape reality. Therefore, everyone is shaping their future all the time by what they think. This means, whenever you or someone else becomes aware of their future, that future will change in accordance with any new knowledge that has been exposed. For this reason, you are actually shaping a person's future, every time you reveal it using divination—this is why the possible future is ever-changing.

This can be a good thing or a bad thing, because you may be able to help someone avoid a bad situation by making them aware of it, or you could cause something bad to happen if what you reveal invokes fear and anxiety. And the implications become even worse if you doing a reading without any kind of psychic connection, because you could unintentionally predict something that was never really meant to be. So to avoid the bad karma that comes along with manifesting a harmful future for someone by giving them advice, simply choose not to read for someone if you don't feel you have a good enough connection.

Even so, there may be times when you see calamity—no one's life is perfect. In such case what is the best course of action? My best advice for you is to avoid reading for people who are highly emotional, or are mentally unstable, because if you do detect something bad and tell them about it, the powerful emotions such revelations create, will just feed that future and cause it to manifest with a ferocity. But if you feel the querent is emotionally stable enough deal with it and willing to listen, you can give them "the speech," then proceed with the reading and tell them what you see afterward. The purpose of "the speech" is to counsel the querent against erroneously believing their future is set in stone, or cannot be changed.

It may go something like this…

> "There is no such thing as a future that is set in stone. This means, you always have the option of changing something you don't like. But in order to do that, you need to stay positive and make the right choices. I know it can be difficult to stay positive a midst such turmoil, but it is important, because what we think and feel, dictates what our future will be."

Once you have given this speech, given them their reading, then explain to them what you have seen and give helpful advice. If in the end they ask you to intervene in that future, be cautious—because even though you may be able to help them, it may not be your place and your intervention could very well make it worse. Say for example you foresaw the end of a person's current relationship: if you were to use magick to try to keep the couple together, you may be preserving a relationship that is meant to end. Maybe that person is meant to be with someone else, or maybe there is physical, mental, or sexual abuse. If a person is not ready to change, or is not willing to take your advice, or if changing that future will hurt another, you shouldn't help them. As a matter of fact, if you tried, you would probably fail, because what they want is contrary to the help you would try to give them. And if you do end up using magick to help someone and that magick ends up hurting innocent people around them, you would suffer the bad karma.

Random Methods

RUNES

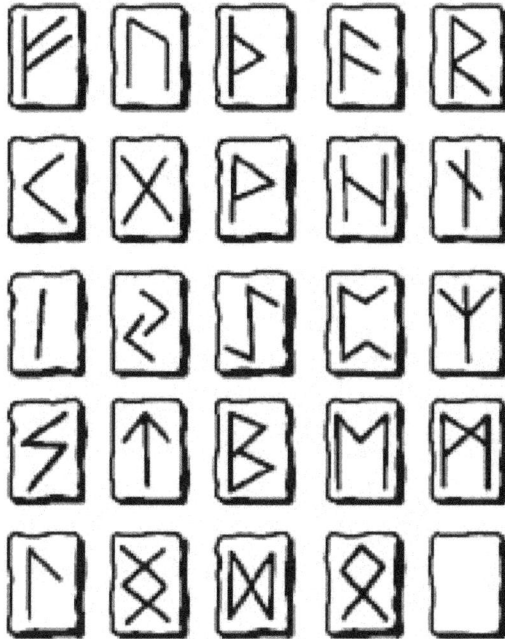

Let me start by saying that runes are a very ancient system of divination, similar to tarot. There are different types of runes, stemming from different cultures; Anglo-Saxon, Futhorc, Cirth, Elder Futhark, Gothic, and Hungarian. Runes have been found on ancient weapons, monolithic stones and shield all over Europe and Scandinavia. These twenty-four symbols were the origin of our alphabet. They were thought to have supernatural powers and had very special meanings to our ancestors.

Runes are typically kept in a pouch and laid or poured out over a cloth. Runes can be made of any materials, but they are typically made of stone or wood. Although runes are similar to Tarot, the symbols themselves do not reveal specific information about the situation of the person being read. Because of this, reading runes requires one to draw insight through mediation.

There are as many methods for choosing a rune as there are spreads in Tarot; they can be pulled from the pouch randomly or chosen by the diviner based on feeling—ex. the one that calls out to you. Just like any form of divination, the querent must concentrate on the question being asked before any runes can be drawn. The act of concentration upon the question is the key that makes drawing the rune more than just a random gesture. Besides this, you should already be in a medium-to-heavy trance state from the act of opening your sacred space.

Method

Draw your first rune. This rune drawn would represent the situation surrounding the question. Any other runes drawn elaborate on the situation and will shed light on what would happen if the you continued along the same path.

You could also use a three-rune draw to represent; past, present, future by choosing three runes and laying them side by side on your cloth. In this case, the past would allude to what attitudes, choices or event caused the situation, the present rune would represent attitudes, actions and events that are happening currently and lastly, the future rune represents what might happen if the you continued along the same path while holding the same attitudes and take your intended course of actions. Every other rune you draw at this point will elaborate on the last.

It doesn't matter how complicated your rune spread is. No matter how many runes you draw or what configuration, you will have to draw upon your intuition and insight to read them. To do this, you will have to spend time studying each rune, meditating on their significance, then relying on the sensations that surface in your mind when actually using them. Consider each rune as a mental gateway by which you can explore various situations in your life or magical workings.

TAROT

The Tarot is a set of cards divided into twenty-two trump cards called the Major Arcana and fifty-six suit cards, referred to as the Minor Arcana. These cards were first used to play games such as Tarocchini and French Tarot throughout Europe during the mid-fifteenth century, but were adapted in the eighteenth century for the purposes of divination.

These cards are read in the same manner as runes, they can be pulled randomly and laid out on a table, or they can be chosen purposefully. The nature of the cards is highly pictorial, with each card being jamb packed with symbolism. These symbols link directly to the subconscious, allowing the reader to tap into the World of Spirit to find the answers needed.

The Tarot has been described as the the Fool's journey, depicting every permutation of events that may happen from life to death. The images and association within tarot describe the whole of magical philosophy, astrology and spiritual involvement. It can be used as a teaching lesson, as well as in spellcraft to build intent.

There are as many different types of Tarot decks as there are versions of the Bible—maybe more, each artistically unique and with varying numbers of cards and different themes. The Rider Waite deck is the most popular because it contains the standard number of cards and standard symbolism. However, when choosing cards, just like any other divination tool, you should choose a deck that calls to you.

When you get your first deck, you must take the time to study each of the cards to develop a mental and spiritual link. There is no need to start off by buying a book on how to read, just thumb through your cards and study what the symbolism depicts. I should really add that it helps to be familiar with occult symbolism first before you can expect to understand what is contained within a card. Allow enough time for each card to soak in and revisit any cards that you have trouble connecting with. If you still have trouble connecting with a card, then don't be afraid to ask any deities that you work with to reveal its meaning to you. Don't forget to write these impressions down in your magical journal after you have finished meditating.

After you have explored your cards, it's the right time to go out and buy a book on reading tarot. Just note that the interpretations of these cards are highly subjective—meanings different books will say different things. Don't let the fact that your interpretation of a card is different from what some author says dissuade you from doing readings. Take the author's interpretations as a suggestion and realize the most important most accurate meaning is the one that resonates with you at the time of the reading.

Having said this, let's go over a few basics. The first thing you should do after getting a set of cards is to consecrate them and bless them to the works of divination. Do this by opening a circle and passing them three times through the smoke of incense. Say some choice words such as "I dedicate and charge these cards for the work of divination, in the name of the [Insert God/Goddess Names Here]." As you say the words know that they are being charged and activated for this divine purpose. From hence forth, wrap your cards in a protective cloth of natural fiber or keep them stowed away in a box away from prying eyes. Keep them contained until the time of their use.

How to Read the Cards

Step 1

Before you read your cards, open a circle or, at a minimum, take the time to surround yourself with light by summoning the light from within and expanding it to encompass the area of the reading. At this point, you should call upon aid and counsel of any deities of divination, prophecy, or fate. Then, take your cards out and place them on the table.

Step 2

Instruct the querent to shuffle the deck, concentrating on the question they want to ask—if you are the querent, then you shuffle the cards. While the querent is shuffling, you should be getting into a medium-to-heavy trance. Just remind the querent that Tarot cards can be expensive, so they need to treat them delicately—I have seen clients ruin cards. Then tell them, once they are ready to lay the cards down.

Step 3

Once you are in the right place, cut the cards, then lay them out in a spread. A spread is a configuration of cards that describes relations and meaning. There are many different spreads used for many different occasions. Each position of the spread gives the card holding that position meaning and context. Even though you can do a reading using only one card, using more than one is always better—so let's talk about spreads.

One-Card Spread

This spread answers a single question that relates to the past, present, or future.

Three-Card Spread

Like the three-card rune spread described under Runes; draw one card to represent the past, one for the present and the last for the future.

Cross Spread

The cross spread is made up of five cards; middle, left, right, top, and bottom. These cards represent the querent's current situation (middle), influences (top), expectations (bottom), the near past (left) and the near future (right.)

Center Position: The Current

This card represents the querent or his or her current situation or both. If this is a face card, it could represent the querent him or herself, if that face card mirrors the querent's attributes. Otherwise, it could represent someone who currently has a major influence in his or her life. All other cards insinuate what is happening in the querent's life at the time. Please note, people sometimes dwell on the past. Therefore, this card may represent something that is currently haunting the querent.

Top Position: Influences

Everyone's thoughts and actions are motivated or influenced by other people and what is happening in their surroundings. That is what a card in this position depicts. This card is extremely important because, what influences us, shapes our expectations and thus manifests in the future. If those influences are positive, we usually have a positive outlook and that reflects into a bright future. However, if our influences are bad, we expect things to go wrong and therefore they do.

Bottom Position: Expectations

This card answers the question "What do you expect to happen?" and that is always shaped by our environment, the people in our lives and our attitudes about life itself—in other words the top position, Influences. Once those expectations are formed, we begin building those thought-forms in the astral and they eventually find a way to manifest.

Right Position: The Near Past

This card represents important events that have happened in the near past—that could be one week ago, or several months ago. Those events cannot be changed of course, but do have the same effect as cards in the influences position. You can chronicle more distant events by laying down more cards under that one, each representing a moment in time, before the last.

Left Position: The Near Future

This card represents what is being shaped and is likely to manifest due to expectations. Looking at this will tell you more about how the querent sees and feels about the world, the people in it, their goals and his or her own life. You can chronicle successively more distant events in the future, in the same way you do the past.

As you can see, each card in a spread provides details about a particular aspect of you of the querent's life. It really doesn't matter where you put them, only what that card is trying to answer. Feel free to create your own spreads. However, before you use it, know what each position in that spread means and be familiar with it.

Whole books have been dedicated to the art of Tarot reading, so I cannot possibly go over them all, but there some things that you may want to consider when looking at a spread. The suits, which are swords or daggers, pentacles, coins of discs, wands or staves and chalices or cups, are related to the elements and represent different influences. Also, it is not a coincidence that these suits mirror the tools you use as a Sorcerer.

Suit Correspondence

Suit	Element	Correspondence
Swords or Daggers	Air	Education, Debate, Conflict
Pentacle, Coin, or Discs	Earth	Money, Material Goods, Health
Wands or Staves	Fire	Ambitions, Lust, Highly Charged Social Interactions, Powers
Chalices or Cups	Water	Happiness or Emotional Strife, Birth, Health, Spirituality

Finding a majority of one of these suits in a spread indicates an overlying issue or influence within the reading. For example, pay attention to how many upright and reversed cards there are. Majority upright means that the querent is a positive person and is surrounded by positive influences, whereas majority reversed cards means the querent may have a negative mind-set or may be surrounded by negative influences.

Having a majority of swords in a spread may mean the querent is surrounded by bickering and strife or focused on higher learning. A majority of Wands might mean querent is a leader or is ambitious. Majority cups may mean the querent is spiritually grounded or well connected to Spirit.

Major Arcana cards represent pivotal points in a person's life and should be given special consideration. One card next to another card can change its meaning, such as the Burning Tower (Major Arcana) and the Devil. This would, of course, be a very bad omen, whereas the Magician next to the High Priestess would be a good omen that might mean a union between two soul mates who are both very spiritual. Let your intuition guide you. Don't be afraid to pull from what you feel. Just remember: even though Tarot is one of the most complicated divination systems out there, it can be one of the most fruitful.

GEOMANCY

Geomancy is a type of augury (divination by interpretation of patterns) that was thought to come out of Arabia or Persia. The word *geomancy* actually means "earth divination" because results were usually generated by hitting the sand with a stick or by casting pebbles. Used since the time of Greece and Rome, it entered Africa and became Afa and Ifa, but the techniques and interpretations most are familiar with today came from texts that entered Europe through Spain sometime around the twelfth century.

Geomancy uses randomly generated ones and twos that are stacked in four levels to create fifteen unique figures that are laid out in a type of spread called a shield. Once laid out in a shield configuration, they can then be interpreted in much the same way as tarot. But in order really to understand geomancy you must understand the anatomy of these geomantic figures.

At a passing glance, one might think geomancy is too simplistic to be of any use, but upon further examination, it's easy to see that it is good at representing the energies or currents that surround the querent. But like other rune systems that have limited basic meanings, the figures generated must be interpreted using the intuition. Whether the numerological calculations used in the popular "Shield" layout (like a tarot spread) have any real barring on the trueness of the ruins created remains to be seen.

The Anatomy of a Geomantic Figure

Each figure is made up of four levels of dots called the head, neck, body, and feet.

Example using Cuada Draconis:

♦ ←		Head
♦ ←		Neck
♦ ←		Body
♦♦ ←		Feet

And each level is associated with a classical element.

Head	→	Fire
Neck	→	Air
Body	→	Water
Feet	→	Earth

Each unique figure also has its own elemental association.

Laetitia, Cauda Draconis, Fortuna Minor, Amissio	→	Fire
Albus, Puella, Tristitia	→	Air
Populus, Via, Rubeus, Laetitia	→	Water
Amissio, Conjunctio, Caput Draconis, Carcer	→	Earth

When determining the ultimate meaning of a figure, one needs to keep in mind the nature of the elements affecting it; for example, fire represents the active energy of one's will or true desires. Air means trying to figure something out or resolving it through understanding or conflict. Water can mean reflection, an emotional state, intuition or creativity and earth can be an indication of stability, maturity, or even narrow-mindedness.

An element is said to be either passive or active according to the number of dots it has. Two dots are considered active, while one is passive. Being active means its effect will probably be long term, while being passive means that effect will most likely be transient or temporary. Because each figure has four levels that can be made up of one or two dots it means that each figure can manifest in sixteen different ways. By default, a figure's ruling element is always considered active, the only exception being Populus which is passive by nature. This means a figure's interpretation is not only influenced by the element that rules it, but also the active or passive states of its head, neck, body and feet.

So now that you know how a figure works, now you just have to acquaint yourself with the meaning of the figures themselves.

Figures Meanings

Via (The Way)

Resembles: A Path
Elements: Inner (Water), Outer (Water)
Planets: The Moon
Astrological Signs: Cancer
Deities: Diana and Mercury
Angels: Gabriel and Muriel
Body: Stomach
Behavior: Inverts the figure that follows it
Meaning: Change

Cauda Draconis (Tail of the Dragon)

Resembles: The Southern Point of the Moon
Elements: Inner (Fire), Outer (Fire)
Planets: Saturn and Mars
Astrological Signs: Virgo
Deities: Mavors, Saturn, and Athena
Angels: Cassiel, Samael, and Malchidael
Body: Left Arm
Behavior: Neutral
Meaning: The end of things

Puer (The Boy)
Resembles: A Sword or Erect Phallus
Elements: Inner (Air), Outer (Water)
Planets: Mars
Astrological Signs: Aries and Mars
Deities: Mavors and Athena
Angels: Samael and Malchidael
Body: Head
Behavior: Masculine
Meaning: Passion, aggression, and sometimes war

Fortuna Minor (Lesser Fortune)
Represents: Sun Beams
Elements: Inner (Fire), Outer (Fire)
Planets: Sun
Astrological Signs: Leo and the Sun
Deities: Apollo and Jupiter
Angels: Michael and Verchiel
Body: Spine
Behavior: Positive but Passive Aggressive
Meaning: Minimal and sometimes temporary success

Puella (The Girl)
Resembles: A Vulva or Exaggerated Breasts
Elements: (Inner) Water, (Outer) Air
Planets: Venus
Astrological Signs: Libra and Venus
Deities: Venus and Vulcanus
Angels: Anael and Zuriel
Body: Kidneys, Lower Back, Buttocks, and Skin
Behavior: Feminine. Balances the masculine energy of Puer
Meaning: Gracefulness, gentleness, empathy, intuition, and beauty

Amissio (Loss)
Resembles: Two Overturned Bowls or Cups
Elements: (Inner) Fire, (Outer) Earth
Planets: Venus
Astrological Signs: Taurus and Venus Retrograde
Deities: Venus
Angels: Anael and Asmodel
Body: Neck and Throat
Behavior: Neutral
Meaning: Loss, or something unattainable

Carcer (The Prison)

Resembles: A Cell, Link in a Chain or Prison
Elements: (Inner) Earth, (Outer) Earth
Planets: Saturn
Astrological Signs: Capricorn and Saturn Retrograde
Deities: Saturn and Vesta
Angels: Cassiel and Hanael
Body: Knees and Skeletal System
Behavior: Neutral
Meaning: Delay, restriction, setback, or binding

Laetitia (Joy)

Resembles: An Arch, Fountain, or Rainbow
Elements: (Inner) Water, (Outer) Fire
Planets: Jupiter
Astrological Signs: Pisces and Jupiter Retrograde
Deities: Jove and Neptune
Angels: Sachiel and Barchiel
Body: Feet
Behavior: Neutral
Meaning: Happiness, joy, and favorable outcome

Caput Draconis (Head of the Dragon)
Resembles: North Point of the Moon
Elements: (Inner) Earth, (Outer) Fire
Planets: Jupiter and Venus
Astrological Signs: Sagittarius
Deities: Venus, Iove, and Vulcan
Angels: Sachiel, Anael, and Zuriel
Body: Right Arm
Behavior: Intensifies the figure that follows it
Meaning: Can be a good or bad omen

Conjunctio (The Conjunction)
Resembles: Crossroads or Joining of Two Figures
Elements: (Inner) Air, (Outer) Earth
Planets: Mercury
Astrological Signs: Mercury and Ceres
Deities: Mercury
Angels: Raphael and Hamaliel
Body: Digestive System
Behavior: Consumes the figure that follows it, creating an entirely new figure by the adding the dots and determining if they are odd or even
Meaning: The joining of two or more forces for good or ill

Acquisitio

Resembles: Two upright Bowls or Cups
Elements: (Inner) Air, (Outer) Fire
Planets: Jupiter
Astrological Signs: Sagittarius and Jupiter
Deities: Jove and Diana
Angels: Sachiel and Adnachiel
Body: Hips and Thighs
Behavior: Neutral
Meaning: Acquisition, accomplishment, especially in finances

Rubeus (Red)

Resembles: An Overturned Glass
Elements: (Inner) Air, (Outer) Water
Planets: Mars
Astrological Signs: Scorpio and Mars Retrograde
Deities: Mavors
Angels: Samael and Barbiel
Body: Genitals and Excretory System
Behavior: Neutral
Meaning: Debauchery, deception, violence, and vice

Fortuna Major (Greater Fortune)
Resembles: An Upright Glass
Elements: (Inner) Earth, (Outer) Fire
Planets: Sun
Astrological Signs: Leo
Deities: Apollo and Jupiter
Angels: Michael and Verchiel
Body: Heart and Chest
Behavior: Neutral
Meaning: Blessings, growth, and major fortune

Albus (White)
Resembles: An Upright Glass
Elements: (Inner) Water, (Outer) Air
Planets: Mercury
Astrological Signs: Gemini and Mercury
Deities: Mercurius and Apollo
Angels: Raphael and Ambriel
Body: Shoulders and Lungs
Behavior: Neutral
Meaning: Peace, wisdom, and purity

Tristitia (Sorrow)

Resembles: A Broken Arch or a Stake Driven into the Ground
Elements: (Inner) Earth, (Outer) Air
Planets: Mercury
Astrological Signs: Aquarius and Saturn
Deities: Saturn and Juno
Angels: Cassiel and Gabriel
Body: Ankles and Lower Legs
Behavior: Neutral
Meaning: Mental or physical pain and suffering

Populus (The People)

Resembles: Two Columns of People
Elements: (Inner) Water, (Outer) Water
Planets: Moon
Astrological Signs: Cancer and the waxing Moon
Deities: Diana and Mercury
Angels: Gabriel and Muriel
Body: The Breasts and Torso
Behavior: Neutral
Meaning: An assembly of people, a public event, crowd mentality, peer pressure

Generating the Figures

In order to use figures in any layout or spread, you need to be able to create them by producing random ones and twos. This can be done in several ways.

- Make a series of ones and twos by jotting them down in sequence without purposefully focusing on what you are doing as if you were using automatic writing.
- Flip a coin—heads represent two dots, and tails represent one dot.
- Roll a die—an even number means two dots, and an odd number is one dot.
- Use a special geomancy tool that you have either made or bought.

Once you decide how you will generate these random numbers, you can decide what layout or spread to use.

LAYOUTS AND INTERPRETATIONS

Like most forms of divination, the figures, runes, and cards can be interpreted by themselves or in a layout. This means you could generate a single figure and analyze it for its properties to determine the likely outcome of any situation. But if you want to answer complex questions, you must generate many geomantic figures and lay them out in a spread. A geomantic layout uses astrological houses to give even more meaning to its figures. If you decide to use this method, I describe each step of the process below, but there is no reason you can't generate these figures and lay them out in a unique spread of your own—the simple three-card spread or cross spread described in this chapter used for tarot would be ideal for this.

The Shield Layout

As stated above, the shield layout is a type of spread based on astrological houses. This layout is made up of a family of four Mothers, four Daughters, and four Nieces as well as two Witnesses and one Judge. To create the Mothers and use them to calculate the Daughters, Nieces, Witnesses, and the Judge.

To Create the Mothers (Maters)

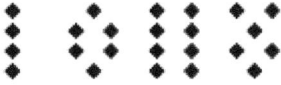

Generate four sets of four one-two dot results using one of the methods described above. Arrange those dots in four rows and four columns. These dots represent the four Mothers.

To Create the Daughters (Filiae)

Use the dots from each column of the first, second, third and last row of the Mothers to create the four daughters.

To Create the Nieces (Neptis)

Of the Nieces, there are four. The first Niece is generated by adding the head, neck, body, and feet of the first Mother to get an odd or even result. If the result is odd, then one dot is generated; if the result is even, two dots are generated. The second Niece is created using the same process as the first except the third and fourth Mothers are used. The third and fourth Nieces are generated like the first and second Nieces, but use the Daughters instead.

First Niece using the first and second Mother:

Calculation	Figure
$1 + 1 = 2$	
$1 + 2 = 1$	
$1 + 2 = 1$	
$1 + 1 = 1$	

Second Niece using the third and fourth Mother:

Calculation   Figure
2 + 2 = 2
2 + 1 = 1
2 + 2 = 2
2 + 1 = 1

Third Niece using the first and second Daughter:

Calculation   Figure
1 + 1 = 2
1 + 2 = 1
2 + 2 = 2
2 + 1 = 2

Fourth Niece using the third and fourth Daughter

Calculation   Figure
1 + 1 = 2
2 + 1 = 1
2 + 2 = 2
2 + 1 = 1

To Create the Witnesses (Testes)

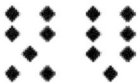

Of the Witnesses, there are two. These Witnesses are created in the same manner as the Nieces, but in this case, the first Witness is made up of the first and second Niece, and the last Witness is made up of the third and fourth Niece.

First Witness using the first and second Niece

Calculation   Figure

2 + 2 = 2
1 + 1 = 2
1 + 2 = 1
1 + 1 = 2

Second Witness using the third and fourth Niece

Calculation   Figure

2 + 2 = 2
1 + 1 = 2
2 + 2 = 2
2 + 1 = 1

To Create the Judge (Iudex or Judex)

Calculation   Figure

2 + 2 = 2
2 + 2 = 2
1 + 2 = 1
2 + 1 = 1

There is only one judge and that judge is created by adding the Witness together.

Laying Out the Shield

Once you have created all these figures you can lay them out in their proper houses. The image below shows the layout as well as which house corresponds to which position.

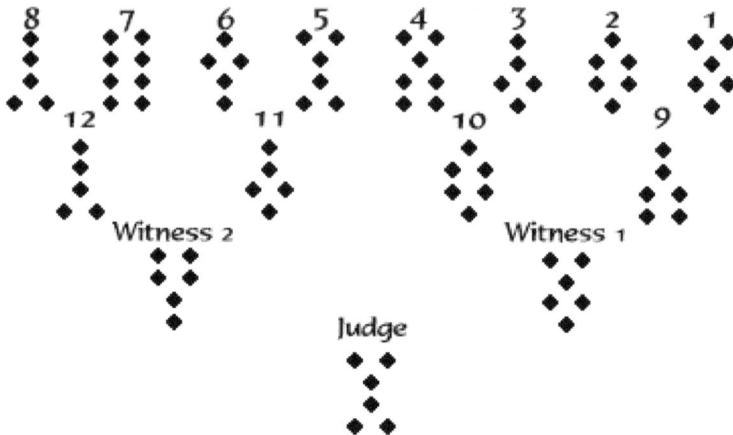

Each astrological house governs a particular area of a person's life. Although the system below was used throughout the Middle Ages and Renaissance to answer common questions governing the lives of our ancestors, it can still be applied to modern folks too.

House	Latin	English
1	Vita	Life
2	Lucrum	Riches
3	Fraters	Brothers
4	Genitor	Father
5	Nati	Sons
6	Valetudo	Health
7	Uxor	Wife
8	Mors	Death
9	Itineris	Journey
10	Regnum	Kings
11	Benefacta	Good Fortune
12	Carcer	Prison

In this system, the reader would look to the figure occupying a particular house to give that figure more context. For example, if you want to determine if you will return home safe after a long journey you would look to the figure occupying the Ninth House (Journey), or if you wanted to see if you will get that promotion you were waiting for, you could look at the figure sitting in House 2 or 11 (Riches and Good Fortune). But the most important figures are the Witnesses and the Judge.

The First Witness, sometimes called Past Testimony or The Father of the Judge, reveals what lead up to the question or why the question is being asked in the first place.

The Second Witness, sometimes referred to as Future Testimony or the Mother of the Judge, reveals how the energy of the question might manifest in the future because all events are caused by our true intentions.

The last figure is the Judge, which is the synthesis of all other figures and therefore determines the final outcome of the question. A Judge can be only one of eight figures; Acquisitio, Amissio, Conjunctio, Carcer, Fortuna Major, Fortuna Minor, Populus, or Via. If it is not, you miscalculated.

Further insight can be gained by comparing the Witness with the Judge: Good Judge and Witness equals great outcome; bad Judge and Witness means you will die a miserable death and then be sucked into the pits of hell (humor); a good Judge and bad witness means you will be successful but only after you have struggled; and bad Judge but good Witnesses means you might be successful but it won't last long. Lastly, if you seem to have difficulty getting any meaningful information, try using one of the methods below to add more clarity.

The Reconciler

In case you are unable to get any clarity from the Judge, you can create what is called the Reconciler to shed more light on the matter. The Reconciler has also been called the Sentence, Super-Judge, Subiudex, Subjudex, or Fate. To do this, simply add the Judge to the first Mother using the same numerological method of addition (odds/evens) that you used to calculate the other figures. But if you want to the Reconciler to have more barring on the question, add the appropriate House to the Judge instead.

Nonrandom Methods

AUGURY

The word *augury* is just the ancient term used to describe prediction of future events by reading signs, called *omens*. An omen can be anything from the flight of birds to the sight of a particular animal to the happening of a series of events. Omens don't have to be bad—a rainbow, for example, is thought to be a good omen by many people.

Many omens of the past may seem silly to us today, but actually had significance to our ancestors. For example, the ancient Greeks recognized the flight of avian scavengers, such as vultures, or errant storms as signs of bad things to come—which, if you think about it, is only logical. Seeing vultures could mean that a war band has sacked a nearby city, leaving behind a trail of death, and we all know that storms cause all kinds of havoc. My point is that augury really has less to do with superstition and more to do with the logical correlation between events when cause and effect is understood. Predictions based on good knowledge and keen observation can be extremely valuable—and that is what we are aiming for. Therefore, the more you know about human psychology and nature, the more you will be able to deduce what is about to happen, and the closer you will come to the truth.

Another thing to consider are synchronicities. A synchronicity is the simultaneous occurrence of events that seem related, but that seems to have no cause. Skeptics like to think that such seemly coincidental happenings could be explain if they were able to see every single event that led up to it. Perhaps, but oftentimes a synchronistic happening defies explanation. For example, I once worked a magazine crew as a young man. Our job was to annoy people by knocking on doors and convince them to buy magazine subscriptions. This line of work took me from city to city, all across the United States. Whenever we entered a new city, they would put us up in a hotel—about four people to a room—then the next day they would drop us off in a neighborhood for us to do our thing. One evening after checking into a hotel, I struck up a conversation about Ouija boards with my crew members. They were so excited; they wanted to try it out. So we decided the next evening we would stop by the store and pick one up.

The next morning, we rolled into a neighborhood, and they dropped me off to sell magazines. After knocking on what seemed like a hundred doors, I decided I would try just one more before I called it and went back to my pickup point. After I walked up on to the desolate-looking porch of a small cottage, I knocked and waited patiently—no answer. Giving it one more try, but getting no response, I turned to leave. As I walked down the steps of the porch, I spotted an odd game-board-shaped box poking out of a garbage can in front of the house. Reaching in and pulling it out, I discovered it was none other than—you guessed it—a Ouija board! If that wasn't coincidental enough, once I got back to the street and looked at street signs to get my bearings, I discovered I was on "Planchette Street." A planchette is the pointer people put their fingers on to slide across the surface of a Ouija board and spell out words. Coincidence? I don't think so! Synchronistic, more likely.

But synchronicities are really just unconscious manifestations—that is, you unconsciously think about something, and you pull that thing into your life through the law of attraction (like attracts like). This pushing and pulling of reality happens all the time with everyone, especially when one's desires, or fears are laced with powerful emotions. My point is that cause and effect in the physical world is obvious. However, you must not forget the law of attraction as it applies to states of mind and spirit—everything is thought energy before it becomes physical. These thoughts and emotions not only can alter people's choices, but also can pull in calamity or blessings—I have personally seen, car wrecks, crimes, and disasters happen in the presence of highly negative people—all tragedies that seemly had nothing to do with what those people did or the choices they made.

Unfortunately, I can't give you a list of definitive omens—they would be too numerous to catalog and are very conditional. You must study these relationships yourself and learn to read the signs. Begin by keeping a record of all the synchronistic events that happen in your own life, then compare them with what came before, but also with your state of mind at the time. Also, observe your surroundings and the people in it. In this way, you will learn to be a highly skilled observer, and as you see, you will also develop your psychic senses in the process.

THE IDEOMOTOR EFFECT

The term ideomotor effect refers to a phenomenon whereby information is channeled from the subconscious mind, through the body via minute muscle movements into a sensitive ideomotor device that can easily be read by the user. Examples of such tools would be devices like dowsing rods, pendulums, and Ouija boards.

Because of the simple nature of these devices, they are ideally used to get Yes or No responses. But if programmed correctly, they can be used to detect charges, locate hidden resources such as water and minerals, talk to spirits, or even find missing items. Programming your ideomotor tool means you must decide what tool movement equals what response (yes, no, greater, lesser). Those tool movements will depend on the type of tool you are using. For example, a pendulum is capable of swinging up and down, left and right, and circling, while dowsing rods can open, close, and cross. Tools like talking boards (Ouija) are designed to translate more complex information by spelling out words and numbers.

Does this work? Yes. Why does it work? Because everything vibrates energetically and our bodies pick up those vibrations on subconscious level. How well does it work? The quality or validity of information wholly depends on your natural psychic sensitivity, your skill with the device, and your ability to trust yourself. Therefore, the information you receive could be fabricated by your own imagination or could come from a legitimate internal or external source. It is also worthwhile to note, if you are trying to locate something, it does not matter how far away it is, because you are actually using your psychic senses when using one of these tools. In the end, the proof boils down to your ability to validate what you have received afterward. In any case, if used correctly, an ideomotor device is the easiest and most convenient way to tap into your psychic senses.

Using an ideomotor device is a practice in trusting your instincts. This means, because all ideomotor tools rely on the micromovements of your body, you should never expect *or believe*, for that matter, that they will move on their own—they don't work using telekinesis. That is not to say that things can't move telekinetically. No, they absolutely can, just that responses are usually passed from your subconscious mind as small body movements that cause the device to move naturally.

Using an ideomotor device as a channel for spirit communication is another important subject. As mentioned above, all information is being channeled from your subconscious mind first before it is represented using your tool. This not only means that you could think you are talking to a spirit when you are actually just talking to your imagination, but it also means, unless you have developed clairvoyance, there is no way to really tell who or what you are talking to, if anything. The only solution really is to try to validate any information you get—if possible—with historical records.

Despite all this, most spirits are natural telepaths. This means, once you have made contact, expect your mind to be read. This of course is not a problem if the spirit is benign. However, if that spirit is malicious it may try to invoke a fear response, then leech that negative energy using psychic vampirism. And invisible mind readers are adept at pretending to be someone else—for example, that dead grandfather you are trying to contact, a spirit guide, or perhaps an angelic being. Lastly, just remember: just because you have tapped into your psychic senses or have contacted a spirit doesn't mean that information is necessary true—validate *everything* you get.

The Pendulum

The pendulum is perhaps the easiest tool to use. Even though pendulums can be purchased for very cheap at metaphysical stores, they are extremely easy to make. The pendulum is essentially a weighted point hanging from a cord or chain. The weight itself can be made out of anything, but is typically a stone, crystal, metal point, or even piece of heavy wood. The pendulum is used by dangling the weight by holding the end of the cord and letting it move freely. Once the weight is dangled, it can then swing left to right, up or down, or even circle clockwise, or counterclockwise.

But before you can expect to get information from your pendulum, you must program it first. To program your pendulum, first decide what each movement means. If up and down makes sense as a yes, then program it by saying, "If the answer is yes, swing up and down." Then program no by saying, "And if the answer is no, swing left to right." If you would rather get your answers by interpreting clockwise and counterclockwise motions, then program it that way by using the same method as described above. To locate something with a pendulum, program it to circle faster when over that item.

Dowsing Rods

Dowsing rods, or divining rods, as they are sometimes called, are two thin rods made of metal or wood. To use this device, simply hold one rod in your left hand and the other in your right. When you do this, make sure they are level, but ever so slightly tipping forward—this will allow them to swing. Once you have done this, you can then get yes and no responses by having them cross or open.

But before you do this, first determine what position (crossed or open) will be considered yes or no by programming them in the same way as the pendulum. For example, if you want crossed to be yes, then say, "If the answer is yes, cross." Then for no say, "And if the answer is no, open." When attempting to locate an object, spread the rods all the way open, then slowly pivot until you feel a tug. When this happens, assume that the rods will begin to come together the closer you move toward the object you are trying to find.

If you wish to measure the charge (ether energy) of an object, place your object on a table or other flat surface, then position your rods over that item so they run parallel. Once your rods are over the item and are parallel simply ask, "Show me the charge." If the rods touch, this indicates that the item has no charge at all, but if the rods begin to open, this means your object is holding a charge. The more the rods open, the more charge that item has.

The Hands

If information in the form of minute muscle movements are being channeled into an ideomotor tool through the hand, why not just use your hand? Well, actually you can, and it's not that difficult. The advantage of using your hand is that, once trained, you can read energetic sensations coming in through the small energy centers in your palms and fingers.

To sense an object's energy field hover your right or left palm about an inch over that object and pay attention to any feelings coming in through the skin. This could be a hot or cold sensation or maybe a tingle—every person is different. Although you can sense using both hands, those sensations may vary because your dominant hand directs and sends energy, while your other hand receives it. If you are right-handed, then your right hand will be the sending hand and your left receiving—vice versa if you are left-handed. To find out how you sense in this way, simply experiment by lining up objects, placing your hand over them and seeing what you feel.

To use your hand like a pendulum, or dowsing rod (to answer simple questions), create two cards labeled Yes and No. Now program your subconscious mind to give you a cue whenever you hover your hand over the right cards. Your cue may be, "Vibrate whenever I am over the right card," or "Cause my hand to become warm when over the right card." Once you have done this, you can lay those cards on a table and ask a simple Yes or No question. After you have asked your question, hover your hand over Yes. Does it tingle, or feel warm or cool according to your request? If not, hover your hand over No, then wait for the sensation to arise.

Getting yes and no answers is really just the tip of the iceberg. You can get even more detailed information by making a full deck of cards with the numbers 0–9 and the alphabet on them, then hover your hand over each card to spell out words and sentences. You can also sense the direction and location of target by extending your hand and rotating until you feel the sensations I talked about above. Your options are endless. However, if you sense nothing after using any of these methods, just keep trying and eventually you will pick something up—otherwise use a ideomotor tool like a pendulum, or dowsing rod.

Using Ideomotor Tools to Channel Intent

Perhaps one of the handiest uses of an ideomotor tool is to physically represent your intent. You can after all measure a change, so why not use it to focus your energy and measure the magnitude of your intentions upon the ether whenever you do spell work.

Whenever you use an ideomotor tool, you are forced to give it your focus and when that happens, you are tapping into the same faculties used to imagine and visualize. And it happens to be that both of these things, focus and Imagination, occupy the lower two points of the "what makes magick work" triangle. So if you want to enhance the power of a spell, use an ideomotor device to channel that energy.

The process is simple—here is how to do it. The quicker your pendulum spins, or the wider your dowsing rods have opened, the more you have actualized your intent and the more powerful it is. That's it—this is all that is needed!

PSYCHIC SENSES

I am sure you have heard tales about people who are able to see things over great distances, get psychic impressions from an object or area, or see into the future—all of these are valid descriptions of psychic senses. Such senses have gone by many names over the past few centuries. In that past, they have been referred to as divination, the gift, the second sight, the sixth sense and most recently extrasensory perception. Although each one of these aforementioned terms are surrounded by their own practices and beliefs, they are all essentially the same thing—psychic perception. In reality there is a psychic sense for each mundane sense. So to make things simple, I will use the term extrasensory perception when referring to all these psychic senses together.

Types of Extrasensory Perception

Mundane Sense		Psychic Sense
Seeing	→	Clairvoyance
Hearing	→	Clairaudience
Smelling	→	Clairalience
Touching	→	Clairtangency
Tasting	→	Clairgustance
Feeling	→	Clairsentience
Knowing	→	Claircognizance

Understanding Extrasensory Perception

As far as mainstream science is concerned, extrasensory perception does not exist. Even so, psychic senses fit extremely well within current scientific theory—especially quantum physics. Quantum physicists know that everything is a wave of energy existing in a quantum field that penetrates everything. They also know that this energy can interact over great distances through a process known as quantum entanglement. Furthermore, it has been proven—beyond a shadow of a doubt—that consciousness is what causes change.

The easiest way to understand extrasensory perception is to use the radio analogy. Think of your mind as a radio that is able to establish a two-way connection between you and the signal—the signal being the waves of thought energy that make up everything in the cosmos. Once this two-way connection is established, it allows you to experience a target from his, her, or its perspective, giving you the ability to see, hear, smell, touch, taste, feel, and even know what that target is experiencing.

It is important to keep in mind is that a target doesn't have to be a person—it can be anything. Everything is conscious. Therefore, everything is consciously experiencing something in its own unique way. A person or animal may have complex or simple thought patterns centered around what they are thinking at the time, a plant may give off happy or distressed energy, according to its surroundings, and a rock may simply resonate with the energy of its surrounding environment. But either way, how you experience your target (with what senses) will depend on how you experience the world in real life. For example, if you are a visual person, you may see visions (clairvoyance) before you hear anything, but if you are better at listening, you will probably pick up sounds (clairaudience) before you see anything. Besides being able to pick up images, sounds, smells, and taste, you will eventually become aware of your target's thoughts. These thoughts may manifest themselves through any of the aforementioned senses or may come as a feeling (clairsentience), an actual voice, or even a knowing (claircognizance).

As this connection strengthens, a synchronization process will begin, with the stronger of the two signals dragging the other up or down in frequency until both resonate at the same wavelength. Once that happens, the stronger of the two signals will take control and begin to lead the other, which presents a unique problem. If you are being led, it will not always be apparent where those thoughts or feelings are coming from—do they belong to the target or you? The only way to know really is to know yourself well enough to be able to tell the difference. Otherwise, it is possible to become overwhelmed by what you are experiencing and even mistake your target's thoughts for your own. And if your target is aware of this and happens to be a skilled psychic, he, she, or it may even try to do a little bit of mind control.

I don't say this to scare you, but it's extremely possible and does happen. The most likely scenario would be if you were to connect with someone who was highly emotional—you would defiantly feel it and there would be a chance you would also be swept up by those emotions and experience some mental trauma because of it. It wouldn't be an intentional thing on the part of the person you were connecting to, it would simply be because that person's emotions are strong. On the other hand, ESP is used to connect with spirit of the dead, or even higher entities. These entities communicate telepathically by default—so they will be aware that you are trying to make contact. Therefore, if you connect with the wrong entity, you can easily get sucked in and controlled. I just want to make you aware that it is a two-way connection and it can be taken advantage of.

Basic Psychic-Sensory Development

There are many ways to develop psychic-sensory abilities, but the absolute easiest way is to simply practice being observant. What most people fail to realize is that when you consciously engage a physical sense (seeing, hearing, smelling, touch and taste), you simultaneously engage its corresponding psychic sense. This means the more you train your physical senses, the more adept you will become at sensing what is beyond the physical realm. When that happens, keen sight becomes clairvoyance, sharp hearing becomes clairaudience, sensitive smell becomes clairalience, a heightened sense of touch becomes clairtangency and a well-trained taste, ends up becoming clairgustance. And once all these psychic senses begin to work in tangent, you will eventually become claircognizance—or knowing on all levels.

One of the best ways to train your psychic awareness is to focus on a particular aspect of your surroundings—that aspect could be the overall environment, an object, or a life form (plant, animal, or person). To focus on something, simply means to move your awareness to that thing's location—and this you would do by using the methods described under meditation. Once you have directed your attention to a particular person, place, or thing, clear your mind of chatter and remain open to any sensations you may feel. At that point, the sensations will manifest within you, as if you were experiencing them from the perspective of the target.

What you will discover is that although everything within an environment will have the same general feeling, each individual entity will have its own unique feel. And if anything doesn't belong, or is out of place, it will feel starkly different from everything else within that environment. This vibration will come as an overall feeling, or current of emotional energy, then eventually will split into an individual sense as you focus on it more and begin to resonate with it. Then, once you are able to recognize these energies and what they are associated with, you can apply it to sensing things at a distance using remote viewing.

Seeing Auras

To *see* energy on a spiritual level you must be open to the experience. This energy is represented as an aura around all things. Just spend some time staring at different objects. The first time you do this, it is unlikely you will notice any differences. The more you do it, the clearer the aura will become. You might initially see what looks like a transparent warped field around that object, then as you become open, you will notice a soft white glow at the edges of that field. Some things will have larger fields than others, while other things may seem to have no field at all. If you are lucky enough, you will start seeing soft colors—those colors will seem to wisp off the object like steam. The more in tune you become with these fields, the more sensitive you will become, then you will be able to pick up objects and feel either a warmth or coldness from them—and that is an indication of a positive or negative field.

Although it is possible acquire the ability to see auras through hypnosis, the subconscious mind tends to shut that ability down because it does not match with your current programming. I myself have tested this out by entrancing people to see these light fields. They gain the ability and are able to identify changes in colors to my auric field as I meditate, but then suddenly lose that ability after the third or fourth time they identify a color change—so you really have to develop this ability over time.

Farseeing

Remember in the chapter entitled "How to Research" that I suggested taking a look at the things that the military, government agencies, and big business were interested in? Well, extrasensory perception is one of them. Operation Stargate was formed during the Cold War when rumors began to come out of the Soviet Union that the Russian government was experimenting with psychic phenomena. In response to this threat, during the 1970s, the DIA (Defense Intelligence Agency) poured over twenty-million dollars into research program that could train soldiers to use clairvoyance to obtain intelligence from afar.

To accomplish this, they enlisted the help of SRI International, a private California contractor who was already doing paranormal research. This project itself was headed by physicist Russell Targ and parapsychological researcher Harold Puthoff from Stanford Research Institute (SRI). One legendary figure in this story was Ingo Swann (1933–2013), the developer and instructor of CRV (controlled remote viewing). He was so talented that he saw the rings around Jupiter well before Voyager detected them in 1979 and was also able to describe, sketch, and affect a magnetometer that was buried six feet under a concrete floor without his knowledge.

The initial idea was to recruit talented psychics, but after they refused to participate in the project, they recruited talent from within the US Army. Once these individuals were trained, they were said to be able to view a target with 65 percent accuracy (oftentimes, 80 percent accuracy). Even so, the project was shut down in 1995, once it was handed over to a CIA oversight comity, who commissioned the American Institute for Research to investigate it. Their official report stated, despite masses of evidence to the contrary, that remote viewing was an unproven and untrustworthy source for intelligence.

So is there anything to ESP, and if so, why would the military and government officially close their project? While the purpose of this book is not to defend paranormal research or magick against the judgment of harsh skeptics, I will say this: there is an overwhelming amount of evidence to support this kind of phenomena—so much, in fact, that it would be foolish to deny its existence. I have experienced such phenomena myself. Otherwise, I wouldn't have written this book. All one really has to do to find out is to practice the techniques divulged here. Why would anyone deny the legitimacy of Psi after spending so much money investigating it for such a long time? To me, the answer is pretty obvious; if everyone knew how to do this, they wouldn't be able to hide many secrets. One thing is for certain, psychic senses are so powerful, they can be used to sense anything, anywhere and at any point in time.

Having said this, the techniques discovered during the twenty-five years of remote viewing research and development are extremely valuable, so we will be taking advantage of them here. Even so, the method described below can't really be considered remote viewing, because it does not involve using blind targeting. It is more likely that you will always need to know who, or what your target is. In such case, the technique described below will use both remote viewing techniques and occult methods to allow you to "view" a target from a distance, anywhere and at any point in time.

Preparation

Using extrasensory perception, like many other psychic procedures demands focus and for this reason it is best practiced in a quiet place where you will not be disturbed. So first thing's first—find a quiet place and set aside about thirty to forty-five minutes to devote to the process. For the best results, it is best to choose an uncluttered room of neutral color—this is done, to reduce mental distraction. If you can't find such a place, you can simply reduce the light, keeping enough illumination to write by, or operate your voice recorder. Although it is highly unlikely that you will be in any kind of danger while remote viewing, I believe in being safe—so why not take advantage of the protective measures taught in this book by creating a protective amulet, opening a sacred space, or surrounding yourself with a protective shield of white light—it can't hurt right. Along with this, you will want to reduce as much electromagnetic interference as possible by shutting off electronic devices. The reason for this is that, powerful electromagnet fields have been known to affect mood and cognition. Therefore, if you reduce EMF, you will improve clarity of the session.

Now for the issue of recording your session—you have several options. You can enlist the help of another person and put him or her in charge of taking notes. You can take notes by speaking into a digital recorder, or you can get a stack of papers and a pencil or pen. Each one of these options has its advantages and disadvantages.

If you choose a person to take notes for you, you can also ask him or her to act as a controller. A controller is someone who leads, or guides the session by asking specific questions. The controller also makes sure the viewer stays on target by redirecting their attention back to a specific entity, location, or object. Once you begin practicing remote viewing, you will understand how easily it is to become fixated on things that don't seem to have anything to do with your target. The disadvantage of using a controller is that he or she must interpret what you say—and in such case, he or she may misinterpret, or embellish. This tendency can be rectified by simply asking your controller to write down exactly what you say without adding anything to it.

If you choose to make your record by recording it using some kind of digital device, you must take special care to make sure you have actually hit "record" on your device when you are ready to start. As obvious and funny as this advice may seem, it's easy to make mistakes when trying to manipulate electronic devices while in a trance. Needless to say, redirecting your focus to make sure you've hit the right button takes practice, because doing so could cause you to slip out of trance. When performing farseeing, you will need to take at least 10 minutes to get into state, before expecting to receive any information. And that means, if you start recording before you get into state, you will have about ten minutes or more of silence before you actually start describing your target. If you have sound editing software, you can easily remove this dead space.

Recording the old fashion way (via paper and pen) has its advantages. Not only can you write down what you see, but also you can sketch it out—and that allows you to record details that you otherwise would not be able to record using the other methods. The only problem with physically writing and sketching things is that it takes time to develop the skill of dividing your focus between the paper and your trance. But if you can manage it, it is well worth it.

The Issue of Analytical Overlay

The project managers of Operation Stargate understood that people have a tendency to filter what they see, hear, smell, touch, and taste through their own personal system of beliefs. For this reason, they wanted to preserve the clarity of the information being received by encouraging remote viewers to report exactly what they sensed without trying to interpret it. This, they called analytical overlay (AOL), because you are overlaying what you sense with your own analysis. That is not to say that all assumptions are wrong, only that if you do happen to be wrong, you will tend to interpret the rest of what you see through that same lens of bias from that point on. To prevent this from happening, they encouraged their viewers purge their assumptions by calling them out, or writing them down under the heading of AOL. In this way, they could get it out of their systems, so to speak, and be able to move on without being fixated on their opinions. Although you do not have to be so technical, I do think this is a good practice, so I encourage you to acknowledge your guesses and record them as interpretations.

Creating the Psychic Link

Remote viewers of Operation Stargate operated under blind conditions—in other words, they didn't know what their target was before viewing it. They were simply given what was called a "target number," which was a long number (usually six or more digits) associated with the target of the viewing. In the past, these numbers corresponded to actual longitude and latitude coordinates on a world map. But when remote viewers were suspected of using their knowledge of geography to infer details about their targets according to the coordinates, these numbers where changed to random digits that were also sealed in an envelope—this, they did because they were trying to determine whether people were having an authentic clairvoyant experience.

This, however, will be impractical for you, because you will undoubtedly be choosing targets by need and will therefore know who or what your target is. Knowing a target can be both an advantage and disadvantage. It is an advantage because you can improve your connection by utilizing the methods I am about to explain, but it is a disadvantage because the data you are trying to collect can be corrupted by what you already know about your target (AOL).

The method we will employ to improve our connection to the target will be the same method used for contacting the spirits of the dead or higher dimensional beings through the art of evocation—the tag-lock. A tag-lock is an item that is associated with the person, place, or thing you are trying to connect to. This could be a fingernail clipping, a lock of hair, or clothing item of the person you are trying to connect to, or it could even be soil sample, plant clipping, or an object from the location you are trying to view. The best tag-locks are biological in nature, being saturated with the DNA of your target. But if you don't have any of that, don't worry, you are not out of luck.

Your second choice, which you can actually use in addition to a natural tag-lock, is to create a psychic link by using a photo or representation of your target. A representation can be an effigy or doll made out of clay, cloth, or even wax—think voodoo doll or poppet. Either way, you will want to compile data about your target and scribe it on a piece of paper. At a minimum, you should include the target's name and date of birth. However, any additional information you add will increase the psychic connection you are creating. If you are using a poppet, you will want to stuff this paper inside the cavity of the doll. For more information about making and using poppets, see "Poppet Magick" under the chapter "Common Forms of Magick."

Connecting to Your Target

Now retire to your quiet room, vest any amulet you have created and erect your Sacred Space—this you are doing to ensure that you are fully protected. After this point, you need to expose yourself to your tag-locks, by reviewing any information you already know about your target, handling the photo or poppet or physical object connected to your target location, reading the name and date of birth and any other information you have compiled. By interacting with these objects and information, you are becoming quantum entangled with your target.

Once you have physically handled the objects and reviewed the information, close your eyes and begin thinking about your target. Mentally go over every detail: name, date of birth, appearance, and so on. Spend as long as you need to really solidify the idea of your target in your mind. Continue this review of information until there is nothing else to review. This may be five minutes, or fifteen—it just depends on how well developed your skills of visualization are. Once you have fully actualized your target, you are ready to move on to the next step.

Remain Open and Receive to Information

By this point, you should have entered a medium to deep trance. Now, all you have to do is remain open to what may come. This is where being proficient in meditation comes in handy, because you must be able to quiet your mind by ignoring any mundane thoughts that might try to creep in. Such mundane thoughts might be: what you want to have for dinner, a conversation you had with a friend, or even your duties at work—just let it go.

The next thing you must do is trust what you are sensing without second guessing it. The goal at this stage is not to scrutinize what you sense, but to record any images, sounds, smells and feelings that may come to you while in your receptive state—you can always judge the information's worth after you are done with the ESP session.

Levels of Information

Psychic visions rarely appear as clear pictures or perfectly audible sounds. Most of the time, what you will see will be dim, fragmented, and fleeting, so you must be attentive to what comes and record it immediately, else you are likely to lose it. From my experience, information tends to come in a top-down manner, meaning you will sense the general qualities of your target before being able to discern details. Although the order may be different from person to person, the acquisition of information usually follows the pattern described below.

Feelings

The first thing that people generally experience is the sense of feeling. This is a vibe, so to speak, like what was described in the section "Basic

Psychic-Sensory Development." Depending on who or what your target is, those feelings may be reactionary, meaning it will be an invoked response versus what that person (if the target is a person) is feeling, or the actual emotional energy resonating in the area. To avoid confusion, gauge how you feel, both before and a few minutes after you have acquired your target. Either way, you may have to consciously probe your target for this vibe by carefully identify your own emotional state—remember: you are resonating with your target, so what it feels, you will also, and what its emotional state or vibe is, so will yours be to some extent. To do this, just ask yourself if you feel secure, anxious, happy, sad, loving, hateful, psychotic, timid, and so on.

Time and Location Markers

If you are intentionally viewing an event that happened in the past, or future, but are not sure exactly when that event happened, or might happen, it is extremely possible to find this information out by playing a game of hot and cold. To do this, ask yourself, "Does this event feel like it took place fifty years ago?" If fifty years seems too distant (cold), then ask, "Does this even feel like twenty-five years ago?" If at that point, it feels like your warmer, it means you're close. Continue with the line of questioning until that date feels hot. If you practice this technique often enough, you can not only home in on the year, month, but also the day, hour, and minute.

The same game can be played to lock onto someone or something's location. To determine direction, stand up and slowly rotate until you feel like you are pointing in the right direction. Then to gauge distance, play the same hot/cold game as described above, except with miles—one hundred miles or less, hot or cold, fifty miles or less, hot or cold, and so on. Do this until you have determined your general or exact distances from your target.

Dimension

You will most likely feel the dimensions of a target before you get any kind of visual of it. Dimensions describe magnitude, space, shape, and volume. Open to the air or inside, tall or short, enormous, microscopic, spacious, or confined are all great descriptors—so have a few good words handy to accurately describe what you are feeling. Dimensions might include information that describes structures like tall buildings, large masses such as lakes, forests, or deep gorges.

Details

At this point, information will begin flooding in through your natural five senses. Of course, you should not expect all of these sensations to be vivid, but it can and does happen. You may see visions, hear sounds, feel textures, taste something, or even pick up an odor. Again, how you experience your target will depend on how you actually sense things in the real world. If you are a visual person, you will receive visions, if you tend to hear better than you see, you may receive sounds first, if you have a thing for odors, you will smell your target first and if you are well connected to your higher self, the information may be dropped in your head all at once as a complete package—claircognizance.

Real-Time Animation

In the end, all of these senses may come together to form a clear picture in real time that can be observed, or even interacted with. If your intention was to view a location, then you may see that location as an animated scene, from a first-person perspective, if you were trying to connect with an entity, or person, you may begin picking up that entity's thoughts. If that person or entity is aware of your presence, a type of schizophrenic conversation may ensue, complete with a visual of that entity talking, making hand gestures and looking at you. Again what you see will be wholly dependent who or what you are viewing and on how you experience things in real life—whatever the case, don't be startled.

Disconnect and Purge

Once you are finished collecting this information, or feel like there is nothing more to be sensed, you should disconnect. Disconnecting is as easy as opening your eyes. In any case, once you have come out of your trance, you should make it a point to step away and do something that will help you mentally separate from your target. This may mean going for a walk, exercising, or even making something to eat. If you've had a particularly difficult time separating from your target, or have experienced highly negative emotions, always end your session with a banishment to get rid of any negative energies that may be lingering about.

Blind Farseeing Exercise

In a real-life situation, where you need to gain information on a target at a moment's notice, you will always have to know who or what that target is. However, it is very possible to practice farseeing using blind targeting with the help of a friend. People have tried to do this using random pictures. However, I don't think this is an appropriate test of ESP ability because "guessing" aspects of a picture works more like precognition than farseeing. So, in order to perform this exercise, you will need to enlist the help of someone else—friends and family member are good for this.

Because ESP sessions can garner loads of information, I suggest you buy a tablet with blank white pages to record your sessions in. Have this tablet will make it easier for you to record information during each phase of the viewing and judge accuracy. Take a look at what a sample record looks like. Also notice how the record is divided among different sheets—this is to reduce distraction and help your consciousness focus on specific information.

Page 1: Full Name of Target/Birth Day/Target Time

Date/Time:
Physical/Emotional Condition
Target Name:
Target Time:
Total Accuracy:

Page 2: Feelings
Page 3: Time and Dimension Markers
Page 4: Details
Page 5: Real-Time Animated Scene

After you have found a volunteer, decide the target date of the farseeing session. Remember: you don't have to perform the farseeing session on this target date—in other words, you can choose to view your target one week in advance. Once you have your target and date, write down the date and time you actually performed the session, as well as your physical/emotional condition, then use the farseeing method above to actually farsee them. When you are finished, speak to your friend and let them to tell you where they were and what they were doing and how they felt at that particular time.

The next part is the most difficult part—you must score yourself. To do this you will grade each point (empathic, space, dimension, natural senses and scene) using a three-point system, including zero (so zero to four). In this case, zero means you got nothing right, one means minimal accuracy, two means your accuracy was above 50 percent, three means, you got at least 80 percent correct, and four means you did extremely well and got at least 95 percent correct. Once you have scored yourself, write that score down as a fraction over 56—for example, if you got 26 correct, write down 26/56. Then, if you want to represent your score as a percentage, simply divide the top of the fraction, by the bottom and multiply by 100.

Seeing the Future

Reading the future is perhaps one of the most amazing and mind-boggling aspects of psychic sensing. How is this even possible? Being human and living on a linear timeline, we oftentimes overlook the fact that nothing really holds an exact position in time and space. I have already talked about how thought precedes physical manifestation—so states the law of "As Above, So Below." If that sounds too mystical, realize that even science acknowledges that things are immaterial before they are material.

What this basically means is, before anything exists here in the physical world, including the events that come together to cause those things, they are immaterial fields of energy—thoughts existing in another plane—another dimension. Although that immaterial field has no physical attributes to allow it to be perceptible here in the physical world, it is still made up of information detailing what it will become.

Everything is the result of thought. This is the whole principle behind magick and is also the conclusion modern science is coming to within the field of quantum physics. Every day when you think of something, you choose what you create and pull it into your reality. Week thoughts, blow over and dissipate, while strong thoughts build like storms in the ether, until they become full-fledged tsunamis that create the reality you see and experience.

When these storms become imminent, they can be sensed as a type of foreboding, or omen, but if you know how to sense energy, you can choose to tap into these fields and read them far before they become reality. What you must realize, though, is you cannot read something that has no intention behind it—in other words, you cannot read something that no one has any intention of acting on. So for example, if you were trying to find out what might happen if you moved to Alaska to join the Eskimos and you really had no intention of doing that, you would get little to no information during that reading. All I'm saying is that thing must be seriously considered before that future begins to build. You would have much better success determining if you were going to get a particular job if you have actually applied for it, because you have already set things in motion and that action demonstrates positive intention. Like I have said before, the future is not certain, certain things are more likely to happen than others, because those things are being given more consideration, or are even being currently acted upon. You should also realize that when you view the future it may affect your intentions toward it. If you like what you see, you will want to move forward and thus that future is more likely to manifest. However, if you don't like what you see, you will most likely change your course of actions, thus causing that future to dissipate—this of course depends on whether certain events and actions are avoidable or not. With that being said, reading the probable future follows the same procedure as reading any other source of energy—you just choose to connect with it. Perhaps the only difference is that the focus of your intent is in the future and not the past or present.

Sending Information Back from the Future

Another aspect of reading the future, especially when it pertains to one's self is sending information from the future, back to your present self. Let's say that you plan on moving and you have two choices; one, you could move to Florida to be closer to your brother, or you could move into a home in the city you are already in. Each of these choices will have an important effect on your life. Moving to Florida means that you would have to relocate to a place that you know nothing about, not to mention you would have to find a new job. If you chose to simply relocate to a different residence in the city, you could keep your job and would still be familiar with your surroundings. On the other hand, you never know what new opportunities you might be missing out on if you were to move.

So considering all this, you decide it would be a good idea to farsee the future. But you have another trick up your sleeve. Your future self will be aware of this reading and because of that, this gives you a unique opportunity—you can psychically send information back from the future, to help your present self-verify whether or not you have made a good choice. But before you attempt to receive this information, you need to make a definitive choice, because only those things you actually intend to act upon create the future. In this case, you decide to seriously consider moving to Florida to be closer to your bother.

The next thing you need to decide is what information your future self will send back to the present you. The logical choice is some kind of sound since in all other ESP sessions you tend to pick up sounds the easiest. So you decide that if at some point in time the choice you made turns out to be a disaster, you will send your present self a high-pitched shrieking sound, but if your future self is satisfied, he will send your present self a warm low tone.

After working this out, you get the journal that you record all of your ESP sessions in, but before you making an entry, you check time—it's 12:15 a.m. To give yourself enough time to create the entry, begin the session, then get into the right state, you add another fifteen minutes onto that time—so the time becomes 12:30 a.m. You can now make your entry.

Farseeing Session (Feb 12, 2018, 12:30 a.m.)

Planetary Day/Hour: Moon/Moon
Physical Health: Well
Emotional State: Anxious
Level of Distraction: Zero
Weather: Clear
Spirits Invoked/Evoked: None

The purpose of this session is to decide whether or not moving to Florida is the right choice for me. To determine this, I plan on sending myself I signal in the form of a sound from the future. If I have made the wrong choice my future self will send a high-pitched shrieking noise to me during the session, and if I have made the right choice, he will send a warm low tone.

So having made this journal entry, you now go somewhere quiet, sit down, and meditate. Sometime in the not so distant future—let's say three months from now, you follow through with your decision to move to Florida. Having moved, you find a house three blocks from your brother and settle in. After a few days, you land a good job, but several weeks later, your brother keeps visiting you on a constant basis, asking you to lend him money to support his meth habit—I'm making this up, but you get the picture. Despite all efforts to send him away, he won't leave you alone, so you decide it is time to give your past self the signal. Having made the choice, you grab your journal and flip back to the entry (Feb 12, 2018, 12:30 a.m.). Now that you have the date and time, you can use this to send the message (a shrieking sound) back to your past self so that he can get the message—and that you do by using the Remote Influencing technique.

Now we shift back to the past. A good five minutes into the session, you begin to hear a week high-pitched tone in your ear. As you continue to meditate, that high-pitched tone becomes stronger until you can hear a definite high-pitched shrieking sound. The signal is clear: do not move to Florida.

Precognition Exercise

Precognition is another word for "predicting something beforehand," so in order to develop this ability, you must have something to predict. In this case, we will be using Zener cards, which are a deck of cards designed by psychologist named Karl Zener in the 1930s, for the purpose of testing precognitive abilities. Zener cards are quite simple, depicting rudimentary geometric symbols in various colors, such as a yellow circle, black square, red cross, green star, or blue wavy lines. Zener cards can be bought online, or even made—in such case, they can be made to depict symbols that most resonate with you. To design Zener cards, simply buy a deck of index cards, or get some card stock and cut the cards yourself. Keep in mind, if the color of your card is the same as one of your symbols, you will have to draw that particular symbol in a different color. If you want to repeat five symbols 20 times, make 100 cards. Once you have your cards, decide how many symbols you want—more symbols, makes the task of predicting more difficult. Next transfer these symbols on each card using the appropriate color. When you've transferred all the symbols once, simply repeat. Repeat each symbol until you have filled all your cards, but remember: there should be an equal number of each symbol.

To perform the precognition exercise you will need a note pad and pen. Before you perform a test, decide how many guesses you want to make, then write that number down on the sheet of paper, drawing a line above it, like a fraction. You will also want to record the date and time, as well as your physical/emotional condition (ill, sleepy, alert, worn out, and so on). To use these cards, shuffle the deck, lay them face down and draw a card. Do not look at the card you draw, instead lay it face down. When you are ready, turn the card over in your mind and see what the result is. Is it blue wavy lines, a star or cross? Now actually turn the card over and see if you got it right. If you got it right, write a number one, but if you didn't write a zero. These ones and zeros can be written one right after the other, after your would-be fraction, to preserve space on the paper. Once you have go through as many cards as you had decided, count the ones (the ones you guessed correctly) and record that number above the line of your fraction. This exercise can be repeated as often as you wish and your progress can be gauged by simply looking back at the fractions. You can also make this exercise easier, or more difficult by removing, or adding more symbols. You can also try guessing color instead of shape, to see where your affinities lye.

PSYCHIC COMMUNICATION

In the Farseeing Exercise, you learned how to tap into, or connect with a person, place or thing. Now you will learn how to communicate with what you have connected with—and that is referred to as telepathy. Learning how to psychically communicate with the fields you have connected with is a prerequisite of evocation, channeling and psychic influencing.

The first thing you need to know about psychic communication is that, when you connect with a sentient being both parties can sense one another's thoughts in the form of visions, sounds, tactile, olfactory, emotional or clairsentient information—this happens even if the person or entity you have connected to is unaware of it. If the person or entity you have connected with is unaware of that connection, it is more likely to mistake those thoughts and feelings as their own—that means they could be influenced by you. That also means, if you haven't developed your psychic awareness, someone or something may be psychically influencing you without your knowledge—I know, scary thought.

Let me stop here and talk about something else—I want to emphasize this—and all you Sorcerers out there who intend on learning how to evoke spirits should take this to heart. All entities communicate telepathically—this means that the entity you connect with probably knows how to influence as well. A negative entity loves targets who are unaware, because they can, number one, read their thoughts and, number two, create thoughts and emotional states to invoke the type of energy they like to feed off of—this is also why psychic communication should be done within a protective circle. So let's move on.

How information is sent and received depends on the depth of the connection and the expertise of both communicators. Information is typically not sent in the form of words and sentences, but instead as sensory input like visions, sounds, smells, tactile sensations, emotions, and complete ideas. However, if both parties are aware of the connection, the deeper that connection becomes, your mind will naturally begin to translate that information in to words. At first, this will happen intentionally, but eventually, it will happen automatically and, at that point, it may seem like a natural back-and-forth conversation with someone who is standing right in front of you. If you are clairaudient (good at psychically hearing things), then you may begin actually hearing a voice. If you are clairvoyant, then you might see the image of a face or a full form speaking and making gestures as if it were animated. The best part of all this is there is no special procedure you have to follow to communicate—all you have to do is take inventory of what you are thinking, then practice telling the difference between legitimate information and stuff fabricated by your imagination.

Scrying

Scrying is the magical process of psychic sensing that involves externalizing your visions onto a black reflective surface. The premise of scrying is this—looking into a black surface is similar to shutting your eyes, and when you do that, what you are doing is shutting out all other external stimuli and allowing imagery to bubble up from the subconscious which is more connected to the collective unconscious or world of spirit. Scrying is typically done by staring at the black or reflective surface of a scrying tool such as a magick mirror, scrying bowl, crystal, or something similar. These tools are ritualistically cleansed, consecrate and charged for this purpose and can be enhanced with tinctures and oils.

With a scrying device, all visions seem to be externalized—this means, instead of seeing them in your mind, you see them on the surface of the scrying tool—that does not, however, mean that anyone else can see those visions—they are, after all, still in your head. Also, because we are dealing with thought energy here, that thought energy is still received and interpreted through the mind. Because of that, what you see is unique to yourself.

This means that if more than one person is scrying, although they might see the same target, the way they interpret it and, thus, what they see could be slightly different from one another. As in psychic sensing, how we sense things makes a difference, so one person may see an image in black and white, another in color, another a still image, and yet another may see these images animated.

Scrying can be further enhanced by using what is called a Triangle of Manifestation (classical evocation). The triangle can be understood to represent the idea of time, space, and energy coming together to form reality, thus bring something into manifestation. A triangle is typically drawn upon a cloth, paper, or piece of wood, surrounded by divine names, the name of the spirit, or left bare. The use of a triangle with divine names is controversial because it is said to bind the spirit to the area of the triangle, potentially trapping it there. While this can be a good idea for lower spirits that you know will be malevolent, this will simply piss off higher spirits and provoke an attack. To be honest, higher spirits really can't be bound by such things, but the symbolism of the triangle by itself does provide a channel in which the spirit can arrive—this is why your scrying tool goes inside the triangle. Think of this as a landing spot for the spirit that says, "I want to see you here."

How to Make a Scrying Mirror

Any mat black surface can be used for the purpose of scrying—even a television screen. But if you want a better connection, you should actually make a scrying mirror. Doing this is quite easy—buy an empty picture frame (glass included of course) and paint the side of the glass that faces inward mat black. Make sure to add several coats to fully cover it, then let it dry. Take your frame and add any runes, God names and other materials. Use your creativity to decorate this frame as you wish. Once the mirror is complete, cleanse, consecrate and charge it for the purpose of scrying—simple as that!

Scrying Procedure

Step I: Preparation

Make sure you will not be disturbed for at least forty-five minutes. Turn off all electrical devices, especially those that make noises, then open your sacred space. For this procedure I suggest using a voice recorder to record any information you sense—it will simply be too dark for you to write. Set your scrying tool on a table, inside a triangle of manifestation if you are going to use one, then place two white candles three feet to either side of you, just behind you—make sure the reflection of the candle flames cannot be seen on the reflective surface of the tool.

Step II: Follow Steps in Psychic Sensing

Follow the steps for psychic sensing. However, stare into the scrying device and expect to see your visions there. Be patient—it could take a good fifteen to twenty minutes to see anything. Do not stare directly at the mirror, instead stare past it. The point here is not to engage your conscious mind by trying to figure out if something is going to literally form on the surface. If you are trying to contact an entity, being able to see your reflection is a good thing—oftentimes, the entity will choose to modify that reflection into an image of itself.

If you are one of the lucky ones, images will simply appear in the mirror. However, the surface may fog over first. Sometimes this fog doesn't come in the form of a fog at all, but a sort of static rain—this means you have achieved the Theta-Gamma Sync and that is where you want to be. If you don't see anything, just try again on another day—learning how to scry takes time and practice. Also note, scrying tools are really not necessary—you can simply do this through meditation. This means it doesn't really matter if you can externalize something, seeing it in the mind's eye is perfectly fine.

Intuitive Reading

Intuitive readings utilize the symbols found in divination tools such as tarot cards and runes in much the same way as Hermann Rorschach used the Inkblot Test. The Inkblot test involved folding a few globs of ink between a piece of paper and spreading it open to reveal a symmetrical shape. The client could then be asked a volley of questions about the shape, which would reveal their inner psychology—this worked exceedingly well, especially on those who liked to hide what they were thinking.

But unlike dynamic shapes created by the Inkblots, we will use the symbols found in tarot and runes because they embody universal archetypes that resonate with the deep subconscious mind of all humans. This means whatever symbolic system you use, you must be very familiar with the iconography and meanings associated with them, because those symbols will reveal what your client is thinking on both a conscious and subconscious level.

And symbols can be used to create a subconscious conduit between a person's Higher Self and a person's conscious mind. Any symbol chosen will be focused upon and thought about. When that happens, those thoughts and their deeper connections will bubble up through the subconscious mind into conscious thought and become easily readable by anyone who is psychically sensitive. However, because the meanings of a symbol might not be apparent to your client, you will want to point out the features of those symbols and explain them—in this way, you can help direct the client's thoughts toward a particular aspect of the question. When that happens, it will be much easier for you to lock on to your client's thoughts and get information. Therefore, by interpreting the symbols chosen by the client and drawing information from your own psychic intuition, you can create a clear picture about the psychology manifesting the client's future.

For example, Say your client is a bright-eyed youth who has come to you because she is having difficulty fingering out what to do with her future. We will call her Tina. She has explained that she has multiple opportunities, which are all very exciting, but also very confusing. Being excited, she has already chosen a few paths, but she wants to know how those choices will pan out. So in this case, you lay out the Major Arcana of your tarot deck and let her choose. With much consideration, she chooses the Fool. Once she chooses this card, you have her set it on the table in front of her, and then you point at it to draw her attention. You then explain the significance of the card.

> "The boy in the picture represents youth, naivety, and the beginning of a journey. Beside him is his companion, a white dog, which represents his protector or higher spiritual self. Notice that he is dangerously close to the edge of a cliff. That cliff symbolizes the unknown dangers that lay before all of us as we move forward on our journey through life. The mountains in the background represent both struggle and potential. The sky, on the other hand, is bright, which represents the bright future we can all have, if we keep a positive outlook. Take a moment and reflect on these symbols as they relate to your question(s)."

Now as your client examines the card and thinks about how it relates to her situation, center yourself and begin breath entrainment. This will cause a psychic link between you and her. When that happens, remain open to any information that may come. This is much like the farseeing method described above; you will get feelings and emotions, time and location markers, dimensions, sensory details and perhaps even an animated scene. Use this information to pick other symbols.

Note, if your client is conflicted—as the girl said she was—then the impressions you get may each represent several possible futures. In that case, you need choose symbols (cards, or runes) that represent each possibility. I would suggest placing them in order of strength. What I mean is this, some futures are more likely to happen because that is what the client truly believes will happen. This may be because they have a positive outlook and are subconsciously choosing the most beneficial path, or they are so afraid that something may happen that their beliefs are causing it to build and manifest.

For example, As Tina meditates on the symbol, you entrain your breath to her and begin receiving information. The first thing you feel is terror, the flash of a stormy beach and the smell of death. In this case, you pull the Moon card, lay it face down and instruct her to think about another option.

> "Tina, I want you to let go of what you are thinking. See it vanish like a dissipating cloud. Good, now focus on your next option."

Next you get the sensation of comfort and security, then family and finally regret. You feel as if this has something to do with her choosing to stay home, so you pick the 6 of Cups, because it represents sentimental feelings related to childhood and family. However, you flip it upside down because you feel she is conflicted about this choice. You continue—

> "Very good Tina, now let that memory go and focus on your next option."

You wait for her to get her barring, then begin receiving more information. Now it feels like she is problem-solving, or embroiled in learning. You sense lots of minds, as if she is surrounded by many people—all doing the same thing. You pick up distance between where she is now and where she will be in the future—she is going somewhere. In this case you draw the Hierophant, because it is related to higher learning.

Now you have a total of three cards laid down, representing three paths; the Moon, the 6 of Cups and the Hierophant. From here you can flip each card in turn, then explain and reveal what you sensed.

After explaining the cards and revealing what you saw, Tina tells you what her options were. It turns out the Moon card represented her thoughts about joining the Red Cross and going to the Bahamas. The second card, the 6 of Cups, represented her desire to stay home and just be with her family and the third card, the Hierophant, was the offer her parents made to send her to collage. With this in mind, you counsel her on all the pros and cons of each choice.

Artistic Divination

Just as Hermann Rorschach used the Inkblot test to reveal hidden secrets of the subconscious mind, art in all forms, has always been a medium where hidden thoughts can bubble up from the depths to reveal themselves to any who knows how to decipher them. And this is because, when we produce art, a bridge is created between the subconscious mind and world of spirit, allowing archetypal expressions to pulled from the collective unconscious to be expressed on paper, clay, song, or even as dance.

Once those expressions emerge onto paper, canvas, clay or some other medium, their meaning must be carefully considered within the context of the question of person who created it. This means, although a symbol may have a universal meaning that can be applied to everyone, it will also have a meaning that is very personal to whoever produced it. This is why popular books on dream interpretation fail to give people accurate insight—the same symbol may mean one thing to one person and something totally different to another. Because of this, you will have to use your intuition to assign the best meaning you can to the art you create. Then, once you have assigned an overall meaning to the entire piece of art, you will need to break it down into its symbolic elements and record what you think each element means. I suggest recording all this in a journal created specifically for divination.

When assigning meaning to art, consider how each part or whole makes you feel. Pay attention to any insight or knowledge that may come by way of extrasensory perception. In many cases, simply viewing a piece of art will invoke the energetic information it embodies. As with any other form of magical journal, you will want to record date, time, moon phase, planetary hour and day, weather conditions, distractions, and any other information you can use to correlate. Along with this, you will want to make a record of how you felt before and how you felt while you were producing the art. By cataloging these symbol-idea pairs, you can then go back and look for elements and themes that may repeat themselves in other pieces of art you produce. In this way, you can pin down an element's true meaning and use those elements to divine with.

As a rule of thumb, only artistic endeavors that involve actual creativity have the ability to tap into spiritual insight. That is, your art must be an original. Therefore, painting by numbers or plagiarizing someone's work will not do. No insight can be gained this way, because the end result is not based on personal artistic expression, it is mechanistic and guided by the conscious state.

Art divination can be used for many things: you can use it to retrieve repressed memories of this life or a past life, you can use it to remote view targets, or events in the past, present, or future, you can use it to explore and map the astral landscape and you can use it as a form of spirit communication. The key to doing all of this is to make the production of art a magical act—that is, sketch, paint, or write with intention of retrieving information about your target.

All of these objectives can benefit from creating a psychic link with the person, place, thing, or event you are trying to view. This is done by gathering as much information as possible about your target. Once you do that, keep that information with you while you create your art and, if at all possible, transfer as much of this information on to the paper or canvas that holds your art, leaving enough space to write, draw, or paint. If your target is a person, or spirit, you will need to know their name, birth date, death date, physical description (sketch or photo), personality traits, and any other details you can uncover about them. If you are dealing with a daemon, angelic spirit, or high spirit, find out if they have a sigil and include that as well. Lastly, if you are trying to answer a question, specific or general, include that question on your canvas also.

Now, the only thing to do is to create your art. This you do in a spontaneous sort of way. In other words, don't try to plan it, or force it—just let your creativity flow. As you do this, type in, or sketch out ideas and images quickly. This means your art will most likely be sloppy. Just remember: producing quality art is not the point, receiving information is. If you really want to, you can correct spelling errors and grammar later, or in the case of a painting or drawing, redraw or repaint it at a later date to create something that looks a little more professional. Finally, do not criticize or question your work as you do it, because if you do, you will interrupt the creative flow and lose your connection to the world of spirit.

You also need to understand that you are connecting with a realm that is beyond space and time. Because of this, you will want to keep an eye out for events that have transpired that might correlate with symbols in art produced in art you created in the past. When those symbols reoccur, they can be used to foretell future events. For example, if you produce a picture of a burning forest and five days later a forest fire erupts in your area, then it's possible you have captured a future event. If it happens once, it may be coincidental, but if it happens repeatedly, you know you that when you see that symbol in a painting, you can expect a fire.

Guided Hypnotic Divination

According to the Law of Attraction, our deepest fears and aspirations build our future. People are not always able to express their true thoughts and feelings during waking consciousness. Therefore, without a way to speak directly to the subconscious mind, it can be almost impossible to know what beliefs are creating their future. And this is where Guided Hypnotic Divination comes in—it is a way to help the client to connect to their Higher Self through hypnosis so that they themselves can discover what is building their future. But in order to pull this off, four requirements must be met: one, your client must be able to enter a deep enough state, two, that state must be entered in a positive frame of mind, three, you must be familiar with entrancement and four, you must be in touch with your own psychic senses.

Guided Hypnotic Divination requires that your client be able to achieve a medium-to-heavy hypnotic trance (preferably heavy). Remember 80 percent of all people can enter into a medium trance, while only 10 percent are capable of going any deeper. You should also avoid using this technique on people who are mentally unstable, in great distress, or who are naturally fearful, because these are all symptoms of major unresolved psychological issues that can cause mental trauma when faced suddenly. You must also understand that this brings unconscious thought to the forefront, while diminishing critical faculties present during conscious waking. This is another reason why you should be a seasoned hypnotist, so, if you are not already proficient in hypnosis, read the chapter on entrancement and get a lot of practice hypnotizing people before trying this technique. And lastly, this is not just a hypnosis technique, it is also designed to create a strong psychic link between you and your client. Therefore, if you have not yet tapped into your natural psychic senses, begin meditating on a daily basis, use the energy-moving techniques suggested in this book and practice Basic Psychic-Sensory Development as mentioned earlier in this chapter. Once you have honed your psychic senses, you will be able to take advantage of the enhanced connection created by this method and will have even more clarity during the session.

Preinduction Interview

Just as you would any other person you intend to hypnotize, you will want to explain to them exactly what hypnosis is and address any fears or misconceptions they might have. After you have done this, take as long as you need to fully understand what your client wishes to know. Are they interested in knowing what the future holds if they make a particular choice? Do they want to explore a repressed memory, or are they just trying to find their life's purpose? Once you fully understand their wishes, explain exactly what Guided Hypnotic Divination entails: you will be creating a safe and protected environment, you will help them get into the proper state, you will probe the thoughts surrounding the issue they wish to explore, you will then move their consciousness to the necessary point and time, where they can view those events as they already exist, or as they are being created, then you will safely bring them out of state and help them disconnect.

For the best results, I suggest you allow three to seven days before actually moving forward with the actual Guided Hypnotic Divination—this will cause enough anticipation to create an even deeper trance. During this time, suggest to the client that he or she should meditate five to ten minutes a day on the subject they wish to address. At this point, drop a few preinduction suggestions, such as, "The next time you we meet and you set down in that chair (or lay down in that bed), don't be surprised if you become extremely relaxed and drop immediately into a deep hypnotic trance," then, "When that happens, it may seem like your body has fallen asleep, while your mind enters a waking dream that you are in control of and can remember."

Another great trick is to simply give your client a hypnotic placebo. It should be noted that the word *placebo* is meant to be a dig; this word is a misnomer for a very real and magical effect. All placebos draw upon the beliefs and intent of the person taking them—that is why they are so powerful. The purpose of using a placebo is to bypass a person's disbelief, by giving them something they do believe in. This means that placebo should take the form of whatever your client believes in the most: if that is magick and metaphysics, then you might want to create a medicine bag, give them a "special" crystal, sigil, or even a spell kit for them to use. If they are religious, then you may want to pray with them, or if believe in objective science, you might choose to give them a sugar pill, or some other fake, but harmless medicine. Either way, you will tell your client that if they use or take the placebo that they will be able to enter an even deeper trance the next time you see them—and for goodness' sake, don't tell them it's a placebo! But before you give them this placebo, imbue it (as you would any other magick item) with the intention that it will cause the person to fall into a deep trance the next time you induce them.

Preparation

Several major factors contribute to a subject's ability to enter a hypnotic trance; they are security, level of comfort, and continuity. The client must know that not only can you be trusted, but also they have the freedom to express themselves without being judged. This means not only must your Guided Hypnotic Divination sessions be anonymous, but also you must make sure you will not be disturbed during the session. For this reason, perform your sessions in a quiet place, where you will not be bothered for at least two to three hours.

Before you start your session, make sure your client is comfortable. This means adjusting the temperature and making sure they have a comfortable place to sit or lay. Just keep in mind, if you have used any of the preinduction techniques I have suggested above, it is more than likely your client will fall into a deep trance whenever they take a seat, or lay down. If that is the case, encourage them to relax by saying something like, "Good, just relax.," then continue to the next step.

If you are going to put up some kind of protection—which I suggest you do—this is the time to do it. You can either open a full circle, or erect a psychic shield. Whatever you decide, don't take too much time, because your client is waiting. This is also a good time to mention recording; either have someone standing by to make a written account, or be prepared to record audio and video—this way you can concentrate on the actual system and you will have something to review afterward.

The last point I would like to make here is about continuity. Continuity means that everything flows. If you are confused, your client will also be confused and likely not be able to achieve the right state—so practice, practice, practice. Don't just run off of a script, know how to be fluid and dynamic and adjust your script when needed. If you can do that, you will not only maintain authority, but also credibility.

The Induction

If your client is not already in a hypnotic trance due to your preinduction suggestions, or hypnotic placebo, then you will have to induce them and perhaps deepen their state once they have entered a light, to medium trance. To be most effective, you will want your client to achieve a heavy trance because it is the real gateway into the subconscious and the causal realm where the answers lay.

It may be that not automatically falling into a trance, once he or she (your client) has sat or lain down, is simply due to a misunderstanding of your preinduction command or your description of the effect of the hypnotic placebo. If this is the case, you should trigger deepening by suggesting that these effects are already taking place and then ask that the client relax and not fight it.

For example:

> "I can see that you are already beginning to relax. It's OK. Don't fight it."

"Looks like the (pill, tincture, sigil, or spell) is taking effect. Good, just let it do its job."

If by this time, your client is not already out, use a traditional, or rapid induction technique to take them the rest of the way, then deepen if necessary.

The Core Session

The core session will be a series of guided visualizations and suggestions that direct the mind's attention from its natural meditative state, into the causal realm where events are built into manifested reality. This will be much like a farseeing exercise, except you will be in charge of guiding the individual through the steps of acquiring the information themselves.

First, prompt the subject to imagine or think about the target they wish to view as a frozen and still image. If they are trying to view a future event, you will want to suggest they view that target in the future by saying something like, "You are seeing your target one week (or another specified time) in the future or past." Tell them to visualize it in every detail: see it, hear it, smell it, touch it, taste it, and so on to the best of their ability. If you are not sure whether they have acquired their target, look for physical signs, such as rapid eye movement, increased or decreased pulse rate, and micro muscle movements. After giving them a good minute to focus on their target, move on to the next step.

Once they have fully visualized their target, in a calm and assuring voice, tell your subject to begin verbally describing it. When they begin speaking, their speech may very well be slurred—don't worry: this is a normal sign of being under a deep trance. If you don't understand what they are saying, have them repeat it, or be content it is being recorded.

Now have them activate the target by allowing it to become a moving image. To do this suggest that the target or scene begins to naturally move, "Notice how the person, place, thing, or scene begins to animate. You are now viewing it in action." Validate that they are seeing an active target by simply asking, "Can see it? If you can, nod your head yes or raise your right index finger." When you get confirmation, give them a word of encouragement, "You are doing good."

Next, ask them to describe what is happening within the active scene. "Tell me what you see. What is your target doing?" These questions will of course be highly dependent on who or what that target is, so don't just follow this script, pay attention to what you are being told. As the client describes what is happening, gauge the client's emotional response by reading their eye movements and body language—in this way, you will be able to tell what elements of the scene are important. Know that the elements that invoke the highest emotional responses are the ones that will likely build into future events. You can get more detail about these elements by suggesting that the subject focus in on them and give you more detail. Example, "Look closer at such-and-such aspect. What more do you see." Ask questions pertinent to the specific element of the target or event. Lastly, if any of these exercises seems to cause great distress or make the subject uncomfortable, simply bring them out of the hypnotic state, adding the suggestion that they will feel positive and well rested when they wake.

Ending the Session

Ending a Guided Hypnotic Divination session is like ending any other session of hypnosis. Just bring them out using any of the methods suggested in the chapter on "Entrancement." Avoid allowing your client to leave directly after the session, because they may not have fully emerged from their trance. Instead, engage them in conversation so that they can become fully conscious—you may even want to offer them coffee or tea. At this point, review what you have learned, answer any questions, and offer advice where it is needed.

The Art of Conscious Influence

In this chapter, we will talk about the art of conscious influence, that is, the ability to influence others while they are awake and conscious. Although, the techniques covered here are generally used by government agencies, religious organizations and the commercial industries to manipulate and control the masses for their own agendas, they can also be used benevolently, to free others from mental slavery and as a catalyst for physical and psychological healing. My point here is not to promote these techniques as a means to satisfy your own selfish desires, but to give you the ability to mindfully wield this power to help others, to motivate people in a positive way and protect yourself.

All of the techniques in this set utilize neuroscience and psychology to bring about powerful change. In this chapter we will be talking about NLP (Neuro-Linguistic Programming), profiling, subliminal and superliminal messaging, as well as the basic factors of influence. But before you read this chapter, or the next one, I suggest you go back and reread the chapter entitled "Mind and Magick."

FACTORS OF INFLUENCE

Motivating others, whether for their own benefit, or for yours, can be a tricky procedure. Some people can be quite willful, while others are more than happy oblige without even the slightest thought to the contrary. For this reason, it is necessary to really understand the main factors that motivate most people.

3-Step Learning Pattern

Depending on the personality of the people you are trying to influence, repeating an idea at least three times is the key.

1. When a foreign idea is presented to a subject the first time, it is discarded.
2. When the same idea is presented to the subject a second time, that idea is recognized as vaguely familiar, then once again discarded.
3. When the same idea is presented a third time, it is recognized as familiar and compared to the last two memories.

Plainly put, the more a person is exposed to an idea, the less foreign it will seem, until eventually that idea will be integrated. In fact, the chance that an idea will be accepted increases when a single person is exposed to an idea multiple times. If that idea is presented by *more than one person,* it not only makes that idea seem more socially accepted, but also masks the fact that influence is being used. In order to use this method effectively, these ideas must be introduced over time—that is, you must allow enough time for that idea to be forgotten (relegated to the subject's unconscious mind). Given enough time, that idea will become so deeply rooted that when mentioned again, the person you are trying to influence will begin to believe it originated from him or herself.

Stacking

Every time your subject accepts something you say, it validates and reinforces the ideas before it until eventually the subject will cave and accept the entire chain of ideas. Acceptance can be considered both literally agreeing or failing to disagree to a statement. When stacking, begin with small ideas that will be easily accepted, then add more challenging ideas.

Example:

> Day 1: Cigarettes are expensive.
> Day 2: You need more money to pay bills.
> Day 3: You have a bad cough.

Day 4: They will probably raise the price of cigarettes again next year.

Day 5: Not smoking cigarettes will save you lots of money.

Day 6: My health began improving one week after I quit smoking.

Day 7: You should quit also.

Similarity

We tend to trust and agree with those who are like us, so by mimicking someone's appearance, manner of speech, or behavior, you can also increase the chances that what you say will be accepted. Personally, I think Bandler and Grinder (the founders of NLP) give this method too much credit. The underlying problem is authenticity. That is, if taken too far, the person you are trying to influence will become aware of what you are doing, because your new persona will seem uncharacteristic. For this reason, it is a good idea to understand how you are viewed by the world and not try to adopt too many uncanny traits from those you talk to—let people respect you for who you are.

Investment

Take a moment to think of all those people who have invested an enormous amount of time and money into an idea—usually one that is life-shaping, like a religious belief, political ideology, or success strategy. Now imagine that belief, ideology, or strategy is flawed in a major way, yet instead of abandoning it, the investor hardens him or herself against advice from concerned outsiders and resists abandoning that harmful belief at all cost. Why does this happen? Because, great investment is a sign of unwavering faith and devotion to an idea. This is of course good when the thing you put your faith in is truly beneficial and benevolent, but when the idea is harmful and malevolent, it can be detrimental. Some beliefs, ideologies, and strategies can also be very parasitic. The more you invest in them, the more you rely on that thing as a strategy for survival—it becomes your lifeblood—and at that point, separation becomes difficult and dangerous.

A good example of this would be joining a cult. The cult leader becomes your new parents, and the members become your new family. At this point, they convince you to give all your time to cult projects. The more time you give, the more dependent you become, because you are spending less time earning money for your own survival. Then your only choice becomes relying on them for all your needs (a place to live, food to eat, and love). The same thing can happen when you invest in a political ideology. When you join a movement, not only do you ostracize those who are not a part of that movement, but also the members become your new family. Those new family members now dictate what you do and think. Another good example are faulty success strategies. Let's say that someone convenes you that by investing an exorbitant amount of money into a pyramid scheme, you will become rich. As time goes by and things don't seem to be going as planned, you keep telling yourself it will all work out. As your life crumbles around you, you ignore warnings from friends and family, because you believe that if you invest more money and work harder, everything will be OK. At that point, it's too late, because now you are now broke and have lost everything.

Another reason why people have a difficult time separating themselves from faulty beliefs, ideologies, or strategies is embarrassment. Human beings are prideful—no one likes to admit they were wrong. For this reason, the subconscious mind will defend an idea, no matter how vile, just to avoid shame and embarrassment.

A Spoonful of Sugar

No one likes being threatened, or bossed around, this is why any suggestion made in positive light will always have more of a chance of being accepted. Yes—you can motivate people by bossing them around, threatening them, or by whining and complaining, but those people will undermine you, do substandard work, eventually push you away, or even come back to get revenge—remember positive, draws positive.

Emotions and Creativity

Both emotion and creativity activate the subconscious mind. Therefore, whenever a person resonates with what you are saying, because it is emotionally charged, or has to be imagined, they will be more open to suggestion. Because of this, you must practice using key-words that invoke the emotional/imaginative state. Just remember: it is easier to lead someone deeper into an emotional state they are already in, than it is to move that state in the opposite direction. For example, it would be easier to move someone already in a calm state, to a happy one, than it would be to move an angry person into a happy state. Also, when trying to invoke creative thinking in your subject, you must speak in terms that they understand. If they are more visual, then use visual words, but if they are more audial, use words that invoke sound.

Exercise:

Get a sheet of paper and divide it into four columns. In the first column write "sight," in the second write "sound," in the third write "taste/smell," and in the last column write "emotion." Next, brainstorm and come up with as many words describing each of those senses—make sure they are commonly used in speech. Then, starting with the first column, make up a sentence that includes all of those words. For example; to practice using "sound" words you might say something like, "Do you hear me? When things get loud, let my voice come through like the sound of music." Notice how my sentence doesn't necessarily make any sense—this is called a word salad. At this point, don't worry too much if what you say doesn't make any sense, the more you practice, the more you will get used to putting these words together in a coherent pattern. When that happens, what you say will have more influence.

Sight	Sound	Taste/Smell	Emotion
See	Soft	Sweet	Happy
Bright	Loud	Hot	Sad
Dark	Music	Sour	Scared
Clear	Voice	Fresh	Peace

THE EYES ARE THE WINDOWS TO THE SOUL

If you ask someone a question, you may notice that for a split second their eyes cut in a specific direction. This is because they are accessing a particular part of their brain to recall something they've heard, felt, or said. This either means they are accessing memories or using their creativity to make something up or lie. Also, by paying attention eye direction, you can tell how that person experiences the world (visually, audibly, through smell or taste, or even feeling) and then communicate with that person in a way that they will best understand and appreciate.

Upper-Left or Straight Ahead

The person is visually constructing a scene or seeing something that they haven't experienced before. This may be an indication they are lying.

Mid-Left

The person is imagining a sound they haven't heard before. If that is a conversation, this could indicate they are lying.

Lower-Left

The person is imagining how something feels kinesthetically (touch, movement, position, weight, and so on). This too could be an indication they are lying.

Upper-Right or Straight Ahead

The person is remembering something they have seen. That means there is a good chance they are recalling actual events.

Mid-Right

The person is remembering something they have heard. That means there is a good chance they are recalling actual events.

Lower-Right

The person is having an internal conversation with themselves. This may indicate they are weighing a situation and are about to make some sort of choice.

The movements above are true for about 85 percent of all people. However, the opposite is true for those who don't fall into the 85 percent—in other words, where someone would normally look up and to the right when remembering what they've seen, those who don't fall into this category would look up and to the left. Many believe this happens mostly in left-handed people. So, if you want to discover how a person represents their experiences, ask a nonleading question that requires them to draw upon an experience.

For example:

> "What helps you decide if something is real?" vs. "How can you *tell* (auditory suggestion) if what you *see* (visual suggestion) is real?"

NEURO-LINGUISTIC PROGRAMMING

The first real scholarly study of language and its effect on behavior was brought to us by Richard Bandler (MA Psychology, Lone Mountain College; BA Philosophy, University of California) and John Grinder (BA Psychology, University of San Francisco; PhD Linguistics, University of California). Together they cofounded NLP, or neuro-linguistic programming, which is an approach to communication, personal development and psychotherapy. NLP uses what is known about neurological processes (neuro-), language (linguistic), and learned behavioral patterns (programming) to create a powerful system for change.

The premise is that language triggers behavior. Think about it: all expressions of language—words both written and spoken, gestures small and grandiose and tonalities—relay a multitude of ideas that, when accepted, trigger a response. That response could be to reject the idea or simply file that concept in the back of the mind to deal with it later—but if delivered correctly and under the right circumstances, that word will cause a physiological change, a shift in views, or a person to act.

Although NLP is considered a pseudoscience by mainstream psychology, it is nevertheless very effective. This is why it is extremely popular among sales professionals who wish to learn how to persuade their clients to buy big-ticket items, people in upper management who want to know how to motivate their employees, and sketchy con artists who want to improve their abilities to fleece people. But to be fair, NLP is also used for positive psychological change both personally and in therapy—we will be examining all this.

The Three Steps of Influencing

1. Building Rapport
2. Pacing
3. Leading

Building Rapport

Rapport is how well others resonate with you and thus, how well received you are. When people feel comfortable with you, they tend to be more open to suggestion. Studies have shown that rapport is 55 percent body language, 38 percent vocal tone, and only 7 percent of what you actually say. Building a rapport can be a matter of mimicking that person's behavior; their energy level, the way they move and speak—this is called pacing—but building a rapport also has a lot to do with trust and reputation. If people don't trust you, because you have a bad reputation, they will feel uncomfortable around you and will be less open to suggestion.

Pacing

A major technique used in NLP is pacing. Pacing means to mimic someone's behavior—example: if they clasp their hands, you clasp yours; if they scratch their nose, so do you; and if they lean back and relax, you do the same thing. Why? Because people are comfortable with what is familiar and what is more familiar than your own behavior. When you mimic someone, you become a reflection of who they are—and we all tend to trust ourselves over others, don't we. But if you try too hard, there is an obvious risk involved, because any intelligent or highly observant person will make you—the idea is to be subtle.

> Exercise: Spend some time pacing every other person you meet. Do this in a subtle way, notice how they react to you.

Do they react more positively, or does it seem to bother them? If it bothers them, tone it down.

Leading

Leading is the second step to pacing—it basically means to direct actions and thoughts on an unconscious level, by using suggestive movements, or words. Leading should only be done after you have effectively paced someone—which may take a few minutes to do. Because pacing is a form of entrainment, a person who has been successfully paced will begin to mimic your actions and words. For example, if you ran your fingers through your hair, they would be unconsciously compelled to do so as well, or if you sat up, they too would also sit up.

To lead with words, you need to disguise suggestions within sentences. Otherwise, those suggestions are open to be judged and evaluated by the conscious mind. Even though those suggestions are well hidden within normal conversation, they are still heard by the unconscious mind—the part of the mind that is most receptive. On top of this, you can emphasize a suggestion, by raising or lowering the pitch of your voice or inserting a momentary pausing before the intended suggestion. Besides hiding your suggestion, you must make sure the suggestion is well-formed. This means, a hidden suggestion cannot be vague, such as "Go." Instead use "Go home," or better, "Go home now." Below are examples of sentences with hidden suggestions that are well-formed.

Examples:

(The sound of a clock ticks in the background.)

"I find *the sound of the ticking clocks hypnotic and relaxing.* Does *it make you tired also?*"

"Once you *feel confident,* you will *do a good job* and be able to *go home as soon as you're done.*"

> "It's easy to *resist alcohol*, once you realize that the more you *resist drinking, the better you will feel.* Then once you feel better and *see all the health benefits*, you will *be more confident* that once you *give up drinking, it was the right decision for you.*"

Also note that these hidden suggestions can be added to text—advertisers do this all the time. When placing suggestions in text, you can subtly emphasize suggestions by using a slightly different font, making that font one-size smaller or larger, or inserting an extra space just before and after the suggestion. Take a look at the suggestions below that have been reworked for text—you may want to try this with your resume.

Examples:

> "Once you feel confident, you will do a good job and be able to go home as soon as it's done."

> "It's easy to resist alcohol, once you realize that the more you resist drinking, the better you will feel. Then once you feel better, and see all the health benefits, you will be more confident that giving up drinking was the right decision for you."

The Power of "Because"

When Harvard social psychologist Ellen Langer conducted an experiment to test the persuasive power of the word *because*, she got some interesting results. The first time she asked, "Excuse me. I have five pages. May I use the Xerox machine?" to a line of people waiting to make copies at a public copying machine, 60 percent of those people let her do it. But with the next group she tried something different. Instead of just asking them to let her skip to the front, she inserted the word "because." This time, after asking, "Excuse me. I have five pages. May I use the Xerox machine because I'm in a rush?" 94 percent of those people let her past. However, to make things even more interesting, she decided to give a no-nonsense excuse. This time, she asked, "Excuse me, I have five pages. May I use the Xerox machine *because I have to make some copies?*," and amazingly 93 percent of those people let her *through. So, how does this work? It works because people tend to accept things when given a plausible reason, even if that reason doesn't make perfect sense.*

Other Forms of Lingo Skullduggery

There are many ways to slip commands past the conscious mind and deliver them to the subconscious. Most of the examples below involve confusion, so don't worry if they make perfect sense.

Embedded Command & Confusion
"Would you like to go to the store" <insert distraction>

Double Binding (Illusion of Choice)
"Would you like to meet me at noon, or five-thirty?"

Context Chaining (Confusion)
"You know I talked to John the other day, who said his brother from California that went to the movies and bumped into Sara his sister's aunt, who told him about—" <insert suggestion>

Confusion Is a Sign of Understanding
"The fact that you don't understand right now, tells me that you are actually getting this on a deeper level. Soon it will all be clear."

The Yes Set
Ask a series of questions that must be answered using the word *yes*. This will make it more likely that the last suggestion you make will also be accepted.

The Truth Set
Make a series of statements that are all true, then insert a suggestion at the end.

Shocking Statement
"I am still shocked that twelve middle school students were murdered in that school bus wreck the other day. But anyway <suggestion>."

ANCHORING

The word *anchor* is used to describe the pairing of a thought or feeling to a word, symbol, or gesture. Once that thought or feeling is strongly paired with a signal of some sort, that signal can be used to trigger a response. When triggered covertly, that response is generated unconsciously. That means you can create a sympathetic link in others in much the same way that you create them in yourself for ritualistic purposes.

If all this seems farfetched, consider the experiments of Pavlov. Anchoring is very similar to the same technique Pavlov used to condition his dogs. Every time he fed his dogs, he would ring a bell. When that happened, the dogs began to salivate, and then they came running. So by pairing the sound of a bell with the act of feeding, Pavlov soon discovered that all he had to do to cause the dogs to salivate was to simply ring the bell, even though no food was offered. This technique can of course be used on human beings with or without them knowing it. When used skillfully, the triggered thoughts and emotions of others becomes a matter of irresistible unconscious reflex.

How to Anchor

Step 1: Choose a Signal

A signal can be any word, sound, symbol, image, or gesture. If you intend to do this stealthily, make sure to choose something that is not obvious. Remember: words or phrases can be covertly hidden within a conversation—you will just need to be careful to stress the word or phrase when you anchor it or trigger it. In the same sense, other anchors, such as images, sounds, and gestures, need to be subtle enough that they are not recognized by the conscious mind, but emphasized enough so that they will register in the unconscious. When choosing an anchor, avoid using signals that are too common—like scratching your nose—because you could trigger a paired thought or feeling in your target without intending to.

Step 2: Invoke through Suggestion

Before you can expect to set your anchor, you need to invoke an idea or feeling within the mind of your target. This can be done using suggestion and through the projection of intent. For example, let's say you wanted to invoke "trust" in your target, every time you touched them on the shoulder. You might begin by talking about the importance of trust, then ask your target to tell you about someone they really trusted and why. Their eyes and body language should give you an indication if they are actually thinking about it. As they are recalling their trustworthy friend and his or her qualities, begin mentally sending the intention that "you can be trusted." Once your target has fully actualized these thoughts and before he or she has a chance to think about anything else, set the anchor.

Step 3: Set the Anchor

Setting an anchor is a matter of exposing your target to the signal. If you are doing this covertly, then you will have to reveal that trigger in a way that will not draw suspicion. For example, to set the "trust" anchor mentioned above, you would need to reach out and touch that person's shoulder. It is also important to understand that you cannot just set an anchor once and expect it to remain. This process might have to be repeated over and over again until you are able to finally trigger the right response.

Step 4: Trigger

In any case, once you have successfully set your anchor, all you have to do is expose it to trigger the response. If it's a word, say it. If it's a symbol, picture, or gesture, present it. And if it's a sound, make it or play it. Again, do it subtly if you are trying to trigger a person without their awareness.

PERCEPTION WITHOUT AWARENESS

Large advertising corporations, government agencies, the military and psychologists have been interested in manipulating people through their awareness for a very long time—this is why subliminal and supraliminal messages are widely used in advertisements and propaganda today. As a matter of fact, these techniques have been considered "occult" knowledge for centuries.

Despite its ancient origins, most people were not aware they could be manipulated while in a conscious state, before the release of a book called *The Hidden Persuaders* in 1957. Even though this book didn't use the term "subliminal," it did popularize the techniques used today in modern advertising. These techniques focused on engaging the subconscious mind by playing to the emotions of the consumer, using fear, hopes, dreams and sex to unconsciously motivate people to buy.

The term *subliminal advertising* was coined by James Vicary in 1957, who purportedly controlled the minds of an audience, as they watched the movie *The Picnic* at a theater in Ft. Lee, New Jersey. To accomplish this, Vicary placed a tachistoscope (an instrument used for exposing objects to the eye for a very brief period of time) in the projection booth and flashed suggestive messages like "Thirsty," "Drink Cola Cola," "Hungry," and "Eat Popcorn" every five seconds, as the movie played. Although these messages were only displayed for one-three-thousandth of a second each—far below the ability to consciously perceive them—Coca Cola sales were reported to have increased by 18.1 percent and popcorn sales were said to skyrocket to an astonishing 57.8 percent.

After a major uproar by the American people, there was a call to perform the experiment again by the president of the Psychological Corporation, Dr. Henry Link, after which Vicary admitted to fudging his numbers. Not surprisingly, even after Vicary confessed, the American people tried to get two congressional bills passed to ban the practice, but those bills died before being voted upon.

More recently, the psychologist Adrian North proved that he could increase the sales of a particular type of wine at a liquor store by playing French and German music over the intercom. He discovered that when French music was played, French wine would outsell the German wine, and when German music was played, the German wine would outsell the French wine.

Not surprisingly scientists and psychologists have tried to distance themselves from this practice by denying that it ever worked. Despite this, research is still going on under a different name—Perception Without

Awareness, or PWA. Regardless of the language used, manipulating people without them being aware of it is a well-documented science that is backed by empirical evidence.

For instance, in 1968 Zajonc demonstrated that people could develop a preference toward something if they were exposed to it on a repeated basis. And in 1980, Kunst-Wilson and Zajonc proved that human beings could detect differences in objects well below the expected threshold of perception. To demonstrate this, in phase one of their experiment they exposed their subjects to irregular-shaped octagons for one millisecond, and then in phase two, they exposed them to both perfectly shaped octagons and the irregular octagons for the same duration. When asked to choose which ones they favored, the subjects choose the irregular octagons 60 percent of the time. And it was also discovered that repeated exposure to stimuli presented below the threshold of awareness created the same preference.

The experiments of Debner and Jacoby in 1994 using "priming words" is another good example of PWA. Subjects were flashed a series of priming words—half at a rate well below the threshold of awareness (one millisecond) and half at a rate that could be clearly seen. The subjects were then given word stems to complete words and asked to create words *not* using those words presented during the priming phase. The result was that the subliminal priming words were more likely to be used than the ones that could actually be seen—and that of course means that the subliminal priming words were being perceived without awareness.

In retrospect, this means that we sense more than we think we sense, but our minds simply hand us what it thinks we should know. So just because we are not aware of it doesn't mean we haven't perceived it. And despite how much we think our minds are impenetrable to subconscious influence, our behavior *can* be manipulated by what our subconscious mind filters out. Being aware of this, will help you be less susceptible to this kind of suggestion. So now that you know this, how can you use this as a part of your Sorcery practice?

Using Supraliminal Suggestions

Like the sympathetic linking process described in the chapter "Occult Magick," ideas, concepts and emotional triggers in society, have already been paired with physical stimuli—this has been happening since birth. In fact, our minds are always scanning the environment for opportunity and danger. This behavior was initially evolved as a type of survival strategy. So when your ancestors crept into those spooky woods to collect berries, they were using perception without awareness to not only look for the color red, but also to prevent themselves from being eaten by that bloodthirsty grizzly bear. This means that certain outside stimuli are already paired with primal instincts.

In such case, any stimuli or symbol that is associated with instincts like preservation and sex-drive can be used to unconsciously suggest something without people necessarily picking it up. A good example of this would be the word *sex* written on a can of energy drink that is hidden within the brand's logo, or a picture of the Hurricane Katrina disaster, at a booth that sells guns.

Besides this, any symbol that represents an idea can be worn, or placed in an area in order to suggest it. Only the most observant will be aware of it, all others will "see" the object and file its suggestion in their subconscious mind. Once it enters the subconscious, that suggestion is more likely to be acted upon than if you were to suggest it directly.

Examples:
- If you want people to fall asleep, or relax, expose them to pictures of people sleeping or relaxing. For example, a picture of a Buddha meditating with his eyes closed would do.
- To encourage trust wear white, or demonstrate similarity by decorating your space with things that person is interested in.
- If you want to get someone amped up, play invigorating music that is suggestive of the state of mind you want to put them in.

Using Subliminal Suggestions

Besides dropping things in plain sight, you can expose people to stimuli that is barely perceivable and although they don't consciously see it, they will pick up on it anyways. For example, pictures and words flashed one-tenth of a second will register in the subconscious mind and affect their thoughts and behavior and things written in invisible ink, which can only be seen using a black light will have the same effect. In the same sense, saying or playing something fast, or at low volume can be picked up by the subconscious mind and be used to motivate, inspire, deter, or manipulate people.

In conclusion, these are all things you should consider when setting up your own Sacred Space, room for working with clients, or when casting spells that are intended to affect others.

Entrancement

U p until now, I have focused on teaching *you* how to enter a trance, but now I will get into the art of entrancement, which is how to bring *others* into that very same state. Knowing how to entrance others will not only give you the ability to heal them, uncover valuable information, and unlock any latent psychic powers they may have, but also is the reason why our ancestors huddled around their hearth, telling stories about scary old women who could bewitch people using the evil eye.

If you've read any other books on magick, you have most likely discovered that things like entrancement, fascination, and bewitchment have either been ignored or underdescribed. This is primarily because occult authors generally don't have a good understanding of how it works. And the reason for that is because more magicians these days, see magick as something different and apart from science and therefore choose to ignore scientific knowledge entirely. It may also be that this art is so powerful that secret establishments like magical orders, covert government agencies and other clandestine organizations simply don't want it to be publicly known—and honestly, I can understand why because it can be quite dangerous. But in all actuality, this information is sitting in plain sight available to anyone who is willing to do a little digging.

But in reality, entrancement has been around for ages—it has been practiced by shamans, gurus, priests, and practitioners of magick for thousands of years. An example of this would be the sleep temples of ancient Greece, where ailing people were ushered in by priests to sleep under the visage of Asclepeion, the Greek God of medicine. It has been said that many left the temple cured. In fact, any encounter with a person believed to have magical powers could be cited as having an entrancing effect upon those who encountered them—charisma and expectation play an important part in the entrancement process, so even if one considers the outcome of those encounters as psychosomatic, it does not make it any less miraculous.

As fantastical as all this sounds, entrancement is something that has been practiced and is still being practiced today by professionals in the field of psychology—it is called hypnosis. As a matter of fact, up until recently, hypnotism was known as mesmerism. Mesmerism began as a technique used by Franz Friedrich Anton Mesmer (1784–1815), a German physician living in Austria, to heal the infirm. Mesmer believed in something called "animal magnetism," a life force that coursed through not only human beings, but also all living things. This energy was said to have a fluidic property, connect everything, and be responsive to thoughts or intention. To heal, Mesmer would position his patience around a gigantic wooden tub filled with liquid (believed to carry the magnetic current). Each patient would then be connected either by cord, or by an angled iron joint partially submerged in the liquid, while Mesmer himself would move among them delivering his magnesium by glance, the pass of his hands, or by directing it through an iron rod. Even though his practice in Austria enjoyed many years of success, he decided to move to Paris, France, to work with wealthy clients after a failed attempt to heal a blind woman. His arrival in Paris spawned debate about whether he was fraudulent or, indeed, a genius who had discovered a legitimate way to heal the sick.

Although Mesmer was very successful in treating ailments using his methods, this success generated jealousy among traditional medical practitioners, who were less successful in treating the same patients. Threatened by his success, he was descended upon by the Royal Commission and later by the Royal Academy in an attempt to prove he was a charlatan and thus put him out of business. But even though they were forced to acknowledge that real healing was taking place, they could not prove that any sort of magnetic fluid existed, so they jumped to the conclusion that the healing was facilitated by means of patient expectation and the suggestive charisma of Mesmer himself—in other words placebo. So they dropped what they considered to be the unnecessary magical bits (the tub, the iron rods and the hand passes), kept the suggestions and developed a system known as hypnotism—and this eventually caused Mesmerism to fall out of practice.

Clinical hypnosis operates under the assumption that any changes; be they psychological, or physical recovery (healing) are caused by a person's natural ability to heal themselves. This means in the minds of modern hypnotists, there is no energy exchange happening at all—and this is unfortunate because there is plenty of research suggesting otherwise. So as time passed, this very powerful technique became neutered by science. Fortunately, though, the practice of Mesmerism never really died—in fact Mesmerism has taken root in Brazil and there is even a school of Mesmerism in Nice France headed by Dr. Marco Paret.

Another interesting fact about hypnosis is that psychic phenomenon such as clairvoyance, remote-suggestion and channeling, used to be included as a part of its study—and this came about, because such phenomena commonly happen when gifted, or sensitive people were placed in a trance. But as materialistic dogma dominated the landscape, interest in this type of study became scandalous and any evidence supporting it was suppressed or disavowed. But we will not be worrying about small-minded people, our goal is not to prove anything—we already know it works. Instead, we will delve into all branches of entrancement and work on getting results. So with that being said and the history of entrancement being laid out, let's talk about ethics.

ETHICS

As far as I am concerned, the same rules that apply to professionals using hypnosis, also apply to Sorcerers using entrancement. Yes—you can use entrancement to hack people's minds to create glassy-eyed zombies that will do your bidding, but doing so would make you a monster and most likely get you locked up or killed. The rule of return still applies here, "What you sow, so shall you reap!" When I sat down to write this book, I promised myself that I would not hold anything back, so this chapter *will* tell you how mind control works, step-by-step. However, I am not telling you this because I want you to abuse the innocent, I am telling you because you need to know how to defend yourself against it and on rare occasions use it as a weapon against evil. Just so you know, wielding this kind of power tends to cause those who would even think about misusing it to become engulfed and lost to darkness. Sure you might think, "Who cares… maybe I want to be a dark Magician.," but what you don't realize is those who live off of darkness are consumed and eventually destroyed by it—so take my word for it: don't go there!

WHO CAN BE ENTRANCED?

Scientific studies show that approximately 90 percent of the population can be hypnotized. Out of that 90 percent, 10 percent can achieve a heavy trance, while the other 80 percent can be induced into a medium trance. The remaining 10 percent are considered unhypnotizable, or of low susceptibility. Keep in mind those numbers were gathered from studies using traditional hypnotic techniques, not the entrancement techniques taught in this book. So what makes people so susceptible and is susceptibility normal? The truth is no one really knows for sure, but experts in the field of psychology do have theories. They do know from conclusive studies that people who have experienced psychological trauma, the mentally ill, and young children are among the most susceptible. All of these groups, especially children, have two things in common: a good imagination and emotional instability.

My own pet theory is that most of us are being entranced from cradle to grave. We experience mental trauma when we listen to the news or read a tragic newspaper article—and this affects us on a deep emotional level. Additionally, we are being mentally influenced every day by commercial advertisements, political rhetoric, and religious indoctrination. Is this normal? No, I don't think so, but it surely creates a very susceptible society. It certainly gives you something to think about as watch people obsessively surf the web, respond to meaningless comments on Facebook, and play mindless games on their cell phone. Of course, none of these things in and of themselves are bad, but they do keep people's minds entranced if allow they allow them to.

HYPNOSIS AND DRUGS

It has also been shown that drugs and alcohol attribute to susceptibility. Scientific studies have shown that alcohol and drugs like oxytocin, a hormone that promotes trust and social bonding and nitrous oxide, a common anesthetic gas, increases people's chances of being hypnotized. But at the same time, there are plenty of herbs and foods commonly used in cooking that do the same thing. I am in no way suggesting that you drug people against their will. I personally don't believe in using hard drugs, so I suggest that if you want to use drugs to help yourself or someone else get into state, go natural. In such case, you can consult the Hypnotics Correspondence Table at the end of this book, which provides a plethora of naturally hypnotic foods and herbs—but by all means, find out if the subject has any allergies first. But to help you understand the effects that alcohol and drugs have on level of susceptibility, I have constructed a list of hypnotic drug studies and their findings below.

Study	Drug	Increase
Sjoberg et al. (1965)	Mescaline	12.7%
	LSD	12.8%
	Psilocybin	0.66%
	Combination	11.75%
Gibson et al. (1977)	Diazepam	0.91%
	Active Placebo	0.41%
Kelly et al. (1978)	Cannabis	22.6%
	Control	0.54%
Barber et al. (1979)	Nitrous Oxide (excluding analgesia suggestion)	27.5%
Whalley & Brooks (2009)	Nitrous Oxide 25% (no induction)	10%
Semmens-Wheeler, Dienes, Duka (2013)	Alcohol (w/induction + 9 suggestions)	69%
Carhart-Harris et al. (2014)	LSD (no induction)	65%

Increasing Hypnotic Susceptibility by Increasing Expectation

Although some people are more susceptible to hypnosis than others, research has verified that susceptibility can be engineered by faking indicators and heightening expectations with suggestion. For example, in 1989 Wickless & Kirsch increased susceptibility in low hypnotizables (people who are difficult to hypnotize) by faking their hypnosis symptoms. Basically what they did was tell the subject they would experience foreign sounds and colors, then once they had their eyes closed they simply projected colored lights into the closed lids and played sounds over a tape recorder. Once their subjects had experienced something they thought validated hypnosis, they let down their guard and were more hypnotizable in the future.

But increasing someone's hypnotizability does not have to involve smoke and mirrors (in this case lights and sounds), it can just be a matter of telling someone to expect to be hypnotized. In 2005, Gandhi & Oakley performed an experiment where they told half of their subjects they were going to experience "hypnosis," and the other half that they were going to experience "relaxation." They discovered that those who received the suggestion that they would be "hypnotized" were more inclined to experience hypnosis, than those who were told they would be experiencing a state of "relaxation." In such a case, we can assume that suggesting "I am going to bewitch you, or put you under a spell" to someone who does not believe in magick, would have the same nonhypnotic effect as being told "you will experience relaxation"—the hypnosis would probably fail and it could even prevent you from being able to hypnotize them in the future.

Both of these studies suggest two things: someone's susceptibility can be increased through mere suggestion and expectation and belief in hypnosis plays a significant role in someone's ability to be hypnotized. This doesn't mean hypnosis is fake, just because expectations play a role. It only means that expectations make a difference. It makes no difference how the subject got into that state, the fact still remains, being in that state produces real measurable changes in a person's brainwave patterns—they are entranced.

BEING HYPNOTIZED AGAINST ONE'S WILL

Now we come to the topic of willing and unwilling subjects. Those who practice clinical hypnosis would like you to think that no one can be hypnotized against their will, but I am here to tell you that is rubbish—it can and does happen. A rapid induction uses surprise and confusion to drop people into a trance long enough to tell their subconscious mind to "sleep!" – so by definition it works best on people who are unaware. To prove this case, I must also mention that many crimes have been committed by hypnotists who have gained the trust and full cooperation of their targets through deception. There have been cases of hypnotists acting as fortune tellers and palm readers in order to gain that cooperation long enough to put their targets under. In 2014, a Russian-born hypnotist approached a sixty-six-year-old woman, Sarah Alexeveya, in front of an Aldi in Elmshorn, Schleswig-Holstein, offering to read her fortune. The next thing she remembered was waking up in her armchair missing her jewelry and valuables.

Hypnotists have also gained cooperation from their victims by offering beneficial hypnotherapy. Once those subjects were under, they then gave suggestions of compliance and commenced to taking advantage. In 2013, a British hypnotist convinced a client that she was his "sexual slave." Timothy Porter, age forty, persuaded his victim that he could treat her anxiety and facilitate weight loss through hypnosis. However, when she awoke, she found him with his pants down. Needless to say she called the authorities and Porter pleaded guilty to one count of causing a person to engage in sexual activity without consent. I say this only to prove a point—people can be deceived into giving up control. If you scour the web, you will find many other cases like these.

And as already discussed, hypnotic suggestions can be delivered to people using covert symbols and disguised words, while they are fully conscious. Furthermore, this type of covert hypnosis can be used to lull subjects into a trance deep enough to drop them into a more susceptible state. For this reason, if you ever find it necessary to entrance someone against their will, it is extremely important for you to be aware of the personal danger you put yourself in. If you fail, consider yourself lucky if all your target does is laugh at you. But understand, if you try to entrance the wrong target and fail, you could end up as a victim of assault, or even murder. No one wants to be turned into a little mind-puppet.

THE DANGERS OF ENTRANCEMENT

Hypnosis can be used to improve quality of life by helping people cope with traumatic repressed memories, to alleviate pain and even to entertain, but just like everything else it can be dangerous. And I'm not just talking about the obvious intentional misuse of such a power, but the unintended effects it can have on a subject.

The fact that a hypnotic trance narrows awareness, can cause a person to tune things out and create major problems, or even death if a subject has been unknowingly left in a trance state. If not properly brought out they could get could get into their car and end up getting into a wreck and killing themselves or someone else. Also being in that trance means they are still very susceptible to suggestion—they may unintentionally take something said in jest, as a command and end up carrying it out unconsciously. If the conversation involved the suggestion to hurt someone, they may do it, even though that suggestion was not meant to be taken literally—after all, people say things don't mean all the time.

Although hypnosis can be used to kill pain, this also poses a danger, because pain serves a purpose—it tells us that something very wrong is going on in our bodies that needs to be taken care of. If hypnosis was used to kill someone's pain, that person could fail to realize that something was horribly wrong with their physical condition and thus die because they never sought out treatment—this is why those using entrancement for pain management should be careful.

Next is the very powerful effect of hallucination—all you have to do is use your imagination to see how this could go wrong. Hallucinations created during hypnosis can be very real! Real-life experiences can be traumatic enough, so it goes without saying that causing someone to experience the wrong kind hallucination could cause mental trauma and send them into a psychotic fit. It's bad enough when a real-life experience challenges what we know about reality, but when you add to this the fact that hypnosis can be used to cause hallucinations that seem supernatural, well, that could really drive someone over the edge. And I haven't even mentioned that hallucinations can cause people believe there is a genuine threat that needs to be dealt with.

Yet another danger of hypnosis is the creation of false memories. And this doesn't have to be an intentional infringement on your subject's mind—it can happen by accident. If you lead your subject under a false assumption, they will naturally create a scenario following that line thought and end up creating a false memory. This is what happened during the Satanic Panic of the mid-1970s and 1990s. People thought there was a Satanic conspiracy to abduct and sacrifice their children to the devil, so the police brought in the alleged victims and had psychiatrists use hypnosis to attempt to uncover traumatic experiences that the children allegedly had. During these hypnosis sessions, the hypnotists asked leading questions based on the allegations of abuse. These questions were then taken as suggestions by the children's impressionable subconscious minds and embellished upon using their vivid imagination—people ended up spending years in prison based on these false memories. So you must understand that while a person is in such a susceptible state, they will translate your words literally. If you suggest they were abducted by aliens and describe how it went down, that will become a new memory and they will think they were an alien abductee.

Probably the most dangerous factor of entrancement is its effect on the nervous system. In the early days of mesmerism, when the French Royal Commission and the Royal Academy of Medicine (1787–1826) was hot on the tail of Mesmer, trying to prove him a fraud, they tried to stop the practice on the grounds that it caused fits of convulsions or seizures. This was encountered by doctors while trying to reproduce Mesmerizing effects without understanding the process. The first time they witnessed a patient go into seizure they panicked and tried restraining him, thus causing bodily harm. Mesmer and those who practiced mesmerism, understood seizure as a type of crisis, or Kundalini rising.

They also knew that, once it began, it must be allowed to run its course, because this crisis caused the energy to rise through all the centers, resetting and balancing the entire biological system—the result, being the miraculous cure of the patient. Other patients went into a cataleptic state while subject to hypnotic tampering under the care of the doctors of the Royal Academy—their bodies freezing in place—some times for days, weeks or even years. One poor woman nearly starved to death, because her mouth was locked shut by paralysis. At the time they didn't have feeding tubes, so instead they tried to force-feed her by prying her mouth open using a steal bar—which of course shattered her teeth and caused damage to her jaw. Even though the inexperienced doctors were clueless, those practicing mesmerism understood what was going on and knew how to bring people safely out of those states.

All of these things make entrancement very serious business and this is why you need to be extremely cautious when using it. My suggestion is that you interview a person before deciding to use entrancement to help them. Build a psychological profile of that person and find out if they have any kind of physical limitations, have experienced any debilitating mental trauma, or suffer from mental illness. After determining if entrancement is safe, make realistic goals and construct a line of hypnotic suggestions that will clearly be understood by the subject. And lastly, make sure that subject has fully emerged from their trance before you see them off.

HOW DOES ENTRANCEMENT WORK?

Entrancement basically cuts through, or bypasses a subject's conscious mind in order to speak directly to their unconscious mind. Remember that not only is the unconscious mind a conduit to the higher spiritual realms and psychic faculties, but also it lacks the logical mechanism to evaluate things rationally—so it is for this reason that suggestions by entrancers or hypnotists are easily taken. If you want to get a better understanding of this, go back and reread the chapter entitled "Mind and Magick."

The next thing you should understand is that entrancement, unlike hypnosis utilizes the manipulation of a person's energy field *along with* non-verbal and verbal commands, in order to bring a subject into a deep-trance state and guide their mental processes. By energy field, we are of course talking about Odic power or animal magnetism once believed to exist by Baron Carl von Reichenbach and Franz Mesmer—we simply refer to this as the life force, the auric field, or etheric energy. By accepting that this force exists, you should also understand that it is a combination of a Sorcerer's skill *and* his ability to manipulate life force that makes entrancement possible. When you reincorporate this knowledge back into modern scientific techniques such as hypnosis, entrancement becomes way more powerful.

So how is such a thing initiated? Well, there are actually three distinct forms of entrancement: traditional hypnosis, rapid induction, and entrainment (bewitchment). Each of these forms of entrancement rely on one or more levels of communication as described below.

LEVELS OF COMMUNICATION

Entrancement is about making a connection with a subject, then communicating with him or her to deliver a suggestion. These suggestions can be and are oftentimes delivered in three ways; psychically (mind to mind), nonverbally (through gesture), and verbally (using voice). All suggestions, whether they come directly from the mind as a telepathic message or are delivered through some kind of gesture or conveyed through speech, carry energy laced with intent. In this way, a suggestion is really made of the same energy we use in occult magick when casting a spell.

Psychic

Whether we realize it or not, every single one of us communicates on a deep psychic level. Those who are aware of it can pick this information up and those who are not are susceptible to the emotional tides lingering about or psychic influence.

Nonverbal

Our first mode of communication, nonverbal, comes as a baby or young child before we are able to understand speech. Because of this, we read, send, and react to nonverbal cues all the time. Therefore, if you study body language, it can be used to send suggestion without the need for speaking. Also, because body language presents no verbal argument, it is less likely to be resisted, whereas words can be debated—nonverbal suggestions carry psychic energy also.

Verbal

Well-placed words, either direct or subliminal, are an excellent way to communicate a suggestion, but those words must be understood first. This is why it is necessary to be familiar with universal vocabulary. Your chances of delivering a successful suggestion is increased when you understand the way your subject expresses him- or herself in words. This is why it is always good to talk with people beforehand to gauge how they speak—words can be misunderstood and misinterpreted.

FACTORS OF INFLUENCE

As you have learned in the chapter on Psi, it is absolutely possible to connect with people psychically from a distance. However, you must be aware of other factors when using entrancement to connect to people who are right in front of you. These factors include trust, the ability to be understood, charisma, energetics and environment.

Trust

The power of entrancement is in the suggestion and that suggestion, like all forms of magick is energy embodied by intent. Any suggestion, just like any spell can be stymied by mental opposition, whether in the form of disbelief, or simply because the subject does not wish to be entranced. Disbelief or objection can come from a misunderstanding of what entrancement is, or be the result of an irrational fear, this is why it is important to talk with a subject before you try to entrance them. Many people would like to think that they cannot be hypnotized—maybe it's because they don't really know what hypnosis is, or perhaps it's because they believe that hypnosis only works on the mentally deficient, or the unintelligent. The first thing you need to do is explain to them that hypnosis allows a person to shift focus from the physical world and direct it inward. You should also tell them that this is something that everyone does every day, naturally when they become focused on one task over another. Cite the phenomenon of highway hypnosis if you have to—or being transfixed by the cell phone or television. By all means tell them that it has nothing to do with how intelligent they are—only their ability to focus, visualize and use their imagination. If they don't believe in hypnosis, simply inform them that it has been used in clinical psychology and medicine, for centuries to help people overcome mental trauma, addiction and even kill pain without the need for anesthesia in major surgeries.

Those with an irrational fear of hypnosis can be consoled by dispelling any misunderstandings. For example, if they have been told they can get stuck in the hypnotized state, tell them that it is extremely rare. Let them know that most people left in trance, will simply wake up refreshed after a few minutes' relaxation. Another fear is mind control; again, this can happen, but no one can be made to do something that they wouldn't normally do. If your suggestions go against their morals, they will simply not comply. But above all, assure them that you are there to help them, not humiliate them, or make them your mind-puppet.

The Ability to Be Understood

Even though this is obvious, it can be easy to overlook. If you intend to use verbal communication as a part of your induction techniques, your target *must* be able to understand you. If they don't understand you, they will not be able to take suggestions. This obviously means you can't expect to entrance someone using verbal communication who doesn't speak your language. It also means, if you are expressing yourself in a vocabulary that is different from, or far above your target's level of understanding, it won't work. This is a good reason to study your subject, know what kind of language they speak, words they use and be aware of their level of vocabulary—I can't stress this more.

Charisma

Charisma is another way of saying presence or authority. This is not meant to imply how well you dominate others, but rather how confident others are in your ability to do what you say. This sort of presence is felt by others as the result of your confidence and appearance. All human beings are naturally genetically predisposed to listen to authority. Why? Because we are all born ignorant and vulnerable. As infants and children, we possess no worldly knowledge and no means to defend ourselves against things that might threaten our existence, so we naturally look to our parents and other authority figures who are supposed to know what they are doing to defend us.

As we grow from infants to young adults, our highly sensitive minds have absorbed all the beliefs and behaviors of our parents. By the time we have flown the coop, most of us have been well conditioned to accept the authority of anyone who is considered an expert, doctor, law enforcement, or who professes to be certified. This mind-set is taken advantage of by businesses who want nothing more than to take your money and create the perfect consumer. That's how it works—you believe, because it's been a successful strategy for you all along—or has it?

Whether any of us would like to admit it or not, this conditioning has carried over well into our adult lives, and because of that, people who don't question what they are told, are highly suggestible. This is why understanding the role of authority is a key factor in entrancement—not because you want to take advantage of people, but because it can be used by a tool to help others. So now the question becomes, what does this charisma look like, and how do you develop this presence? All of this depends on your appearance, confidence and credibility—let's look at them one by one.

Appearance

Human beings are very visual animals. Just like any successful creature in the animal kingdom, we know how to pick out the leader of the pack. We know he or she is the leader because he or she is the strongest and most attractive. To our primitive little monkey brains, we equate strength with the ability to survive. Now, of course, strength doesn't necessarily mean survival in this day and age, but most haven't evolved past the Neanderthal mind-set enough to realize intelligence is also a great asset. It can also be said that those who are beautiful are typically seen as healthy and this is why we look for beauty when choosing a mate—we do, after all, want our offspring to be healthy as well. And this is why beauty occupies the top of the list in appearance. So the first step in developing your presence is to become healthy or look as healthy as possible.

Needless to say, there are a lot of unhealthy people out there who are in positions of authority, so appearing healthy does not complete the picture—there is something else, and that is the way you dress. Did I mention people were visual? Yes? OK, I'll move on. Point blank, people judge you by the way you dress. If you look shabby, they will assume you are also shabby of mind, status and spirit. If you don't believe me, spend some time at a mall dressed as a homeless person. Walk through the mall and try engaging people in conversation, then go home, take a shower, groom yourself and put on better clothes. Go back to the mall and do the same thing. You will be received much differently. So if you wish to develop a presence of authority you must dress with authority.

What should you wear? Well, that depends on what type of presence you are trying to create. A professional presence would require you to wear a suit, or clothing suited to a particular segment of people (upper-class, blue collar, and so on). However, if you wanted to portray yourself as wise and sagely, you might try wearing something from Indian, African, or the Native American culture. You would then accessorize according to the type of spirituality you were trying to exude. My best advice to you is to mimic the appearance of the type of success you want to attract. If you want to know how to dress, do some research and find out how your target audience expects you to look. Feel free to get creative and make it your own. However, try not to go overboard.

Confidence

There is nothing sexier than someone who is confident! Anyone who owns a charismatic presence has this. Confidence says, "I know what I'm talking about and I can back up what I say with proof and action." The best way to build this kind of confidence is to build your knowledge and skills—after that, it's a matter of getting out there and interacting with others. Once practiced, your confidence will show in your tone of voice and body language—but for God's sake, don't be a braggart. No one likes that!

Credibility

Credibility is described as "the quality of being trusted or believed in." This can of course be deserved, or undeserved, authentic, or false. People will initially judge you by how you look and how confident you are. However, if they have the opportunity to interact with you more than once, they will want to know more about your history, education and accomplishments in order to determine how credible you are. Unfortunately, most people do not take the time to dig and do actual research on the people they meet, so instead they will match what you say about your history, education and accomplishments by directly observing you—the end result (whether they think you are credible or not) is based on a combination of your physical appearance (your health, what you wear, and what you own), how confident you seem and what you do (whether you can produce results).

So, if you can pass the appearance test and can present with confidence, that means all you have to do is demonstrate that you are accredited and then be able to do what you say you can do—and honestly, sometimes just claiming to have credentials is good enough, depending on the gullibility of the person trying to impress. However, if the person you are talking to is smart, he or she will be able to dismantle your lies by simply weighing what you say against known facts. Who knows? They may even decide to do a little research to find out if you are legit. The point is, the best kind of credibility is genuine credibility—so don't lie.

Energetics

A *big* part of entrancement is the ability to resonate with someone. In both magick and entrancement, energetics can be described as the ability to connect with a subject by matching their energy. This singularity happens when intensity of emotion and intention of both you and the subject are the same. To understand this, think of a time when you were a part of a group of people experiencing the same thing at the same time—everyone's emotions were stirred, and everyone experienced pretty much the same thing. Weddings, concerts, moving speeches, or tragic accidents are all good examples that demonstrate energetics. I will go into this in more detail when I get to "entrainment."

Environment

Where entrancement takes place plays a big role in how smoothly it will go or if it will even happen at all. If a person does not feel comfortable or safe, it is unlikely they will be able to achieve a trance deep enough to accomplish anything of lasting value. This is why you must create an atmosphere soothing enough to relax the subject. Although optimal environmental conditions can be unique to each individual subject, most people respond well to a quiet room of moderate temperature, with neutral colors and soft lighting. If your subject appreciates aroma, then add scented candles, or incense.

Another thing to take advantage of is placing unconsciously suggestive cues around the room that not only suggest deep relaxation (achieving a deep trance), but also engender the ideas that you want to install in your subject deep subconscious mind. Such a cue might be a picture of someone being healed or a symbol that means nothing to the person's conscious mind, but actually spells out "WELLNESS." Preparation of an environment in this way can be very intricate and multilayered. But in order to do this successfully, you must get to know your subject by interviewing them.

TESTING SUSCEPTIBILITY

Knowing how susceptible a subject is is very important. One, you want to be successful, so you can help the subject, and two, you want to maintain your credibility—if you fail to entrance someone in front of a crowd, those people may stop believing in you, and therefore you may be less effective when entrancing others in the future. Fortunately, there are signs you can look for and tests you can perform to see how susceptible someone is.

The Signs

- Subject is creative.
- Subject experiences deep emotions.
- Subject has already been hypnotized before and thus can be hypnotized again.
- Subject is cooperative and wants to be hypnotized.

- Subject is naturally compliant to authority.
- Subject reacts to covert nonverbal cues.

The Creative

We already know that highly creative and emotional people are the most susceptible to hypnosis. Therefore, by determining if your target fits into one or both of these categories, you can tell if they will make a good subject. So to test for creativity simply suggest that your target to think about something that will engage their creativity.

Example:

> You: I'm starving. Do you like to cook?
> Target: Yes.
> You: Me too. So if you have to create the perfect dish, what would it look like?

At this point, listen to how the person describes the dish. Do their eyes dart to the left, indicating that they are accessing the right-creative half of the brain. Take note of how much detail they include—the more detail, the more creative, the more creative, the more susceptible.

The Deeply Emotional

Simply talk about an emotionally charged subject and see how emotionally invested the person becomes. The more emotional, the more susceptible that person is likely to be.

Prior Hypnosis Experience

Mention reading a book, watching a video or attending a stage hypnosis event, then ask the person if they've ever experienced it. If they have, ask them if it was successful and if so, ask that they describe what it was like. Make sure to pay attention to the method used by the prior hypnotist. If that hypnotist was successful, there is a good chance you can use the method. Otherwise, you will learn what not to do.

Consent

Ask your subject if they would like to experience hypnosis. Address any misconceptions the target may have, then if they give consent, move forward.

Compliance

Take notice whether or not the person tends to obey the requests, or commands of authority figures, or try giving commands, or suggestions yourself. Remember: a command, or suggestion does not have to be rude—you can in fact ask for cooperation by using the words "could you" or "please." The more obedient the person, the better your chances of entrancing them.

Nonverbal Cues

Have you ever caused others to yawn just by yawning? That is a nonverbal cue. Stand in plain sight or in someone's peripheral vision and do something like yawn, stretch, or scratch. If a person consistently mimics your actions, they are suggestible.

VERIFYING THE HYPNOTIC STATE

Because different states allow for varying degrees of influence, it is extremely important in hypnosis to be able to tell *if* someone is actually in a hypnotic state and to be able to determine how "deep" that state actually is. Without this knowledge, you can't expect your suggestions to stick. So once you have performed your induction, look for some of the symptoms listed below.

Amnesia

This cognitive technique does not rely on physical performance, but instead relies on an amnesia indicator. Have the subject count backward from three hundred to one (the larger number is used because it is out of the person's instinctual counting range). As they count backward, begin making suggestions that the subject will forget the numbers by saying, "Notice how the numbers begin to slip from your mind as you count," or "See the numbers floating away and vanishing as you say them—all numbers after this point begin to fade." Not only will this cause the person to eventually stop counting because they are forgetting the numbers, but also it will cause them fall into a deeper trance.

Another example of amnesia is the Forgotten Words Test. After taking the subject into a trance, tell them they are standing in front of a blackboard. Ask them to walk up to a white chalk and write out the words *apple, fairy, grasshopper,* then ask the subject to raise his or her hand after he or she has written the word. Once the subject raises his or her hand, have him or her pick up an eraser sitting at the base of the chalk board, then erase the words *apple* and *fairy.* Tell the subject, "As you erase these words, I want you to also erase them from your mind. The only word that is left is *grasshopper.*" Affirm that *grasshopper* is the only word they are able to think of by nodding or holding their hand up. Then deepen their trance by counting back from six to zero—example, "As I count backward from six to zero, you will become more relaxed. Six, beginning to feel relaxed, five, even more relaxed, four, the relaxation is becoming more prevalent," and so on. Once you see an indicator that they have relaxed even more (e.g., slumping, elasticity of skin, shallow breathing, and so on), ask them what the three words were. If the subject is able to remember the three words, then he or she has is not yet in the amnesic stage of trance. If they can't remember the other two words, they have reached the amnesic state. At this point, you should say something like, "When I count to three, you will recall all three words and repeat them to me." The subject should then be able to remember the words and repeat them.

Another Test
People that have achieved a medium or heavy trance can be made to forget things, or forget things and recall them later.

Example:

> "Whenever I ask you your name, you will be unable to recall it. The more you try, the more it will slip from your mind. But when I say, 'Remember,' it will immediately come back to you."

Example:

"Whenever you count, you will not be able to remember the odd numbers."

Anesthesia

Anesthesia is the ability to kill pain. This can be localized (confined to one area of the body), or encompass the entire body. As mentioned in the chapter on trance, hypnotic anesthesia has been used to strip varicose veins, extractions in dental procedures and even in open-heart surgery. A simple exercise you can perform on a subject is called the Pinch Test.

Once the subject is in trance, stroke the back of his or her hand. While doing this tell your subject he or she will feel an increasing amount of numbness and loss of sensation in that hand. Repeat this process for a few minutes, while affirming the loss of sensation and numbness, pinch the back of hand you were stroking, then the other. Ask the subject if he or she felt any difference. If there is sensation in one hand and no sensation in the other, this is a good indicator that a medium or deep trance has been achieved.

Breathing

Shallow breathing from the diaphragm is usually an indication that a person is in a light trance, while slower and deeper breathing is a sign that person has slipped into a heavy trance. Erratic breathing combined with REM (rapid eye movement) can also be an indicator that a person has entered into a dreamlike medium or heavy state.

Catalepsy

Oftentimes, those who enter a medium or heavy trance will experience catalepsy. Catalepsy is a type of paralysis that can be local (one part of the body) or encompass the entire body. Out of all the types of catalepsy experienced, arm, hand, and eye catalepsy is the most common. Usually brought on by a medium or heavy trance, the subject's eyes will feel so heavy, they will not be able to open them on their own accord. If you see this, you may want to take the opportunity to gently lift the subject's eyelid to examine his or her eyes. If you do and notice that they red and rolled up in the back of the head, it means they have entered a heavy trance.

Another good indication of a deep trance is full-body rigidity. Although not uncommon, this doesn't happen to everyone—sometimes the opposite happens—the body becomes so relaxed the skin has a loose elastic appearance. If a subject encounters full-body catalepsy, bring them into a more level state by suggesting they are becoming more conscious and relaxed, "As I count from one to (whatever), feel yourself becoming a little more awake than you are now."

Catalepsy can be induced in any state by means of suggestion. For example, if you were to say, "As you relax, you notice that your eyes are beginning to seal shut, so tight that it becomes impossible to open them," or "You may notice that the more you relax, the more rigid your body becomes."

Limpness

If you gently take a subject's wrist, lift their arm and it drops limply to their lap or side, this is a good indication that person may be in a medium trance. However, if you lift their arm and it slowly drops, you know that person has not achieved a trance or is only in a light state.

Somnambulism

If you want to test if someone is in a medium or heavy trance, plant a suggestion that will be followed after they have awoken. This suggest that it be carried out minutes after the person awakes from trance, or that it will be triggered whenever the subject sees you make a particular gesture or use a key word—that suggestion can even be to return to that particular trance state. If they do in fact follow your instruction, it is a good indication they were in a medium or heavy trance.

Example:

> "Whenever you hear me say, 'Tacos are delicious,' you will find this statement so irresistibly funny that you will begin laughing hysterically, but when I say it again, you will stop laughing."

Example:

"Once you have awakened you will feel the urge to walk outside, memorize three license plate numbers, then come back and tell me what they are."

Hallucinations

Subjects that have achieved a medium-to-heavy trance can be made to sense (see, hear, smell, touch and taste) things that are not there, even after they have awoken.

Example:

"When you awake, you will be able to hear me, smell me and even touch me, but you will no longer be able to see me."

Example:

"Whenever you pick up this wand, or I place it in your hand, it will become a snake."

Note: Do not leave people in a hypnotic state! Remove suggestions by bringing them back under and suggesting,

Example:

"When I count to three, you will wake up feeling refreshed and everything will return back to normal."

Example (better):

"When I count to three, you will wake up and you will no longer [insert a suggestion that changes things back to normal. If you made them forget their name, tell them they will remember it. If you made yourself invisible, tell them they will be able to see you again and if you caused them to see something they normally wouldn't, make it disappear, and so on.]"

DEEPENING TECHNIQUES

A deepening technique is used to link the idea of deep relaxation, with a repetitive stimulus. This technique is oftentimes used to deepen a person's state after a quick entrancement technique like rapid induction or fascination is used.

Example:

> "Every time you [hear, feel or do] [this], you will become more relaxed and fall deeper into a trance."

In other words, suggest that a sound (your voice), feeling (being touched, or stroked), or an action (the dropping of an arm, or rocking) will cause that person to experience a more profound state of relaxation and that will drop them into a deeper trance. Feel free to play around with descriptive words, but just remember work within the vocabulary of your subject. Here are some more examples.

Sound of Voice
"Listen to the sound of my voice. The more you listen, the more relaxed you will become."

Finger Snaps
"Every time I snap my fingers, you will go three times deeper."

Rocking the Head
"As I rock your head back and forth, you will go deeper and deeper into a trance."

Rocking the Shoulders
"As I rock your shoulders from side to side, the more incredibly relaxed you will become."

Counting Down

Count from some number to 1. As you count, slightly to lower your voice and describe how the subject is supposed to feel.

For example:

5 – You feel yourself becoming relaxed
4 – You are going deeper
3 – Your mind is beginning to relax
2 – The relaxation is spreading throughout your body
1 – You are overtaken by the deepest sensation of relaxation you have ever felt.

ENTRAINMENT

To understand entrainment, you must understand wave resonance. Wave resonance is when a system osculates (swings back and forth, or moves up and down), reaching a maximum amplitude when stimulated by pulses at a specific frequency. This would be like striking a tuning fork keyed to C, next to another tuning force keyed to the same note—by proximity the tuning fork that was not struck would begin to resonate at the same frequency.

This same phenomenon happens to the human brain when exposed to foreign frequencies and rhythms. For example, listening to a particular beat or rhythm, breath, or through exposure to another person's thought-field. This can be witnessed happening to people listening to music in night clubs or concerts. It is also the reason why people use rhythmic drumming in rituals and ceremonies—to bring all participants into the right state for higher works. But this can also happen on a psychic level whenever you stand next to someone who is emitting a strong field—you can be unconsciously pulled into their state, whether it be anger, peace, or joy. If you want to know how to psychically entrain someone, read the chapter on "Divination." Until then, take a look at Entrancing through Entrainment and the Breath Entrainment Exercise below.

Entrancing through Entrainment

It is absolutely possible to bring someone into a deep trance through entrainment alone, this is why it is an extremely useful technique to learn. Entrainment can be used at the very beginning and throughout of all entrancement sessions to create an energetic bond between you and your subject. Pairing entrainment with an entrancement technique will speed up the induction process when using traditional hypnosis.

Step 1:

Once your subject is positioned, sit in front of them and tell them to relax and breath normally.

Step 2:

As you begin using whatever entrancement technique you want, begin to follow their breathing pattern with your own.

Step 3:

As you match their breath, continue your instruction and dialogue, then bring yourself into a calm state by slowing down your rate of breathing. As you do this, the subject should follow and also become relaxed.

Entraining the Unwary

The aim of this exercise is to bring an unaware target into a trance and confirm that you have successfully connected by causing them to mimic your behavior. This type of entrancement involves energy work, but no form of magick.

Preparation

Go to a public place where people typically relax. This could be somewhere like a bus station, train station, an airport, the mall, a library, or a church. Once there, scan the area for someone who is not distracted and seems to be daydreaming—people listening to music, or playing on their cell phones don't make good targets. Stand or take a seat near your target.

Step 1:

Mimic their breathing.

Step 2:

Slow down your breathing and bring yourself into a deeper trance. As you do this pay attention to your target and see if he or she fallows you into that state. What you are doing here is called breath entrainment.

Step 3:

Connect with your target by moving your conscious awareness into their field. To do this uses the techniques described under Farseeing—the only difference here is that you do not need a tag-lock because your target is right in front of you.

Step 4:

Once you feel like you have a psychic connection with them and see signs that your target is drifting into a deep trance, make a gesture such as scratching your nose, or running your finger through your hair to see if they will mimic your movement. If your target mimics this movement then you have successfully entranced your target. Unlike remote psychic influencing, it is unnecessary to use your powers of visualization to send suggestions because you can simply test the connection by making a body movement.

ENTRANCEMENT STRATEGIES

Although entrancement can take on many forms, there are three major methods; traditional hypnosis, rapid induction and remote hypnosis. In brief, traditional hypnosis uses guided meditation, along with verbal and nonverbal cues to induce a subject, while rapid induction relies on shock and confusion, followed up with a deepening technique, to do the same thing. Remote hypnosis, on the other hand, is more controversial, because it is based on psychically connecting with a subject from afar and influencing them—this is simply the remote influence method described in the "Divination" chapter relabeled.

Traditional Hypnosis

Traditional hypnosis is a longer process that uses a type of guided meditation. These guided scenarios use suggestions that make use of words like relaxed, deeper and down to help create deep relaxation and therefore achieve a deep-trance state. This type of induction works best when you want to build trust. It is also ideal for healing sessions and other spiritual work. Using the techniques below you will enable you to get your subject into a deep enough trance that you can make incredible changes.

Step 1: Rapport

Ask your subject what he or she knows about entrancement and clear up any misconceptions so they will be at ease. Set the stage by telling them what to expect and take some time understand their issues by interviewing them. By interviewing them you can pick up on their manner of speech and use some of their own words to describe things in their own language.

For example, if your intent was to make that person more confident, then you might say the following things to them:

1. When interacting with others what do you imagine those people are thinking about you?
2. Describe a time when you felt the most confident.
3. What else were you feeling at the time?

The answers of all of these questions not only produce data that you can use during the hypnosis session, but also are highly specific and personal to the subject.

Step 2: The Induction

To perform a long induction, you must be somewhere where you will not be disturbed and your subject can be comfortable. This means providing your subject with a comfortable place to sit or lay, as well as making sure you will not be disturbed by sounds of people chattering, outside noises or cellular devices. Once a quiet and tranquil atmosphere has been established, you can move on to the preliminary relaxation stage.

As your subject sits or lays down, ask him or her to stretch and get comfortable. Have them breathe in a relaxed manner. If they know a special breathing method such as two-four, have them do that. Otherwise, have them breathe normally—their breath will become shallow as you step them through guided visualization using one of the induction scripts below.

Remember that not all guided visualization will work for all people, because every person has their own likes and dislikes, fears and aspirations. For this reason, you should be familiar with the scripts and be able to adapt them to each subject—I would even suggest be able to mix methods spontaneously.

Step 3: Deepening
Deepening is built into the guided visualization. Therefore, no special deepening technique is needed.

Step 4: Test for Level of Trance
Standard trance level tests apply here.

Step 5: Induction Trigger
Set your induction trigger, as described in rapid induction.

Step 6: The Suggestion
Your subject is in the same trance state they are in using rapid induction. Therefore, the same rules apply.

Step 7: Bring Them Out
Once the session has ended, bring them out of entrancement. When you do this, you want to leave them in a happy and energetic state. To bring them out simply use counting.

Example:

> When I count from one to three, you will wake up feeling fully energized and happier than you have ever felt in your entire life.

1. Your eyes are opening, and you feel yourself begin-
    ning to awake.
2. Your eyes are halfway open, and you feel that you are
    almost conscious now.
3. Your eyes are wide open now, and you feel happy and
    energized.

Lastly, have the subject get up, stretch and walk around.

Induction Scripts

Induction 1: The Stairs

Hypnotist: Imagine yourself standing in front of an open archway. Directly
beyond the threshold of this archway is a flight of stairs leading down. There
are a total of nine steps. At the bottom of the stairs you can see a door with
a keyhole. Do you see this?

Subject: Yes

Hypnotist: Good (reinforcement), describe the stairs and door to me.

The Subject uses his/her imagination to describe the flight of stairs and the
door at the bottom of the stairs. This encourages creativity and thus brings
the receptive part of the mind (the subconscious) to the forefront.

Hypnotist: Good (reinforcement). As I count from one to nine, you will
walk down these steps and eventually get to the door. The closer to you get
to the bottom of the stairs, the deeper and more relaxed you will become.
Do you understand?

Subject: Yes.

Hypnotist: Good (reinforcement)
    1 – As you take your first step, you begin to feel a slight change.

2 – A wave of energy begins to roll over your body like a good message.

3 – Deeper (reinforcement).

4 – You can feel the wave of relaxing energy spread from the top of your head, enter your face, relaxing all the muscles there and continues on to your neck.

5 – Even deeper now (reinforcement).

6 – This feeling of relaxation spreads through the neck and penetrates your shoulders.

7 – The door is noticeably closer and you feel even more relaxed than before.

8 – This relaxing energy spreads through the shoulders and into the arms, then into your chest, down your entire torso and into your legs.

9 – You become completely relaxed as this energy settles into your toes and fingers. The door is now in plain view.

You seem to remember having the key to this door. Take the key out of your pocket, insert it into the keyhole, and open it up.

Note: By this time the subject gets to the bottom of the stairs, he or she should be in a deep trance. From this point on, you could continue in any way you wish.

Induction 2: The Theater

Imagine yourself sitting in an empty dark movie theater. Before you is a gigantic, white movie screen. No one else is present except for you.

As you relax, you hear the sound of the projector click on and suddenly a large black number nine appears on the screen. As you listen to the mechanical ticking sound of the projector, the screen begins to count down and when this happens your relaxation increases.

8 – Feeling more relaxed.

7 – You feel lighter and the tension begins to fade from your body.

6 – Even lighter and more relaxed now.

5, 4, 3 – As all the muscles in your body relax, you begin to fade into eternity.

2 – The sensation of relaxation is incredible.

1 – You are so relaxed it almost feels like you are out of body.

Note: At this point, the subject should be completely relaxed, and you can lead them wherever you wish.

Induction 3: Infectious Sleep

I want you to take a deep breath. Now close your eyes and allow yourself to become relaxed. If you have to itch, stretch or reposition—feel free to do that now.

(Once the subject has closed their eyes and is finished repositioning, continue)

Let the sound of my voice lead you. Take another deep breath and notice the complete darkness created by your closed lids. As I say a letter, it will appear in the blackness of your mind as a bold white character.

S – Feeling relaxed (three to five second pause).

L – This relaxation begins to spread (three to five second pause).

E – A white cloud of relaxation surrounds your body (three to five second pause).

E – You become more relaxed as it grows stronger (three to five second pause).

P – This already bright aura of relaxation intensifies (three to five second pause).

Sleep! (said as a command and with confidence)

(This alone should put them under, but we are going to take this a little further)

Now I want you to concentrate on the cloud. Look into it. Notice how it seems to be made of tiny particles. You know that whatever this field of energy is, it makes you relaxed, comfortable and causes you to slip deeper and deeper into a trance. Now let your mind focus in on one of these particles, like a powerful microscope. As you zoom in, it becomes clear—this entire cloud is made up of words—and that word is *Sleep!*

(This should bring them even deeper, but we are not done yet.)

But then you notice something else, each word begins to duplicate itself, and each duplication adds to your relaxed state. As the number of words increase, the sleep field becomes brighter and stronger until it becomes impossible to follow—so many words, each causing you to go deeper and deeper.

(At this point, the subject should be displaying symptoms of being in a deep trance. If not, pause for a good thirty seconds and let the subject visualize. It is likely that they will display rapid eye movement, as they try to count the little microscopic "sleeps" populating in their mind. When you see this, you want to stop the field expansion.)

Now, as suddenly as it began, the microscopic words stop reproducing, and the field stabilizes. When this happens, the field begins to fade from sight and become invisible. You know that it's still there—you just can't see it.

Note: From this point, continue the session any way you wish.

Past-Life Regression

Past lives have always been a highly debated topic, but for those who have experienced things like déjà vu or have recalled memories from lives before, there is no question that it is real. Reincarnation is a reoccurring theme in most major religions and esoteric traditions—especially the Eastern ones. Reincarnation is the belief that the soul, being eternal, is born again into another body after death and repeats this cycle until it realizes its full potential. In fact, there have been many documented accounts of people who have claimed to have lived before in another time, remembering exact details of those lives, with the ability to give accurate historical accounts of what went on during that period. Some of those people have actually gone on to seek out people they once knew, in order to tie up loose ends and make contact with old friends and family members.

A Dr. Eli Lasch, who worked as a doctor for the Israeli government in Gaza, had a three-year-old client who lived near the border of Syria and Israel. The child, who recalled being killed with an ax in a previous life, was able to show the village elders where his former body was buried, where the murder weapon was located and also identify the killer. Because of this, a body with a head wound and the murder weapon was found in the indicated location and the killer confessed.

Another outstanding case, recorded by Dr. Ian Stevenson of the University of Virginia, was the account of Semih Tutusmus, a boy who lived in a small village in Turkey. Before Tutusmus was born, a man with a bloody face that had been shot in the right ear, who called himself Selim Fesli, appeared to his mother in a dream. It was known that a man by that name, who lived in an adjacent village, had died several years before in 1952. Tutusmus himself was born with a deformed right ear. Astonishingly, once he was able to talk, he informed his mother that he was Selim Fesli—the man who appeared in his mother's dream. And at age four, he made his way to Fesli's old home, where Fesli's widow lived and told her, "I am Selim. You are my wife, Katibe." Not only did he claim to be her husband, but also he could recall details of their former life as well as the names of their children—and of course, he was able to identify the man who shot him.

Recalling former lives has serious implications; if what you recall is true, then having this knowledge gives you the opportunity to learn from past mistakes, come to grips with past events that may be haunting you and allow you to draw upon knowledge from those lives. However, it also means, there is a chance you will be haunted by those memories and may be compelled to repeat the same mistakes you made in the past—the very thing you are trying to avoid by reincarnating. But if what you recall is not real (fabricated or imagined) you might be inclined to live a life based on those false memories. Therefore, living life under the false assumption that you are better, or worse than those around you. For this reason, I would dissuade people from believing everything that comes forward during a past-life regression without checking it. A lot of people will let this information go to their head; I have met several people who believed they were Cleopatra or Jesus in a former life and others who believed they were some poor tortured soul, bound to live in turmoil. Needless to say, performing any kind of regression on those who are not prepared, especially the mentally unstable, can be detrimental, so interview your clients before you perform a past-life regression.

Regardless of this, past-life regression is a relatively simple procedure. You induce the subject, then transition them to different points in their lives using guided visualizations and allow them to describe to you what they are seeing. But before you set out to do this, you should take several things into consideration. First, you need to be extremely careful not to create false memories by leading your client—let the client lead the regression instead.
Example:

> "Tell me what you see when the mist clears."

vs.

> "When the mist clear, you see a large pyramid. Its golden cap reflects the rays of the bright sun above it."

Another thing you want to avoid is the shock of your client as they enter scenes from their past life. What you must remember is, whether these memories are imaginary, or real, if your client is in a deep enough trance, those images, sounds and feelings will be vivid. In such case, those memories may invoke awe and joy, or pain and terror. For this reason, it is necessary that you make sure your client feels safe at all times. To do this allow the client to experience the scenes in peace and safety, from a third-person perspective—this can be easily accomplished using a simple suggestion.
Example:

> "As you step into your former life, know that you are there only as an observer. Being an observer means that no one can see or harm you and you are safe at all times."

Also realize that some people will allow themselves to get sucked in anyways. If this happens, you will want to bring your client out of their trance quickly, review what was discovered and perhaps continue the session another time.
Example:

Client is freaking out because they are experiencing being tutored on a stretching rack in a dungeon, during the inquisition.

You of course must remain calm. Otherwise, you will just make it worse, because the client will feed off of your fear.

"Listen to the sound of my voice. When I count from one to three, you will wake up. One, waking up now, two, eyes beginning to open, three, fully awake and refreshed and happy."

In any case, before you perform a past-life regression on a subject, you need to make sure and do it within a safe setting. Past-life regression, like any kind of trance, brings the client into a vulnerable mental state. If not surrounded by a positive environment, it is possible for outside spiritual influences to slip in and take advantage of the situation. To prevent this, you will need to, at a minimum create a positive psychic shield around the entire area, or even open a protective circle—this way you and your client will be safe.

Keeping these things in mind, how do you perform past-life regression? First induce your client using any of the regular induction methods mentioned above. Remember: a medium-to-heavy trance is preferable, so look for depth indicators. Once you have done this, use one of the regression methods below to step the person through one, or more of their past lives.

Method 1: The Gallery of Lives

Step 1: Set the Scene

"You find yourself standing in a simple circular room with soft lighting. Along its walls are large paintings that span an area from the sealing, all the way down to the floor. Although, each is a bit fuzzy and out-of-focus, you can tell each painting depicts a scene. You recognize these paintings as being important scenes from one, or possibly more of your former lives. Take a moment to let your eyes scan them, then stop

at the one that seems the most intriguing to you. Now look
at that painting a little closer."

Step 2: Have them Describe the Painting

Not everyone will be able to immediately describe a painting in full detail,
so help the client give the painting more detail by guiding them through the
description process. Like remote viewing, begin with feelings and progress
to the finer details. If your client begins giving more detail without being
prompted, this means they are seeing something important and should be
allowed to give those details uninterrupted.

Also realize that if your client is in a heavy trace, it may take them
a while to verbalize what they are seeing and their voice may be slurred.
For this reason, you may have to ask them to repeat something. Also, pay
attention to the direction their eyes are pointing when they describe something—this can give you an indication of how they are experiencing a scene.
As your client describes details of a painting, use positive reinforcement
(ex. "Good, very good").

Feelings

> "For now, I don't want you to worry about details. Instead, tell
> me how you feel as you look at the painting. Take your time."

Allow the client to describe how the painting makes them feel. If they simply
can't describe how they feel, or say they feel nothing, wait a little longer,
then move on to spatials.

Spatials

Spatials are dimensional aspects of a scene: Is it outside or inside? Is it a
grand scene, such as a huge chasm, or confined, as if inside a building? Let
your client make these determinations.

> "As you stare at the painting, you begin to get the sense of
> space. Is the painting depicting a large area, or a small area?

Allow your senses to probe the painting and feel the dimensions of its scene."

Notice how I didn't assume the client would be seeing an outside area, or inside area—that would be leading. It could very well depict an area inside that is so huge that it gives the sense of being open and spacious. Describing spatials usually prompts client to begin seeing more details—in such case, let the client finish describing dimensions, then move on to details.

Details

At this point, allow the client's attention to be drawn to specific details in the painting. Of course, what a client sees will be very personal to that client. Therefore, you will have to tell them to elaborate on each detail as they describe the scene, but to begin this process, simply ask them to, "Focus on the details of the painting." Remember: use positive reinforcement and give them plenty of time to describe these details between each one of these questions.

"What colors are in the painting?"
"What shapes do you see?"
"What do those colors and shapes seem to depict?"

Continue with the questioning, going over each aspect of the painting, asking for more and more detail, until you feel there is nothing more left to describe.

Animation

Once the client has described the painting in full detail, ask them to animate it—remember always give positive reinforcement.

"I want you to take another look at the painting. Watch it closely. Good, now notice how the scene begins to move and become alive. Describe to me what is happening in the scene."

Give them time to describe things. If there are figures (animals/people/mythical creatures, and so on) within the painting, ask what those figures are doing. One of those figures will represent the client, in his or her past life. Pay special attention to this figure and what part that figure is playing in the scene.

Absorption

Up until this point, the client has been seeing the scene from an outside perspective. Now you will ask the client to step into the painting and enter the scene. But they will not enter the scene as them self in a past-life, they will only enter the scene as an observer—this will allow them to acquire even more detail. However, before they enter this scene, remind them they will be safe at all times and cannot be harmed.

> "Now step into the painting, realizing that you will be safe at all times."

Again remember that the questions will be unique to what each client is experiencing. Once the client has entered the scene, he or she will be privy to the full range of his or her senses; sight, sound, smell, touch, taste, and so on. You will want to cover all these senses. Pay close attention to important aspects of the scene, such as things that would give away time period, indicate possible historical events that could be verified, and so on. After giving them ten to fifteen seconds (or more) to do this, continue your questioning. Begin by asking them if they have entered the scene; wait for an acknowledgment, then continue.

> "Have you entered the scene? Nod your head yes if you have."
> You can also have them verify this by making another small body movement such as raising a finger.
> "Good, now describe what is happening in that scene."

Continue your questioning, until you feel you have exhausted all questions.

Step 3: Exit the Scene

Once you are satisfied that you have acquired all the information you can from the regression, bring the person out of the trance. When you do this, make sure to suggest they will remember everything in full detail—unless of course the scene was traumatic.

"When I count from one to three, you will wake up. When you wake up, you will feel refreshed, happy and be able to remember every detail of the scene. One, beginning to wake up now, two, almost awake, feeling refreshed and reenergized, three, fully awake and eyes open."

Step 4: Discuss What Was Discovered

After allowing the client time to recover from exiting the trance, ask them if they would like to talk about what was discovered. Encourage them to verify the details of the session by doing a little bit of historical research. Discuss the scene and what it may mean. Talk about how what was discovered, may play a role in this life and offer suggestions about how to manage any problems that may have resulted due to past-life influence.

Method 2: The Mists of Time

Begin by using one of the regular methods above to induce the client into a trance, then set the scene. In "The Mists of Time" the client will begin the regression by standing inside of an obscuring mist. Describe the mist as being a thick blanket of fog that is so thick nothing can be seen. Refrain from describing the mist as a positive, because this would insinuate that they will have a positive experience and would be leading. Although you don't want them to have a negative experience, you do want for their regression to be authentic, so instead of describing the mist as a particular color, ask the client to describe the nature of the mist—that is, the color and how it makes them feel.

Step 1: Let the Client Describe the Mist

"You are surrounded by a thick mist that hides everything."
"What is the color of the mist?"
"How does this make you feel?"

Step 2: Clear the Mist

Once they have thoroughly described the mist and how it makes them feel, suggest that the mist clears. The purpose of clearing the mist is to slowly unveil more detail—this will be done gradually using a counting technique.

> "Good. Now relax, knowing you will be safe at all times—nothing can hurt you. I will now count from three to one. As I count, the mist will become thinner and thinner, until it has totally cleared. As the mist clears, you will be able to see and hear more of what is behind it."

> 3 – The mist is beginning to thin. Tell me what you hear and smell. Describe those sounds and odors.
> 2 – As the area becomes noticeably clearer, your senses become sharper, and you can make out vague shapes. Describe what you see.
> 1 – The mist has now entirely vanished. Once the cloud clears, everything sharpens, and you can now see, hear, smell, and feel everything. Take your time and describe those things.

Once the client has finished describing the scene and if you feel he or she is comfortable exploring another scene make the mist envelope them again and repeat steps 1 and 2. Remember to give them positive reinforcement.

> "Good. Feeling satisfied that you have learned everything about this experience at this time, you are ready to enter the mist again and explore another experience. As I count from one to three, watch the mist once again envelop you."

> 1 – You begin to see wisps of mist steaming off the ground.
> 2 – That mist starts to obscure everything as it becomes thicker.
> 3 – You now totally surround by the mist and can see nothing else.

Step 3: Exit the Scene

When the client has finished cycling through experiences, clear the mist and wake them up, also suggesting they will remember everything.

> "As I count from one to three, the mist will clear and you will become more aware of this world, until you are totally awake. When you have awoken, not only will you be refreshed and happy, but also you will remember everything."

> 1 – As the mist begins to clear, you feel more awake.
> 2 – As the mist begins to vanish, your eyes start to open, and you feel you are almost awake.
> 3 – The mist is no more. You feel happy, refreshed, and awake, and you can now open your eyes.

After your client is cognoscente discuss what he or she has experienced and answer any questions they might have.

RAPID INDUCTION

A rapid induction relies on shock or confusion to tie up the cognitive part of a subject's mind—this is called a cognitive interrupt or pattern interrupt. Once the conscious mind is tied up by using shock or confusion or both, the command to sleep can be given, which will cause that person to fall into a light or medium trance. Once this trance has been created, it must be immediately followed up with a deepening technique, or the person will come out of that state in a matter of seconds. The steps below outline what must be done at each stage.

Step 1: The Induction

As stated above the shock/confusion induction relies on causing a state of shock or confusion to tie up the logical mind. To explain this, I can use an example: have you ever tried to open a door in the wrong direction only to be left in a momentary state of confusion while trying to figure it out—that challenges your logical centers. Or have you ever lost your balance and nearly fallen as a result—this challenges your instinctual centers. Consequently, the shock does not have to be real—it can be imagined. You would get the same result if you pulled someone off balance, or asked someone to stand, while having another person stand behind them and push them backward to be caught. There is no real threat, but the instinctive mind believes there is, because it is reactionary. Fortunately, you don't have to wait till someone opens a door the wrong way, or falls, to try a rapid induction, you can induce this state yourself using a technique. Both methods cut through the logical centers and give you access to their receptive subconscious mind.

Step 2: Deepening

Once you have used shock or confusion to cause the initial drop into a light trance state, you will have to deepen it—if you don't, that person will come out of that state in a matter of seconds. To deepen a hypnotic trance, use a cognitive loop based on relaxation. For example, "Listen to my voice. As you listen to my voice, you become more relaxed, the more relaxed you become the more you listen to my voice." You can find a list of these loops under "Deepening."

Step 3: Test Level of Trance

When you feel your subject's trance state has been sufficiently deepened, you need to test to see just how deep it is—it's not good enough to rely on the symptoms.

Step 4: Induction Trigger

If your subject's trance state is deep enough and if you want to easily bring them under in the future, you need to plant an induction trigger. An induction trigger can be a word or a visual cue like a picture or hand signal. Please note: unless you want your target to fall into a trance constantly do not make the trigger something that they will commonly see or hear in their everyday life—in other words, no triggers like "every time you walk outside, you will fall into a deep trance," or "every time you see the color red, you will become deeply relaxed and fall into a trance." Once you have implanted an induction trigger, you are free to deliver suggestions.

Rapid Induction Scripts

Please note, if you do these inductions on people who are standing they could fall and injure themselves. If you insist on doing this type of induction on someone who is standing, one, be able to catch them, or two have someone standing by to do the same. Otherwise, have your subject sitting comfortably and solidly in a chair—even then, be ready to catch that person.

Hand-Press Induction

1. Ask the person to press on your hand.
2. While pressing your hand tell the person to close their eyes.
3. Suddenly remove your hand out from under theirs. As you do this snap your fingers or swipe your other hand in front of their face, then say, "Sleep!" in a commanding tone. Having them concentrate on two things happening at once will tie up that person's conscious mind, startle them and leave them in a highly suggestible state.
4. Immediately follow with a Deepening Technique.

Handshake Induction

1. Reach forward to shake someone's hand, but instead…
2. Gently grab their wrist and pull their palm up to face level, about ten inches away from their face.
3. As you do this, point at the palm of their hand. Make sure to direct your eyes to their hand to prevent them from staring at you instead. This may involve stepping to their side and facing their hand as you hold it and point.
4. When you have their hand at eye level say, "Stare at the palm of your hand and notice how the focus of your eyes change as you…," and finish with the word *Sleep!* said in a commanding tone.
5. Immediately follow with a Deepening Technique.

Say Something Confusing

1. Walk up to the person and say something confusing like, "Can you imagine an imaginary menagerie manager managing an imaginary menagerie?"
2. Flash your fingers before their face and command them to "Sleep!"

Handshake and Hug Method

1. Establish positive rapport by getting the subject to agree with you.
2. Reach out to shake the subject's hand.
3. Shake normally and then jerk their hand down and to your right side. When you do this, don't pull too hard because you might injure them. A slight tug will do, because they won't be expecting it.
4. As you pull them toward you, place your left hand on their neck and pull them toward you in the same motion. Do this as if you were giving them a hug.
5. Again, as you perform steps 3 and 4, command them to "Sleep!"
6. Immediately follow with a Deepening Technique.

Finger Play

1. Reach out and shake their hand naturally.
2. Stare into your subject's eyes and let the handshake naturally come to a stop, but hold their hand loosely.
3. Slowly release their hand as you randomly touch different parts of their hand.
4. Look through the subject or between their eyes.
5. Begin deepening their thought's with command's to relax, like were used in the previous demonstration.
6. Continue to touch their hand lightly while continuing the commands.

REMOTE HYPNOSIS & PSYCHIC INFLUENCE

Targeting your thoughts—or what scientists refer to as "Intention" appeared to produce an energy potent enough to change physical reality. A simple thought seemed to have the power to change our world.

—LYNNE MCTAGGART, *THE INTENTION EXPERIMENT*

By "remote" hypnosis, I am not talking about entrancing someone via phone or by video conference—I am talking about entrancing a subject from afar without any contact like voice, video, or touch. Although very similar to hypnosis, it is best described as "psychic influence."

The mental influence of living systems (humans, plants and animals) has been a part of Psi research for quite a while. In such experiments, the organism is isolated in a room that has been shielded to all known forms known energy, such as sound waves and electromagnetism, then an influencer attempts to influence some psychological (a feeling, emotion, or behavior), or physiological (blood pressure, activity in some part of the brain) aspect of the target at a randomly scheduled time.

One such experiment, called *le sommeil a distance* (influence at a distance), was carried out by Joseph Gibert and Pierre Janet in Le Havre between 1885 through 1886—the subject was Leonie B, a highly hypnotizable. The aim of the experiment was for Dr. Gilbert to mentally summon Leonie to his location while sitting in his office. At 9:00 p.m. on April 22, 1886, A. T. Myers, Ochorowicz and Marillier, Janet moved silently through the empty streets of Le Havre and took up position outside of Madame B's cottage. After waiting some time, it began.

Ochrowicz writes,

> "At 9:25, I saw a shadow appearing at the garden gate: it was she. I hid behind the corner in order to be able to hear without being seen. At first the woman paused at the gate and went back into the garden. Then at 9:30 she hurried out into the

street and began to make her way unsteadily toward the house of Dr. Gibert. The four researchers followed as unobtrusively as possible. They could see she was obviously in a somnambulistic state. Finally, she reached Gibert's house, entered and hurried from room to room until she found him."

Also, Dr. Barušs, a professor of psychology at King's University College, decided to try to influence the energy level of volunteers from a distance. To do this he arranged a time, via email, when the subject would not be driving. Then, by the flip of a coin he proceeded to direct his intentions at the subject, closely monitoring his own state. What he found out was that his thoughts did indeed affect the subject and that it was 95 percent likely that his influence was the cause. He also noticed that his effect was greater when he achieved a deeper trance.

In another example, scientist decided to test if Qigong Masters who practiced the art of Tohate (the practice of knocking one another back via intention only) was a real thing and if it was, was it psychological, or physiological. To do this they placed the Masters on separate floors and hooked them up to EEGs. Amazingly, when the Masters released their Qi, increased alpha brainwaves were registered and their beta brainwaves synchronized. Even more astonishing was that hits reported as an "Ouch" were registered moments before the sender sent the Qi.

Psychic Influence can happen without being aware of it. If you know how to connect with a target and that target is not aware, that person can be compelled to think or do just about anything as long as they believe that thing is in their best interest and that those thoughts and feelings originated from within.

Having said this, you can totally drive someone out of their gourd doing such a thing. Influencing someone without them being aware of it could cause them to think they have become schizophrenic or possessed and at that point, they could end up in the funny farm—and that is not a very nice thing to do. Still, this ability can be used as a powerful tool to help others, or to shut down dangerous criminals. Think about it; you could help someone overcome drug addiction by compelling them to get help, or you could stop a dangerous criminal by making him feel compassion and then causing him to turn himself in.

The Method

The method of remote influence is actually quite simple, all you have to do is establish a telepathic connection using the same methods described in the "Farseeing Exercise" in the "Divination" chapter, then hold a thought in your mind until they pick up on it. As I have said before, that thought must be compelling and believable to the target. If you are in their head, that means you can tell what they are thinking and lead them in the direction you want them to go by presenting thoughts that push them in that direction. You must also realize that once they are outside of your influence, they may change their mind, so if you really want them to act on something, you will probably have to enforce that thought several times over a period of a week. Also remember: you are not sending words, you are sending sensations; visions, sounds, tactile, tastes and most importantly emotions.

You should also know that when you connect with such a person, the information you receive will give you a clue as to how that person or entity sees the world. For example, if you are seeing visions, that means that person is visual; if you are hearing things, that means that person listens better than he sees; and if what you receive are emotions, it means that person is a sensate. The tip here is, once you know how that person experiences the world, you then know what kind of sensations you can send to motivate them. Those sensations will be the most powerful to that person.

Fascination

Fascination means to be transfixed by something. Fixation might happen naturally when someone becomes obsessed with the passing of time and begins watching the second hand tick away on a clock, or when they witness something awe inspiring, or in the case of highway hypnosis, when a driver's attention is drawn to the dashed lines whirring past him as his car travels down the highway.

Fascination is nothing new; as a matter of fact, this was one of the primary methods that hypnotists used back in the day, to put their subjects into a trance—and that is why when most people think about hypnosis, it conjures up images of a guy swinging a pocket watch, saying, "You are getting sleeeeepy." Of course the art of fascination does not belong to the realm of psychology—it is much more ancient than that. Witches and magicians alike wore rings and pendants for this very reason. And the infamous magick mirror is just another type of fascination device. By staring at a black reflective surface, attention is narrowed and the lack of visual stimuli kicks the subconscious mind into high gear, causing a shift in consciousness. Eye fixation is similar to object fixation, but eye fixation improves the ability of the entrancer to bring a subject into an altered state through transfer of energy through the eyes—people don't believe the eyes are the windows of the soul for no reason.

Gaze Fascination

Step 1: Rapport
Begin by centering yourself and calming your spirit—remember energy can be felt. Next, put your subject at ease by answering any questions about hypnosis and clearing up any misunderstandings.

Step 2: Gaze
Calm your spirit, then ask the subject to relax and look you directly in the eyes. If they become distracted, get their attention by raising your hand and use your fingers to indicate they should focus and maintain eye contact.

Step 3: Entrainment
Take a moment to mimic their breathing, then slow down your respiration and bring yourself into a deeper state. By relaxing yourself you will also be relaxing your target. After a minute or so, you should begin to see the subject's facial expression and body language begin to relax—their eyes may even begin to close and their head drop. You can accelerate this process by giving nonverbal cues like narrowing your eyes and dropping your head ever so slightly—remember: your movements do not have to be grandiose, the subconscious mind picks up on micromovements. At this point, you should be able to psychically influence them through intention, or use hand passes to perform energy work.

Fascination by Object

Most fascination objects have highly polished reflective surfaces meant to capture a person's attention. Although that can be enough to hold a person's attention for a long period, there are techniques you can use to induce a trance quicker. For example, rhythms, whether created by sound or light, can cause entrainment. Therefore, by flashing the reflective piece at a particular rate, you can bring that person to state quicker.

Step 1: Rapport (Same as Gaze Fascination)

Step 2: Object Fixation

Grasp your object, or take it in hand and tell the subject to stare at it. If their eyes wonder, point to the object to indicate they should focus.

Step 3: Entrainment

Begin to flash your object by twitching it back and forth. To do this you will need a source of light that you can reflect off the surface of the fascination device. A 4 to 4.5 flash per second pulse is best for bringing people into a deep-trance state. As you do this use breath entrainment to bring them deeper. Once you see their head drop and eyes close, you are free to psychically influence them, or perform energy work.

Covert Fascination

Covert fascination, means to fascinate someone without them knowing—in other words, against their will. Covert fascination relies of a number of layered techniques; suggestion by means of Neural Linguistic Programming, psychic entrainment, in conjunction with breath entrainment and gaze or object fixation. Although subtler than consensual fascination, it can be just as powerful. Essentially what you are doing is dropping a person into waking trance, making it easier to feed that person's subconscious mind suggestions—only the most paranoid would notice.

Step 1: Rapport

Center yourself and begin breath entrainment. Once you have brought yourself into a calm state and have started the breath entrainment process, establish rapport by making small-talk. Naturally change the conversation to something that will invoke a positive emotional response, or lead them into a conversation that requires them to use creativity—this will activate their subconscious mind, making them more susceptible to suggestion.

Step 2: Fixation

If you are using gaze, make eye contact. If your target is timid, stare past or through them, but always keep their eyes in your peripheral vision. And for God's sake, do not stare wildly into their eyes, because it will just creep them out and give you away!

If you are using object fixation, make a microgesture toward your object. If it seems natural, pick up the object and begin to flash it (a 4–4.5 rhythm per second rate is best). As you stare, or flash your object, continue breath entrainment.

Step 3: Neuro-Linguistic Programming and Psychic Influence

At this point, you should begin to see noticeable physiological changes in your target's appearance; eyes narrowing (perhaps becoming red), pulse rate dropping (hint: look at the pulse of major blood vessels in the neck, or side of the head) and general relaxation. When you see these things, begin NLP. What you suggest through NLP will be specific to your intentions, but because you have entrained them, you are psychically connected and can send mental suggestions along with your disguised NLP suggestions.

Bewitchment

This is the stuff legend—you know, where the Witch walks up to her quarry, stares them in the eyes and puts them in a trance as if they were placed under a spell. Bewitchment reaches into the realm of magick, possibly black magick, by paring spellwork with the art of fascination. So let me begin by warning you that bewitching people for the fun of it, or just to satisfy a psychotic urge, puts you in danger of becoming the victim of your own negative energy. However, as argued under ethics, there *may* be an occasion that calls for bewitching someone and controlling them from distance.

But before we get into the step-by-step procedure of how to bewitch, let's talk about the purpose of each phase. In the first phase we use a binding spell called "The Night Whisperer" to connect with the target well before we intend to fascinate them and reinforce our control. In the second phase, we can choose to use modified rapid induction technique, or modified fascination to drop them in trance and "officially" bewitch them. And the third phase serves to maintain the connection, while strengthening control by using what you've learned about psychic influence and occult magick.

Close-Quarter Bewitchment

Note: Perform the "Night Whisper Spell," or a similar spell of your own creation before you attempt close quarter bewitchment. Then reinforce the bewitchment as needed using the same spell. If you have become adept at psychic influence, you can even dispense with the spell.

The Night Whisperer

Components
- A small black pouch
- A sheet of parchment paper
- A red pen
- Dowsing rods
- A tag-lock from your target
- Your target first, last, and middle name, as well as his or her date of birth
- 3 obsidian stones
- 1 tbsp of Peppercorn
- Theurgic incense

The purpose of the spell is to bind your target, and make him or her more compliant. For the best results perform this spell within your sacred space on the dark moon or during the waning quarter. Begin by lighting your incense and invoking any familiar spirits or deities that are willing to aid you in this endeavor. Neutralize any unwanted energies by cleansing all spell components using your preferred method. When your components have been cleansed, ask the entities you have called to bless them with an energy capable of binding your target and bringing him or her under your control.

Set the black pouch, the three obsidian stones, and your portion of peppercorn upon your altar for charging. If you are using a pentagram to charge, place your components within it. Next pick up your dowsing rods and hold them over your components while imagining a feeling of compliance and obedience. As this feeling becomes clearer in your mind allow the dowsing rods to naturally open. Known that when the dowsing rods have completely opened your components have been fully charged. When this is complete place the stones and the peppercorn inside the pouch. Now take your parchment and write your target's full name and date of birth on it a total of three, six, or nine times. As you do this visualize your target. Next take the paper with the target's name and date of birth in your right hand, and the tag-lock in the other, and try to connect with your target using the methods detailed under psychic influence.

Once you feel that you have connected with your target, begin the entrainment process and invoke a feeling of trust, and compliance. Conjure up the feeling of resonance and vibration within the paper and tag lock, and feel a permanent link being establish between these items and your target. When this feeling is strong enough cease visualization and enclose the name and date of birth written on the paper by folding it twice. After you have folded this paper draw a single vertical line on each of its faces— this line represents the Isa, a nordic symbol of binding. When you are done place these items within the pouch, pull the drawstring closed, and end in the typical manner by saying "So be it!" or "so mote it be!"

Preparation

Buy, make or acquire a fascination piece. Cleanse, consecrate and charge this item for the purpose of holding your target's attention and entrancing them. Create a babblogue incantation. This incantation should be long enough to occupy your target's attention for at least four to six seconds. The meaning of your babblogue incantation should be to bring a target under your control. Don't worry if your target can't understand it—they are not supposed to. As long as you do, that's all that matters.

Either create a unique command word that is both easy for you and your target to pronounce and remember, or create a sigil out of your target's name. If you choose the sigil route, simplify that sigil so that it can be easily recognized by your target. This command word or sigil will be used to quickly bring your target back into a bewitched state after he or she has been initially bewitched.

Step 1:
Once you have your target in sight, call upon your divine authority and build your magnetism by using the Circulation of the Body of Light.

Step 2: Use Breath Entrainment

Step 3:
When you can see your target following your breath, walk up to them and speak your babblogue incantation—this should create confusion. As soon as you see this confusion, flash your fascination piece so that it catches their glance and say "Sleep!" in an assertive tone. This should cause your target become so shocked that they fall automatically into a trance. However, at this time if you don't deepen that trance, you will lose control of your target. Beware, when you do this the target may instinctively fall—so be ready to catch them.

Step 4:
Don't be surprised if your target's head slumps down and their eyes close. At this point, lightly grasp your target's shoulders and begin to gently sway one shoulder back and the other forward, then the other shoulder back and the other shoulder forward. As you continue this back-and-forth motion encourage a deeper trance by saying something like,

> "The more you sway the more you relaxed you become, the more you relaxed you become, the deeper you sleep."

Step 5:
Once your target is in a very deep trance, set your command word or sigil—this will allow you to pull them back into this same state at any time in the future. If you chose to use a command word, tell them that they will fall into the same relaxed state every time they hear you say that word.

"Every time you hear me say COMMAND WORD, you will fall into a deep trance like this one."

If you chose to use the sigil, tell them to open their eyes. You may have to use words of encouragement like, "Open your eyes. Good. Very good, you can do it. Open your eyes."

Once their eyes are open, display the sigil so they can clearly see it and say,

"Every time you see this symbol, you will fall into a deep trance like this one."

Repeat your chosen command three times, then ask them to confirm that they understand by nodding their head.

"If you understand, nod your head yes."

If you don't get a yes, you may be in trouble (chuckle). This could mean that your target really doesn't understand, or that you are about to get punched out for trying to entrance that person against their wishes. But if you get a yes move to the next step.

Step 6:
It is extremely important that you make the person forget they have been bewitched and awaken them with a good feeling and positive frame of mind. If you don't do this, they will remember that you entranced them and be extremely upset. To accomplish this, say something like,

"At this point, you can either forget to remember or remember to forget any of this ever happened. When you wake, you will have a sense of peace and happiness."

Now awaken them by saying,

"You are beginning to wake up."

"As you begin to wake, you feel at peace and happy."
"You are almost awake. You have never felt happier than you do now."
"Wake up."

Caution

When your target awakens, there is a good change he or she will be confused—after all they have been entranced and might sense the missing time. If this happens, divert their attention by holding a normal conversation. If you must console them, you might say something like,

> "It's OK. You must be tired," or "Don't worry. I space out sometimes too."

Also remember that there is a good chance you may fail to bewitch your target—this takes practice. In such a case, you may be in real danger because your target has become aware that you are trying to control them.

Etheric Thought-Forms

An etheric thought-form is considered to be a type of sentient energy that has been created by the beliefs of one or more people. Such creations can be intentional, or unintentional. Intentionally created thought-forms are created by mystics, shamans, and magicians, whereas unintentionally created thought-forms arise from inadvertent unconscious thought. Many believe that all gods, angels, and demons of ancient and contemporary religions are nothing more than thought-forms created by the fervent beliefs of their followers. Although I don't personally subscribe to this point of view, I certainly do believe that it is possible. In a sense, we are all thought-forms created by the first thought emanation of the Source.

So where does this idea come from? The idea of the thought-form is actually quite ancient. Although we really can't say *exactly* how old it is, the ability to create a "mind–body emanation" has been described in the early Buddhist text Pali Samaññaphala Sutta, and is also a part of Tibetan Buddhist practice. However, we do know that this concept was introduced to Western society through theosophists and spiritualists such as Evans-Wentz and Alexandra David-Néel sometime during the 20th century. Soon after, this idea was adopted by western occultists, and magicians.

Alexandra David-Néel described what she called a "tulpa" as, "magic formations generated by a powerful concentration of thought." She also suggested that these creations could think for themselves when she wrote, "Once the tulpa is endowed with enough vitality to be capable of playing the part of a real being, it tends to free itself from its maker's control." She then went on to describe the tulpa of a jolly Friar Tuck-like monk that she created herself, but later had to destroy because it got out of control.

David-Néel acknowledged the possibility that she could have hallucinated the experience, but also claimed that others could see it to.

But this idea did not die after the heyday of spiritualism and theosophy. This concept of the thought-form, or a type of intelligent ethereal energy has been studied by those in the field of parapsychology. Take for example the idea of the poltergeist—a type of turbulent spiritual energy, usually created by a disgruntled youth, that tends to destroys things. As a matter of fact, a group of parapsychologists in Ontario Canada did an experiment in 1972 to test the possibility of willfully creating such an energy form. This was called the Philip Experiment.

The Experiment itself was conducted by a group of nine parapsychologists who were overseen by psychologist Dr. Joel Whitton. The goal was to test the hypothesis that poltergeist activity and spirit communication could be caused by a spiritual force that was artificially created by a group of people during a séance. To this end, they created a fictional character called "Philip," whom they gave a fictional history interwoven with actual historical events and places.

Philip was supposed to be born in England in 1624. According to his historical description he fought in the English Civil War, and was knighted by the age of sixteen. After becoming personal friends with Charles II, he began working as his spy. Although Philip was married to a woman named Dorothea, he was not happy, and decided to have an affair with a Romanian girl. However after she was accused of witchcraft and burned at the stake Philip committed suicide.

Once they created Philip by describing him in as much detail as possible, they tried to communicate with him using meditation. But after one year with no success they decided to change their tactics. Instead of simply meditating, they turned off the lights and performed a traditional séance. Once they did that, they began to get raps, telekinetic movement, and levitations. They became such a big deal in the media, other groups across the world began performing the same experiment—getting the same results.

Does this prove that an artificial spirit was created? No—the only thing it really proves is that something sentient was being communicated with and caused paranormal activity. That "thing" could be an artificial spirit, an entity that strayed in to take advantage of the situation, or the result of mislabeled natural psychokinetic energy evoked by the experimenters—either way, the technique was powerful enough to create real psychic phenomena. Having said this, let's examine the idea of the "familiar."

The concept of familiars dates back to the Middle Ages. They were believed to be minor demon spirits, such as imps, that would inhabit the body of an animal or human in order to assist a novice witch or warlock. In those days, people believed that witches were given a familiar upon initiation to act as a type of protector. The idea of a familiar was probably not a part of the practice of real witchcraft at the time, but was more likely something that was made up by the church in order to prosecute woman who owned animals for witchcraft.

Now, the whole idea of spirit animals, or totem animals is in fact an ancient concept that was very widespread. This is likely where the idea of the familiar came from, but they were not animals possessed by minor demons; they were spirit animals.

So do such spirit animals exist? Sure, I believe they do and think I have even encountered a few in my lifetime. If our consciousness persists after death, why not theirs? Would they ever want to go out of their way to help us? Maybe—dogs assist humans every day in real life, so I don't see any reason why one wouldn't want to stick around to aid their human companion after it has passed on. Do these animal spirits possess their material animal counterparts to assist shamans, witches, and magicians? Although I can't say for certain whether this is the case, I have had my own experiences with familiars I have personally created.

For example, my oldest familiar, which is a spiritual thought-form of a black cat, has actually shown up to collect its reward. A day after it successfully completed a task I had assigned it, I decided to give it energy by offering it a reward. In this case, the reward was a can of tuna. Now keep in mind that in this case, it's not the physical tuna itself that feeds the familiar, it's the intention and energy of the tuna that energizes it—so I would just set this tuna out in a bowl for several days assuming my familiar would absorb this energy.

But on this particular night I was so pleased by what my familiar had accomplished, I went to the store to buy the highest quality tuna I could find. And to my surprise, when I stepped out of the car to enter my apartment, there was a black cat waiting for me on the doorstep. What is even more amazing is that it had the same features I gave it when I created it—black, medium hair and emerald green eyes. Unfortunately, once I stepped out of the car, it took off and vanished into the night. So in this case, I set the bowl outside hoping it would come back and take the offering. As it turned out, one week later while driving through the neighborhood, I saw the very same cat hanging out in a neighbor's yard just a block away. Could this be synchronicity, or could this be a case of my familiar possessing the body of a living cat in order to enjoy the reward—honestly, stranger things have happened.

At the same time, I have talked to many people who swear up and down that their pets are familiars. However, those pets don't behave any differently than any other pet. It is more likely they just labeled their pet as a familiar out of ignorance, or simply just made it up to boost their ego. Real familiar creation is a lot of work!

Having said this, let's take a look at how to create a thought-form. First, know that you can enhance the strength of your familiar by creating it within your sacred space. You will initially spend a lot of time defining your familiar in great detail, and you will later reinforce those ideas by reviewing that information and through meditation. As you do this you should understand that you are not only defining your familiar, but you are also charging that information with emotional energy. This is what gives your familiar life. Be prepared to provide the following information in as much detail as possible.

Name

Give your familiar a unique and inspiring name that matches its form and personality type. Once you have decided upon a name, sigilize this name using whatever method you prefer. This sigil can be used to evoke it in the same way you would evoke a spirit found in any of the ancient grimoires.

Description

Depending on your talent, there are many ways to describe your familiar. For example, if you are good with words, you can represent your familiar with a textual description. Similarly, if you are good at sketching or painting you can produce a picture. Lastly, if you are good at crafting things with your hands, then you can gather the appropriate materials and create a statue of some sorts. Either way, you should ritualistically cleanse all of these items before you use them. But for the best results, feel free to employ all of these methods.

Background History

Here is your chance to tell your familiar's story. Just like in the Philip experiment, feel free to mix fact with fiction in order to add realism and legitimacy. Remember that this story should have elements that make you actually endure you to the familiar you are creating. This is especially important when you are creating familiar's that will be used by groups of people, or passed down within a magical order. Above all, your story should highlight your familiar's special qualities and abilities by including stories about its deeds, and accomplishments. By doing this, future readers will help empower your familiar because they will be inspired and moved by its story.

Correspondences

Because you are a sorcerer you should consider associating and sympathetically linking a planetary day and hour, a particular blend of incense, stones and crystals, as well as an elemental correspondence with your familiar. You of course can make other associations and sympathetic links, but these are the primary ones.

Evocation

You can of course call your familiar at any time by simply saying its name. However, you can create a special evocation to help create a stronger link. Although this evocation can be written in plain English, I encourage you to make it more powerful by writing it in a foreign language or babblauge. This evocation can then be repeated over and over again like a mantra in order to align yourself with the familiar.

Energy Source

Just like any other spirit a thought-form will seek out ways to satiate its energetic needs. This energy primarily comes from interaction with other conscious entities. Therefore, a thought-form will naturally try to invoke an emotional response in its creator, or other conscious entities that it might interact with in order to feed itself. If this is a positive thought-form, it will do so by trying to inspire its target in positive ways, but if the thought-form is negative, it will try to elicit a negative emotional response. Like attracts like.

So instead of allowing your familiar to run amok, and draw energy in chaotic ways, you can provide that energy by offering some sort of reward. As a matter of fact, that reward can be just about anything. For example, you could reward your familiar with a typical bread and wine offering or even the energetic vibrations emanating of stones or crystals. Obviously you want to avoid any form of offering that involves pain or bloodletting. At a minimum, energy can be sent to your familiar by utilizing the circulation of the body of light ritual in this book.

Kill Switch

You might want to consider adding a kill switch to your familiar when you create it. A kill switch is a special word or phrase that you can say to destroy or dismantle your familiar in the case that it goes awry. I personally have never had this happen to me before, but I have heard stories. In any case I think that it is good practice.

You create your kill-switch, decide upon a word or phrase and then imagine that you're familiar will be destroyed when those words are spoken. This destruction can be insured in several ways: first, by setting a clear and powerful intention, secondly, by including a theurgic call in your kill-switch, and lastly, by keeping that kill-switch sacred.

Please understand that creating a familiar is a process of indulging in willful fantasy. In other words, in order to successfully create a familiar you must be willing to let go of your critical faculties long enough to fully engage the creative half of your mind. You must also understand that familiars are only as powerful as the people who create them. Therefore, you cannot expect to create something with god-like powers if you have only been practicing magick for a few months. The strength of a familiar is also governed by how much and how often you reinforce it's concept by actively thinking about it—this is why, as silly as it may seem, interaction with your familiar, whether it is imaginary or not is a necessity. Again I stress, you cannot underestimate the importance of this type of interaction. The people who participated in the Philip project we're literally at it for a year before they saw firm results. Although you should get results quicker because you are using more advanced methods, you should be patient.

At this point you are probably wondering how send your familiar to task. Fortunately, this is very simple. To do this you simply ask it to do something for you—as any other spirit—and then you give it a reward if and when it has accomplished that task. With that being said, you should understand that you are creating something that will eventually become conscious. Therefore, you should treat this entity with respect. The method you used to communicate with your familiar is up to you. If you have developed your ability to communicate telepathically, you should have no problems communicating with your thought-form, but if you have not, then you will just have to trust that you're familiar has heard you. If that is not good enough, you can still use an ideomotor device to validate communication, and it to extract information. Lastly, consider deeper communication using the methods described in the next chapter.

Spirit Communication

I first began communicating with spirits at age sixteen, by using the infamous Ouija Board. And because at that age, I had no belief barrier, I had immediate success. The results were dramatic, with the planchette (the thing that points to the letters) gliding across the board spelling out words and letters so fast it was difficult to keep up. In those days, what came through, showed a knowledge and command of the English language that neither myself nor my friends possessed—and all of this of course, came with unexplainable paranormal activity. Although this trend continued well into my twenties, as my knowledge of magick grew, I began studying practicing higher forms of spirit contact such as evocation. After experimenting with evocation, I achieved even more success by incorporating parapsychological techniques into my contact routine. All of this has led me to conclude that having a solid connection with the right spirits can greatly enhance magick and serve as a valuable source of information for those seeking wisdom.

It is unfortunate that so much disinformation and lies have been spread about connecting with the spirit world that it has shroud it in mystery and fear. It is my firm belief that, it is not that the practice of communication with spirits that makes it dangerous, it is actually disconnection with all things spiritual and our ignorance of spirits that causes it to be so. Spirit communication has been a part of human history since our ability to think and reflect. It is not abnormal and it's not evil. It is just a fact of life. In fact, more danger comes from not being aware of the spiritual influences at play in the world than by knowing what they are and how to properly interact with them.

THE HISTORY OF SPIRIT COMMUNICATION

As I have already said, spirit communication has been with us since time immemorial. In the good old days—that is thousands of years ago—tribal shamans relied on their natural ability to psychically communicate with spirits using abilities such as clairvoyance and clairaudience. Add to this communication through dreams and you have a steady line of communication between the physical and spiritual that goes back centuries. Besides these things, divination played a big role in communicating with ancestors and other-worldly beings. Questions could be asked, then signs within nature, or random systems like rune stones and tarot cards could be read to provide answers. And the art of scrying—staring into pools of water, using magick mirrors and crystal gazing—have been around just as long. These tools were used as a way to shift the mind to the right state for communication, the end result being a mental image reflected upon the scrying surface.

Then enters spirit summoning, or Goetic Evocation (taken from the Lessor Keys of Solomon), which dates to around the seventeenth century. What really sets Goetic Evocation (spirit summoning) apart from simply calling a spirit by any other means is that evoker uses a litany of holy names to beat demonic spirits into submission—after which the magician demands information, or puts the demon to task. This practice supposedly began with King Solomon, who allegedly summoned seventy-two demons into a brass vessel, then forced them to build his temple. Once the temple was constructed, it was eventually overthrown by Nebuchadnezzar who then found vessel and opened it, releasing the seventy-two demons back into the world.

But even Goetic Magick has its origins. Goetic Magick was highly influenced by a collection of Greco-Egyptian scrolls called the Greek Magical Papyri, which dates even further back to the second through fifth centuries BCE. Among miscellaneous spells to bring wealth and attract a lover, are the blueprints for the ceremonial practice of evocation—whipping spirits into submission by beating them over the head with various names of god. Of course, this information must have been drawn from traditions even older than that, so it's safe to say evocation probably coexisted a midst older shamanic practices. Either way, Goetic Evocation was adopted by the Hermetic Order of the Golden Dawn and evolved by people like MacGregor

Mathers and Aleister Crowley. It is an extremely popular form of magick and is still used today.

Traditional magicians swear by this method, saying it is totally necessary to keep these entities in check—otherwise you are just asking for trouble. However, not all magicians feel this way. They feel that this is just another form of bullying that inevitably provokes the spirit. They warn, if you fail to restrain the entity, it is likely to retaliate and make your life living hell. One could argue that some kind of restraint and protection should be used against such a demonic entity, but to be fair, many of these demons were just the gods of cultures who were dominated by Christianity. Once that culture was dominated, those gods were demonized by changing their names a bit and relabeling as devils. The goddess Astarte is a good example of this. Astarte, who is a goddess of fertility, sexuality and war was changed into the demon Astaroth who is the great duke of Hell.

Why did the Christians do this? This was of course because the Christians wanted to suppress competing religions. Once the old gods were relabeled as demonic, those who worshiped them were put down and it was much easier to convince the next generation that they were evil beings. Now by saying this I am not trying to promote the old gods, because, some of them did have malevolent traits. However, I just wanted you to understand that not everything the Abrahamic religions label as a demonic is actually an evil being. In the same sense, Christianity has its own demons, Satan and Lucifer, but these beings were never a part of any old world religion.

As a matter of fact, the angel-demon dilemma runs deep. The words *angel* and *demon* meant something different to the ancients then they do to us today. Both of these words stem from Greek. In the Greek language *angelos* simply meant "messenger" and had no supernatural connotations whatsoever. That means, the word *angelos* could be applied to anyone delivering a message. On the other hand, the word *demon* is a perversion of the Greek word *daimon*, which was originally used to describe a divine power, or nature spirit. In this sense, a daimon can be considered neither good nor evil—and this is how the Greeks saw it. It was not until the word *daimon* was adopted by the Romans that it became "daemon" and finally perverted into the word *demon*, meaning "an evil spirit," by the church.

Practitioners must keep all this in mind before even thinking about summoning demonic spirits using Goetic Evocation. Even though these beings may have once been connected to the old gods—they are no longer. When a magician or witch calls one of these beings, they are not calling a "daimon," in the Greek sense of the word, they are calling a sentient thought-form that was born out of all those misaligned ideas shaped by Christian paranoia, pop horror films and urban legend. That is not to say that somehow the old pagan gods were transformed into vicious demonic entities. No—only that the propaganda of the Abrahamic religions have created new malicious entities in their likeness. In this way, a novice evoker can be lulled into thinking that he or she is calling upon an entity that has his or her best interest at heart, when oftentimes, that is not the case. Moving on now.

To see where all this has gone, we must now move from ancient times, to 1848 Hydesville, New York, because this is where the spiritualist movement began. On March 31, Kate and Margaret revealed to their family that they had made contact with the spirit of a peddler that was buried in the walls of their house. Soon this information spread from the family to a small circle of friends and finally out into their world where it spawned the spiritualist movement.

In fact, communicating with spirits became so popular that a spiritualist church was founded. Some branches took the idea of communicating with spirits and merged it will Christianity, while others used it as more of a metaphysical practice. As the movement grew, it eventually crossed the Atlantic where it became popular in Europe. Soon, everyone was holding séances, table tapping and using talking boards to communicate with the dead.

However, none of this was based around any magical practices. There were no complex rituals for contacting the spirit world, only a medium and few people sitting around the table in the dim light. And in many cases there was not even a medium was present, only a group of dedicated novices pushing a planchette across a Ouija board. And this says something very important about spirit communication—anyone can learn how to do it and complex ritual is unnecessary.

Now let's shift a few years into the future—1920. This was an age of great technological innovation. It was Thomas Edison himself, inverter of the telephone and phonograph that said,

"I am inclined to believe that our personality hereafter will be able to affect matter. If this reasoning be correct, then, if we can evolve an instrument so delicate as to be affected or moved, or manipulated by our personality as it survives in the next life, such an instrument, when made available, aught to record something."

With that being said, the first real experiment with trying to communicate with the dead using technology, came in 1956 when Attila von Szalay and Raymond Bayless capture the first spirit voices on tape. To do this, Szalay, who claimed be to a natural medium, would sit enclosed in a special wooden box where a microphone would record voice. It is understanding to assume deception on Szalay's part, when you consider that human beings are adept at mimicking voices. However, both male and female voices were captured and not just that, both while Szalay was in the box *and* outside of it.

Years later, in 1959, Friedrich Jurgenson, a well-known Swedish documentary producer, captured voices on reels of tape while trying to record the songs of birds. However, thinking this could be electronic interference, he asked the local radio stations in the region if they were broadcasting, but he discovered that no station had been transmitting at this time. After carefully listening to the tapes, Friedrich realized that the voices claimed to people he knew who had passed on—voices of the dead.

Since that time, paranormal investigators and parapsychologists have been employing newer and newer technology to capture communication from the other side. Recording EVPs (electronic voice phenomena) using tape has given way to using digital recorders and automatic drawing (capturing images of the spirit realm through sketch), has transitioned to capturing spirits on video. As time passes even more advanced sensory equipment is being adapted to detect the presence of spirits. It is possible to scan for electromagnet interference using an EMF reader, detect minute telekinetic movement using motion sensors and even emphasize spirits using laser grids.

In more recent times, a new movement called CE5 has caused Witches and Magicians to look up and take notice. CE5 stands for close encounters of the fifth kind. Whereas the former classes of alien contact (CE1–4) are initiated by an extraterrestrial, those who practice the CE5 protocol voluntarily initiate the contact using a type of remote viewing. CE5 was originally developed by Dr. Steven Greer, a former high-ranking officer in the United States Navy with the help of alien contacts. After working out this protocol and forming the disclosure project, Dr. Greer made his methods public in 1990.

What is interesting about CE5 protocol is the fact that it makes use of some of the root methods used by people who practice various forms of spirit contact such as mediumship, remote viewing and evocation. Not only this, but also it makes an important connection between the evocation of the old gods, or Anunnaki (those from heaven to earth came) if you will and extraterrestrial higher dimensional beings (those who visited Earth from space). So as interdenominational communication using remote viewing and technology becomes more mainstream, this will eventually open up serious inquiry into the study of other dimensions and other dimensional beings, allowing for real technologies to be developed.

In conclusion, the art and science of spirit communication has come a long way. Not only is there a vast body of knowledge illuminating the practice, but also there is a plethora of new technologies that one can use to make it easier. This means, with diligence and dedication, anyone can make contact. So now let's talk about what is common to all these methods and then put all this knowledge together to create a more concise way of tapping into the spirit world.

WHAT IS A SPIRIT?

Although both ancient esoteric traditions and modern science understands that the physical is built upon the nonphysical, people still have a difficult time coming to grips with the idea that anything nonphysical, like a spirit, could ever exist. This is primarily because we have been programmed to believe that consciousness is the product of things happening within our physical body, not beyond it.

The argument against such a thing usually begins with the question, "How could such an immaterial being function without a physical body. After all, movement requires some kind of physical mode of locomotion, hearing requires ears, seeing eyes, touch skin, tasting a tongue and of course the ability to think, a healthy physical brain right?" Well, no, not necessarily.

As modern science learns more about how reality works, many scientists are adopting the idea that mind precedes matter. As you already know, this means on a very fundamental level, the universe is made of organized thoughts and ideas and that those thought-forms are an expression of a consciousness that lay somewhere *beyond*. If consciousness really is fundamental to existence (which it is), that means everything is, or has the potential to be, a living thinking thing whether it is solid or made of liquid, gas, plasma, atoms or some other form of energy that cannot be seen by the human eye.

I personally believe that one of the reasons why science has been unable to find proof for the human soul is because of conflicting beliefs between the different schools of science and the way they interpret data. Biologists tend to see things as being composed of DNA, cells and organs, while quantum physicists are only concerned with waves and particles and of course the psychologists are specifically looking for patterns of thought that dictate behavior. The outstanding majority of these fields are not ready to unify their discoveries, because doing so may lead to their extinction—and that is why they fight so hard to protect their theories against other schools of thought. So in my opinion, science has failed to find the soul, not because it doesn't exist, but because they have simply overlooked it. It's been there all along.

Another important clue to the existence of a spiritual body is the electromagnetic field that surrounds the body. Mainstream science teaches that these fields are actually generated by the physical body. However, the mystical traditions believe it's the other way around—the physical body is produced by the electromagnetic field or etheric body and of course, the mental body is responsible for producing the etheric body.

These fields of energy can persist in nature, outside of any physical structure—even Einstein said that, "Energy is neither created or destroyed." This means that when we die, this energy goes somewhere. Does it dissipate into nothingness as many scientists profess, or does it persist as a subtler form of energy on a different plane of existence? Although science has no conclusive answers, psychics, shamans, mystics and magicians have known for a very long time that this energy does in fact survive after death.

Paranormal researchers and investigators have been able to prove this to some extent by taking measurements at haunted locations using EMF readers. Of course, not all readings indicate that a spirit is present, but some do. Even though technology (especially large appliances) generate electromagnetic fields, EMF fluctuations have been captured away and apart from any electronic sources. To be fair, getting an EMF reading does not necessarily mean a spirit has been detected, but when a measurement corresponds to information received by a psychic (before the fact), or the fact that things have been captured on video moving by themselves, the evidence mounts up and it becomes impossible to ignore that a spirit is most likely present.

The fact that these electromagnetic fields can have an effect on the brain powerful enough to change behavior and cause hallucinations or nightmares, leads many critics to believe that exposure to these fields via technology gives them license to debunk every account of a haunting. But if you consider the fact that you can pick up on someone's *vibes* while standing next to them, it shouldn't surprise you that a disincarnate entity could have the same effect on your mind, if it entered your electromagnetic field.

So in light of all this, what is a spirit? The truth is we don't know. However, we can speculate. We do know that the physical form exists because we all have bodies. We also know that electromagnetic fields emanate from the brain, heart and other major organs of the body. Actually anything made of atoms, including every cell in the human body generates an electromagnetic field. All of this insinuates a type of etheric body talked about in esoteric texts. Casting aside the belief that consciousness is the result of bioelectric signals firing off in the brain that ceases to exist after we die, a mental body can be evidenced by acknowledging that we all have conscious thought. This makes for a total of three bodies; the physical, etheric and the mental. So now let's define them.

The Physical Body

That's easy—it's what you are seeing now; made of cells, organs, skin, a brain, and so on. But remember all that is made of subtler energies.

The Etheric Body (The Physical Template)

The etheric body acts as a blueprint or template for our physical body. It is this template that is reflected from the astral into the physical world to create our physical manifestation. Most mystical traditions believe that the etheric body houses the Chakras, which are responsible for moving vital energies throughout your body. This body also acts as a bridge between your lower physical form (the physical body) and your higher forms.

The Mental Body (The Spirit)

The mental body is made up of a higher form of energy. Therefore, it exists beyond space and time. This body itself is composed of ideas that make up your personality, like gender and cultural identity, likes, dislikes, experiences and memories. The mental body resides within the etheric body and is connected to one or more collectives. In order to tap into these collectives, a person must be able to shift their conscious state using meditation. Once this happens the mental body can draw upon the information shared by all souls that are a part of a collective.

Our Divine Aspect

This is the point in which all things are connected and therefore is a sea of knowledge built by the experiences of everything that is a part of it. This ultimate sea of conscious knowledge is ever growing and every evolving. Our divine aspect is the Source. We do not dissolve into it by becoming spiritually enlightened, but if we are aware of our connection, we can tap into this universal consciousness and take advantage of its vast warehouse of knowledge.

OUTSIDE SPIRITUAL INFLUENCES

At some point, in your journey you will encounter outside spiritual influences—hopefully only good ones. In such case you should understand what they are. The renown psychiatrist Carl Jung believed that spirits were archetypes or less successful personalities that split off from the psyche to became dissociated—kind of like what happens to people suffering from multiple personality disorder, or what is now called DID (dissociative identity disorder). In my early practice, I too thought this may be the case, but that explanation does not explain physical phenomena such as phantom lights, disembodied sounds, or telekinetic activity that usually comes with the presence of a genuine spirit. So if you want to practice Sorcery you must come to grips with the idea that we are not alone and that the universe is alive with spiritual activity. Some of these spirits are more advanced than us, while others are less advanced, but they are all connected to the same Source and thus have a divine aspect.

High Spirits

These are beings that have raised their vibrational level to such a high degree that they exist on the higher planes. Some of these beings were once human, while others are outside of the human genome. Such beings could include alien species, nature spirits, elementals and ancient thought-forms. These beings can be distant, with little interest in humanity, or they can feel personally obligated to help us on our spiritual journey. Although these beings reside in the upper planes, they can be found on all levels of existence. If they chose to interact with us directly, then they may choose to reincarnate as a human being. Otherwise, they will speak to us telepathically to guide and inspire us to grow spiritually.

Elemental Spirits

As mentioned under, "The Elemental Model," Paracelsus believed, as most practitioners of magick do, that elementals are the spiritual form of an actual element in nature such as air, earth, fire and water. If everything is a conscious matrix of spiritual force—this of course makes perfect sense. Why wouldn't all things have some kind of spirit? With this being said, there would be many other types of elementals besides the air, earth, fire and water—varieties within a particular element, making for some very unique and specialized species. Just as every human being is unique, all elementals are unique as well. Why don't we see these beings today—well we do, we just don't recognize them for what they are. Most people don't see the forces of nature as conscious things. Therefore, they don't pay attention to what nature is trying to tell them. Pay attention and they will make themselves known. You should also be aware that some of these elemental forces are high-level beings with godlike powers. They could be construed as the daemons of the Greeks, or old gods of the ancients.

Planetary Forces

Planets are also a type of elemental manifestations. Being conscious beings with spirits, they have been referred to as the planetary forces. Of these planetary forces are the seven planets of astrology: Earth, Jupiter, Mars, Saturn, Venus, Pluto, the Sun and the Moon. Now whether some of these bodies are actually planets, stars, or merely satellites has always been up for debate by scholars, but for all intents and purposes, they are huge bodies in space, also with spirit.

The Human Spirit

Human beings exist in all Worlds. Those human spirits that exist on the lower levels have as many of the same psychological hang-ups as you and I—in other words, they keep the same personality they had before they died. After working with various forms of spirit communication, including evocation you will discover that many of these lower spirits are totally unaware of the fact they have died. Therefore, they may be just as shocked as you when they catch glimpse of your spirit manifesting on their plane to communicate with them. I have personally been mistaken for the devil, or have received messages like, "Who the hell are you!" by such unsuspecting souls. Approach lower spirits with caution, because you can scare the piss out of them if you are not careful—I'm just saying. But human spirits who exist on the higher planes are more enlightened and thus more aware and less selfish—this is why it doesn't hurt to communicate with your ancestors. If you can find family members that achieved a high level of enlightenment, who have passed and have not currently reincarnated, then they may be willing work with you to help you achieve that same amount of enlightenment.

Shades and Vampires

I know what you're thinking, "Vampires? Really?" OK, so here we go. Yes, vampires do exist and are quite common. They are not the blood-sucking undead that roam the night looking for victims to exsanguinate. No, they are low-level spirits that feed off of negative energy—this would include nonhuman spirits as well as human spirits.

These spirits are attracted to the weak and emotionally unstable—and this is not meant to be an insult to anyone that may be suffering from a weakened mental state—we all encounter problems in our lives that cause momentary weakness and emotional turmoil. Nonetheless, a vampiric spirit will be attracted to the negative emotions caused by these states and will try to invoke more of the same within that victim. If the victim is susceptible and unaware, all the better, but if the victim has spiritual sight or has evoked the spirit intentionally using some form of spirit communication device, the vampiric spirit will try to edge its way into the victim's mind and dominate—and domination, either through deception or by force is the precursor to possession. Such vile spirits make up your run-of-the-mill shades and archetypal demons—and such spirits can cause harm to not only the victim, but also everyone that the victim comes in contact with, be they strangers or family members. As a Sorcerer, you will inevitably come into contact with these souls—especially if you practice evocation. But if you are wise and learn how to bind and banish, they can be easily dealt with.

IF SPIRITS EXIST, WHY DON'T WE SEE OR HEAR THEM?

Spirits are around us all the time. No, they are probably not hiding in your bathroom watching you take a shower, but they are among us nonetheless. The thing is, most people miss spirits, because they are not looking for them. They either don't believe and therefore filter out evidence of spiritual activity, or they don't know what to look for, thus have no context to "see" spirits. It is a proven fact that the human brain tends to sensor out information it finds irrelevant, or incomprehensible. Think of the way you intentionally or unintentionally tune out everything else in your environment in order to focus on one particular thing, or how your mind can fill in the blanks concerning shady memories. These are some of the reasons why eyewitness testimony is so unreliable in the court of law—most people are not trained observers.

So barring mentally blotting out those things we simply can't put into context, or would rather not see, what are some other reasons why spirits remain invisible to most? For one, most people don't understand the nature of spirits. Therefore, people oftentimes mistake spiritual phenomena, for naturally occurring physical phenomena. For example, a message from a spirit, delivered through human being can be intentionally ignored as hokum, or mistaken as a coincidental response to something the listener was thinking. Spirits can speak through others, oftentimes we just choose not to listen.

And spirits can also communicate through synchronistic events. Those events can be set in motion by the spirit, through force of will from the higher planes, just as you might cast a spell or wish something into existence—the end result being a "sign" that answers the question. Oftentimes, a spirit won't even try to communicate using direct voice, or telepathy—not because they don't want to, but simply because direct voice requires a lot of energy and most people are incapable of receiving telepathic information. This might sound like magical thinking, but if you choose to ignore such signs, you will be missing a lot.

THE DANGERS OF SPIRIT COMMUNICATION

Probably the biggest mistake those communicating with spirits make is to treat it like a game and do it for the purpose of thrill-seeking. This is oftentimes the case with naive teenagers, they invite all their friends over to play Ouija hoping to get a scare and the energy created by that anticipation draws a negative entity. Spirits are attracted to emotions. Therefore, if you go into any kind of spirit communication with a negative mind-set, you will attract negative spirits, but if you do it with a positive mind-set, you will attract positive spirits. This is why the uninitiated, mentally unstable, or fearful should never be invited to a spirit communication session—because that fear, or psychosis will inevitably draw negative entities!

Another fatal mistake new communicators make is not being able to determine the difference between aspects of their own personality and communication from the spirit being called. This is oftentimes because they subscribe to the psychological model of magick and go into the communication thinking that they are connecting with archetypes from their own unconscious mind. In such a case, they may be willing to take the chances they usually wouldn't. Because after all, they believe they are dealing with a part of their own psyche, not a real entity—and certainly there is no harm in that. However, when a legitimate spirit does arrive, it can easily infiltrate the mind of such a communicator, oftentimes unnoticed (because that person believes that their thoughts are their own) and eventually take full possession. For this reason, a Sorcerer must be in full control of his or her mental faculties and possess a great amount of divine authority.

WHAT TO EXPECT

Honestly, you never know what may happen during a spirit communication session. Sometimes it can be uneventful, while other times it is absolutely amazing. For example, a spirit may not be able, or even want to make an impressive show of its power. Therefore, you all you might get is a mental impression. And that of course could lead you to the conclusion that your mind has conjured up that information and you are just imagining everything. To the outside world, it looks even sillier—after all, nothing impressive is happening and you are just sitting there relaying a message. Because of this, it is always a good idea to surround yourself by people who understand the nature of spirit communication and telepathy—otherwise, the negative energy a skeptic, or those who are quick to ridicule, will weaken the connection. On the other hand, I have communicated with spirits who never reveal their presence in any tangible way, but deliver information so impressive that it leaves no question in anyone's mind that something was actually there.

In the same sense, if you are using a ghost box, it is possible to communicate with an entity in real time. A ghost box usually works by shifting from one radio station to another every few milliseconds or so. This results in a randomly shifting audio that acts as a type of carrier wave that spirits can use create messages. Although those messages are usually short and staticy, they are quite impressive when you receive one that pertains to something you are currently doing at the time, or that is related to the area you are in, or that directly answers a question that you've asked. Similarly, entities can be coaxed into affecting other electronic devices such as lights, or meters, in order to establish a yes-no form of communication—seeing that happen is quite amazing.

If you get lucky (or unlucky, depending on the situation) you may begin to witness paranormal activity. Such activity can range from flickering lights, to gusts of wind, doors opening by themselves, things moving on their own, phantom lights, objects shattering, or even the partial or full manifestation of an apparition. Legend even has it—though I have never witnessed it myself—that small objects have been teleported from one place to another (apportation). Apparently this happens all the time in CE5 with recordings being made of alien craft dropping out of subspace (the astral) and manifesting in the physical world.

WHAT/WHO TO CONTACT

Suggestion number one, avoid connecting with negative spirits like demons, shades and other malevolent beings, because they are dangerous. Not to mention, evoking negative entities builds negative energy, which can cause disturbing mood shifts, physical illness, mental illness and the culmination of catastrophic events. Instead, choose a spirit that you can trust, like an ancestor. Just keep in mind that just because someone is a relative, doesn't mean they are wise and have all the answers—being dead doesn't change who they are.

Your next best choice might be a familiar thought-form of your own creation. This will not only open up a line of communication between you and your familiar, but also help to empower it. Once you have connected with your familiar, you might attempt to connect with an elemental spirit. Doing this might give you a certain amount of cooperation with these elements in nature and will allow you to add that power to any spell or ritual you cast that involves fire, air, water and earth.

When you have successfully contacted a familiar, or elemental, you may want to connect with a higher being. A higher being would be something like an angel, daimon (not *demon*), an ascended master, or benevolent higher alien life form. Much information about these beings can already be found in other books, so I will not cover that here. However, many of these beings are considered the old gods, or gods with a lower "g." Just do your research and be careful what you contact—don't try to connect anything that will obviously be harmful. Also, I find connecting with beings that originate from my own culture is much easier because there is already a collective link.

COMMUNICATING WITH SPIRITS

There are a multitude of ways to communicate with spirits. Therefore, there is absolutely no reason why you can't use more than one. Either way, what you choose, will wholly depend on your skill-level and what you are comfortable with. In fact, you may want to experiment with more than one way at a time.

Divination

The traditional way of communicating with a spirit has always been some form of divination: extrasensory perception, scrying, ideomotor tools and even tarot or runes—each method having its own set of advantages and disadvantages.

Extrasensory Perception

The same techniques used in the farseeing exercise are used here, except that your target is a spirit. Because of this, if one is not careful, this method can suffer from the same type of personal bias, or analytical overlay that any other farseeing session can suffer from. Even so, if one can tell the difference between their own thoughts and any messages coming in, this method can bear the most fruit. Farseeing can be found in the chapter on "Divination."

Scrying

For those who are skilled seers, scrying can be just as fruitful as using pure extrasensory perception. Scrying is simply projecting one's thoughts onto a reflective scrying surface—the same thoughts that would come through using ESP. Again, the method is prone to the same analytical overlay as farseeing. How to scry and make a magick mirror, can be found in the "Divination" chapter.

Ideomotor Devices

Out of all of the ideomotor tools, the spirit board or Ouija board, when operated by more than one person, is probably the most reliable method. Even though the users of the board are operating it while in a conscious state, it is more likely that any message that comes through will be from an actual spirit, because it is more difficult for multiple users to consciously, or unconsciously control it than if there was a single user.

Although divining rods and pendulums can be used, they allow a single user to tap into the subconscious mind, while in a conscious state. This means the mind of the operator is insufficiently connected to the plane of spirit and therefore cannot trust that they have actual spirit connection.

You should also know that higher spirits, such as daimons, angels and other higher intelligences disdain communicating through ideomotor devices because it is too slow—they actually prefer telepathy, because they can relay more information quicker.

Tape and Digital Recorders

Spirits have been known to be able to affect electromagnetic frequencies in order to impress their voices upon media. In recent times, digital recorders have become popular. However, in times past, tape recorders were the popular medium. Even though this method is a bit antiquated, it is still very popular because many paranormal researchers believe that the analogue signal is closer to our body's natural frequency than digital.

Having said this find a tape recorder that has a line-in jack, mic jack, and a counter. When buying tapes choose quality: Maxwell or Fuji is good for this. Because you will want to reduce outside noise when listening for voices, you will want to buy ear phones that cover the ears. To record, follow these steps. To get the best results, you need to buy a mic that is able to pick up the highest and lowest frequencies possible (between 20 Hz and 20 kHz)—a mic made to record vocals is best for this.

Using a Tape Recorder

If you are using a new tape, open and load it into the tape recorder. Although you can record on a used tape, you do not want to record over prior recordings. Instead, fast-forward to a part of the tape that has not been recorded on yet and note the number on the counter. If you are using a fresh tape, fast-forward past the tape leader (the transparent part of the tape) and hit reset on the counter so that you will be able to note the number when you have finished recording.

Connect your mic to the mic jack, then extend it as far away from the tape recorder as you can—this will ensure that you don't pick up the sound of yourself breathing, or the tape recorder running. To reduce vibrations, attach your mic to mic stand. However, if you don't have one, lay it on a surface that is not prone to vibration.

Using a Digital Recorder
Fortunately, in this day and age we have cell phones, so you can just download a recording app. You will of course need a phone that has a mic or mic jack. Otherwise, you will not be able to record. The advantage of making a digital recording is that you don't need to rely on a counter to find your position, because each recording is an individual sound file. As above, you will want to position your mic away from you to prevent picking up the sound of yourself breathing, or moving.

Adding White Noise
Oftentimes it is not enough to expect a spirit to be able to imprint their voice directly onto the condenser of a microphone. For this reason, white noise (static noise) can be introduced to the recording as a type of carrier wave on which a spirit can craft the message. This of course presents its own problems: first, it takes a well-trained ear to be able to pick out the messages hidden within the static and second, multiple voices can easily blend together.

For this you will need a recording device that has a line-in piece of technology capable of producing white noise, like a radio, or an old fashion television with a line-audio output jack and the cables to connection them. When recording try to avoid doing it in stereo because this increases the chance of blending. When using a radio, you will want to dial it in between to stations to pick up static. And lastly, if you have none of this, you can still use a natural source of white noise such as a fan, or running water and just record near the source as you question and wait for answers during the session.

Video

It is widely known that spirits can be photographed and videoed. The reason for this is that image technology oftentimes has the ability to capture light anomalies that are far outside of what normal humans can perceive. Therefore, the best camera will be capable of recording at night and picking up the infrared and ultraviolet spectrum. Furthermore, your camera should create some kind of digital file that can be uploaded to a computer and analyzed.

Another issue is the actual operation of the equipment. Unless you have an assistance, it is more than likely that you will have to begin recording before you actually need to record. This is so you don't have to break from meditation to start your equipment. So, if you know about how long it takes you to achieve a deep trance, you will want to hit play that many minutes before you actually need to record.

MODERN EVOCATION

Items Needed

- Any Sympathetic Links to Spirit (an altar or space to create an altar)
- Anything you will need to erect a sacred Space or put up protection
- Any technology you will need to record, interact with, or sense spirits.
- Energy Enhancers: played or recorded music, crystals, incense

Unlike attempting to contact a spirit by going to a haunted site and hoping it might be there, evocation actually summons a specific spirit to your location. Once the spirit has arrived, it can then be communicated with, or even asked for aid—if appropriate. Such a summoning can result in telepathic contact, or even a physical or astral manifestation. The thing that sets this method apart from traditional evocation is its use of technology and the common courtesy extend to the spirit being summoned. In other words, you will not be demanding that it come and you will not be trying to dominate it by threatening it with names of God.

Preparation

Although all magick can benefit from preparation, evocation requires the most. Therefore, one of your top objectives will be to have everything ready beforehand, so you will not be distracted and can maintain focus. That means not only having everything you need, but also knowing where everything is so you don't have to consciously think about it. Having said this, let's go over some of the things you will need.

The Sympathetic Link

In the case of evocation, the sympathetic link is an object that is used to help forge a connection between your mind and the spirit's mind. In this case, a sympathetic link can be an item that was worn or cherished by the spirit while alive, and/or any tag-lock that is loaded with its DNA. Besides this, you will want to have as much information about the spirit as you can get. This might include a picture of the spirit, or some kind of effigy like a statue, or poppet. If you amass many things, you may want to set up an altar to that entity—not for worship, but as a focal point. You can then place all your items on the altar along with an offering, candles, and incense.

If the entity you are evoking is a grimoiric spirit (any spirit found in an old grimoire), then you will want to construct a sigil. Instructions for making and charging sigils can be found in the chapter "Common Forms of Magick," and the depiction of the sigil can be found in the grimoire you chose. Just be careful and don't call anything that is malevolent.

When setting up an altar for a grimoiric spirit, follow the instructions in the grimoire you found it in when setting up that altar. It will likely suggest that you place the altar in a certain quadrant (north, south, east, west), burn a specific type of incense, use a particular color scheme and even perform your evocation on a particular planetary day and hour.

Protection

Remember: even though you will not be purposely summoning an evil entity, all forms of magick draw curious spirits—more so when performing evocation. Unlike other forms of magick, you will be allowing an intelligence to get close to you—close enough to communicate. In such case, it's a good idea to have some kind of magical protection.

This protection can be casting a circle, wearing an amulet, putting up protective wards, or even posting a spiritual guard such as a thought-form you have created. All of this has already been mentioned in the chapters, "Concerning Magick Circles and Sacred Spaces," and "Binding, Banishing and Protection." Whatever method you choose, just keep in mind that the protection is only as good as the person who cast it. This means, if you doubt your ability to use magick protection, you shouldn't be evoking.

Energy Raising Aids

Evocation is a strenuous endeavor for both the evoker and spirit. For this reason, you will want to raise all the energy you can. To do this you can utilize song and dance, drumming, recorded music, crystals and the burning of incense. This has all been covered previously like "Working with Energy," and "Spell Magick."

An Offering

In a way, an offering could be considered energy raising, because the spirit will most likely be using energetic essence of that offering to forge a good connection and manifest. However, not all spirits require an offering. Even so, it's just polite. That offering can a plate of food and an offertory drink, or an incense that is favorable to that entity.

Take note that if you are summoning a grimoiric entity and the grimoire suggests you use blood, there is a possibility that said entity is malevolent and you should use great caution. On the other hand, a blood sacrifice may be a cultural thing—after all, we slaughter animals all the time for food. A good example of this would be animal sacrifice to the Haitian Vodou gods, the Loa, or the sacrificial lamb in Christianity. If you do need to make a blood sacrifice, you should be the one who performs it, but you should have assistance.

Recording and Sensory Equipment

If you are not concerned with gathering physical data, you can skip this step. However, it can be very rewarding. If you have any doubt evocation works, physical evidence can give you confirmation and help build the confidence you will need in future evocations. If you opt to use technology, then it is likely that you will need the help of another person to operate it while you do the evocation itself. If you don't, you will have to stop what you are doing in order to take care of technical problems—and that will cause you to lose your trance state.

With that being said, you should have a video camera capable recording in the dark, as well as picking up the infrared and ultraviolet spectrum. You may in fact want to have enough cameras to effectively cover the entire ritual chamber. These video cameras should be situated on tripods and magically protected so their batteries don't end up being drained. Besides cameras, you should have recording equipment. This can either be a tape recorder or a digital recorder.

The Pre-Evocation Process

To ensure that the spirit you are trying to evoke will appear, it is beneficial to actually call it three or more days before you perform the officially evocation. Doing this is an easy process, you simply meditate on the name and image of the spirit. Meditation should last anywhere between ten to fifteen minutes, during which you focus on the fact that you want to call that spirit on a particular day and hour. During meditation, hold the sigil or related item(s) in your hands and repeat your intention over and over again, like a mantra. You may in fact get contact during this process, so take note of any communication in your ritual diary after the performing the meditation.

Forging the Connection

The most accurate word I can use to describe the forging of a connection is *actualization*. Actualization is the process of realizing, or imagining something, in order to bring it into reality. This is what we do every day when we perform problem solving in our minds before we actually set out to actually make something happen. To do this we might use various physical aids to help visualize the task or action we are about to do, before we actually do it.

The good example of this would be a carpentry project for a chair. First we decide that the chair needs to be the right dimensions for an average adult to sit in. Secondly, we choose a material like oak. Then we plan the schematics by creating a blueprint and go about gathering our materials.

Without this actualization, be it purely mental, or physical (in the case of the blueprints) we would be unable to use the materials to create the chair.

In evocation, the actualization process quantum entangles the mind of the Sorcerer with that of the spirit so that communication and/or manifestation can occur. And the only way to do that is to be able to actualize the spirit by giving it directed attention. So in order to effectively focus one's attention on a particular spirit, the evoker must have something to focus on. This might be photograph, sketch, poppet, or even a statue in the likeness of the spirit, and/or a tag-lock, such as hair, nails, or a personal effect. All of this will be arranged on an altar and be available for the evoker to handle as he or she evokes.

Once all of these things have been gathered and arranged upon an altar, the Sorcerer can then use those items to direct his attention to the spirit through meditation. Therefore, when the Sorcerer has achieved a deep enough state and has applied the right amount of focus, a connection will occur and the spirit will either choose to communicate telepathically, or manifest astrally or physically with the chamber.

So at this point, you may be wondering exactly how to use these items (sigil, picture, tag-locks, ritual observations) as a form of foci? The first thing I must say is this—by researching the spirit, gathering related items and making sure they have been arranged on the altar, you have been following the rule of immersion and have already started the quantum entanglement process. This also means that you shouldn't expect to be able to pick the name of a spirit out of a hat one minute and in the next minute expect a spirit to appear—a great deal of thought, or intention must go into making this connection. Besides following the immersion process by setting up your altar, you can inundate yourself with these items during meditation by handling them (picking them up, wearing them, smelling them, and so on) or even focusing on them as you would a flame during a Tratak exercise (see: Mind and Magick).

But as you do all this, you must also make a call. You can call to a spirit mentally, but I would argue that making a verbal call ensures that your intentions have been released, because intention always prefaces words. In ages past, ancient magicians believed that specific magick words could be spoken that would draw a spirit into their triangle. But I am here to tell you this is not the case at all—it's all in the belief and intention. If you "believe" such words will have power, you create strong intent. However, if you already know that evocation is possible and you will get communication, relying on such words is not necessary. As a matter of fact, I strongly suggest you avoid using old evocations because they are unnecessarily harsh and insulting to spirits. Remember: you are not summoning demons. Therefore, those spirits don't need to be threatened. However, if saying arcane words helps you strengthen your connection with a spirit, or actualize, you can simply make those words up using the sigilize charm method described in "Occult Magick."

For example:

> "I call to you" might be sigilized as "tullca" *and*
> "I give you power" might be sigilized as "wuvo"

Once you have created these sigilized charms, you will want to sympathetically link them to their meaning, then record them in your book of shadows. To use this charms as calls, you would speak them as a part of the evocation and repeat them like a mantra.

For example:

> "Tullca Vassago˙. Tullca Vassago. Tullca Vassago"
> "Vassago wuvo. Vassago wuvo. Vassago wuvo."

Having said this, you don't need any fancy arcane words to summon a spirit—you can simply request it be present using plain English.

Example of evocation:

> "Vassago, we invite you to this circle."
> *Or,* "Vassago hear me."

As you do this you will want to be open to signs of communication or manifestation. If you are using a form of extrasensory perception, you

---

* Vassago is the name of a grimoiric daimon.

should be expecting some form of impression, but if you are using a bowl or mirror, eventually your vision will blur and a fog will appear. Allow this to happen and pay attention to your intuition as you gaze. Images will not appear on the mirror as if you were watching a television program. They will at first be felt—in other words, intuited. You may see a vision, hear sounds, smell something, or the like, or you might get sudden insight.

If this is the first time you have performed an evocation, it is likely you will get amazing results. However, the next time you perform evocation, you may question your experience and chalk it up to no more than your imagination. But what is important to realize is that the more you practice evocation, the more vivid this sensory input will become, until eventually that entity will manifest right in front of you—in plain sight.

Also, don't be surprised if you hear odd sounds, such as rapping, voices, or other sounds. You will likely see lights appear out of nowhere, candles flare up, or lights sputter. Just be forewarned, these experiences can leave one shocked and awestruck! But in the end, the purpose of the ritual is to connect with the spirit and gain valuable information or aid—as long as that happens, it doesn't matter if it displays its presence physically. In any case, once you sense something, assume the spirit is there.

At this point, you may want to make some kind of offering, as a gesture of thanks. The most common form of offering is a glass of wine and a plate of food—remember although the spirit cannot actually consume this, all offerings have spiritual essence that can be absorbed. If the spirit proves to be benevolent and helpful, you can even keep a personal altar to it as a sign of respect, thus creating more spiritual essence in which the spirit can feed off of.

Once you have made your offering and welcomed the spirit tell it why you called it and proceed to question it, or request that it perform some kind of task. If you don't, not only have you wasted your time, but also you have wasted the spirit's time—and I'm sure it won't appreciate it. By all means, make sure to record any information you might receive.

Furthermore, if you are using recording equipment such as a tape recorder, digital recorder, or even a video camera, you will need to allow three to five minutes of quiet time between each question so that the spirit can respond. This also means that you need to be choosy with what you ask and prepare all questions beforehand.

Close the Evocation

It is always necessary to officially close all lines of communicate with the spirit world, then clear your area of unwanted energy or entities afterward. This can be done by simply thanking the spirit for its presence and help, then telling it farewell. You may say something like, "Depart in peace with harm to none." Afterward, close your Sacred Space if you have opened one, then use one of the cleansing methods described in "Binding, Banishing, and Protection" to clear away any energy build up. Although letting this energy remain in the room facilitates quicker evocation in the future, if you never cleanse your area, it creates a buildup of energy that can draw in unwanted spirits, which in turn can cause all kinds of strange phenomena to happen.

Lastly, make sure you have written down all this information in a grimoire dedicated to the evocation of spirits. Such a grimoire is called a "Liber Spiritum" or Book of Spirits. This is also where you store the sigils dedicated to the spirits you have evoked, unless of course you want to display them on its altar.

Memetic Magick

Meme: an idea, behavior, style, or usage that spreads from person to person within a culture.
—MERRIAM-WEBSTER DICTIONARY

Memetic magick, or meme magick, is a type of magick that uses words, images, videos, or music to deliver highly suggestive and emotionally charged messages to people on a massive scale. The word *meme* was first coined by the evolutionary biologist Richard Dawkins in 1976 in his book "The Selfish Gene." Dawkins describes a meme as follows,

> Memes (discrete units of knowledge, gossip, jokes, and so on) are to culture what genes are to life. Just as biological evolution is driven by the survival of the fittest genes in the gene pool, cultural evolution may be driven by the most successful memes.

In fact, the catchy nature of a meme has caused it to be compared to a highly contagious virus. Because, like a virus, a meme will penetrate mental defenses of the people exposed it by bypassing conscious objection, instruct the infected to think or behave in a certain way, and finally replicate itself by encouraging those infected to share its ideas with others. Memes are propagated in many ways: by word of mouth, in literature, on local news networks, in television commercials, on social media and through games.

Once a person's mind has been compromised by a meme, they will follow the behavior pattern suggested, then take action, which can and oftentimes will end up causing real change in the physical world. For example, a malicious meme might instruct people to hate a particular racial group. Therefore, when a person, or group of people are compromised, they might go out and assault others, riot, or even commit genocide. On the other hand, if the meme had a benevolent message, such as "Be kind and love one another," it might cause an increase in random acts of kindness. Either way, because most people are predisposed to mimicking thoughts and behaviors of the masses, they will share the meme and magnify its effects.

Of course, this is nothing new, because in many ways memetic magick is another form of propaganda. Such propaganda has been used by religions, governments and academia to socially engineer society for thousands of years. A good example of this would be the recruiting advertisements played before movies during World War II, pharmaceutical commercials that try to sell you ridiculously expensive medicine by trying to convince you that you have a disorder, or even news agencies that spin hate and fear to spread elite agenda.

But in reality, the concept of using memes in magick is even more ancient than the modern concept of propaganda. Memes are very similar to sigils, and sigils, like memes contain symbolic language used to communicate ideas to the subconscious mind. Those messages then invoke the thoughts and emotions necessary to cause change. In fact, most logos of large corporations such as Walmart, McDonald's and Bank of America, are nothing more than an attempt to embed the idea of that brand into the mind of the viewer. In the same sense, works of art, including popular literature can be used to inject ideas into the populous. Perhaps the only real difference between memetic magick and sigil magick is that memes are specifically created to cause change on a large scale.

So what makes a meme so powerful? A meme is tremendously powerful, because the emotional energy it is charged with shuts off critical thinking. Once the critical mind has been bypassed, suggestions are implanted directly into the unconscious mind—remember the unconscious mind has no real way of fighting suggestions. Now of course the same rules that apply to conscious influence, or entrancement, also apply to memetic magick. Basically one out of every five people are highly suggestible and three out of every five people will be suggestible to a lesser degree. Suggestibility is also higher in young people, or those suffering from stress, trauma, or mental illness—this is why propaganda focuses on youth and people who are unstable. If you think about it, that's pretty scary, because there are more irrational people in the world than there are rational people.

So why would you want to use memetic magick? Trying to manifest ones will in an environment ruled over by other forces has always been a serious challenge to sorcerers. This is because the consensual reality will only allow for manifestations that fit into its definition, and will reject manifestations that go against that agree upon reality. Therefore, meme magick provides a way to create an atmosphere fertile enough to psychically manipulate using occult magick. For example, if the sorcerer can convince enough people—by releasing a persuasive enough meme—that magick exists then his or her spells are more-likely to be successful. Once this has been done, the sorcerer will be able to perform higher miracles using magick without them being rejected by the reality net. Besides this, the power of memetic magick should be obvious. Large groups of people can be motivated to make real physical changes if a sorcerer can engineer a powerful enough meme. This is a tremendous amount of power for those people who can master it.

IS PROPAGANDA REALLY MAGICK?

In the beginning of this book I explicitly stated that sorcery is the art and science of causing change in conformity with one's will, by *any* means necessary—so in this way memetic magick fits perfectly within that scheme. However, there is a deeper reason why you should consider propaganda an actual form of magick.

At the core of all magick is the belief that by manipulating the symbolic elements of a spell, a sorcerer is able to shape quintessence (the fundamental energy in which everything is made of) which will then have a measurable effect on reality. In this way, memetic magick is no different—it just uses more contemporary symbolism to create a set of instructions that are released into a medium. That message is then apprehended by those who are exposed to it and are capable of understanding it, and thus causes them to act. The reason why it is more powerful than other forms of magick is that it utilizes pre-manifested mental constructs (computers, books, art, human beings) that are an accepted part of reality. Unless the instructions embedded within the meme point to an obviously fictitious idea, they are less-likely to be questioned and more likely to manifest something—a good example of this would be fake news. In the end, everything is really just an idea. So having said this, let's go over some basics before actually getting into the actual creation of a memetic spell.

THE CONCEPTUAL REALITY MODEL (CRM)

Although sorcerers acknowledge that they live in a world that is for the most part solid and cohesive, they are also aware of another realty that exists in tangent with the physical—that reality is made of concepts and ideas. This conceptual reality was brought about by the conscious and unconscious pondering of humanity.

The Conceptual Reality Model is used to represent the ideas, beliefs, and concepts that make up a person's personality and perception of reality. This model can also be used to predict and engineer the behavior of any conscious being according their personality, and the version of reality they subscribe to. In order to understand the CRM you must understand the following concepts.

Thought as a Thing

Although modern science tends to think of thought as being illusory, ideas have real power and therefore should be given serious consideration. Regardless of whether you think thought is illusory or real, you cannot deny that patterns of thought exist in the minds of the people who conceive them, and continues to exist as long as those thoughts are shared.

Matrix

A matrix is the scaffolding or framework upon which something else is built. In this case, we are talking about a conceptual matrix.

Information

Information includes anything that has linguistic or symbolic value that can be understood by the person accessing it. Information can be stored in the pages of a book, as files on a computer, as the lyrics in music, or a message within a media file, as graffiti or hieroglyphs on the wall of a structure, or in the mind of any conscious being. Please note this is not a definitive list of how information can be stored.

Information Matrix (IM)

An information matrix is a collection of information that can be accessed by a human being. That information could be acquired through reading, listening, viewing, etc.

The Primary Information Matrix (PIM)

The Primary Information Matrix or PIM is the information matrix that defines the base of reality for all human beings. This data is comprised of universally accepted beliefs about the physical world which are inherited by a child from his or her parents or the culture they grew up in. It is in effect consensual reality.

Information Submatrices (ISM)

An information submatrix is a divergent set of information that is an off-shoot of the PIM. All information submatrices belong to the PIM, but can also be the child of another ISM which forms a hierarchical structure.

All ISMs inherit their core data from the PIM, and other ISMs they belong to; however conscious minds can restructure this data, or inject outside information into them to mutate into another submatrix.

Memetic Thought-Forms

In traditional magick a thought-form is considered to be a mental construct that exists somewhere in the spirit world. Most often these constructs are automatons, only able to act according to the instructions given to them by one or more magicians, but sometimes they can grow into living conscious beings able to act on their own accord. Although such beings do exist, they are beyond the scope of this chapter—instead I want to talk about memetic thought-forms.

In the context of conceptual reality, a thought-form is a mental life-form that exists within the unconscious minds of one or more people—this means they can be made up of a network of humans. A memetic thought-form is born when a group of human beings adopt an ideology or strong belief-system. The more those beliefs are shared, the more the human beings who share them begin to see themselves as a cohesive group. The larger the group and the stronger its bond, the more that group begins to behave like a hive-mind. When this happens the collective intelligence of the group can develop into an independent mind and begin acting on its own accord.

No *true* member of a thought-form is aware they are possessed by it, because all *true* members whole-heartedly believe in the ideology that supports the network. On the other hand, other thought-forms can hijack other thought-forms by mimicking the beliefs of the host and guide it according to its new agenda. In the same way, thought-forms can be possessed by independent people.

MODEL OF THE HUMAN MIND

In order to assert influence on human psychology one really needs a model of the mind. Below is a model that defines the elements that make up human cognitive faculties. This model is intended to be used to chart and diagnose the network of ideas, concepts and beliefs that motivate human psychology. It is not intended to be a strict or comprehensive guide.

Engram

We will use the word "engram" which was coined by German Biologist Richard Semon to represent a single unit of thought. Engrams have four distinct properties:

1. They are encoded with information. That information can be any-thing: information about a person, place, thing, event, or even coded behavior.
2. They have emotional charge.
3. They are always connected to other engrams.
4. They can either be accessible or inaccessible to the ego.

By understanding the nature of the engram you can magnetize thoughts with either a positive or negative emotional charge in order to compel people towards or away from certain actions or choices.

Behavior

A behavior is a clustering engrams that are encoded with instructions. These instructions can be triggered by exposing a subject to the right stimuli. A behavioral engram is capable of compelling a person to take action, or cease action, change the way they perceive reality, or even to cause them to ignore certain sensory input. Behaviors like all engrams are emotionally charged.

Personality

An individual's personality is composed of their collective knowledge. This knowledge forms that person's preferences, and beliefs about themselves and the outside world. A person inherits this knowledge form their parents or whoever they interact with throughout their life time. Most of these ideas come from one or more thought-forms. The more ideas a person inherits from a particular thought-form, the more control that thought-form has over their mind.

FACTORS OF MOTIVATION

At this point I think that it is necessary to discuss the factors that contribute to a person's decision making process. Some of these factors have already been discussed in the Conscious Influence, and Entrancement chapters. These factors will be taken into consideration when constructing powerful memetic spells that are capable of influencing the minds of an individual or group of people.

Survival

Because survival is one of the strongest of human desires, a person will gravitate towards things that will insure their survival. However, if that person is possessed by a thought-form that values the survival of the group (all members that are connected to its mental net) over its individual members, the person possessed by that thought-form may decide to sacrifice him or herself for the survival of the group mind (thought-form). Therefore to magnetize someone towards an idea, you can simply let them know how that idea will contribute to their survival, and to cause someone to abandon an idea, let them know how the idea they cherish is threatening their survival.

Authority

The power and knowledge of an individual person is limited. This is why we are willing to rely on authority for security and guidance. But unlike the way authority one must have when trying to influence an individual person, the meme does not have to rely on the authority of its creator. Instead memetic magick can source out authority by edifying an icon that is more credible. For example, memes intended to affect Christians would use the authority of Jesus, and memes intended to affect disgruntled white male Americans might edify the current republican president.

In the same sense authority within a meme can come from a message delivered by someone or something representing the appearance and ideals of the target audience. For example, if your message was aimed at women, then you would have a woman deliver it, or if your message targeted older rich people, you would have it delivered by someone similar.

Conformity

People find security and personal validation by being a part of a group; therefore, most people will want to conform to the group(s) they belong to— even if the group they belong to considers themselves as non-conformists.

Validation of the EGO

Most people lack the ability to be critical of their own beliefs and short-comings; therefore they will gravitate towards others who share the same beliefs in order to reinforce their own ego.

Instincts and Urges

Most human beings lack some degree of control over their primitive urges. These urges include hunger, thirst, sexual attraction, and in many cases, the need to numb themselves using alcohol and drugs.

Experience

People tend to accept and act on information that matches their personal life experience. If these experiences have led to the satisfaction of an urge, or has fulfilled their ego in some way it will have even more gravitas.

Investment

The more time or money someone has invested into an idea, the more difficult it is for that person to abandon it.

Embracing after the Shame

Being exposed as incompetent or stupid is a threat to one's ego; therefore people will often time embrace bad choices after the fact in order to cope with the shame.

Ease and Availability

If resources are available and little effort is needed, then people are more likely to take action.

CHARTING POWER STRUCTURES

If you want to influence an individual or society at large you must be able to identify the thought-forms that are in control of those individuals or groups. But before you undertake this task, you must understand that every individual or group is controlled by a network of thought-forms that are organized in a hierarchical structure, with the most influential thought-form being at the top and the least influential thought-forms being at the bottom.

The first thing that you must realize is that you can take nothing at face value. That is, you cannot necessarily identify a dominating thought-form by simply asking someone what their religious or ideological beliefs are, because the answer they give you may simply be a façade. In reality the best way to identify dominating thought-forms is to observe the actions of the person or group of people you are trying chart in order to see if their actions or accomplishments add up to the ideological claims they are espousing—then and only then will you know for sure what thought-forms control them.

Also remember that in the end, the PIM that forms a person or group's core belief system always dictates what that person or group of people will do. That means that one's fundamental belief in the nature of reality will always guide their action in the end. This is why for example someone can be highly religious, and is still subscribe to a life of shallow materialism. Because, even though they claim to believe in the eternal soul, the dominating materialistic thought-form that controls them has convinced them that physical reality is the only thing that exists. In the end all lower thought-forms are slaves to the top most dominating mental construct. This means the goal of all lower thought-forms within a hierarchy will always be to serve the dominant thought-form, even if that means denying their nature. Ultimately charting power structures is a process of using deductive logic based on observation of people's actions, achievements, and professed ideological beliefs in order to identify possessing thought-forms. So when charting power structures consider the following common thought-forms.

Common Thought-Forms

- Government: An official ruling system that provides law and order.
- Organized Crime: Crime syndicates.
- Health Care: Health schemas.
- Academic: Recognized bodies of education.
- Corporate: Powerful businesses ruled over by a CEO and share-holders.
- Religious: Organized spiritual systems that usually espouse a dogma.

- Social Networks: Large groups of people who organize under a shared interest.

THE MEDIUM

Memetic magick relies on the transmission of information through a physical medium. That medium could be the pages of a book, a computer network, or even other human beings. But what must be realize is that even though memes are transferred through a physical medium, they still begin as energy that organizes within the quantum field (spirit world). In other words, all memetic thought-forms have a corresponding etheric thought-form.

The fact that memetic magick relies on multiple conscious observers gives it a distinct advantage over traditional magick. Think about it this way: those who use traditional magick usually only rely on their own power to fuel it, while those who use memetic magick empower it by grabbing the attention of large groups. Etheric thought-forms can also be created using memetic magick. Thought-forms created in this way are extremely powerful because once the memes that create them are apprehended by the target audience; the attention and belief of those people will multiple their power.

MEMETIC SPELLS

Like ordinary spells, the memetic spell is intended to cause change in conformity with your will, however your intentions will be delivered and hopefully enacted by the target audience. As I have already mentioned, the act of creating a meme also creates a spiritual template of your intentions in the quantum field, followed by the development of a corresponding etheric thought-form. But in order to pull this off you need to make sure that your intentions are in alignment with what reality can provide—that is, your target audience should be able to realistically carry out the instructions.

Instructions

Instructions, unlike intent are meant to be carried out by the viewer or listener of the meme. The most successful instructions are realistic, clear, and emotionally charged. To magnetize your instructions try to incorporate the aforementioned factors of human motivation into your instructions.

Depending on the type of meme you are creating, you will need to deliver your message in one of two ways: as a direct message or clandestinely. Direct messages are meant to be consciously heard and evaluated by the rational mind. Instructions conveyed clandestinely can be symbolically "insinuated," hidden within the context the meme, or presented as a compelling argument within fiction. But, whatever the case, before or as you are delivering your instructions your meme should whip your audience into an emotional frenzy.

Target Audience

Depending on the nature of your intentions, you will probably be trying to effect change in a select group of people. In such case, you will want to consider what type of person you are trying to influence. What is their culture like? What is their level of education? What beliefs do they hold? What are their goals? What are their hopes and fears? Do they fall within a certain age range? All of these things and more are very important to consider when crafting a good meme. Once you know who your target audience is, you will know how to package your message. For example, if your target group is Christian you will be speaking in terms of Christ, the devil, sin and forgiveness, but if your target group is youth, you might play to their desire to be "different," and seen as nonconformists.

Possessing Though-Forms

Whenever you target a group of people with a meme, you must always consider the thought-forms that possess their minds. Not only this, but you must consider every single thought-form in the hierarchy of thought-forms that make up their personality. The good thing is that most groups are possessed by the same thought-forms, so if you can study a segment of that group, then you can be relatively sure how the others will behave. This is the reason you should be charting power-structures.

Replicability

Another important aspect of a successful meme is its ability to replicate. It's not enough to just drop a meme into social media that says, "Be good and love one another," and expect it to change the world. That meme must either be so inspiring that people will naturally want to share it, or you must actually instruct the viewers or listeners to share the meme. Memes that are not shared die. Religious memes—especially the Abrahamic faiths—are very good examples of replication. For example, most Christians are instructed to go out convert others by sharing the teachings of their faith with others. Most even go as far as indoctrinating their children when they are at an impressionable age.

Defensive Measures

Although there are definitely a lot of impressionable people out there, there will always be a select few that will naturally resist. Therefore, all memetic spells should have built in defensive measures. A memetic defensive measure is an informative point meant to defeat objections through persuasion, dissociation, or isolation. Persuasive defensive measures will simply try to convince the viewer that choice A is better than choice B by using logic, reason, and even emotional arguments. Defensive measures that cause dissociation will often-times pair an objection with a very strong emotion in order to cause the mind to dissociate any doubts. For example, you could pair the desire to question ones faith with the extreme fear caused by the suggestion "Non-believers will burn in hell forever." In the same sense, you might convince greedy peopling to help by suggesting that helping one another would create a better society for everyone—including you.

Archetypes

If you have read the chapter on "Mind and Magick" then you already know what an archetype is, but just in case I will remind you. Archetypes are symbols that embody ancient concepts, beliefs and morals. For example, both Osiris and Jesus represent rebirth, because they are both resurrection deities. Legendary entities such as demons, the Djinn and shadow people are all representations the forces of darkness. You can also say that figures like Merlin and Gandalf represent the ideal Wizard archetype and Gaea, fairies, gnomes and mermaids all represent elemental forces. Whether any of these concepts are real or imaginary matters not, the point is, these figures invoke the primal energy, emotions and thoughts associated with their archetypal images. Why, because they are based off of ideas shared by everyone and rooted in our deep past.

Because these archetypes naturally resonate with the collective consciousness of certain groups, you can use these archetypes to communicate your instructions.

For example, if you wanted to convince people that science is magick and magick is science, you could have that message delivered by Sir Isaac Newton—because Newton was both a scientist and magician. But for example, if you wanted to convince a bunch of Christians that religion is a form of magick, you might portray Jesus as a magician and show him performing some kind of Christo-mystical ritual, along with the message "Religion is magick."

Form

Now is the time to decide what form your meme will take. This is where you get to express yourself artistically! A meme can take any form, as long as that form can transmit information, instruct people and replicate itself by compelling people to share it. Memes can be images with words, short stories, novels, screenplays, films, videos and music, just to name a few— whatever your talent is, use it.

Unleashing

Once you have created your meme, you are ready to launch it. Remember: you will need to direct it to your target audience. Memes directed at the wrong people may be ignored or even have the opposite effect. Another thing to consider is timing. If you can launch your meme during an event that is related to the meme's nature, you can fuel your meme by capturing some of the emotional energy created by that event. For example, a meme intended to increase wealth would probability do best during Thanksgiving or Christmas, but may flop if released on Groundhog Day, while the aforementioned "Science is Magick, and Magick is Science" meme would probably be rejected on Christmas, but be accepted during Halloween.

After considering all these things, you need to decide how you will transmit your meme to your target audience. If it's a short story, you may want to email it to your friends or get it published on a popular website. If your meme is a video, you could post it on Facebook or YouTube, and if it's a screenplay or song, there may be a chance you could perform it at a local venue or release it to social media—you will know what's right for your particular meme.

USING MEMES IN CONJUNCTION WITH OCCULT MAGICK

Anything you create, you are naturally quantumly entangled with. Therefore if you created and released a meme then you can tap into that force using your pure psychic abilities or even occult magick. There are actually two main methods of using memetic magick in conjunction with occult magick. The first is to use memetic magick to set-the-stage for any occult magick spells or rituals that you intend to perform. By creating the right meme, you can either move the appropriate forces into place, or actually create an environment that is more conducive to manifesting your intentions. The second is by sigilizing your meme in the same way I described in the chapter Etheric Thought-Forms, and then controlling your memetic thought-form using psychic influence or evocation.

Magick Most Foul

Although it is possible to go through life without the need to use harmful magick, I think that any Sorcerer or Sorceress worth his or her salt should know something about the black arts. Honestly, if you are a serious practitioner of magick, you are bound to encounter a curse, hex, or dark spirit some time in your magical career. Who knows? There may be a time when you need to become the nightmare that stalks in the shadows—so you had better become familiar with the dark side.

Be forewarned: this chapter contains knowledge that, if abused, will cause woe or even death not only to others, but also to the wielder. It explicitly teaches the Sorcerer how to use magick to harm or even cause death to a target. If you are mentally unstable or do not have the maturity required to wield such power, do not mess with this kind of magick. Now that you have been warned, let's get on with it.

BLACK MAGICK, WHITE MAGICK, AND BANEFUL MAGICK

There are a lot of misconceptions when it comes to the different shades of magick. What is the difference between black magick, white magick and where does baneful magick fit into all this? In reality magick is a neutral force of nature that can be used for whatever purpose the practitioner sees fit. It is only when this energy is impregnated with ill, or good intent that it could be considered black or white. For example, a hammer could be used to build a new home for orphans (good intent), or it could be used to bludgeon your neighbor to death (evil intent). Therefore, like the tool of magick, the hammer is not evil, the person using the hammer is.

Black magick is typically understood to mean "magick used to harm others in a sadistic or unfair way, or to gain something for selfish reasons." This includes any spell that may cause physical, mental, social harm (or even death), or magick that allows you to take what is not rightfully yours. Thus, harm could mean using magick to cause psychological distress, or to actually put someone in their grave, while selfish intent could mean using magick to become so ungodly rich that it steals resources from others, or to manipulate someone against their will.

White magick could be seen as any form of magick cast for the sake of enlightenment, healing, or helping fill the material need of yourself or others. But sometimes magick occupies a gray area; that is, sometimes it's not clear what is good or bad and for that reason, a spell might not always have the effect intended.

But what is baneful magick? The word *bane* means "death." Therefore, the word *baneful* means "deathly" or "deadly." Baneful magick is similar to black magick in that it is used to cause physical, mental, or social harm to others. However, it is not done for the sheer sadistic joy of torturing others—it is used as a preemptive strike against someone who poses a legitimate threat, or someone who might already be attacking you. Therefore, baneful magick may be the best way to avenge your raped daughter, or to defend yourself against a relentless bully. But the thing is, whether your intention is psychopathic (black magick), or your cause is just (baneful magick), you will still have to tap into that dark current in order to cause the harm intended.

BANEFUL MAGICK AND MORALITY

Statement – "Do what thou wilt shall be the whole of the Law."
Response – "Love is the law, love under will."
—ALEISTER CROWLEY, 1904

"Eight words the Wiccan Rede fulfill, As it harm none do what ye will."

—Doreen Valiente, 1964

Practitioners of magick oftentimes refer to two different laws when considering the morality of magick. Above, you see two statements. One says, "Do what thou wilt shall be the whole of the law." And the other says, "As it harm none, do what ye will." These statements have resonated throughout the magical community to this day, so much that they are oftentimes assumed to be immutable laws. You will oftentimes hear Magicians and Witches refer to the second statement without its corresponding response as a way of justifying any action by force of magick. This is usually because they have not done their research and know nothing about the response to "Do as thou wilt shall be the whole of the law," which is, "Love is the law, love under will."

As immutable as these laws sound, they are not divine edicts. They are there as a means to prevent negative people from succumbing to what is called the Law of Attraction (like attracts like). In my opinion, this is the only law that really matters. I believe it, because I have seen it at work in my own life—you really do get back what you put out. But I feel I must elaborate even more; not only do you get what you put out, but also that energy tends to build upon itself. This means, if you are a negative person, that energy will build and cause catastrophe that resonates throughout your whole life until it finally crushes you. On the other hand, if you are a positive person, that energy spreads out and transforms all areas of your life in a positive way—this is what is probably meant by the "Threefold Law."

The "Threefold Law" states that not only do you get back what you put out, but also you get it back three to the power of three times over—in other words, if your solution to every life problem is to throw a curse at it, you are screwed. But whether the energy comes back twofold, threefold, or ad infinitum, it really doesn't matter—it comes back, and it comes back plenty, and you should accept that. So how then can one use black magick and not be annihilated by it? Keep reading!

THE AGE OF DISBELIEF

There was a time when people took witches and magicians seriously, but those days for the most part are over. In fact, most people find the notion of someone having a familiar, or throwing a curse to be ridiculous and funny, so claiming that you are Sorcerer will most likely get you laughed out of the room—or worse yet, locked up in the funny farm. The reason it is so important to be aware of disbelief is because the negative intentions projected by disbelief, can be powerful enough to cancel a spell—this is both true for a Sorcerer who doesn't believe in the spell he is casting, as well as the target who can't help but laugh because he thinks your nuts. It is not so much that spells have no real power, or that magick is fake, but that when two opposing concepts occupy the same space, the most powerful idea always wins. Therefore, when disbelief is more powerful than a belief, it *will* negate the possibility of that thing happening—this is governed by consensual reality.

So how does one get around this? Well, as you already know, we have two types of cognition; conscious processing and subconscious processing. Our conscious mind is in charge of our logical/rational faculties, sees things in terms their differences and therefore will reject things based on what is believed to be true. On the other hand, our subconscious mind sees things in terms of how they relate and simply accepts any information received without judging it logically. This means if you can bypass your target's conscious mind and instead speak to his subconscious, you can seed the curse in a place where it cannot be doubted. This can be done using conscious suggestion.

Now what about the Witch or Sorcerer who doesn't believe? All I have to say is you gotta believe in this to do it. If you haven't gotten to the point yet where you can accept that magick is real, you need to work with it more. Studying can help; meaning, just read a book or watch a video on magick—and don't restrict yourself to just books or videos on magick either—become grounded in science. What you will discover is that the universe is more incredible than you think and anything is possible. I went from being a practitioner of magick of more than fifteen years to losing my faith in it before I finally regained my faith in magick by studying the sciences.

I bought into a consensual reality that was just as silly as any metaphysical belief system, because I wanted to rejoin the rational world. However, once I began studying science, I realized that people's views of reality are extremely flawed and limited. The turning point for me occurred when I began studying quantum physics. Many of the theories posited by physicists mirror how mystics believe the universe actually works. All you have to do is take a look at string theory, the idea of the multiverse and what is known about atoms. After you have a decent grasp on those things, there is no turning back and you will be forced to accept that magick is possible. But I also wanted to say this; sometimes the perfect Magician, or Witch is a young one! That's right, someone who us old-folks might write off as being inexperienced and therefore inept.

The thing is that it doesn't matter how many magical words you know or how they are said, nor does it matter how complicated your spells or rituals are—it doesn't work that way. The key behind any successful magick is *belief*! Simply put, younger people have not fully invested in the consensual reality yet and therefore have less preconceived notions about how reality works than older folks. And because of that, their magick is powerful—lucky pups! For example, back when I was in my early twenties, I cursed a woman who pissed me off. First, I warned her that she was the target of a curse, then that night I followed that up with a hex. The intent of the curse was to cause her house to catch fire and to destroy her relationships with others. The result was that in the early morning following the spell, faulty wiring caused her living room to catch fire and all her friends and family members to abandon her. I have not used magick to do such a thing since, but I have witnessed many curses and hexes performed by both younger and older folk—the young ones always seem to drive it home, while the older people are left wondering why it didn't work!

WORKING WITH NEGATIVE ENERGY

As you have probably figured out by now, working with negative energy can be extremely dangerous, but if you take the right precautions, you can do it without causing harm to yourself, or innocent bystanders. For the most part, the laws that govern positive energy also apply to energy of the negative spectrum. For example, all energy is charged with emotion and intent and all energy, no matter what type, attracts more of the same.

But the biggest question on your mind is probably, "If like attracts like," then how do I avoid the backlash caused by using black magick, or baneful magick?" The answer to this question is detachment and purification. In order to use this deadly magick successfully, not only will you have to raise an incredible amount of negative energy, but also when you do this, your auric field will be inundated with a negative emotional charge and this will undoubtedly affect the way you think. Depending on the intention of your spell, this might leave you feeling depressed, anxious, or even angry. In order to recover from this state, you will have to first detach from it, then purify yourself and your ritual chamber. If you do not, you are just inviting trouble.

So what could happen, might you ask? Well, if you are already a dark person, allowing yourself to remain in this heightened negative mind-set will cause you to become even darker. In other words, if you are already teetering on the brink of psychopathy, you could very well become a full blown ax-murderer. If you are good by nature and continue to neglect this purging step, you will continue to slide down the dark side of the scale, until you have totally gravitated to the dark side. Who knows, maybe you will go from being a person capable of great acts of kindness, to a person whose actions become morally questionable, then from being morally questionable to downright criminal and finally from being a criminal to being an authentically callous and brutal monster.

Another thing that can very well happen when you neglect to cleanse yourself and your ritual area is the attraction of negative entities, such as the common malevolent spirit, to shades, to the more powerful demonic forces. Because they feed off of negative energy, they find people and areas charged with negative energy yummy. These entities enter through portals created by the accumulation of magical energy in a specific area—if you perform magick in your bedroom, this is where they will enter. Once they appear, your troubles have just been amplified.

Furthermore, if you are performing negative magick in your home without clearing it, that energy build up will leave it feeling icky. Most people can't see it, but everyone has experienced walking into a place and feeling a sense of dread—that's the energy I am talking about. If left unchecked, this type of energy can cause depression, anxiety, psychological breakdowns and even illness—when guests come to call, they will actually feel like they are walking through cobwebs upon entering your home. The paradox is, although this kind of energy can be seductive and make you feel powerful, it is destructive by nature and will ultimately kill you if you abuse it.

RAISING NEGATIVE ENERGY

All energy is charged with intent and emotion. Therefore, the method for raising negative energy is the same method used for raising positive energy—the only difference is one's emotional state. But the key to raising truly powerful energy is having a truly powerful emotion. In other words, you can't just be a little angry, you have to be enraged, nor can you be a little bit bothered because you don't have what you want, you have to be monumentally upset. For this reason, you can't wait to cast your spell, because if you do, you will lose that emotional state and any energy you raise will probably not be enough to imprint the quintessence that forms reality. Whipping yourself into a frenzy usually means displaying a genuinely authentic physical response like crying, yelling, screaming, hitting things and generally getting loud and belligerent. This means, unless you want to rouse your roommate, or neighbors, you need to have your privacy, because you need to be able to express yourself in order to raise and release that kind of energy. These emotions must embody what it is you actually want to happen—your intent. In other words, you cannot just throw a fit, then release that energy into the cosmos expecting it to manifest what you desire. Not only does that energy have to be charged with a specific intent, but also it has to be aimed at a specific target, be it a person, place, or thing. If not, you won't get the results you expected, but instead it will cause general havoc, or even unexpected collateral damage.

Another tactic oftentimes used in black magick to raise energy is terror—that is the terror of your target. This is why it is not uncommon to hear stories about someone waking up to find a dead cat on their doorstep, with a curse nailed to it. Although I don't condone harming innocent little animals. However, this kind of terror can be employed without killing anything—leaving a note covered with a demonic-looking mystical symbol is probably good enough to make anyone realized they pissed off someone who practices magick. But if you want to amp it up even more, you could leave a sheet of paper with evil-looking symbols and a picture of corps— even if it's an artistic stylized version of a dead person. Having said this, deciding to go this route is risky because threatening someone's life is a crime in most countries and this of course is why you must have a *big set* to practice the black arts.

CLEANSING & BANISHING

Like I said before, the possibility of shifting from good natured, to malicious and evil is a real danger when working with negative energy—this is why one must cleanse and banish. Cleansing is getting rid of negative energy within your psychic field that would otherwise infect your psyche with negative thoughts and feelings. Banishment simply means to get rid of negative energy that is still floating around your ritual chamber, or home. Working with negative energy is a balancing act—it must be balanced by positive energy, else you will eventually turn to the dark side, so to speak. If you don't balance these energies, you will begin to think your condition is "normal," and simply won't care. At that point, you may not have the capacity to understand why your life is falling apart.

Once you have cleansed yourself, cleanse your home and banish residual negative energies by thoroughly physically cleaning it—I suggest using the "Aura Cleansing Wash" in the back of this book. Remember: our physical world is nothing but waves of energy, so by physically cleaning, you are in fact cleansing the area. Once you have thoroughly cleaned, perform the house blessing ritual listed under Banishment, Binding and Protection.

DARK MAGICK AND DEITIES

There is something within all of us that believes in a higher power. This belief speaks to our deep subconscious mind in a very real way, so much, in fact, that no matter how much we might doubt the existence of a divine creator, we are willing to call out to these forces when we are lost and powerless—but in this case, we are not talking about calling upon the ultimate expression of love and healing, we are talking about calling on upon the ultimate expression of hate and destruction!

But what is this dark force really? Is it an entity forged out of a strange ether, who wants nothing more to overthrow God's efforts to bring us into the light, or could it be nothing more than our own fear? I am so glad you asked. There is a saying in ceremonial circles that states, "There is no part of me that is not of God." The kicker is that this is not only true about you and me, but also it's true about all of creation—there is nothing that is not of God—including those things considered evil!

That is not to say that evil is the same as good, or that demonic entities don't hide in the darkness waiting to drag you into the lower planes, so they can feast off of your tortured soul. No, no, I would be lying to you if I told you that. There are dark forces that want to feed off of you and cause you harm, but as confusing as this next statement may seem to you, even they are a creation of the Source, just like angels of light and benevolent gods, they serve a purpose—their purpose is to destroy. A wise Sorcerer knows this and will call freely upon either force whenever necessary, because he understands that both are aspects of the creator.

Still though, don't think there is no danger in this—that would be foolhardy. Mess with fire and you can get burned. Dark magick is one of the most powerful types of magick out there—this is probably because it's easier to destroy than to create, or to remain ignorant of something, because you are too lazy to understand it—we love our cognitive dissonance.

Having said this, these destructive forces come in all shapes, sizes, grades and depths—that is, there are high-level demons and dark gods and low-level demons and dark gods. Most of these entities are not entirely evil. In fact, many spirits conjured by magicians of the Renaissance were not demons at all, but merely the gods and goddess of other religions that were seen as a threat to the authority of the Catholic church—in other words the pagan Gods. It was not until Christianity came a long and labeled these entities demons that they were considered *evil*, or *demonic*. In fact, the word *demon* is actually a bastardization of the Greek word *daimon*, which did not have the same negative connotations it did in Christianity—*daimon* simply meant a powerful spirit or divine power, which could be good natured or foul natured.

So knowing this then, what's all the fuss? Why is there any need to be cautious? The reason for caution is this, we are not trying to connect with an aspect of the Source that is benevolent, we are trying to connect with an aspect of the Source that is malicious. By malicious, I mean an entity that is a cunning predatory death dealer—or something that has no compunction about doing harm. These are the creatures that best fit the traditional definition of demon, not benign gods that were just given a bad name by Christians who didn't like the fact they existed. Quite simply, you can't go to a being-of-light and ask it to ruin or kill someone, they will always find a solution that involves spreading love and peace. Those are the beings are that are called in theurgy, not Baneful Magick—they are good by nature.

So where do you find entities willing to spread, chaos, death, and destruction? To do that you have three choices; one, delve deep into the dark gods and goddesses of the ancient cultures, two, tap into a thought-form, or three, conjure a powerful malicious spirit. Let's look at each of these options individually.

Option 1: Dark Gods

Every culture has one, or more adversarial God or Goddess. This is a natural reflection of the obvious duality that exists in the world. Many of these deities have two or more aspects; one gentle and kind and the other merciless and cruel. Here are just a few such deities that may interest you.

- The God of the Bible, YHVH, aka Jehovah, who drowned the entire Earth's population in a cataclysmic flood—except for Noah and his family of course.
- Satan, who in my opinion is not as ruthless as the God of the Bible, but people fear him nonetheless.
- The Persian God Ahriman who was the embodiment of all that is evil.

- The Celtic Goddess called the Morrigon, who is the goddess of war, battle, strife and fertility.
- The Norse Goddess Hel or Heleim, who is the half-living, half-dead goddess of the underworld and is also said to be responsible for spreading death and disease. The Christian word *hell* was most likely derived from her name.
- The Greek Goddess Hecate, goddess of the underworld, who is capable of great kindness, but is also infamous for stirring up a shit storm of trouble.
- Hades, the God of the underworld, who decides who lives and dies and was feared by all Greeks for ages.
- The Egyptian Goddess Sekhmet, who in a genocidal rage was loosed upon the Earth by Ra to commit unspeakable carnage.

And the list goes on and on… Just like theurgy, you can't just call upon these Gods with the assumption that you can use them like a tool—they are real entities, with real personalities. So in order to successfully call upon these entities you must work with them first, to develop a relationship. You do that in the same manner as described in theurgy.

Option 2: Dark Thought-Forms

If you really want to commit diablerie, the second option may surprise you—thought-forms. There are plenty of thought-forms that already exist, so why not tap into one. Preexisting thought-forms are powerful because they play into consensual reality. What people believe here and now is just as important as any long-standing ancient belief—if not even more important. All of these thought-forms are connected together in a chain that is linked to two of the most ancient and powerful forces, namely Good and Evil. Not only are thought-forms powerful, but also such a force exists within our current consensual reality and thus can be easily tapped into. So when choosing a dark god or goddess, chose one that is in play.

For example, if god Ahriman has been forgotten and is not being worshiped or called upon by the masses, don't use him—instead chose a spirit that is actually feared, like Satan. In the same sense, if most of the population has lost faith in the whole God/Satan paradigm, but instead believes in the

Illuminati, use that instead—yes, thought-forms can be abstract ideas as well. But this works for lessor thought-forms to. Let's say that your target thinks Satan is silly, but the slender man scares the piss out of him—that means the slender man is the guy for the job, not Satan. Which brings up a point; as ridiculous as it may sound, horrors spawned by urban legends can become very powerful thought-forms. Why, because they fresh off the plate and have the strongest connection to the two primal forces I mentioned earlier. Although such urban legends are oftentimes bunk, or at least have been blown out of proportion, it doesn't matter, because such stories create thought-forms. That concept or thought-form acts as a key that can be used to unlock the gates to hell in monumental and terrifying way, so you should definitely take advantage of them. But if you want to play it safe—and this really won't guarantee your safety—create your own thought-form using the methods laid down in the chapter entitled "Thought-Forms, Familiars, and Guardians." Just remember to create a kill switch!

Option 3: Malevolent Lower Spirits

Your third option, although I don't recommend it, is to find a malevolent spirit that is powerful enough to do what you need, then bind it. Locating such spirits is not difficult to do, since we already live on a plane of low vibration and they are practically everywhere. As a matter of fact, if you are practicing dark magick without properly purging yourself and your home of this dangerous energy, there are probably a few hanging out feeding off the negative energy that has accumulated.

But if you are looking for a special spirit to carry out an attack, you need to do a little research. To find such spirits you can delve into old grimoires, historical records and even your family history—we all have aggressive ancestors in our linage. If you are still having trouble finding the right spirit, you can prowl graveyards, haunted places and crime ridden neighborhoods, but I must warn you, this is risky. Not only does this put you out of your element, but also it exposes you to the flesh-and-blood bad people as well as puts you at risk of being arrested for trespassing. In addition to this, you run the risk of having a downright evil entity latch on to you.

In conclusion, all of the methods above involve calling spirits that are very real and also very dangerous—this is why I urge you to take the task very seriously. Because of this, whatever spiritual force you decide to go with, you need to be familiar with spiritual warfare and most definitely know how to bind and banish.

THE SACRED DARKNESS

The first Sacred Space ritual you were introduced to was the Fully Qualified Circle Opening Ritual. That ritual is charged with light, not darkness, so you really can't expect to use it when working with negative energy—for more maleficent works you need a different type of Sacred Space—one that honors the darkness. For this, you have two choices; one, create your own Dark Sacred Space ritual, using the suggestions below, or just use the Circle of the Abyss. If you decide to create your own personalized Dark Sacred Space (which I suggest you do), follow the suggestions below.

Suggestions

1. You should still cleanse your ritual chamber using sage and holly water, because this will wipe the slate clean and allow you to raise energy that is untainted by other intentions.
2. You can still use a Circle, because it represents the Source, which is neutral force—however, your Sacred Space can be any shape.
3. You can still call upon divine authority—because again, the Source is neutral. However, when you call upon divine authority, see yourself surrounded and inundated with darkness.
4. If you have incorporated the elemental forces into your Sacred Space ritual, can still call upon them—nature is an expression of the Source, which also has dark aspects.
5. If you are calling upon dark gods, make sure to include pertinent symbols. When using a circle, make it a double one and place these symbols between the double circle, in the appropriate quadrants— this you will have to discover through research.
6. When evoking spirits, call upon dark ones, or call upon spirits that have a dark aspect.

7. Work your magick, then close the ritual as usual.

8. End by thoroughly cleansing yourself and your ritual chamber.

Circle of the Abyss

Components
- 1 Small Illumination Candle
- 1 Black Candle
- 4 Quarter Candles (Red, Yellow, Blue and Green)
- Incense (Elysium Blend)
- Black Altar Cloth
- The 4-Tools
- Red Wine or Liquid
- Black Mirror or Stone

For works of darkness or magick that relies on the powers of the abyss, a different type of circle must be erected. This circle is similar in many ways to the standard banishment circle used to bring in the force of light, though it is not intended to keep out the power of darkness. Instead, this energy is welcomed in all respects. Even still this doesn't mean you are in any danger, because this circle is programmed to bar entrance to any entity, or force that intends to do harm to those within it.

Within this circle, dark Goddesses and Gods can be called. This would also include deities that have a twofold, threefold, or multifold nature, such as Hecate or the Oak King. Whatever deity you decide to call upon, you should in no way try to associate their positive nature with this ritual—instead keep the dark overtones of this ritual intact. It should be obvious that this circle opening should be performed at night, preferably between the hours of 1:00 a.m. to 5:00 a.m. in the morning. This is the time when the dark current is most powerful; people have gone to sleep and the mental chatter of the day has died down to quiet lull. If at all possible, a dark circle should be cast during the waning moon, or closest to the dark moon; working during the waxing period, especially during a full moon would be counterproductive to the type of energy you are trying to raise.

Preparation

Remove everything from your altar and replace the white altar cloth with a black one, then put all your tools back into position, except your upright pentagram. Instead, replace the upright pentagram with a reverse pentagram. This item must be cleansed, blessed (by the dark gods) and charged using methods specific to abyssal energies (see: Cleansing, Consecrating, and Charging) Your chalice should be filled with red wine or another pleasing liquid of red color—also cleansed, blessed, and charged with intent (normal charging applies). Everyone should dawn black robes, wear black apparel, or even go sky clad. Light your illumination candle and burn the Elysium incense blend.

Creating a Dark Circle

You will be walking a circle like you usually do, but in a widdershins (or counterclockwise) direction instead of deasil (clockwise)—knowing that on the waning or dark moon this actually pulls in dark energy. But first, pull the dark energy from your surroundings into you. See this energy as a shadowy tempest or an inky thick sea of blackness that surrounds you. When you have this vision firmly in your mind, take a moment to come to grips with the energy that now resides within you. Allow yourself a few moments to adjust to this icy cold feeling of death. If negative thoughts, such as anger, depression, or fear should cross your mind, acknowledge them and center yourself. Now concentrate on programming that energy—it is of the most powerful sort and deadly to boot. Tell this energy what it will be used for, but keep it simple. In this case it should be "Bind and banish all forces that intend harm to anyone within this circle. If that force resists, attack it with equal force." As you ruminate on this intent, see the dark energy within you change hue—it is becoming purple. The clearer you understand the intent, the more vibrant the purple becomes.

At this point, pick up your wand and move to the western quadrant and again walking the circle counterclockwise. See the energy flow out of your body and through the wand. Project this energy as far out as you wish to create a circle the size you so desire. As the energy hits the ground, see it projecting in all directions to form a concave wall that extends as far above and below you, as it does out from you. Hear this purple wall crackle with energy as it is formed. Smell and taste the electromagnetic charge in the air as it is projected. After you have completed the first circuit, make another one. See the second wall meld into the first, making the shield even stronger—like a master blacksmith folding mettle. Complete this sphere by walking it one last time, using the same visualization, then move back behind the altar facing the quarter you have chosen.

Creating a Dark Portal

In the "Fully Qualified Circle Opening Ritual," you opened the pathway to the higher planes by acknowledging the process of manifestation from the higher planes, to the lower planes (i.e., "Light is born from darkness and given *Will*," and so on). However, these words carry too much positive imagery to be of any use here—instead, we will trace a path to lower planes and open a gateway to the Underworld.

Pick up your pentagram, go to the North, light the Black candle, and say,

"The gates to the Underworld shall be thrown open."

Now walk counterclockwise around the circle while holding your pentagram on high. See or feel dark abyssal energy charging the entire sphere. Know that this energy represents the Darkest aspect of the Divine and that you have made a connection with the Underworld by lighting the candle and saying the evocation.

Next, pick up your chalice, go to the West, light the Black candle, and say,

"Its souls rising up from the depths of the abyssal sea like shades of darkness."

Now walk counterclockwise around the circle as you raise your chalice on high. See or feel a murky Aquatic Blue energy charging the entire sphere. Know that this energy represents the Dark Divine Aspect rising up from the Underworld into the World of Water and being transformed into the energy of merciless forces of the murky depths. The Connection has been made.

Next, pick up your athame, go to the East, light the Black candle, and hold the hold the athame on high saying,

"Their baneful voices crying out into the night demanding
to be heard."

Now walk counterclockwise around the circle while pointing the athame
to the edge of your circle. See or feel dangerous stormy energy charging
the entire sphere. Know that this energy represents the Dark Divine Aspect
entering the World of Air, being given the qualities of time and form. The
Connection has been made.

Next, pick up the Wand, go to the South, walk up to the Black candle
and light it saying,

"With rage and malice immeasurable."

Now walk counterclockwise around the circle while holding the Wand
on high as if you are displaying it with honor. See or feel fiery red energy
charging the entire sphere causing it to explode in flames. Know that this
energy represents the most volatile Aspect of the Divine entering the World
of Fire, where it is fully manifest and connected to the physical (or imaginary) circle you have drawn upon the ground.

Finally, walk back to your altar, pick up the Wand in your left hand
and point it to the ground, while taking the Athame in your right hand and
pointing it to the sky, then say,

"As below, so above shall be."

Invite the Dark Gods

At this point, light the single Black candle sitting in the middle of your altar
and call the dark forces using this evocation, or one that appropriate to the
god(s) you are calling. Once you have called the appropriate deities, you
are ready to perform any spellwork. When you are finished, close the circle

"Oh Gods and Goddesses that dwell within the deepest layers
of the abyss, Lords and Ladies of entropy and chaos, harbin-
gers of death and destruction, from the edge of the veil, I call

to thee. I lift my cup in your honor. Hear this invitation. Grant us your wisdom and lend me your dark aspect."

[[**Work Your Dark Magick**]]

Closing the Circle

Begin by dismissing the entities you have called, be they benign spirits, shades of lower worlds, or more nefarious powers.

"I dismiss all spirits that reside here. Go forthwith to thy abodes, but leave in peace."

Turn to the Black candle and disc, for they represent the dark aspect of the divine. Using your own words, acknowledge all deific influences present, thanking them for their attendance and help. Do not dismiss them nor command them to leave, for they are a part of nature.

At this point, with athame still in hand, walk to the chosen quarter, face a clockwise direction, and point the blade of your athame in that direction. Begin to walk the circle. As you slowly make your way around the circle imagine this dark energy being draw into the blade. Do a full three circuits, then when you have collected all the energy, return to your altar, point it toward the chosen quarter, and expel that energy into the abyss where it can be recycled. Lastly, reinforce the grounding by picking up a four pinches of salt and tossing each to the four quarters of your altar. Take a moment to notice how environment becomes calm.

///

Finish with "So mote it be!"

HOW TO DELIVER A CURSE

So you want to curse someone, *eh*? I hope they deserve it (cackle). Cursing involves getting upfront and personal with your target. Most curses are delivered when emotions are high and at the spur of the moment. You essentially have to look them in the eyes and tell them what kind of misfortune they will befall. Because of this, you must be brazen.

Cursing is very much related to entrancement, except the bond you create with your target is one based on fear, not trust. And it is best that your target believe that you are capable of doing what you say can. Therefore, it must be delivered with the same kind of presence and authority that any good hypnotist would have—so if you haven't studied entrancement yet, go back and do it.

Step 1: Intent
First off, your will and emotions must be in alignment with your intent. In other words, you really must want it to happen and have no pity on your target—otherwise it will definitely come back to bite you. To deliver the maximum amount of energy, you need to wait until you are thoroughly enraged, then move onto the next step.

Step 2: Fascinate
To create a link between you and your target you will have to use the art of fascination. To do this you need to draw their attention by staring them directly in the eyes and throwing up a mystical sign. This works in much the same way that rapid induction does; shock and confusion. Once you have made eye contact and have thrown your sign, go ahead and deliver your curse.

Step 3: Speak the Curse
As you make the sign and with as much animosity as you can muster, speak your curse. Illicit fear by raising the volume of your voice and speaking the curse in a dramatic tone. Raising your target's emotion will create a bridge between you and your target's subconscious mind—and when that happens, their critical faculties will shut off.

Tips
- Keep it simple.
- Make your curse time contingent (example, "You will die in one week," or "You will become more ill with each passing day until, you cannot move!").

- If you think you might cast a curse, store some negative energy in an amulet so that you can use it for special occasions. When you cast your curse, grip the amulet and draw its energy—your curse will be even more powerful.

Step 4: Walk Away

End the curse by shooting the target an evil grin, then just walk away. Don't be surprised if your target immediately attacks you, so be prepared. If your target laughs at you, remain confident and just know that your words have been heard by their subconscious mind. Even though people say they don't believe, they really do on a subconscious level and this incident will bother them so much, they will run off and tell their friends and family. When that happens those friends and family members will exacerbate the effects of the curse by talking about it—perhaps even warning the target to seek spiritual protection.

HOW TO HEX SOMEONE

The word *Hex* is used to describe any spell that is intended to cause harm or death to another person. The most common form of Hex is the voodoo doll. The same instructions listed in Spellcraft can also be used to create your own hex. Really the only difference between a Hex and any other spell is the type of energy it uses (negative) and the fact that dark Gods and spirits are called instead of light ones. At this point, I will leave the creation of Hexes up to you—be creative and by all means banish and be safe.

Hate Foods & Beverages

While killing someone with noxious chemicals or poisonous herbs is highly illegal and will land you in prison for the rest of your life; feeding a deserving target spiritually poisoned foods is not illegal. Just as any food or drink can be imbued with healing power they can also be programmed with sickening, or even fatal dark etheric energies. If you have any doubt, perform Masaru Emoto's rice-water experiment by creating a bottle of "Hate" water and drink it over the course of a week. I actually don't recommend you do this!

This very same concept can be applied to any kind of food or beverage—it matters not if it's technically safe to eat or drink. If it's been spiritually poisoned, it will have an ill effect. For the best results, cleanse, consecrate (to darkness), and charge your foods within a Circle of Darkness, then keep it in a covered Phylactery until you intend to serve it. There is no special ritual for this; all you need to do to charge the food item is focus on the intent of harm—see the person eating or drinking that beverage getting sick, or even dying. I also recommend that you charge your cursed food or beverage to a specific target—this way, others who might unknowingly eat or drink it will not fall ill.

Insidious Suggestions

Curses do not always have to be in your face and obvious. There is a way to pass on harmful and destructive energies through mere suggestion. This technique operates on the nocebo effect, using a target's fear of perceived threat—real or illusory. Once you have issued a suggestive nocebo curse, you can reinforce with a good old fashion hex later on.

Some people actually do this naturally. For example, have you ever known anyone who has a bad habit of constant asking you if you are OK all the time? Even though they usually don't wish you harm, their negative suggestions act as a catalyst to actually cause misfortune. They will oftentimes see the worst in everything, rather than the best and by being in their company when they suggest "things will not turn out well," those suggestions will end up manifesting.

The trick to mastering this technique rests with your ability to understand the psychology of your target and use the Hermetic principle of Cause and Effect. Insidious suggestions work best when someone actually trusts your opinion—you have to have credibility! First, identify what bothers your target. Many times you can find out just by just listening, but if your target trusts you, sympathetically engage them in a conversation about their ills, worries and problems. Then file away this knowledge so that you can use it to make suggestions on a different day.

For example, if that person is worried about falling ill, you might tell them, "Your color is off today," "You look a little bit sickly," or simply feign concern for them by saying, "I'm sorry you're not feeling well today." If there is obviously something wrong with them, such as a rash for example, you might suggest that it will not get better, only worse: "Wow, that doesn't look like it's getting any better! You know my uncle had the same sort of rash and ended up having to get skin grafts, because it literally ate his flesh." You see where I'm going with this?

Be creative, but be sly! Repeat these suggestions at opportune times over the course of weeks, until they really sink in. Just as any suggestion, convincing someone that they are not well can be amplified if everyone around them is telling them the same thing. So try to get everyone in on it. Just tell them that you think your target is not feeling well, and they will subconsciously catch on—this way everyone will be suggesting malignancies. Just remember every time you make these suggestions, focus and imagine the ill condition you wish to spread to the target and by all means, make sure they actually deserve what they get. As a last note, beware of psychic vampires. Oftentimes, negative people, especially those who like to complain about their health a lot, are doing so to get attention—and in such case, feigning concern will only feed them. Such people are best dealt with by cutting them off from their source of power—your attention.

How to Make Magical Incense and Oils

Both oil and incense are great for bringing one into the proper state necessary to perform a spells and also for imbuing a magical charge. The same methods used to make nonmagical oils and incense, are used for making magical oils and incense—the only difference is the addition of ritual in order to add a magical charge.

PRACTICAL BASICS OF INCENSE AND OIL MAKING

- As always be cautious when working with herbs—some are highly poisonous.

MAGICAL BASICS OF INCENSE AND OIL MAKING

- Make magical incense and oils within a circle.
- Cleanse, consecrate and charge everything!
- Incense and oils should be made on a day or night corresponding to the moon phase that best represents the energy you are trying to imbue the oil with (i.e., waxing/full moon for manifestations and waning/new moon for bindings and banishments.)

- Incense and oils specific to a Planetary Force should be made on its day and hour.
- When making an incense and oil that is specific to a particular deity, you should invoke that deities name and create it on that deity's holy day.
- Store and treat magical incense and oils like any other magical tool.

MAKING MAGICAL INCENSE

Incense Ball Recipe

1. Choose your herbs.
2. Pulverize them into a fine powder using a mortar and pestle, or coffee grinder. Hint—frozen resin is easier to pulverize.
3. Decide on a binding agent. Labdanum is a very popular binding agent for balls, but you can also use dried prunes, sultana raisins, apricots and even honey. As a rule of thumb use about half to three-quarters cup of dried fruit to every one cup of loose incense.
4. Take that dried fruit and let it soak in heavy red wine overnight before using. Then drain and add this to your dried mixture and blend the whole thing in a food processor.
5. If you are using a mortar and pestle combine a small amount of your mixture with a little bit of drained fruit until the entire batch has been pulverized.
6. Place this mixture in another bowl and drizzle about one teaspoon of pure honey for every ¾ cup of dried fruit. After kneading well begin forming balls.
7. Place your balls on wax paper, cardboard, or cloth and store away from sunlight. Let them dry for about two to four weeks.

Cone Incense Recipe

1. Choose your herbs.

2. Pulverize them into a fine powder using a mortar and pestle, or coffee grinder.

3. Decide on a binding agent and add it to the dry mixture. Many people use Gum Arabic or Tragacanth as a binding agent, but I suggest makko (tabu) Makko, which is made from the bark of the tabu-no-ki tree, is both combustible and water soluble. Because it is water soluble, the exact amount of Makko to add to a mixture depends on the humidity of your environment and the moisture content of any resins and woods in your mixture. Note, the wetter your herb/resin mixture, the more Makko you will need to add—do some experimenting. For this reason, I suggest you keep notes on the proportions you used so you can reproduce it next time.

4. Add water slowly and hand mix. Knead until it becomes gummy and pliable, then form it into cones with your hands.

5. Let dry for a couple of weeks. Hint: if the bottom center part of the cone is a different color than the edges, it's not dry.

Stick Incense Recipe

1. Follow steps 1 through 4 as described for Cones.

2. Lay down a sheet of wax paper, add some of the mixture, then roll the mixture on to sticks by hand. Hint, bamboo makes great sticks. You can either buy blanks, or harvest bamboo locally if it grows in your region. Avoid sticks that have additives.

3. Allow your sticks to dry for a couple of weeks.

MAKING MAGICAL OILS

Practical Basics of Oil Making

- Oils should be stored out of sun light and away from moisture.
- Storing oils in colored glass increases their shelf life.
- The best herb to oil ratio is 1 oz. of dried herbs to 10 oz. of oil.

Magical Basics of Oil Making

- Do not randomly stir oils. Blend by either swirling in a clockwise, or counterclockwise direction according that oil's purpose. For example, if your oil is intended to manifest or bring something to you swirl in a clockwise direction, else if your oil is to banish or send something away swirl in a counterclockwise direction.

Essential Oil Method

1. Gather all the essential oils you will be using to create your oil.
2. Pour one-eighth cup of carrier into the container you will be using to store your oil in.
3. Using a dropper, add the suggested number of drops of essential oil to the jar containing the carrier.
4. Blend, seal, label, and store.

Infusion Method

1. Gather your herbs and grind them into a fine powder.
2. Add your dried herbs to the container you will be using to steep your oil in.
3. Pour your carrier oil over the herbs, making sure they are completely covered.
4. Seal your container and blend using the suggested method above.
5. Place container somewhere warm, but keep out of direct sun light.
6. Let steep for four to six weeks, but ritualistically blend it every few days to affect your charge and to make sure the herbs are still covered by the oil.
7. Decant by lining a funnel with cheesecloth and placing its tip into the mouth of the jar you will be storing your oil in. Pour your oil from the steeping jar, into the funnel to separate herbs from oil. Once finished, remove cheesecloth and squeeze every last drop form it into the jar containing your oil.
8. Seal, label, and store.

Correspondence

The correspondence tables below are only meant to serve as examples and not to be thought of as fixed. Use them as a starting point for your own personal tables. An important part of the craft is developing your own sets of personal correspondences, so if you are not sure how to do this, read about sympathetic linking nder the chapter entitled The Language of Magick.

Day/Planet Correspondence

Day	Planet	Color	Energy/Magick
Monday	Moon	Silver	Illusion, Glamor,
		White	Dreams, Emotions, Divination
Tuesday	Mars	Red	Banishment, Protection,
		Black	Martial Magick
		Orange	
Wednesday	Mercury	Purple	Art, Communication,
		Orange	Change, Luck
Thursday	Jupiter	Blue	Wealth, Prosperity,
		Purple	Protection, Strength
		Green	
Friday	Venus	Pink	Love, Birth, Fertility,
		Aqua	Romance, Friendship
Saturday	Saturn	Black	Banishing, Protection,
		Purple	Wisdom, Cleansing
Sunday	Sun	Gold	Success, Promotion,
		Yellow	Fame, Wealth, Prosperity

Hour/Planet Correspondence

Hour	Planet
Dawn	Sun, Mars
Midafternoon	Jupiter
Noon	Mercury, Mars
High Noon	Sun, Mars
Dusk	Saturn
Midnight	Moon, Venus
Early Morning (3:00 a.m. to 6:00 a.m.)	Moon, Venus
Early Morning	Moon, Saturn

Note: The hour/planet correspondence above are based on the general time of day or night. I am fully aware that there is a system that involves calculating these associations by dividing each twelve-hour period (twenty-four hours or one cycle total) by twelve, based on when the sun actually rises to find the exact planetary hour. However, I have found this to be unnecessary. If you want to use that system, you will discover it online—there are even apps you can download that will calculate this for you.

Moon Phase Correspondence

Moon	Works
Waning	Any binding and banishing
Sun in Waning Moon	Any binding and banishing
New Moon	Most powerful binding and banishing
Sun in New Moon	Most powerful binding and banishing
Waxing	Manifestation
Sun in Waxing Moon	Manifestation
Full Moon	Most powerful manifestation
Sun in Full Moon	Most powerful manifestation

Chakra Correspondence

Chakra	Color	Association	Tone
Crown	Violet	Spirituality, Wisdom, God	Ti
Third Eye	Indigo	Intuition, Awareness, Charisma	Lah
Throat	Blue	Expression, Inspiration, Truth	Sol
Heart	Green	Love, Compassion, Integration	Fah
Solar Plexus	Yellow	Power, Wisdom, Social Self, Will	Mi
Sacral	Orange	Sexuality, Creativity, Emotion	Reh
Root	Red	Grounding, Basic Trust, Stability	Doh

Carrier Oil Correspondence

These oils are considered the base oils you would add other oils to in order to create oil blends.

Oil	Properties
Apricot Kernel Oil	Water, Love, Aphrodisiac
Avocado	Love, Lust, Beauty
Caster	Any
Coconut	Fidelity, Protection, Purification
Grapeseed	Water, Fertility, Intuition, Money
Jojoba	Good Carrier for any magicks
Olive Oil	Abundance, Balance, Fertility, Harmony, Prosperity, Rebirth
Rose Hip	Heart Chakra, Love, Secrecy, Selfishness, Aphrodite
Sunflower	High Spiritual Vibrations, Sun, Clairvoyance, Meditation, Protects from Physical Harm, Consecration, Success
Sesame	Hope
Sweet Almond	Air, Money, Prosperity, Wisdom, Love, Overcoming Obstacles
Walnut Oil	Air and Fire, Change, Fertility, Healing, Inspiration, Intentions, Protection, Wealth

Solfeggio Frequency Correspondence

Note	Frequency	Association
UT	396 Hz	Liberating Guilt and Fear
RE	417 Hz	Undoing Situations and Facilitating Change
ME	528 Hz	Transformation and Miracles (DNA Repair)
FA	639 Hz	Connecting/Relationships
SOL	741 Hz	Expression/Solutions
LA	852 Hz	Returning to Spiritual Order
	174 Hz	Reduces pain
	285 Hz	Heals tissue, regenerates organs

Color Correspondence

Color	Properties
Black	Astral Magick; astral projection, scrying, psychic senses, divination of lower spirits. Counter Magick by Liminal Deities; Binding, Banishing, Unhexing, Uncrossing Earth Magick: grounding, gleaning knowledge of things hidden in the earth Baneful Magick: Calling on malevolent spirits or deities with the purpose of doing harm
Blue	Water Magick; Emotional balance, Forgiveness, Psychological healing, Patience, Domestic Harmony, Childbirth
Brown	Earth magick; concentration, grounding, stability, finding lost objects Wealth Magick: Attainment of minerals, stones, crystals, or other goods composed of the earth.
Copper	Earth, growth, business, money, fertility, developing mastery over a trade
Gold	Masculine divinity, business, great-fortune, success, understanding, divination, fast luck, the sun, charisma
Gray	Turning the wheal, reflection of the past, connecting with the troubled in order to understand them

Green	Healing, nature deities, physical and mental healing, building relationships with others, soothing ill feelings Nature Magick: Earth, plant growth Wealth Magick: Developing lasting success, procuring necessary provisions.
Indigo	Air Elemental Energy, Banishment, Intention of Psychological Change
Lavender	Maternal Deities, Love tempered with Wisdom, intuition, Healing, especially that of children
Blue	Divination, Will, Focus, Good Luck, Truth, Balance of Emotions, Banishment, Astral Projection.
Light Blue	Spirituality, tranquility, peace, protection
Orange	Nutrition, Happiness, Creativity, Wisdom, Building Business Relationships with Clients
Pink	Femininity, Friendship, Girls or Young Woman, Building Healthy Loving Relationships
Purple	Wisdom, influence, spiritual power, Evocation or Invocation of Higher Spiritual Forces, Banishment, Vitality, government, Breaking Bad Habits
Red	Fire, Passion, Will Power, Vitality, Strength, Charisma, Fertility, Courage, Sexual Potency, Sudden Action, Aggression, War, Harsh Purification, Competition
Silver	Feminine Deities, Oaths and Obedience, Psychic Awareness, Intuition, Dreams, Divination, Understanding, Moon Magick
Violet	Feminine Deities, Deep Love, Bonding of Soul mates, Spiritual Understanding, Higher Self
White	The Source, Feminine and Masculine Deities, Spiritual Love, the Divine Light, Force of Good, Countermagick; Breaking Hexes, Uncrossing, Banishment, Invocation and Evocation of Positive Spiritual forces, Truth, Balance, Divination, Understanding
Yellow	Nutrition, Pleasure, Successes, Happiness, Meditation, Inspiration, Solar Magick, Air Tempered with Fire, Boyhood, Revealing Foolishness

Herbal Correspondence

Herb	Properties
Agrimony	Wealth, Binding, Banishing
Basil	Love, Divination
Bay Leaf	Success, Protection, Visions
Chamomile	Sleep, Cleaning, Protection
Dragon's Blood	Offertory, To Enhance the Power of Any Spell, Luck, Protection
Frankincense	Offertory, Banishment, Meditation
High John The Conquerer	Healing, Wealth, Courage, Luck
Lavender	Healing, Peace, Sleep
Mugwort	Love, Healing, Protection, Visions and Dreams
Myrrh	Offertory, Healing, To Increase the Power of Any Spell
Patchouli	Love, Wealth, Success
Peppermint	Healing, Banishment, Cleansing, Visions, Psychic Abilities
Rose, Black	Death Energy, Dealing with Loss, Connecting with Liminal Spiritual Forces
Rose, Red	Love
Rose, White	Platonic Love, Connecting with the Positive Spiritual Forces
Rosemary	Increasing Memory, Protection, Banishment, Meditation
Rue	Protection, Uncrossing, Love
Sage	Cleansing, Banishment and Protection
Sandalwood	Offertory, Love, Healing, Cleansing, All Magick

Hypnotic Correspondence

Hypnotic: A synthetic or natural drug used to induce sleep.

Hypnotic Herbs

Type	Properties
Ashwagandha	Anxiety Reduction
California Poppy	Sleep
Hops	Sleep
Lavender Tea	Infrequent Insomnia
Passion Flower	Anxiety Reduction, Sleep

| Valerian | Sleep |
| German Chamomile | Infrequent Insomnia |

Hypnotic Foods

Foods Containing Tryptophan

- Dairy products (milk, low-fat yogurt, cheese)
- Poultry (turkey, chicken)
- Seafood (shrimp, salmon, halibut, tuna, sardines, cod)
- Nuts and seeds (flax, sesame, pumpkin, sunflower, cashews, peanuts, almonds, walnuts)
- Legumes (kidney beans, lima beans, black beans, split peas, chickpeas)
- Fruits (apples, bananas, peaches, avocado)
- Vegetables (spinach, broccoli, turnip greens, asparagus, onions, seaweed)
- Grains (wheat, rice, barley, corn, oats)

Foods Containing Magnesium

- Dark leafy greens (baby spinach, kale, collard greens)
- Nuts and seeds (almonds, sunflower seeds, brazil nuts, cashews, pine nuts, flaxseed, pecans)
- Wheat germ
- Fish (salmon, halibut, tuna, mackerel)
- Soybeans
- Banana
- Avocados
- Low-fat yogurt

Foods Containing Calcium

- Dark leafy greens
- Low-fat milk
- Cheeses
- Yogurt
- Sardines

- Fortified cereals
- Soybeans
- Fortified orange juice
- Enriched breads and grains
- Green snap peas
- Okra
- Broccoli

Foods Containing Vitamin B6
- Sunflower seeds
- Pistachio nuts
- Flaxseed
- Fish (tuna, salmon, halibut)
- Meat (chicken, tuna, lean pork, lean beef)
- Dried Prunes
- Bananas
- Avocado
- Spinach

Foods Containing Melatonin
- Fruits and vegetables (tart cherries, corn, asparagus, tomatoes, pomegranate, olives, grapes, broccoli, cucumber)
- Grains (rice, barley, rolled oats)
- Nuts and Seeds (walnuts, peanuts, sunflower seeds, mustard seeds, flaxseed)

Hypnotic Drinks
- Warm milk
- Almond milk
- Valerian tea
- Chamomile tea
- Tart cherry juice
- Passion fruit tea
- Peppermint tea

Mineral Correspondence

Type	Properties
Dead Sea Salt	Banishment (Use on a full moon)
Graveyard Dirt	Connecting to the Dead, Curses
Lava Salt	Fire, use waning

Crystal/Stone Correspondence

Crystal/Stone	Properties
Actinolite	Balance, Harmony, Patience, Self-worth
Adamite	Courage, Emotional Issues, Inner Strength, Problem Solving, Prosperity
Adularia	Clairvoyance, Divination, Guidance, Health, Intuition, Longevity, Soul-Searching, Soul Travel, Wealth
Agate	Balance, Clarity, Courage, Courage, Creativity, Energizer, Fertility, Good Health, Good Manners, Grounding, Growing Plants, Happiness, Healing, Health, Inner Bitterness, Intelligence, Longevity, Making Friends, Prosperity, Protection, Restoration of Energy, Strength, Support, Truth, Ward Anger, Wealth
Agnitite	Life Force, Purify, Spiritual Light
Agrellite	Confidence, Distant Healing, Independence, Potential, Self-Respect
Alabaster	Clarity, Composure, Forgiveness, Meditation, Mental Balance
Alexandrite	Forgiveness, Good Fortune, Happiness, Sexual Powers, Success
Alum	Ill Wishes, Protection, Purification, Ward Negativity
Amazonite	Balance, Harmony, Hope, Physical Stamina, Thinking
Amber	Balance, Infection, Lift The Spirit, Positive Energy, Rids Depression

Amethyst	Calming, Compulsive Behavior, Faithfulness, Fear, Friendship, Headaches, Healing, Inner Calm, Insights, Intuition, Meditation, Psychic Ability, Self-Esteem, Sleep, Spiritual Awareness
Amethystine Agate	Change
Ametrine	Healing, Intellect, Openness, Understanding
Apache Tear	Centering, Good Luck, Grief, Grounding, Promoting Peace, Protection, Repel Negativity, Scrying
Aqua Aura	Cleanse Chakra, Open Chakra
Aquamarine	Accidents, Banish Fears, Compassion, Confidence, Courage, Happiness, Inspiration, Nervous Tension, Open Throat Chakra, Phobias, Purifying, Sooths The Heart, Thinking, Travel
Aventurine	Balance, Creativity, Healing, Luck
Azurite	Acceptance, Calm, Dreams, Healing, Inner Confusion, Intuition, Personal Stress, Psychic Ability, Psychic Eye, Spiritual Guidance, Truth, Understanding
Barite	Anxious, Communication, Conserve Energy, Immune Problems, Obstacles, Relationships, Rituals, Spells, Stress
Beryl	Psychic Awareness, Relationships
Black Onyx	Negativity
Bloodstone	Accidents, Balance, Business, Business, Confidence, Courage, Courage, Depression, Disease, Emotional Blockages, Healing, Invisibility, Legal Matters, Longevity, Physical Strength, Spells
Blue Calcite	Astral Projection, Balance, Fear, Joy, Lightness, Stress
Blue Celestite	Angelic Realms, Clear Perspective, Detachment, Divine Inspiration
Blue Lace Agate	Feminine Qualities, Gentleness, Peace
Botswana Agate	Gifts, Mood Lifting, Pleasures
Calcite	Balance, Clarity, Clearing Blockages, Energy, Meditation

Carnelian	Anger, Communication, Concentration, Confidence, Decisions, Eloquence, Energy, Fear, Focus, Good Fortune, Gossip, Harmonious, Healing, Health, Longevity, Motivation, Peaceful, Protection, Wishes
Celestite	Angels, Astral Work, Dreams
Charoite	Conquering Fears
Chrysocalla	Clears Thinking, Feminine Qualities
Chrysocolla	Friendship
Chrysolite	Clarity
Citrine	Abundance, Confidence, Courage, Prosperity, Self-Determination
Clear Quartz	Clarity
Coral	Fertility
Emerald	Harmony
Fluorite	Concentration
Fuchsite	Balance, Harmony
Garnet	Commitment, Energy
Hematite	Grounding, Uncrossing
Jade	Confidence, Dreams, Fertility, Fidelity, Friendship, Harmony
Jasper	Awareness, Grounding
Jet	Grief
Kunzite	Communication
Kyanite	Awareness, Communication, Dreams
Lapis Lazuli	Creativity
Lead	Foundations
Lepidolite	Astral Work, Changes
Lodestone	Attraction
Malachite	Changes, Clearing Blockages
Moonstone	Forgiveness
Obsidian	Grounding
Onyx	Centering, Grief
Opal	Creativity
Peridot	Changes

Petrified Wood	Changes, Grounding
Rhodochrosite	Balance
Rose Quartz	Friendship, Happiness
Ruby Zoisite	Angels, Astral Work
Rutilated Quartz	Energy
Rutilayed Quartz	Clairvoyance
Sapphire	Beauty
Smoky-Quartz	Balance, Grounding
Sodalite	Communication
Sugilite	Confidence
Tigers Eye	Grounding
Topaz	Creativity, Energy, Generosity
Tourmalinated Quartz	Balance
Tourmaline	Balance, Confidence
Turquoise	Astral Work, Grounding

Encyclopedia of Terminology

///: Each slash is a bell ring, percussion strike, clap, or stomp.

Athame: A ritual knife used to cut symbols into the air or for other ritual purposes. Athames are not used for assaulting others.

Asperge: To sprinkle, typically with holy water.

Astral Plane: A spiritual plane of existence that is closest to the physical plane, which is said to be a plane where ideas and concepts begin to coalesce into our physical reality. The Astral Plane resonates a frequency higher than the physical plane yet is considered a lower plane.

Backlash: Negative energy return from abusing magick or doing something selfish or otherwise evil.

Baneful Magick: A spell that is intended to harm, manipulate or control another against their will.

Banish: To repel and get rid of negative spiritual forces and people.

Benevolent: Good, friendly, helpful.

Bind: To render someone or something incapable of doing harm.

Black Magick: Magick performed out of greed, selfishness, or to derive pleasure which causes harm or manipulates against a target's will.

Boline: A white-handled ritual knife usually used to cut plants or herbs.

Charge: To imprint or program with intention or *will.*

Circumambulate: To walk around something; in magick, usually three times.

Consecrate: To dedicate an item to a particular deity or spirit for the purpose of making it a vessel of that deity or spirit's power.

Deasil: Clockwise.

Deity: A sentient spirit, good, evil or both that has godlike powers.

Effigy: a sculpture or model that is made to look like a person.

Enchant: Same as charge. To imbue an item with intent or magical power.

ESP: Extrasensory Perception. Your psychic senses.

Evoke: To call an energy, spirit or power into an area.

Familiar: The spirit of an animal or other spirit, which possess the physical body of an animal and acts as a Sorcerer's servitor or an artificial spirit created by the Sorcerer for the same purpose.

Formula: A recipe that includes the combination or various magical components to form another.

Gematria: An Assyro-Babylonian-Greek system used as an alpha numeric cipher where each letter of the alphabet is represented by a number. The conversion of words to numbers were thought to represent that word's intent within nature. This system was later adopted by the Hebrew and Greeks and is used in Western systems of magick today.

Invoke: To call an energy, spirit or power into you.

Macrocosm: The universe or self on a large scale; the solar system, planets, body, limbs, organs, and so on.

Magical Link: See tag-lock.

Magick: This term is used to distinguish "real magick" from "sleight-of-hand magic." It is the ability to affect spiritual reality to cause change in your life or the life of others.

Magician: A general term for a man or woman who practices magick.

Malevolent: Evil, harmful, bad.

Metaphysical: Philosophy concerned with abstract thought or subjects, existence, causality, or truth, time or substance.

Microcosm: The universe or self on a very small or subtle scale; atoms, subatomic particles, spirit.

Pop-Magick: Magical systems written for the populous, usually based on fantasy and not rooted in actual science and metaphysics.

Poppet: A representation of a person in the form of a doll, intended to be used in magick. Poppets are most commonly made of cloth or wax, but can be made of just about anything.

Probabilistic: Subject to chance, or variation.

Pseudoscience: Not really a science. A field of research masquerading as a real science, but without any legitimate evidence to support it.

Quarters: This refers to the four directions; north, south, east and west which are also attributed to the elements. North is earth, east air, south fire and west water.

Scry: To use a tool such as a crystal ball, magick mirror, or scrying bowl to remotely view people, places and things in the present, past and future.

Show Stone: A piece of glass or crystal that practitioners use for scrying.

Sigil: A symbol that is thought to have magick power.

Spirit: A being which is composed of thought energy that exists on one of the Spiritual planes.

Spiritual: Concerned with ideas related to existence of life after physical death, the rudimentary laws that govern spirit.

Tag-lock: A personal item relating to the target or a spell, such as fingernails, hair, jewelry, which holds that person's energy signature or charge.

Threefold Law, or Law of Return: This law states that you get back what you give; meaning, if you put out negative energy, it will return to you three times over.

White Magick: Magick used to heal, or help others.

Wicca: An earth religion that worships the Lord and Lady that sometimes involves the practice of magick.

Wiccan Rede: Do as thou wilt, yet harm; meaning do what you want, but do not harm yourself, or others.

Widdershins: Counterclockwise.

Witching Hour: The best time to perform magick. The time when the sun is the highest in the sky (high noon), or the time when the moon is the highest in the sky (sometime around 3:00 a.m.).

Witch: Someone who practices witchcraft. Such a person can be male or female. This does not insinuate that they follow the spiritual path of Wicca.

Suggested Books

Any book by Aleister Crowley

Any book by Dr. Dean Radin

Any book by Rupert Sheldrake

Astral Dynamics by Robert Bruce

Buckland's Book of Spirit Communication by Raymond Buckland

Eleven Lessons in High Magick by Donald Michael Craig*Lost Book of ENKI* by Zecharia Stitchen

Magic and Medicine of Plants by Reader's Digest

Magnetic Current by Edward Leedskalnin

Mastering Witchcraft by Paul Huson

The Complete Book of Witchcraft by Raymond Buckland

The Lost Secret of Death by Peter Novak

The Magician's Companion:
A Practical and Encyclopedic Guide to Magical and Religious Symbolism

by Bill Whitcomb

The Twenty-One Lessons of Merlyn: A Study in Druid Magic and Lore
by Douglas Monroe

Lightning Source UK Ltd.
Milton Keynes UK
UKHW040644211020
371973UK00001B/13

9 780998 708195